WITHDRAWN

AMERICA
DIVIDED

AMERICA
DIVIDED

The Civil War of the 1960s

SECOND EDITION

Maurice Isserman
Michael Kazin

NEW YORK   OXFORD
Oxford University Press
2004

Oxford University Press

Oxford   New York
Auckland   Bangkok   Buenos Aires   Cape Town   Chennai
Dar es Salaam   Delhi   Hong Kong   Istanbul   Karachi   Kolkata
Kuala Lumpur   Madrid   Melbourne   Mexico City   Mumbai
Nairobi   São Paulo   Shanghai   Taipei   Tokyo   Toronto

Published by Oxford University Press, Inc.
198 Madison Avenue, New York, New York 10016
http://www.oup-usa.org

Oxford is a registered trademark of Oxford University Press

Library of Congress Cataloging-in-Publication Data

Isserman, Maurice.
America divided : the civil war of the 1960s / Maurice Isserman, Michael Kazin.—2nd ed.
p. cm.
Includes bibliographical references (p.   ) and index.
ISBN 0-19-516046-0 — ISBN 0-19-516047-9 (pbk.)
1. United States—History—1961–1969. I. Kazin, Michael, 1948– II. Title.
I. Title.
E841.I87 2003
973.923—dc21
                                                                    2002044968

9 8 7 6 5 4 3 2 1
Printed in the United States of America
on acid-free paper

To
Daniel Kazin
Ruth Isserman
Maia Kazin
David Isserman

THE EIGHT YEARS IN AMERICA FROM 1860 TO 1868 UPROOTED INSTITUTIONS THAT WERE CENTURIES OLD, CHANGED THE POLITICS OF A PEOPLE, TRANSFORMED THE SOCIAL LIFE OF HALF THE COUNTRY, AND WROUGHT SO PROFOUNDLY UPON THE ENTIRE NATIONAL CHARACTER THAT THE INFLUENCE CANNOT BE MEASURED SHORT OF TWO OR THREE GENERATIONS.

—*Mark Twain and Charles Dudley Warner,* The Gilded Age:
A Tale of To-Day *(1873)*

Contents

Preface

"History," a great scholar once declared, "is what the present wants to know about the past." We have written this book to make sense of a period that continues to stir both hot debate and poignant reminiscence in the United States and around the world. The meaning of the '60s depends, ultimately, upon which aspects of that time seem most significant to the retrospective observer. We have chosen to tell a story about the intertwined conflicts—over ideology and race, gender and war, popular culture and faith—that transformed the U.S. in irrevocable ways. The narrative does not remain within the borders of a single decade; like most historians, we view "the '60s" as defined by movements and issues that arose soon after the end of World War II and were only partially resolved by the time Richard Nixon resigned from the presidency.

Our own friendship is a creation of the long 1960s and its continuing aftermath. We met in 1970 in Portland, Oregon—two young radicals of college age who cared a great deal more about changing history than studying it. For a while, we lived in the same "revolutionary youth collective" and wrote for the same underground paper—signing only our first names to articles as an emblem of informality. We then left to attend graduate school on different coasts and found teaching jobs at different schools. But a passion for understanding and telling the story of the '60s brought us together as writers. In the late '80s, we coauthored an article on the failure and success of the New Left and began to consider writing a study of the period as a whole.

That shared past animates our story but does not determine how we've told it. While still clinging to the vision of a democratic Left, we certainly do not endorse all that radicals like ourselves were doing in the 1960s. And, unlike some earlier scholars and memoirists, we no longer view the narrative of the Left—old, new, or liberal—as the pivot of the 1960s, around which other events inevitably revolve. What occurred during those years was too important and too provocative to be reduced to the rise and fall of a political persuasion. We intend this to be a book for people who were not alive in the '60s as well as for those who may remember more than they can explain about that time in their life and in world history.

A variety of people were indispensable to the making of this book. At Oxford University Press, Nancy Lane convinced us to embark on it, and Gioia Stevens inherited the assignment and handled both the developing manuscript and its authors with intelligence and grace. Stacie Caminos and Karen Shapiro, artisans of the book trade, prodded and instructed. And Brenda Griffing copyedited splendidly. Peter Coveney and Lisa Grzan guided our work on the second edition with great skill, generosity, and humor.

We got essential aid on the illustrations from Lisa Kirchner and a few good shots from David Onkst, Todd Gitlin, Jefferson Morley, Pamela Nadell, David Weintraub, Paul Buhle, and Paula Marolis.

Three of America's finest historians helped us avoid at least the most obvious errors. Leo Ribuffo critiqued a draft of the religion chapter, Nelson Lichtenstein gave the entire book a perceptive and encouraging read, and Stepen Whitfield discovered a number of errors in the first edition.

We thank our families for continuing to persevere through yet another '60s story. As always, Beth Horowitz was a demon on bad prose and sloppy thinking. Marcia Williams took time off from her law school education to remind her husband of the importance of the Warren Court. We dedicate the book to our children. Now it's their turn.

Introduction

We have not yet achieved justice. We have not yet created a union which is, in the deepest sense, a community. We have not yet resolved our deep dubieties or self-deceptions. In other words, we are sadly human, and in our contemplation of the Civil War we see a dramatization of our humanity; one appeal of the War is that it holds in suspension, beyond all schematic readings and claims to total interpretation, so many of the issues and tragic ironies—somehow essential yet incommensurable—which we yet live.
—*Robert Penn Warren,* The Legacy of the Civil War, *1961*[1]

As the 1950s drew to a close, the organizers of the official centennial observances for the Civil War were determined not to allow their project, scheduled to begin in the spring of 1961 and to run through the spring of 1965, to become bogged down in any outmoded animosities. Among other considerations, much was at stake in a successful centennial for the tourism, publishing, and souvenir industries; as Karl S. Betts of the federal Civil War Centennial Commission predicted expansively on the eve of the celebration, "It will be a shot in the arm for the whole American economy."[2] Naturally, the shot-in-the-arm would work better if other kinds of shots, those dispensed from musketry and artillery that caused the death and dismemberment of hundreds of thousands of Americans between 1861 and 1865, were not excessively dwelt upon. The Centennial Commission preferred to present the Civil War as, in essence, a kind of colorful and good-natured regional athletic rivalry between two groups of freedom-loving white Americans. Thus, the commission's brochure "Facts About the Civil War" described the respective military forces of the Union and the Confederacy in 1861 as "the Starting Line-ups."[3]

Nor did it seem necessary to remind Americans in the 1960s of the messy political issues that had divided their ancestors into warring camps a century earlier. "Facts About the Civil War" included neither the word "Negro" nor the word "slavery." When a journalist inquired in 1959 if any special observances were planned for the anniversary of Lincoln's Emancipation Procla-

1

mation three years hence, Centennial Commission director Betts hastened to respond, "We're not emphasizing Emancipation." There was, he insisted "a bigger theme" involved in the four-year celebration than the parochial interests of this or that group, and that was "the beginning of a new America" ushered in by the Civil War. While memories of emancipation—the forced confiscation by the federal government of southern property in the form of 4 million freed slaves—were divisive, other memories of the era, properly selected and packaged, could help bring Americans together in a sense of common cause and identity. As Betts explained:

> The story of the devotion and loyalty of Southern Negroes is one of the outstanding things of the Civil War. A lot of fine Negro people loved life as it was in the old South. There's a wonderful story there—a story of great devotion that is inspiring to all people, white, black or yellow.[4]

But contemporary history sometimes has an inconvenient way of intruding upon historical memory. As things turned out, at the very first of the scheduled observances, the commemoration of the Confederate attack on Fort Sumter, the well-laid plans of the publicists began to go awry. The Centennial Commission had called a national assembly of delegates from participating state civil war centennial commissions to meet in Charleston. When a black delegate from New Jersey complained that she was denied a room at the headquarters hotel because of South Carolina's segregationist laws, four northern states announced they would boycott the Charleston affair. In the interests of restoring harmony, newly inaugurated President John F. Kennedy suggested that the state commissions' business meetings be shifted to the nonsegregated precincts of the Charleston Naval Yard. But that, in turn, provoked the South Carolina Centennial Commission to secede from the federal commission. In the end, two separate observances were held, an integrated one on federal property, and a segregated one in downtown Charleston. The centennial observances, *Newsweek* magazine commented, "seemed to be headed into as much shellfire as was hurled in the bombardment of Fort Sumter."[5]

In the dozen or so years that followed, Americans of all regions and political persuasions were to invoke imagery of the Civil War—to illustrate what divided rather than united the nation. "Today I have stood, where once Jefferson Davis stood, and took an oath to my people," Alabama governor George Wallace declared from the steps of the statehouse in Montgomery in his inaugural address in January 1963. From "this Cradle of the Confederacy. . . . I draw the line in the dust and toss the gauntlet before the feet of tyranny . . . and I say . . . segregation now . . . segregation tomorrow . . . segregation forever!"[6]

Six months later, in response to civil rights demonstrations in Birmingham, Alabama, President Kennedy declared in a nationally televised address:

Mock confederates fire on mock Union soldiers during the centennial reenactment of the Battle of Bull Run, July 1961. Source: *Associated Press*

"One hundred years of delay have passed since President Lincoln freed the slaves . . . [T]his Nation, for all its hopes and all its boasts, will not be fully free until all its citizens are free."[7] Two years later, in May 1965, Martin Luther King, Jr. stood on the same statehouse steps in Montgomery where Governor Wallace had thrown down the gauntlet of segregation. There, before an audience of 25,000 supporters of voting rights, King ended his speech with the exaltedly defiant words of the Battle Hymn of the Republic:

> Mine eyes have seen the glory of the coming of the Lord, trampling out the vintage where the grapes of wrath are stored. He has loosed the fateful lightning of his terrible swift sword. His truth is marching on. . . .
>> Glory, glory hallelujah!
>> Glory, glory hallelujah!
>> Glory, glory hallelujah![8]

To its northern and southern supporters, the civil rights movement was a "second Civil War," or a "second Reconstruction." To its southern opponents, it was a second "war of northern aggression." Civil rights demonstrators in the South carried the stars and stripes on their marches; counterdemonstrators waved the Confederate stars and bars.

The resurrection of the battle cries of 1861–1865 was not restricted to those who fought on one or another side of the civil rights struggle. In the course of the 1960s, many Americans came to regard groups of fellow countrymen as enemies with whom they were engaged in a struggle for the nation's very soul. Whites versus blacks, liberals versus conservatives (as well as liberals versus radicals), young versus old, men versus women, hawks versus doves, rich versus poor, taxpayers versus welfare recipients, the religious versus the secular, the hip versus the straight, the gay versus the straight— everywhere one looked, new battalions took to the field, in a spirit ranging from that of redemptive sacrifice to vengeful defiance. When liberal delegates to the 1968 Democratic convention in Chicago lost an impassioned floor debate over a proposed antiwar plank in the party platform, they left their seats to march around the convention hall singing the Battle Hymn of the Republic. Out in the streets meanwhile, watching the battle between Chicago police and young antiwar demonstrators, the middle-aged novelist Norman Mailer admired the emergence of "a generation with an appetite for the heroic." It pleased him to think that "if it came to civil war, there was a side he could join."[9] *New York Times* political columnist James Reston would muse in the early 1970s that over the past decade the United States had witnessed "the longest and most divisive conflict since the War Between the States."[10]

Contemporary history continues to influence historical memory. And although as the authors of *America Divided* we have tried to avoid political and generational partisanship in our interpretation of the 1960s, we realize how unlikely it is that any single history of the decade will satisfy every reader. Perhaps by the time centennial observances roll around for John Kennedy's inauguration, the Selma voting rights march, the Tet Offensive, and the 1968 Chicago Democratic convention, Americans will have achieved consensus in their interpretation of the causes, events, and legacies of the 1960s. But at the start of the twenty-first century, there seems little likelihood of such agreement emerging anytime in the near future. For better than three decades, the United States has been in the midst an ongoing "culture war," fought over issues of political philosophy, race relations, gender roles, and personal morality left unresolved since the end of the 1960s.

We make no claim to be offering a "total interpretation" of the 1960s in *America Divided*. We do, however, wish to suggest some larger interpretive guidelines for understanding the decade. We believe the 1960s are best understood not as an aberration, but as an integral part of American history. It was a time of intense conflict and millennial expectations, similar in many respects to the one Americans endured a century earlier—with results as mixed, ambiguous, and frustrating as those produced by the Civil War. Liberalism was not as powerful in the 1960s as is often assumed; nor, equally, was conservatism as much on the defensive. The insurgent political and social movements of the decade—including civil rights and black power, the

New Left, environmentalism and feminism—drew upon even as they sought to transform values and beliefs deeply rooted in American political culture. The youthful adherents of the counterculture shared more in common with the loyalists of the dominant culture than either would have acknowledged at the time. And the most profound and lasting effects of the 1960s are to be found in the realm of "the personal" rather than "the political."

Living through a period of intense historical change has its costs, as the distinguished essayist, poet, and novelist Robert Penn Warren observed in 1961. Until the 1860s, Penn Warren argued, Americans "had no history in the deepest and most inward sense." The "dream of freedom incarnated in a more perfect union" bequeathed to Americans by the founding fathers had yet to be "submitted to the test of history":

> There was little awareness of the cost of having a history. The anguished scrutiny of the meaning of the vision in experience had not become a national reality. It became a reality, and we became a nation, only with the Civil War.[11]

In the 1960s, Americans were plunged back into "anguished scrutiny" of the meaning of their most fundamental beliefs and institutions in a renewed test of history. They reacted with varying degrees of wisdom and folly, optimism and despair, selflessness and pettiness—all those things that taken together make us, in any decade, but particularly so in times of civil warfare, sadly (and occasionally grandly) human. It is our hope that, above all else, readers will take from this book some sense of how the 1960s, like the 1860s, served for Americans as the "dramatization of our humanity."

CHAPTER 1

Gathering of the Forces

WE HAVE ENTERED A PERIOD OF ACCELERATING BIGNESS IN ALL ASPECTS OF AMERICAN LIFE."

—*Eric Johnston, U.S. Chamber of Commerce, 1957*[1]

Seven years after it ended, World War II elected Dwight David Eisenhower president. As supreme commander of Allied forces in Europe, "Ike" had projected a handsome, confident presence that symbolized the nation's resolve to defeat its enemies. After the war, both major parties wooed the retired general before he revealed that he had always been a Republican.

In many ways, the country Eisenhower governed during the 1950s was still living in the aftermath of its triumph in history's bloodiest conflict. Millions of veterans and their families basked in the glow of a healthy economy—defying predictions that peace would bring on another depression. Long years of prosperity allowed Americans to dream that, for the first time in history, the problem of scarcity—which bred poverty, joblessness, and desperation—might soon be solved. But they also feared that a new and even more devastating world war—fought with nuclear weapons—could break out at any time. Affluence might suddenly give way to annihilation. The backdrop to the '60s was thus a society perched between great optimism and great fear.

As he prepared to leave the White House in the early days of January 1961, Ike was reasonably content with his own record in office. His final State of the Union address, read to Congress by a lowly clerk, boasted of an economy that had grown 25 percent since he entered the White House in January 1953. A recession that began in 1958 had hung on too long; over 6 percent of American wage earners still could not find a job. But, with unemployment insurance being extended for millions of workers, there seemed no danger of a return to the bread lines and homelessness of the 1930s.

Moreover, Eisenhower could claim, with some justification, that his administration had improved the lives of most Americans. During his tenure, real wages had increased by one-fifth, the system of interstate highways was rapidly expanded, and new schools and houses seemed to sprout up in every middle-class community. To counter the Soviet Union, the Congress had found it necessary to boost defense spending and create what Eisenhower, a few days later, called a "military–industrial complex" whose "unwarranted influence" citizens should check. Nevertheless, the budget of the federal government was in balance. America's best-loved modern general had become one of its favorite presidents. Ike left office with a popularity rating of nearly 60 percent.

Dwight Eisenhower's America held sway over a Western world that, since the late 1940s, had been undergoing a golden age of economic growth and political stability in which the lives of ordinary people became easier than ever before in world history.[2] U.S. political and corporate leaders dominated the noncommunist world through military alliances, technologically advanced weaponry, democratic ideals, and consumer products that nearly everyone desired—from Coca-Cola to Cadillacs to cowboy movies. At home, American workers in the heavily unionized manufacturing and construction industries

Workers and engineers complete production of Atlas ICBM missiles at a General Dynamics Plant near San Diego, 1958. Source: Dwayne A. Day Collection

enjoyed a degree of job security and a standard of living that usually included an automobile, a television, a refrigerator, a washing machine and a dryer, and long-playing records. A generation earlier, none of these fabulous goods—except, perhaps, the car—would have been owned by their working-class parents. TVs and LP disks were not even on the market until the 1940s.

Most economists minimized the impact of the late-'50s recession and predicted that all Americans would soon share in the benefits of affluence. In 1962, after completing a long-term study of U.S. incomes, a team of social scientists from the University of Michigan announced, "The elimination of poverty is well within the means of Federal, state, and local governments."[3] Some commentators even fretted that prosperity was sapping the moral will Americans needed to challenge the appeal of Communism in the Third World. In 1960, the *New York Times* asked "How can a nation drowning in a sea of luxury and mesmerized by the trivialities of the television screen have the faintest prospect of comprehending the plight of hundreds of millions in this world for whom a full stomach is a rare experience?"[4]

Only the omnipresent Cold War tarnished the golden age for the comfortable majority. Beginning a few months after the end of the Second World War, the United States and Soviet Union had employed both the force of arms and ideological conviction to persuade the vast majority of nations and their citizens to choose up sides. The two superpowers fought with sophisticated propaganda, exports of arms and military advisers, and huge spy services—an ever growing arsenal that burdened the poorer countries of the Soviet bloc more than the prosperous, industrial nations in the West. Since 1949, when the USSR exploded its first atomic bomb, the specter of nuclear armageddon loomed over the conflict.

In preparing for that ultimate war, the overarmed combatants exacted a terrible price. The United States and USSR tested nuclear weapons in the open air, exposing tens of thousands of their soldiers and untold numbers of civilians to dangerous doses of radiation from fallout. Both powers helped quash internal revolts within their own virtual empire—the Caribbean region for the United States, Eastern Europe for the Soviets. In Guatemala and Hungary, the Dominican Republic and Poland, local tyrants received military assistance and economic favors as long as they remained servile. For the U.S. State Department, any sincere land reformer was an incipient Communist; while, on the other side, any critic of Soviet domination was branded an agent of imperialism. The two blocs were not morally equivalent: in the United States, the harassment of dissenters violated the nation's most cherished values, while in the USSR, the routine silencing and jailing of political opponents conformed with Communist doctrine.

By the late '50s, the death of Joseph Stalin and the end of the Korean War had diminished the possibility of a new world war. But anxiety still ran high. The United States, a commission funded by the Rockefeller brothers reported in 1958, was "in grave danger, threatened by the rulers of one-third of mankind." Two years later, Democratic presidential candidate John F. Kennedy warned, "The enemy is the communist system itself—implacable, insatiable, unceasing in its drive for world domination. . . . [This] is a struggle for supremacy between two conflicting ideologies: freedom under God versus ruthless, godless tyranny."[5] Western European countries were rapidly shedding their colonies in Africa and Asia, and American leaders feared that native pro-Communist leaders would fill the gap.

By the end of the decade, the most immediate threat to the United States seemed to come from an island located only ninety miles off the coast of Florida. Cuba had long been an informal American colony; U.S. investors owned 40 percent of its sugar and 90 percent of its mining wealth, and a major American naval base sat on Guantanamo Bay, at the eastern tip of the island. On New Year's Day, 1959, this arrangement was disrupted: a rebel army led by Fidel Castro overthrew the sitting Cuban government, a corrupt and brutal regime that had lost the support of its people. At first, the new rulers of Cuba were the toast of the region. The bearded young leader—handsome, well-educated, eloquent, and witty—embarked on a speaking tour of the United States, where he met for three hours with Vice President Nixon.

But Fidel Castro was bent on a more fundamental revolution than American officials could accept. His government soon began executing officials of the old regime and confiscating $1 billion of land and other property owned by U.S. "imperialists." When the Eisenhower administration protested, Castro signed a trade agreement with the USSR and began to construct a state socialist economy. Anticommunist Cubans, many of whom were upper class, began to flee the island. By the time Ike left office, a Cuban exile army was training under American auspices to topple the only pro-Soviet government in the Western Hemisphere.

At the time, communism appeared to be a dynamic, if sinister, force. Since the end of the world war, its adherents steadily gained new territory, weapons, and followers. U.S. officials were also concerned over reports that the Soviet economy was growing at double the rate of the American system. The other side was still far behind, but the idea that the USSR and its allies in Cuba, China, and elsewhere might capture the future was profoundly disturbing. Another high-level commission announced that the Soviets had more nuclear missiles than did the West. And, in 1957, the USSR launched *Sputnik*, a tiny unmanned satellite that seemed to give them a huge edge in the race to conquer space. All this threatened the confidence of Americans in their technological prowess, as well as their security. The year before *Sputnik*, Soviet Premier Nikita S. Khrushchev had boasted, "We shall bury you." It didn't seem impossible.

Responding to the perception of a grave Communist threat, Congress did not question the accuracy of the missile reports (which later proved to be false) or the solidity of the alliance between Moscow and Beijing (which was already coming apart). Lawmakers kept the armed services supplied with young draftees and the latest weapons, both nuclear and conventional (which also meant good jobs for their districts). The space program received lavish funding, mostly through the new National Aeronautics and Space Administration (NASA), and positive coverage in the media. Billions also flowed into the coffers of American intelligence agencies. In the Third World, any stalwart nationalist who sought to control foreign investment or questioned the value of U.S. bases was fair game for the Central Intelligence Agency's repertoire of "covert actions."

The Cold War also chilled political debate at home. Liberals learned to avoid making proposals that smacked of "socialism," such as national health insurance, an idea their Western European allies had already adopted. To question the morality of the Cold War sounded downright "un-American." The need for a common front against the enemy made ideological diversity seem outmoded if not subversive.

But not all Americans at the dawn of the decade shared a world view steeped in abundance at home and perpetual tension about the Cold War abroad. "The American equation of success with the big time reveals an awful disrespect for human life and human achievement," remarked the black writer James Baldwin in 1960.[6] Emerging in the postwar era was an alternative America—peopled by organizers for civil rights for blacks and women, by radical intellectuals and artists, and by icons of a new popular culture. These voices did not speak in unison, but, however inchoately, they articulated a set of values different from those of the men who ruled from the White House, corporate headquarters, and the offices of metropolitan newspapers.

The dissenters advocated pacifism instead of Cold War, racial and class equality instead of a hierarchy of wealth and status, a politics that prized direct democracy over the clash of interest groups, a frankness toward sex instead of a rigid split between the public and the intimate, and a boredom with cultural institutions—from schools to supermarkets—that taught Americans to praise their country, work hard, and consume joyfully. Dissenters did not agree that an expanding economy was the best measure of human happiness and tried to empathize with the minority of their fellow citizens who had little to celebrate.

To understand the turbulent events of the 1960s, one must appreciate the contradictory nature of the society of 180 million people that was variously admired and detested, imitated and feared throughout the globe. To grasp how and why America changed economically, politically, and culturally in the 1960s, one must capture something of its diverse reality at the start of the stormiest decade since the Civil War.

We set out a few material facts, benchmarks of what had been achieved and what was lacking in American society. Of course, the meaning of any

particular fact depends upon where one stands, and with what views and resources one engages the world.

A massive baby boom was under way. It began in 1946, right after victory in World War II, and was ebbing only slightly by the end of the '50s. In
that decade, an average of over 4 million births a year were recorded. Teenaged
wives and husbands in their early twenties were responsible for much of this
unprecedented surge. The baby boom, which also occurred in Canada and
Australia, resulted from postwar optimism as well as prosperity. None of these
English-speaking nations had been damaged in the global conflict, and most
of their citizens could smile about their prospects. Western Europe, in contrast, was devastated by the war, and people remained wary of the future.
Economies there recovered quickly and then grew at a more rapid pace than
in the U.S.—but birthrates in England, France, Germany, and Italy still lagged
near prewar levels.

Millions of young American families settled in the suburbs—in new developments like Levittown on Long Island and in the previously agricultural
San Fernando Valley adjacent to Los Angeles. Large contractors erected acres
of tract houses whose inexpensive price (about $7000 each) and gleaming
electrical appliances almost compensated for the absence of individual character. Hoping to create instant communities, developers also built schools,
swimming pools, and baseball diamonds. The federal government smoothed
the way by providing low-interest, long-term mortgages, and new highways
to get to and from work and shopping centers.

Thus, millions of men and women who had grown up in crowded urban
apartment houses or isolated, agrarian towns now possessed, if they kept up
their payments, a tangible slab of the American dream. Tract names like "Crys-
tal Stream," "Stonybrook," and "Villa Serena" lured city dwellers with the
promise of a peaceful, bucolic retreat. By 1960, for the first time in U.S. history, a majority of American families owned the homes in which they lived.[7]
Home ownership did seem to require an endless round of maintenance and
improvements. "No man who owns his house and lot can be a Communist,"
quipped developer William J. Levitt, "He has too much to do."[8]

The suburbs were more diverse places than their promoters' publicity
suggested. White factory workers and their families joined the migration along
with "organization men" who rushed to the commuter train, ties flying and
briefcases in hand. And suburbanites tended to live near and socialize with
others of the same class. Status distinctions by neighborhood, lot size, and
the quality of parks and schools defied the notion that every suburbanite belonged to the same "middle class."

However grand or humble the house, most Americans were earning
enough to pay the mortgage. By 1960, the real hourly wage of manufacturing workers had doubled since the beginning of World War II. The rise in
personal income, which occurred despite periodic recessions, was accompa-

A white working-class family outside their suburban home in the late 1950s. Source: George Meany Memorial Archives

nied by a steady increase in the number of women entering the paid labor force. Women over 45 led the way, swelling the professions and the ranks of office workers. The number of married women with jobs had risen since the war. But the family "breadwinner" was still assumed to be male; fewer than 250,000 women with small children worked outside the home.

American women, no matter their circumstances, were still expected to become cheerful housewives and mothers. In 1951, *Seventeen* magazine advised its young readers to be "a partner of man . . . not his rival, his enemy, or his plaything. Your partnership in most cases will produce children, and together you and the man will create a haven, a home, a way of life."[9]

But the growing number of women in the workforce was beginning to undermine the domestic ideal. In 1960, CBS televised a documentary about the "trapped housewife," and the *New York Times* described a class of educated women who "feel stifled in their homes. . . . Like shut ins, they feel left out." With more children around, even new appliances didn't lessen the time spent on housework. Family "experts" counseled every wife to help her husband "rise to his capacity." In response, journalist Marya Mannes criticized the suppression of intelligent women by calling up fears of their advancing Soviet counterparts: "We have for years been wasting one of the resources on which our strength depends and which other civilizations are using to their advantage."[10]

In their bedrooms, some women did enjoy a new kind of freedom. The widely read Kinsey Report on female sexuality suggested that as many as half of all American women had intercourse before marriage and reported that one-quarter of married women had had sex with someone besides their husband. By decade's end, over 80 percent of wives of childbearing age were using some form of contraception; the total was higher among women with at least a high school education. And, in 1960, the federal government allowed marketing of a birth control pill—the first reliable contraceptive that did not interfere with "natural" intercourse.[11]

The spread of prosperity encouraged most citizens to identify themselves with the "middle class." The mass media and leaders in business and government assured Americans that the days of backbreaking labor for little reward were over. Supposedly, getting to and from the job was now more arduous than anything one did while at work. In 1960, *Time* published a cover story entitled "Those Rush-Hour Blues" in which a psychiatrist stated that commuters (their maleness assumed) actually enjoyed traffic jams and crowded trains. "The twice-daily sacrifice of the commuter to the indignities of transportation satisfied something deep within the husband's psyche," explained Dr. Jose Barchilon. "In modern society, there are few opportunities for the breadwinner to endure personal hardship in earning the family living, such as clearing the forest or shooting a bear."[12]

In reality, for millions of workers—in mines, in factories, and at construction sites—work remained both hard and dangerous. But, thanks to newly powerful labor unions, it was better compensated than ever before. The labor movement helped lift millions of wage earners into the middle class. A third of the nonagrarian labor force was unionized, and smart employers learned that the best way to stave off pesky labor organizers was to improve the pay and benefits of their own workers before unions gained a foothold. Even the barons of the mighty steel industry could not humble Big Labor. In 1959, industry spokesmen announced they would no longer permit the United Steel Workers to block job-eliminating technological changes. But the union called a strike and, after a four-month walkout, its members prevailed.

Heavy industries like steel were still the core of the American economy. Metals and automobiles produced in the U.S. dominated world markets—although the West Germans were beginning to pose some serious competition. And the technological auguries were excellent. Such new inventions as digital computers and Tupperware were propelling electronics, aircraft, and chemical firms to growth rates superior to those of older companies like Ford and U.S. Steel.

The Cold War was also helping to transform the economic map. Military contracts pumped up the profit margins of such high-tech firms as Hewlett-

George Meany, the first president of the AFL-CIO and a symbol of the power and pragmatism of organized labor. Source: *George Meany Memorial Archives*

Packard and General Electric. Opportunity shone on entrepreneurs and skilled workers alike in a vast "Gunbelt" stretching from Seattle down through southern California and over to Texas. This was the civilian half of the military–industrial complex Eisenhower had warned about—and it was drawing population and federal money away from the old manufacturing hub in the East and Midwest.

And all over the country, more and more Americans were working in "white-collar" jobs. Gradually but surely, the economy was shifting away from the industrial age toward an era dominated by service and clerical employment. In 1956, for the first time, jobs of the newer kind outnumbered blue-collar ones.

The term "white collar" masked huge differences of pay, skill, and the autonomy allowed a worker on the job. A kindergarten teacher's aide had neither the comfortable salary nor the freedom to teach what and how she liked that most college professors took for granted. And sharing an employer was less significant than whether one managed investments for a huge commercial bank or, instead, handed out deposit slips or cleaned its offices. "My job doesn't have prestige," remarked bank teller Nancy Rodgers, "It's a service job . . . you are there to serve them. They are not there to serve you."[13]

In any economy, however successful, there are losers as well as winners. For a sizable minority of citizens, the American dream was more a wish than a reality. State university branches multiplied, as the number of college students increased by 1960 to 3.6 million, more than double the number 20 years before. Yet less than half the adults in the U.S. were high school graduates. Lack of schooling did not disqualify one from getting a job in a factory or warehouse, but the future clearly belonged to the educated. Already, a man who had graduated from college earned about three times more than his counterpart who had dropped out at the lower grades. Where union pressure was absent, wages could be abysmally low. In 1960 farm workers earned, on average, just $1038 a year.[14] In the Appalachian Mountains and the Mississippi Delta, many poor residents owned a television and a used car or truck—but lacked an indoor toilet and a year-round job.

The central cities many Levittowners had quit were already on the road to despair. African Americans who moved to the metropolises of the North seeking jobs and racial tolerance often found neither. Black unemployment stubbornly tallied nearly double the rate for whites. Following World War II, black migrants filled up old industrial cities like Detroit and Chicago that were steadily losing factory jobs to the suburbs. Few white settlers on the crabgrass frontier welcomed blacks as prospective neighbors. In 1960, not one of 82,000 Long Island Levittowners was an African American—even though New York state had passed a civil rights law in the mid-1940s.

Out West, Mexican Americans—the nation's second largest minority—were struggling to achieve a modicum of the economic fruits that most whites enjoyed. Less than one-fifth of Mexican-American adults were high school graduates (a lower number than for blacks), and most held down menial jobs—in the cities and the fields. During World War II, to replace citizens drafted into the military, the federal government had allowed U.S. farmers to import workers from Mexico, dubbed *braceros* (from the Spanish word for "arms"). The end of the war alleviated the labor shortage, but the political clout of agribusiness kept the *bracero* program going—and it severely hampered the ability of native-born farmworkers to better their lot.

These problems remained all but invisible in the business and political centers of the East. Outside the Southwest, Americans regarded themselves as living in a society with only two races—white and black. The federal census did not even consider Mexican Americans a separate group.

A growing chorus of intellectuals blasted the hypocrisies of the era. In their eyes, America had become a "mass society" that had lost its aesthetic and moral bearings. Critic Lewis Mumford condemned surburbia, too broadly, as "a treeless, communal waste, inhabited by people in the same class, the same income, the same age group, witnessing the same television performances, eating the same tasteless pre-fabricated foods from the same freezers." Sociologist C. Wright Mills indicted a "power elite" for fostering a system of "organized irresponsibility" in which "the standard of living dominates the style of life."[15] Mills joined with radical economists Paul Sweezy and Seymour Melman in arguing that "a permanent war economy" geared to fighting the Cold War was imperiling democracy even as it promoted growth. But such criticisms did not engage most Americans, for whom private life was all consuming.

Nor did they convince the most powerful politicians in the land. The primary business of government, Democratic and Republican leaders agreed, was to keep the economy growing and the military strong. Conservatives and liberals in both parties squabbled over details: whether, for instance, to fund a new wing of B-52 bombers or more science programs in the public schools. But rarely did any senator question the wisdom of policing the world (as had Robert Taft, the GOP's leading conservative, in the late '40s).

The previous generation of lawmakers had fought bitterly over the social programs of Franklin D. Roosevelt's New Deal and Harry Truman's Fair Deal. But the first Republican president since Herbert Hoover accepted a limited welfare state as the new status quo. Dwight Eisenhower wrote from the White House to his conservative brother Edgar, "Should any political party attempt to abolish social security and eliminate labor laws and farm programs, you would not hear of that party again in our political history."[16]

By the end of the decade, FDR's party was making something of a comeback. In the 1958 congressional election, Democrats gained their biggest margins since the beginning of World War II. In the midst of the recession, Republicans who ran against union power went down to defeat in the populous states of Ohio and California. Liberals in Congress and in advocacy groups like Americans for Democratic Action (ADA) got busy drafting plans for higher minimum wages, government health insurance for the elderly, and other extensions of the New Deal. Meanwhile, the Supreme Court—headed, ironically, by a chief justice (Earl Warren), whom Eisenhower had appointed—was aggressively expanding the definition of individual and group "rights" to favor demonstrators against racial inequality and persons convicted on the basis of evidence gathered illegally. A public which, according to polls, admired Eleanor Roosevelt more than any woman in the world, seemed amenable to another wave of governmental activism.

But despite the Democrats' surge, the party remained an uneasy coalition of the urban, pro-union North and the small-town, low-wage South. Big city machines, originally established by Irish Catholics, continued to wield a measure of power in the two largest cities—New York City and Chicago—as well as in Pittsburgh, Cleveland, and Buffalo. Below the Mason–Dixon line, most whites still voted against the ghost of Abraham Lincoln—although in 1956, Eisenhower, who assured southerners he wanted "to make haste slowly" on civil rights, did win the electoral votes of five former Confederate states.[17] In 1960, the GOP could count only seven congressmen from the South—and virtually no state or county officials. American women had won the vote in 1920 but rarely did they figure significantly as candidates or campaign managers.

Republicans were still the party of Main Street and Wall Street—of American business, large and small, and of voters who cherished the rights of private property and were leery of "big government." Party allegiance tended to follow class lines. The wealthiest stratum of Americans voted heavily for the GOP, as did most voters with college degrees and professional occupations. Blue-collar workers, particularly those who harbored bitter memories of the Great Depression, favored the Democrats by a 4–1 margin. The legacy of old battles over restricting immigration and instituting Prohibition also played a part. Outside the white South, native-born Protestants tilted toward the Republicans, while Catholics and Jews—who were closer to their foreign-born roots—usually favored the Democrats.

The result of these alignments was a legislative system unfriendly to serious change—whether in a liberal or conservative direction. Key posts in Congress were held by southern or border state Democrats who had accrued decades of seniority: the Speaker of the House, the majority leader of the Senate, and the chairmen of committees with power over tax and appropriations bills. Howard Smith of Virginia, who had first been elected to Congress in 1930, headed the mighty Rules Committee. Smith was able to block most proposals he disapproved from even coming to the House floor. And he *despised* civil rights bills. Like all but a handful of Southern congressmen, Smith represented a district in which few blacks were allowed to vote—and he intended to keep it that way.

Not every southerner was so uncompromising. Both House Speaker Sam Rayburn and Senate majority leader Lyndon Johnson were shrewd Texas moderates who retained their power by balancing demands from different wings of their party. But most southern Democrats and nearly all Republicans routinely united to defeat new programs to aid big cities, racial minorities, and the poor. The mechanisms of government were purring along nicely, so why disturb them? As even liberal McGeorge Bundy, then a Harvard dean (and soon to become a federal policymaker) intoned, "If American politics have a predilection for the center, it is a Good Thing."[18]

If mainstream politics in the 1950s lacked fire and daring, the same could not be said of popular culture. The postwar absorption with leisure generated a feverish search for new ways to spend all that free time and disposable income. In the past, Americans had fought major battles over who would control the workplace and how to distribute the fruits of their labor. Mass movements of small farmers and wage earners had pressured the powerful to recognize unions, subsidize crop prices, and establish Social Security and a

minimum wage. Cultural differences motivated some earlier mass movements, the prohibitionists being a prime example. But after World War II,
public conflicts often turned on matters of cultural taste—in music, in styles
of dress and hair, slang, drugs, and sexual behavior.

Popular music—especially rock and roll and the rhythm and blues from
which it sprang—became a major arena of generational strife. The young people who listened to, danced to, and played rock and rhythm and blues were
implicitly rejecting the notion that creativity obeyed a color line. Leaping
over racial barriers were black artists like Willie Mae (Big Mama) Thornton
and Chuck Berry, Mexican Americans like singer Richie Valens (born Valen-
zuela), Greek-American bandleader Johnny Otis (who identified himself as
black), white Southern Baptist Elvis Presley, and Jewish-American song writers Mike Stoller, Jerry Lieber, and Carole King. Lieber and Stoller wrote
"Hound Dog" for Big Mama Thornton, who made it a hit with black audiences in 1954 before Elvis covered it in 1956—and sold millions of copies.

Established record companies tried to resist the onslaught. National music awards usually went to more innocuous recordings, despite the higher
sales of rock. In 1960 Percy Faith's "Theme from *A Summer Place*," a string-
filled waltz, won the Grammy for best song of the year—beating out Roy Or-
bison's "Only the Lonely," the Drifters' "Save the Last Dance for Me," "Stay"
by Maurice Williams and the Zodiacs, and Chubby Checker's "The Twist."
Faith's music would soon be heard mainly in elevators; while the other songs
became rock classics and are still played by disk jockeys throughout the world.

Satire also appealed to growing numbers of adolescents. *Mad* comics published clever putdowns of advertisements, Hollywood movies, television
shows, suburban culture, and the military. Edited by Harvey Kurtzman (who
had once drawn cartoons for the Communist *Daily Worker*), *Mad* ridiculed
nearly everything that established middlebrow magazines like *Life* and
Reader's Digest took for granted—particularly the mood of self-satisfaction.
"What, Me Worry?" asked Alfred E. Neuman, the gap-toothed idiot with over-
sized ears and freckles whose comic image beamed from every issue of *Mad*.
High school readers also snapped up novels about alienated youth. One of
the most compelling was *The Catcher in the Rye* (1951), J.D. Salinger's tale
about a teenager named Holden Caulfield who drops out of his prep school
to wander dyspeptically around New York City. "Phonies," Caulfield called
the adults who plagued his unhappy, if materially privileged, life.

Even World War II was becoming grist for farce. Joseph Heller's best-
selling 1961 novel, *Catch-22*, signaled a new eagerness to question the logic
of established authority. The protagonist, named Yossarian, is an American
bombardier in Europe who wants to be grounded after having risked his life
flying dozens of missions over enemy territory. But, according to military regulations, he can opt out of the war only if he is crazy. So Yossarian goes to
his unit's medical officer, Doc Daneeka, asking to be grounded on that basis.

But the rules don't permit it. "You mean there's a catch?" Yossarian asks:

Sure there's a catch," Doc Daneeka replied. "Catch-22. Anyone who wants to get out of combat duty isn't really crazy. . . . Yossarian was moved very deeply by the absolute simplicity of this clause of Catch-22, and let out a respectful whistle.
"That's some catch, that Catch-22," he observed.
"It's the best there is," Doc Daneeka agreed.[19]

Some young whites were attracted to a more extravagant style of alienation. They sought refuge among and enlightenment from America's most dispossessed and despised groups—tramps, migrant laborers, black criminals—as well as jazz musicians. In 1957, the novelist Norman Mailer published a controversial essay, "The White Negro," in which he celebrated hipsters of his own race who "drifted out at night looking for action with a black man's code to fit their facts." Mailer romanticized black men who "lived in the enormous present . . . relinquishing the pleasures of the mind for the more obligatory pleasures of the body." He predicted that "a time of violence, new hysteria, confusion and rebellion" would soon come along to "replace the time of conformity."[20]

Cultural innovation is usually the province of the young. But prime-time television, perhaps the most significant cultural force in the 1950s, was an infatuation that bridged the generations. During that decade, TV developed from a curiosity into a staple of the American home. By the end of the '50s, close to ninety percent of families owned at least one set, and the average person watched about five hours a day. In 1960, the most popular shows were westerns starring male characters who were strong, violent, and just (*Gunsmoke* and *Have Gun, Will Travel* headed the list) and a crime show about the 1920s whose heroes were latter-day gunslingers in suits (*The Untouchables*). Dominating the medium were the three national networks—CBS, NBC, and ABC—whose evening offerings provided the only entertainment experience most Americans had in common.

Not all was right in TV land, however. In 1959, Charles Van Doren, a handsome young English professor who had thrilled viewers with his victories on the quiz show *Twenty-One*, admitted to Congress that the program had been fixed. The show's producer had given Van Doren the answers in advance. President Eisenhower remarked that the deception was "a terrible thing to do to the American people," revealing how strong a grip the relatively new medium had over the nation.[21] The exposé, that same year, of disk jockeys who accepted "payola" (bribes) from record companies for playing their records on the air was, by comparison, a minor matter. Television was admired as clean family entertainment that promoted "togetherness." Rock and roll had an outlaw reputation; one almost expected it to be tarred with corruption.

Sports too had an occasional scandal—college basketball players shaving points or boxers throwing fights. But, in 1960, the world of gifted athletes and their fans was still conducted on a rather simple scale and did not yield large profits. College football got more attention than the grittier professional variety; major league baseball had recently placed its first two teams on the West Coast; and there were a scant eight teams in the National Basketball Association, and only six in the National Hockey League. Although baseball was the most popular spectator sport, the average major league player earned only about twice the salary of a skilled union worker—and seldom, if ever, was asked to endorse a product.

The sports world was more racially integrated than American neighborhoods and schools, yet it too often mirrored the attitudes of the larger society. During the 1960 Cotton Bowl game, a fight broke out after a player on the all-white Texas team called one of his Syracuse opponents "a big black dirty nigger." Syracuse won the game and, with it, the national championship. Magazine headlines about "A Brawling Battle of the Hard-Noses" implied that racist taunts were just part of a manly game.[22]

For solace from the imperfections of the secular world, Americans turned to organized religion. A majority of Americans were affiliated with a church or synagogue—the highest total ever. The popular evangelist Billy Graham staged televised revivals in major cities in which he preached a fusion between godliness and Americanism. Millions bought books by Rev. Norman Vincent Peale, who believed that "positive thinking" could release the potential for spiritual joy and worldly success that lay inside every Christian soul. Not all Roman Catholics accepted the conservative views of the church hierarchy, but most basked in a new legitimacy secured by the stalwart anticommunism of their bishops and their own rising fortunes. It even seemed possible that a Catholic could be elected president. For their part, many Jews, now relocated to prosperous suburbs, turned to Conservative and Reform synagogues to find a substitute for the vigorous community their parents had found either in the Orthodox faith or in the socialist left. In the "return to God," one could glimpse elements of both the pride and the anxiety emblematic of the U.S. at the dawn of the '60s.

No area of national life was more highly charged than the relationship between black and white Americans. Racial segregation was still firmly established in much of the U.S. in 1960. Across the South, thousands of public schools had closed down rather than allow black children to sit alongside whites.

Official racism had many faces—all of them immoral, some also ludicrous and petty. South of New Orleans, a local political boss named Leander Perez told a rally of 5000 people that desegregation was a conspiracy by "zionist Jews" and the National Association for the Advancement of Colored People (NAACP). "Don't wait for your daughter to be raped by these Congolese," warned Perez. "Do something about it now." The next day, a race riot broke out. The city fathers of Montgomery, Alabama, sold off the animals at their municipal zoo rather than obey a court order to allow black people to enjoy them. Meanwhile, in the nation's capital, the *Washington Post* routinely printed want ads that specified, "Stenographer—White, age 20 to 30 . . . " and "Short-order cook, white, fast, exper."[23]

The movement that would lift this burden—and catalyze many other jolts to American culture and politics—was gathering force in black churches, schools, and homes. Its funds were meager, and it had, as yet, little political influence. But the sounds of hope, preached in an idiom both militant and loving, were swelling up from picket lines outside Woolworth stores in New York City, in the small towns of the Mississippi Delta, and from a Masonic temple in Richmond, Virginia—former capital of the Confederacy.

On New Year's Day, 1960, Rev. Martin Luther King, Jr. came to Richmond to speak to a mass rally against the closing of the public schools. "It is an unstoppable movement," the thirty-year-old King informed segregationists. "We will wear you down by our capacity to suffer, and in the process we will win your hearts. . . . Nothing is more sublime than suffering and sacrifice for a great cause."[24] Before that movement—and King's own life—had run their course, the self-satisfied tones of Dwight Eisenhower's last State of the Union address would seem a murmur of lost illusions. The greatest social upheaval in America since the Civil War was about to begin.

CHAPTER 2

Black Ordeal, Black Freedom

I'VE GOT THE LIGHT OF FREEDOM, LORD,
AND I'M GOING TO LET IT SHINE,
LET IT SHINE, LET IT SHINE, LET IT SHINE!
—Traditional spiritual

One morning in July of 1944, a civilian bus driver at Fort Hood, Texas, ordered a black army lieutenant to "get to the back of the bus where the colored people belong." The lieutenant refused, arguing that the military had recently ordered its buses desegregated. MPs came and took him into custody. Four weeks later, the black officer went on trial for insubordination. If convicted by the court martial, he faced a dishonorable discharge—which would have crippled his job opportunities for the rest of his life.

The lieutenant's name was Jackie Robinson. Three years later, Robinson would don the uniform of the Brooklyn Dodgers to become the first African-American in the twentieth century to play major league baseball.

Robinson's bold defiance of racial custom, his appeal to federal authority, and his acquittal by that military court in 1944 all indicated that significant changes were in spin. World War II was a watershed in African-American history, raising the hopes of people who, with their children, would build the massive black freedom movement of the 1960s.

The urgent need for soldiers to fight abroad and for wage-earners to forge an "arsenal of democracy" at home convinced a flood of African Americans to leave the South. Mechanized cotton pickers shrunk the need for agrarian labor just as the lure of good jobs in war industries sapped the will to stay in the fields. Metropolises from Los Angeles to New York filled up with dark-skinned residents—and, after the war, the flow persisted. Between 1940 and 1960, 4.5 million black men and women migrated out of Dixie; African Americans were fast becoming an urban people.

This second great migration (the first occurred during and just after World War I) helped pry open some long-padlocked doors. Before the war, all but a few blacks were excluded from access to good "white" jobs and the

Jackie Robinson being tagged out on an attempt to steal home. Source: *National Baseball of Fame, Cooperstown, NY*

best educational institutions. After the war, increasing numbers of blacks finished high school and gained entrance to historically white colleges; the number of African Americans in the skilled trades and in professions like medicine and education shot up.

Before the war, the black freedom movement was a small and fragile entity, repressed by southern authorities and shunned by many African Americans fearful of reprisals if they took part. In 1941, labor leader A. Phillip Randolph vowed to bring masses of demonstrators to Washington, D.C., unless the government opened up jobs in defense plants to black workers. His threat persuaded President Franklin Roosevelt to establish a Committee on Fair Employment Practices (FEPC) and to bar discrimination by unions and companies under government contract. During the war, the NAACP, the oldest national civil rights organization, increased its membership by a thousand percent. Many a black veteran returned from overseas with a new determination to fight the tyranny under which he'd been raised. "I paid my dues over there and I'm not going to take this anymore over here," stated a former black officer.[1]

Centuries of bondage and decades of rigid segregation (called "Jim Crow," after a bygone minstrel character) had taught African Americans hard lessons about the barriers they faced. A maxim of Frederick Douglass, the nineteenth-century abolitionist who had freed himself from slavery, seemed self-evident: "Power concedes nothing without a demand. It never did and it never will." The demand in the post–World War II era was for "freedom." But what did that mean?

Their history as a nation within a nation left most black people with both a deep sense of alienation from the society of their birth and an intense longing for full and equal citizenship. The black activist and intellectual W. E. B. DuBois wrote, in 1903, that the black American "ever feels his two-ness—an American, a Negro; two souls, two thoughts, two unreconciled strivings. Two warring ideals in one dark body, whose dogged strength alone keeps it from being torn asunder."[2]

The thousands of men and women who joined the freedom movement in the two decades after 1945 continued to live in perpetual tension between the two ideals. They demanded equality under the law—to be judged as individuals and not as members of a minority race. Yet, at the same time, their strength rested on ideas, relationships, and institutions that sprang from their own African-American community—one in which illiterate laborers and a small core of black professionals were bonded (not always happily) by race. The result was that a black individual—whether cook or physician—would rise from the community or not at all. The cause of civil rights was thus always, by necessity as much as design, also a demand for black power.

The legal effort that culminated in the most famous court ruling of the twentieth century illustrated the dual longings that DuBois described. In 1950, Thurgood Marshall and his talented team of NAACP lawyers decided to challenge the principle of segregated schools. But they were not acting from an abstract belief that black children should mix with whites. NAACP attorney Robert Carter later explained, "I believe that the majority sentiment in the black community was a desire to secure for blacks all of the educational nurturing available to whites. If ending school segregation was the way to that objective, fine; if, on the other hand, securing equal facilities was the way, that too was fine."[3]

Marshall's team was convinced that white authorities would always treat all-black schools as neglected stepchildren, denying them needed funds and other support. Research by psychologists Kenneth Clark and Mamie Phipps revealed that black children confined to segregated schools "incorporated into their developing self-image feelings of racial inferiority."[4] Young African Americans, the couple insisted, would never learn to respect themselves if they were barred from learning alongside members of the dominant race. On May 17, 1954, the Supreme Court unanimously agreed with NAACP attorneys who argued that separate schools violated the Fourteenth Amendment's guarantee of "equal protection of the laws."

The case that gave the ruling its name—*Oliver Brown, et al. v. Board of Education of Topeka, Shawnee County, Kansas, et al.*—illustrated the kind of demeaning irritations that marked daily life for most American blacks. In Topeka, training and salaries were roughly equal for teachers of both races. But black children had to ride buses to classrooms located miles away; their white peers could simply walk to school.

As DuBois understood, "two-ness" often entailed a painful bargain. Thousands of black teachers lost their jobs after school systems were desegregated. And when Jackie Robinson began playing the infield for the Dodgers, the two Negro baseball leagues made up one of the largest black-owned and -operated enterprises in America. Black fans took pride in the fact that sluggers like Josh Gibson and pitchers like Satchel Paige had skills equal or superior to those of white stars like Joe DiMaggio and Bob Feller.

But Robinson's success with the Dodgers (he led the team to the World Series in two of his first three years), followed by the gradual integration of other clubs, destroyed the Negro leagues. Their demise left an ironic legacy: it is likely that fewer black men earned a living as baseball players in the late 1950s and 1960s than during the era of Jim Crow. But not many African Americans mourned the old order. "Nothing was killing Negro baseball but Democracy," wrote journalist Wendell Smith in 1948.[5]

The changes that occurred during World War II and in the decade immediately following it were, by and large, encouraging ones. As black people filled the workplaces and streets of urban America, whites were finally beginning to grapple with "the problem of the color-line," which DuBois had predicted would be "the problem of the twentieth century." Academics and journalists increasingly condemned the belief in and practice of white supremacy. In 1948, President Harry Truman ordered the armed forces to desegregate. At its nominating convention that summer, the Democratic Party, for the first time in its long history, took an unambiguous stand for civil rights. Most of the southern delegates walked out in protest.

Still, such advances were only a first step toward liberating black people from the lower caste to which law, custom, economic exploitation, and vigilante violence had confined them. At midcentury, the income of black families averaged only 55 percent that of white families (and black women went out to work at higher proportions than did white women). Segregation remained the rule in most of America. After the war, African Americans began to have a realistic hope that their long night of hatred and economic abuse might end. But it would require two more decades of arduous, heroic effort—and intermittent support from sympathetic authorities—to bring about serious change.

In the South, the odds remained particularly formidable. By the 1950s, slavery had been dead for almost a century, but its legacy remained disturbingly alive in the hearts and minds of most white southerners. They had always treated black people as their social inferiors and saw no reason to change. Few members of the majority race questioned the demeaning etiquette that accompanied this tradition. When greeting a white person, black southerners were expected to avert their eyes. Blacks were required to address all whites, even adolescents, as "Mr.," "Miss," or "Mrs.," while whites routinely called blacks, whatever their age, by their first names or used such demeaning terms as "boy" or "aunty."

A large number of fiercely guarded prohibitions and exclusions defined the Jim Crow order. Whites and blacks were not supposed to drink or dine together, in private homes or restaurants. They did not attend the same schools or churches or live in the same neighborhoods. Public toilets and drinking fountains were restricted by race. And, in nearly every industry, there were strict lines dividing "white" jobs from "black" ones.

Behind such rules was a lurking dread of interracial sexuality. Many southern whites viewed black men as possessed of an insatiable desire for white women. Segregated institutions were designed to keep intimate contacts across the color line to a minimum. A black man who made a sexual comment to a white woman was considered tantamount to a rapist. The slightest transgression of the code might lead to a lynching tree.

The hypocrisy was glaring. In fact, many white men patronized black prostitutes and those who could afford it sometimes took black mistresses—practices resented by black men and by women of both races. For white women, the pedestal of purity could be an emotional cage. Willie Morris, a white writer from Yazoo City, Mississippi, was shocked during World War II when he encountered a woman of his own race who actually enjoyed sex. "I had thought that only Negro women engaged in the act of love with white men just for fun."[6]

Segregation enforced injustices that were economic as well as interpersonal. In rural areas, black elementary schools were usually open only during the winter months (when there was no planting or harvesting to be done) and suffered from ill-trained teachers, a paucity of supplies, and crowded classrooms that mixed students of different ages. The main housing available to blacks was cheaply built and distant from most sources of employment and commercial recreation. Interracial labor unions were rare in the South, and blacks could seldom find jobs that paid a secure income and held out the possibility of advancement. A black laborer could teach himself to master a craft such as carpentry or machine building, only to see a younger white with little or no experience gain a skilled position and the coveted wage that went with it.

As before the Civil War, when whites blamed abolitionists for stirring up their slaves, Southern authorities after World War II claimed "their Negroes" were a contented lot, that only "outside agitators" with Communist proclivities sought to overturn the status quo. But belying such confident words were the measures taken to keep black people from voting, especially in Deep South states where they were most numerous. Poll taxes were raised or lowered, depending on the race of the applicant. Alabama gave county registrars the power to determine whether prospective voters could "understand and explain any article of the Constitution of the United States" and were of "good character and [understood] the duties and obligations of good citizenship under a republican form of government." Mississippi officials came up with ludicrous questions for aspiring registrants such as "How many bubbles in a bar of soap?"[7]

As the authorities in rural areas, white registrars set their own working hours, bent election laws at will, and made it as difficult as possible for blacks to acquire the necessary documents. In 1946 a black army veteran from McComb, Mississippi, testified to a congressional committee that a county voting clerk had required him to describe the entire contents of a Democratic primary ballot. The prospective voter was not allowed to see the ballot and so had to decline. The clerk disdainfully rejected his application, telling him "You brush up on your civics and come back."[8]

Throughout the long decades of Jim Crow, southern blacks had fashioned many ways to cope with such outrages. In crossroads towns, "juke joints" offered the thrills of liquor, conversation, and a blues whose bent chords and bittersweet lyrics expressed the pains and joys of life at the bottom of society. Sharecroppers moved frequently to find a better landlord or a larger piece of land; a hardy minority saved their money and purchased their own acres. In cities, the protection of numbers led to sporadic street protests and some threats of violence against recalcitrant white authorities.[9]

For a fortunate few, upward mobility was more than a dream. Segregated educational institutions—poorly financed by individual states and white philanthropies—trained a black elite. At places like Tuskegee Institute in Alabama and Morehouse College in Atlanta, men and women studied to be engineers and pharmacists, preachers and social workers, historians and linguists—excited about using their talents but rueful about the restricted sphere allotted to their race.

The most durable force in the shaping of the black community was the church. Since emancipation, Protestant congregations had been meeting in converted barns or more prosperous brick structures, the only durable institutions owned and controlled by black people themselves. Free from dependence on white benefactors, black ministers often spoke more freely than did the administrators of black colleges; from the pulpit, they could mobilize their congregations for protest. On the other hand, many a preacher avoided speaking out against injustice, lest it jeopardize his hard-won status. Black churches also helped sponsor a number of black-owned small businesses—community banks, mutual insurance companies, funeral parlors, and newspapers. And it was within church bodies like the National Baptist Convention of America that thousands of black people learned such skills as fund-raising and political campaigning that were denied them in secular society.

Driving church activities, of course, were matters of the spirit. Black Protestantism mingled West African styles of worship with texts and denominational creeds initiated by English colonists—particularly Baptism and Methodism. From Africa sprang the distinctive emotional tenor of a southern church service. The shouts from the pews, the call-and-response ritual that made the sermon a participatory event, and the synchronized movements and singing of the choir all had their origins on the black continent. But ministers drew their moral lessons and social metaphors from the King James Bible and Reformation theology.

The content of sermons was closely tethered to the black ordeal in America. Since the days of slavery, the story of Exodus had held a special significance; black people, like the children of Israel, were sorely tested. But, someday, they would escape to freedom and see their oppressors, like Pharoah, humbled and scorned. The Crucifixion symbolized the suffering of the righteous, especially those who dared to criticize the powerful; while the Resurrection was glorious proof of divine justice.[10]

Regardless of whether a black minister favored open resistance against Jim Crow, the texts on which he relied gave his people hope for collective redemption. A favorite passage came from Paul's Epistle to the Ephesians: "Put on the whole armor of God, that ye may be able to stand against the wiles of the devil. For we wrestle not against flesh and blood, but against principalities, against powers, against spiritual wickedness in high places." Given their worldly status and mastery of Christian discourse, it naturally fell to black preachers like Martin Luther King, Jr. and pious laypeople such as John Lewis, who had attended a seminary, and Fannie Lou Hamer to lead the freedom movement in many parts of the South. In contrast, well-educated activists from the North, such as Stokely Carmichael and Bob Moses, tended to draw their inspiration from secular sources.

The black freedom movement arose at different times and unfolded at different paces in thousands of communities across the South. Only a few of these could be sighted, sporadically, on TV screens during the '60s. But its remarkable local presence gave the movement the power to transform the nation's law and politics—and to catalyze every other social insurgency that followed it through that decade and into the next.

The Supreme Court's ruling in the *Brown* case gave black people and their northern white allies a jolt of confidence, but it was up to the executive branch, under the reluctant leadership of Dwight Eisenhower, to enforce the ruling "with all deliberate speed." The first sign that a grassroots movement could make headway against Jim Crow appeared in 1955, in Montgomery, Alabama—the original capital of the Confederacy.

On December 1 of that year, a 42-year-old seamstress and longtime NAACP activist named Rosa Parks refused to give up her seat on a municipal bus to a white patron. Bus segregation was a particularly odious feature of urban life in the South. Blacks were the majority of customers in Montgomery (most whites had cars), but none were hired to drive buses, and they typically had to pay their fare at the front of the vehicle and then get off and enter again through the back. Rosa Parks, who supported her family on $23 a week, had defied the law on several occasions—as had a scattering of other black riders, to no avail. But this time would be different.

As soon as she heard of Parks's arrest, Jo Ann Robinson, leader of the local Women's Political Council, a black group, wrote a leaflet calling for a boycott of city buses and then stayed up all night to reproduce 50,000 copies. The enthusiastic response she got convinced E. D. Nixon, a union official who led the local NAACP chapter and had bailed Parks out of jail, to help organize the protest.

Robinson and Nixon recognized that Rosa Parks was an ideal symbol of the injustices of Jim Crow. She had a high school education but could find only menial work and, despite a courteous and reserved demeanor, was still called "nigger." Most important, Parks, after more than a decade of activism, was determined to break the back of Jim Crow. "Having to take a certain section [on a bus] because of your race was humiliating," she later explained, "but having to stand up because a particular driver wanted to keep a white person from having to stand was, to my mind, most inhumane."[11]

The bus boycott began on Monday, December 5—a day after black ministers had endorsed the idea from their pulpits. That evening, a 26-year-old preacher who had been in town for little more than a year assumed leadership of the embryonic movement, whose main arm was the new Montgomery Improvement Association (MIA). Martin Luther King, Jr. told thousands of black people packed inside the Holt Street Baptist Church and an equal number listening on loudspeakers outside that the boycott would be a "protest with love," a peaceful, if aggressive, way to oppose centuries of official, frequently violent coercion. If the boycott succeeded, he predicted, "when the history books are written in future generations, the historians will have to pause and say, 'There lived a great people—a black people—who injected new meaning and dignity into the veins of civilization.' This is our challenge and our overwhelming responsibility."[12]

King himself had been raised in segregated comfort, son of one of Atlanta's leading black ministers. His mother's father and grandfather had also been prominent preachers. After considering a career in either medicine or law, the young King decided to enter the family profession. He went north to study theology at Boston University and spent part of his first year in Montgomery writing his dissertation.[13] On summer jobs, he had experienced the harshness of racism and, in the North, had patronized integrated restaurants.

Dr. Martin Luther King Jr., Coretta Scott King, and their baby daughter in the 1950s. Source: *Archive Photos*

As an idealistic student in the wake of World War II, King came to believe that the church should throw itself into the fight against injustice. But he was nominated to be leader of the MIA for less glorious reasons: as a newcomer in town, he had no enemies, and older ministers feared taking the post might weaken their positions and endanger their lives.

Over the winter, the mass protest slowly gathered force. Adopting an approach used two years before by bus boycotters in Baton Rouge, Louisiana, blacks in Montgomery organized mass carpools or walked to their jobs. Some white women, out of conviction or reluctance to clean their own houses, helped drive domestics to and from work.

It wasn't easy to keep spirits high or to persuade people to adhere to the principle of civil disobedience. Montgomery police arrested numbers of boycott organizers on the pretext they were "intimidating" passengers. The White Citizens' Council held big rallies that stiffened the resolve of the authorities. Early in 1956, a bomb planted at King's house almost killed his wife, Coretta, and their children. When the young minister rushed home, he heard an angry black resident snarl to a policeman, "Now you got your .38 and I got mine; so let's battle it out."[14] A race riot was barely averted.

But, supported by every institution and leader in their community, the black citizens of Montgomery stayed off the buses through the spring, summer, and early fall. Finally, in mid-November, the U.S. Supreme Court came to their aid; segregation on Montgomery buses was ruled unconstitutional.

"Praise the Lord," cried a black Alabamian, "God has spoken from Washington, D.C."[15]

Federal assistance to the fledgling black movement enraged a growing number of southern whites, ordinary citizens and politicians alike. Echoing their Confederate forebears, they accused the Supreme Court and liberals in Congress of trying to destroy a cherished way of life. In 1957, after Congress passed a rather weak civil rights bill, Young Democrats in one Texas town wrote to their senator, Lyndon Johnson, "The boys at the barber shop understand what [this] . . . bill has done to them and they don't like it. They will not long stand for a federal dictatorship."[16]

During the late '50s, following the *Brown* case and the Montgomery boycott, southern state legislatures moved quickly to block any efforts toward school desegregation. They attempted to ban literature issued by the NAACP and other civil rights groups. Several legislatures voted to insert a replica of the old Confederate battle standard into the flags of their states. In 1959 the Alabama legislature even authorized the burning of a children's book. The inflammatory volume, seized from public libraries, was *The Rabbits' Wedding*; it featured a marriage between a white bunny and a black one.[17]

Nearly all white southern politicians began to preach an undiluted version of the gospel of white supremacy. When Orval Faubus ran for governor of Arkansas in 1954, he had promised to boost spending on public education and to give blacks more state jobs. But, in the fall of 1957, the governor publicly defied a court order to integrate Little Rock's Central High School. Faubus became a hero to whites when President Eisenhower—who privately disagreed with the *Brown* decision but could not allow a deliberate defiance of federal authority—called in the 101st Airborne Division to protect the constitutional rights of nine children threatened by a rock-throwing mob. In other parts of the South, local governments avoided integration by transferring school property to private academies reserved for whites. This move left thousands of black children with no schools at all.

The growth of "massive resistance" by whites presented the black freedom movement with a challenge. In 1957 King and other leaders of the Montgomery boycott had founded the Southern Christian Leadership Conference (SCLC) to coordinate the political activities of black churches. But how would black activists, preachers or not, push forward their agenda of integration and economic justice against what seemed a solid front of southern whites and the ambivalence of both the president and a majority in Congress?

A big part of the answer came from the prosperous city of Greensboro, North Carolina. To most of its white citizens, Greensboro seemed one of the least likely places to become a hotbed of civil rights activity. The thriving textile and insurance center boasted excellent public schools, two of the best black colleges in the South, and a reputation as a "progressive" island in a Jim Crow sea. African Americans were free to vote and run for office. In 1951, a black candidate had been elected to the city council, with substantial support from white neighborhoods. One day after the Supreme Court's ruling in the *Brown* case, the Greensboro Board of Education voted to implement desegregation. "It is unthinkable," said the superintendent of schools, "that we will try to abrogate the laws of the United States of America."[18]

Still, the whites who controlled Greensboro had no more intention of disrupting the racial status quo than did Orval Faubus. Only a thin trickle of black students entered previously all-white schools, and separation remained the rule nearly everywhere else. Relegated to "Negro jobs," African-American residents earned, on average, only 40 percent of what whites did.

Greensboro city fathers prided themselves on maintaining a pleasant, civil environment. Good manners were expected of both races, and violence was abhorred. But, such civility among unequals was clad, as elsewhere in the South, in a fabric of deception. Prominent whites, hearing no protests from their black maids and janitors, assumed they were content. A white attorney acknowledged the contradiction, "We're just like Georgia and Alabama," he said, "except we do it in a tuxedo and they wear suspenders."[19]

Early in 1960 four freshmen at North Carolina Agricultural and Technical (A & T), the local black state college, took a daring step away from a system based on lies. Ezell Blair, Jr., Franklin McCain, Joseph McNeil, and David Richmond had been debating for several weeks about the best way for a "moral man" to resist injustice. Their discussions were inspired by the oratory of Martin Luther King, Jr. and the example of Mohandas Gandhi, the pacifist leader of India's struggle for independence from British rule. On the first day of February, the four students walked downtown to a Woolworth's department store. They bought toothpaste and a few other sundries. Then they sat down at the lunch counter and politely tried to order something to eat. They were refused service and, after waiting for 45 minutes, left the store.

The next day, they came back with 23 of their fellow students. The following day, they returned with enough supporters to occupy every seat in the store. By the end of the week, a group of white students from a local women's college joined in. And when the protestors were heckled and jostled by a knot of young, white working-class men brandishing Confederate flags, burly members of the A & T football team, American flags in hand, rushed to their defense. "Who do you think you are?" asked the astonished whites. "We the Union Army," came the response.[20]

The concept of mass civil disobedience spread quickly. By April, lunch counter sit-ins were under way in 54 different southern cities. And, before the year was over, most had achieved their limited objective. All over the country, young black people heard about the sit-ins and decided to join the movement. "Before, the Negro in the South had always looked on the defensive, cringing," remembered Bob Moses, then a 26-year-old math teacher in a New York City high school. "This time they were taking the initiative.

They were kids my age, and I knew this had something to do with my own life. It made me realize that for a long time I had been troubled by the problem of being a Negro and at the same time being an American. This was the answer."[21]

That April, 200 young activists came to Raleigh, North Carolina from all over the South to discuss the future of their infant crusade. They applauded Martin Luther King, Jr., who counseled them to force the authorities to fill the jail cells with demonstrators or relax the grip of segregation. But their highest regard went to two little-known figures: Ella Baker, a veteran organizer in her mid-fifties, who was critical of black ministers (including King) who sought to control the sit-inners; and James Lawson, a former missionary, who denounced the NAACP for focusing on the courts and representing only the interests of "the black bourgeoisie." Lawson urged the participants to behave as "a people no longer the victims of racial evil, who can act in a disciplined manner to implement the Constitution." And, following Baker's lead, he called for a new, independent student group to mount disruptive campaigns all over the South. The participants responded by forming the Student Non-Violent Coordinating Committee (SNCC).[22]

The organization that became known as "Snick" was an innovation in the black freedom struggle. Never before had college students possessed the numbers or the confidence to take a leading part, nor had nonviolent action been viewed as the chief device with which to dismantle the Jim Crow order. And, as during the heyday of the abolitionist movement, thousands of young whites signed up for the cause. SNCC's vision was of a "beloved community" that would gradually replace a culture of hatred and inequality. Only through an integrated movement could an integrated society be built.

In the late spring of 1961, a few SNCC workers took part in the Freedom Ride, a courageous argument for the efficacy of non-violent interracial protest. Thirteen people—seven black, six white—boarded a southbound interstate bus in Washington, D.C., to begin an effort planned by the Congress of Racial Equality (CORE). They were aiming to test a recent Supreme Court ruling that prohibited the segregation of bus terminals. "At every rest stop, the whites would go into the waiting room for blacks, and the blacks into the waiting room for whites, and would seek to use all the facilities, refusing to leave," CORE leader James Farmer recalled. "We felt that we could then count upon the racists of the South to create a crisis, so that the federal government would be compelled to enforce federal law. That was the rationale for the Freedom Ride."[23]

It proved a most perilous voyage. At a terminal in Rock Hill, South Carolina, John Lewis of SNCC was clubbed and beaten. In Anniston, Alabama, white vigilantes set upon a bus carrying nonviolent protestors. They pelted it with rocks, then set it on fire as the riders fled. In Montgomery, a mob kicked and pummeled everyone involved, including a cameraman for NBC television. Officials of the Kennedy administration pleaded with CORE and SNCC to call off the bloody affair lest it damage America's image at a time of rising tensions with the Soviet Union. But the rides continued into the summer, ending only when Attorney General Robert Kennedy quietly negotiated an end to separate facilities.

SNCC was never intended to be a mass membership organization like the NAACP; it was a fellowship of the dedicated few. Soon after setting up their headquarters in Atlanta and electing the group's first chairman—22-year-old Marion Barry, the son of a Mississippi sharecropper—SNCC workers fanned out to small towns and rural counties across the Deep South. They survived on salaries of $10 a week, boarding with black families and confronting the rage of local whites. Like a band of peaceful guerillas, SNCC would assist black people to free themselves from the shackles of segregation—by challenging Jim Crow laws, registering to vote, and educating themselves and their children.

Mississippi became the main testing ground. Most whites in the still largely rural Magnolia State were averse to any hint of racial equality, indeed to any black person who meant to advance beyond the status of field hand or manual laborer. Fewer than 5 percent of black Mississippians were high school graduates; about the same number were registered to vote. In 1950 there were but 5 black lawyers and 64 black doctors in the entire state.

In contrast to Greensboro, whites in Mississippi neither preached nor practiced a gospel of civility. The state's most powerful politician was Senator James Eastland, a rich landowner from Sunflower County. Eastland regularly accused the civil rights movement of wanting to destroy "the American system of government" and to promote "the mongrelization of the white race."[24]

Acts of terror enforced such savage words. In 1944, near the town of Liberty, the Reverend Isaac Simmons was lynched because he refused to sell a local white man his 220 acres of land, on which oil had been discovered. In 1955 Emmett Till, a 14-year-old Chicagoan who was visiting relatives in Money, Mississippi, was mutilated and killed after he either whistled at a young white woman or called her "baby." Till's murderers, who were positively identified, won acquittal after their attorney prodded the jurors (all white and male), "I am sure that every last Anglo-Saxon one of you will have the courage to free these men."[25]

SNCC workers believed that if they could crack Mississippi, the more permeable barriers in the rest of America would follow. It seemed an urgent task, as well as a moral one. Since World War II, thousands of black Mississippians had abandoned the state for points north, and the political impotence of those who remained only deepened their poverty. Children and the elderly—those who could not easily get out—outnumbered able-bodied adults.

Into this cauldron stepped a team of young organizers, headed by Bob Moses. Moses was not the typical activist, hard-driving and exhortatory. His manner was precise, gentle, almost shy. Brought up in a housing project on the fringe of Harlem, Moses had excelled in mostly white schools and earned a master's degree in philosophy from Harvard. He spoke with quiet authority about the problems of southern blacks, and no one doubted his absolute dedication to the cause.

During the summer of 1961, Moses moved into Amite County—a particularly violent corner of the state where Isaac Simmons had been murdered and where only a single black person was a registered voter, although African Americans were 55 percent of the population. There and in a number of towns in the Mississippi Delta, Bob Moses began a campaign to win back the constitutional right to the franchise.

Fortunately, Moses and his fellow crusaders did not have to fight alone. For decades, local activists, inside and outside the NAACP, had waged a lonely battle to register voters. Gaining access to the ballot was a direct way to pressure the white establishment—and one that did not raise sensitive issues of sexual purity. SNCC organizers gradually gained the support of black Mississippians who enjoyed the respect of their communities—particularly independent farmers and small businessmen whose modest economic success was itself a challenge to the system. "The importance, the quality of the person, the local person, that you go to work with, is everything in terms of whether the project can get off the ground," Moses learned.[26] Black churches provided the movement with space for meetings, mimeograph machines, and occasionally a refuge from violence.

One of the local people Moses came to admire most was Fannie Lou Hamer. Born in 1917, the youngest of 20 children, Hamer had spent most of her life working on Delta cotton plantations in conditions little better than those of slavery. Her mother had gone blind after an accident in the fields because no doctor was available. A similar case of medical neglect had left Hamer herself with a bad limp. She and her family had no working toilet; one day, while cleaning her boss's house, Hamer noticed that the family pet had his own bathroom. "Negroes in Mississippi," she concluded, "are treated *worse* than dogs."[27]

But Hamer determined not to remain a victim. She was active in her Baptist church and, like countless African Americans before her, converted her faith into a sword of redemption. In a deep, strong voice, Hamer led movement gatherings in "freedom songs" set to such spiritual tunes as "This Little Light of Mine" and "We Shall Overcome." And her experience as a lay preacher helped make her a memorable orator in a movement filled with fine speakers. "God is not pleased with all the murdering and all the brutality and all the killing," she told a 1963 gathering. "God is not pleased that the Negro children in the state of Mississippi [are] suffering from malnutrition. God is not pleased because we have to go raggedy and work from ten to eleven hours for three lousy dollars!"[28]

The collaboration between SNCC organizers and local people in Mississippi yielded mixed results. Together, they mobilized thousands of rural blacks to learn about and attempt to exercise their legal rights. "Freedom schools" taught reading, math, and history, while advising students how to surmount the various hurdles erected by white voting registrars. Led by activists like Hamer and Moses, farmers and laborers trooped repeatedly down to the county courthouse to take tests designed to frustrate them.

Mississippi whites did their worst to dissuade potential black voters from exercising their rights. In the summer of 1962, armed men attacked a SNCC office in Greenwood; organizers had to escape through a second-story window. The next year, SNCC's Jimmy Travis was shot in the head while driving with Bob Moses on a Delta highway, and Fannie Lou Hamer was badly beaten with thick leather straps by jail guards in the town of Winona. The number of black registrants barely inched upward. By 1963, the transformation of Mississippi—and of the South—had just begun.

The North was supposed to be different. African Americans who flocked to cities like New York and Chicago, Philadelphia and Cleveland, Oakland and Los Angeles had expected, if nothing else, an end to routine indignities. In certain ways, the promise was fulfilled. Northern blacks were free to vote, run for office, and sit next to whites in buses and at lunch counters. They could also discard the demeaning etiquette required of blacks in Mississippi. Some found work in department stores and city government, expanding sectors of the economy that usually paid double the wage earned by an agricultural laborer or domestic back in Dixie.

A number of powerful white liberals joined in pushing for further improvements. Walter Reuther, head of the 1.5-million-member United Auto Workers, which had a sizable black membership, frequently denounced racism and contributed union funds to the SCLC and NAACP. Prominent figures in both major parties spoke out for equal employment and an end to all segregationist laws and practices. Although most blacks voted Democratic, some, like Jackie Robinson, stuck to the GOP, where Governor Nelson Rockefeller of New York was a strong advocate for civil rights.

To black newcomers, the North represented progress, a place where the swift changes that symbolize modernity might work for them (unlike the mechanical cotton picker). In a 1948 essay, novelist Ralph Ellison wrote from Harlem, "Here it is possible for talented youths to leap through the development of decades in a brief twenty years, while beside them white-haired adults crawl in the feudal darkness of their childhood. Here a former cotton picker develops the sensitive hands of a surgeon, and men whose grandparents still believe in magic prepare optimistically to become atomic scientists."[29]

A few achieved such lofty goals. Local black newspapers and black magazines like *Ebony* and *Jet* heralded every success story they could find, particularly when the first member of the race achieved some cherished honor: Ralph Bunche, the UN diplomat who was the first black to win a Nobel Peace Prize (in 1950); poet Gwendolyn Brooks, the first black to win a Pulitzer Prize (also in 1950); Lorraine Hansberry, the first black dramatist to have a play produced on Broadway—*A Raisin in the Sun* (in 1959).[30]

Life in the North, however, remained difficult for the mass of African Americans. The rhetoric of liberal tolerance did little to pry open the tight network of institutions—the Catholic Church, building trades unions and apprenticeship programs, and downtown law firms—that groomed many young white men in cities like Chicago and Boston for good jobs and professional careers.

Moreover, a terrible irony greeted those blacks who migrated from the rural South to the industrial heartland. Manufacturing plants were no longer hiring large numbers of unskilled workers, and new factories tended to be built in the suburbs, close to interstate highways and subdivisions, where few blacks lived. Most migrants could find work in the thriving economy, but jobs of the kind available to men and women without much formal education paid low wages and promised little or no advancement.

Nor could hopeful rhetoric persuade white homeowners to open their neighborhoods to newcomers of a different race or white politicians to jeopardize their careers for the cause of racial equality. Residential segregation meant

A street corner in Harlem, New York City, in the early 1960s. Source: *George Meany Memorial Archives*

that the public schools were also divided by race; and whites who dominated school boards tended to channel funds disproportionately to schools attended by children who looked like them. The small but growing black middle class—made up largely of school teachers and other public employees—kept trying to push back the boundaries. But no breakthrough was yet forthcoming.

Dashed hopes fueled a resentment that burned even hotter than in the South where no illusions were possible. Lorraine Hansberry, who grew up in Chicago, borrowed the title of her prize-winning Broadway play from a Langston Hughes poem that asked, "What happens to a dream deferred? Does it dry up like a raisin in the sun? Or does it explode?" Ralph Ellison compared Harlem dwellers, to "some tragic people out of mythology" who "aspired to escape from its own unhappy homeland to the apparent peace of a distant mountain; but which, in migrating, made some fatal error of judgment and fell into a chasm of mazelike passages that promise ever to lead to the mountain but end ever against a wall."[31]

In Harlem, that wall had many faces. The starkest was segregated housing, which remained ubiquitous even where new local and state laws prohibited it. In New York City, the measures needed to prove a case of housing discrimination were lengthy, precise, and cumbersome. As two sociologists explained:

> One needs a respectable-looking white friend to find out first that the apartment is available; a Negro who really wants it and is ready to take it then asks for it and is told it is not available; a second white is then required in order that he may be told that the apartment is still available, so as to get a sure-fire case; then direct confrontation plus rapid action in reporting all the details to the City Commission on Human Rights is required.[32]

Not surprisingly, few landlords were ever found guilty.

In Chicago, resistance to open housing took a nastier form. From the late 1940s on, white mobs regularly attacked black families who attempted to move out of slums and into private homes and public housing developments. "A working man purchases a home . . . , secures a mortgage, improves the property and enjoys the fruits of his labor and then . . . city planners and do-gooders decide to dump a project in his back yard," complained one white community newspaper in Chicago.[33]

Mayor Richard Daley, to avoid antagonizing his white base, sought to preserve what one critic called a "cordon of hostility." Tall, fortresslike projects were erected where black people already lived, a cluster of neighborhoods that everyone began calling "the ghetto." African Americans were not legally confined, as were Jews in the seventeenth-century Italian cities where the term originated. But whenever they managed to move into a white neighborhood, the most they could hope for was that the other residents would refrain from violence and hurry to move out.

Black people in the North could never escape the psychic dilemma
W. E. B. DuBois (who was born and bred in Massachusetts) had so memo-
rably identified. They saw the dream of equal citizenship and opportunity
dangled before them, yet every day their skin color marked them as individuals to be mistrusted, feared, and/or pitied.

Some African Americans in the expanding ghettos turned this image on
themselves, "processing" (straightening) their hair and bleaching their skin
with chemicals to look more like members of the dominant race. They were
well aware that, since the days of slavery, privileges had accrued to Negroes
of a paler hue. Others rejected the moral code of family and church and became lifelong criminals, committed to a life of dangerous pleasures. Gam-
bling, drug dealing, theft, and prostitution were thriving industries in ghettos like Harlem—as they were in poor neighborhoods from London to Naples
to Rio de Janeiro, whatever the skin color of the perpetrators. In the U.S.,
most victims of these predatory trades were also black, and many suffered
from a kind of desperate lassitude. "Yes, we've progressed," mocked writer
James Baldwin. "When I was a boy in Harlem, Negroes got drunk and cursed
each other out. Now they become junkies and don't say anything."[34]

Attempting to keep the ghetto orderly, if not quiet, was the job of municipal police, the overwhelming majority of whom were white. Their job
bordered on the impossible. Ghetto residents saw cops as the embodiment
of a society that, despite official rhetoric, seemed determined to keep them
in their place. "Their very presence is an insult," wrote Baldwin in 1960, "and
it would be, even if they spent their entire day feeding gumdrops to children." So the normal relationship between urban blacks and the police was
full of tension and violence, suggested or actual. "Rare, indeed, is the Harlem
citizen, from the most circumspect church member to the most shiftless adolescent," continued Baldwin, "who does not have a long tale to tell of police
incompetence, injustice, or brutality."[35]

Frustration bred a variety of solutions. Many ghetto dwellers flocked to
churches old and new. Most establishments were storefront affairs whose
part-time preachers shared the unsteady fortunes of their parishioners. But
the ministers at impressive brick churches like Abyssinian Baptist in Harlem
and the Institutional A.M.E. Church in Chicago were men of substance and
influence. In addition to their spiritual leadership, they ran soup kitchens,
boosted politicians, and collected funds for civil rights organizers in the South.
The migration north also produced a variety of unorthodox bodies that mixed
the gospel of self-help with apocalyptic visions of social deliverance. The
largest of these included Father Divine's Peace Mission, Daddy Grace's United
House for Prayer for All People, and Elijah Muhammad's Nation of Islam.

The fervor of southern rural evangelism strengthened and deepened in
the cities, even if regular church attendance was no longer a universal experience. Amid the frustrations of change, the old-time black religion stood as

a rock of inspiration—and no black-owned business could yet rival the resources or cultural resonance of the major churches.

Starting in the 1940s, gospel music—religious lyrics set to blues arrangements—spawned a generation of such black performers as Mahalia Jackson and the Sensational Nightingales. Some second-generation gospelers like Aretha Franklin and Al Green later earned wealth and fame as singers of "soul" music—whose very name denotes the spiritual roots of the music (though its lyrics speak of more secular passions). Even though gospel performances tended to convert congregations that had previously joined their voices in song into mere audiences, the music had a binding and healing power. In the words of the great hymn by Thomas A. Dorsey, the musician and songwriter who gave gospel its name:

> Precious Lord, take my hand
> Lead me on, Let me stand,
> I am tired, I am weak, I am worn;
> Through the storm, through the night
> Lead me on to the light,
> Take my hand, precious Lord,
> Lead me home.[36]

Politics offered another outlet for grievance and hope. By the 1950s, black council members were helping to govern a handful of northern cities, and African-American voters had become a critical part of the Democratic coalition. Two black congressmen—New York's Adam Clayton Powell, Jr. and Chicago's William Dawson, both of whom were first elected during World War II—wielded more power than did any other elected officials of their race. They were of quite different minds, however, on how that power should be exercised.

Dawson was a skillful lieutenant in Mayor Daley's Democratic machine. He quietly made deals that secured jobs, contracts, and a degree of police benevolence for key segments of his huge South Side constituency. At the same time, Dawson discouraged public demands for civil rights, lest they alienate white power brokers. The local NAACP chapter, leading ministers, the *Chicago Defender* (America's most popular black weekly), and kings of the thriving numbers racket routinely obtained favors from the congressman; all Dawson asked in return was their loyalty.

Powell, in contrast, was a vigorous and talented, if self-aggrandizing, advocate of black equality. As pastor of Abyssinian Baptist, the largest church in Harlem, Powell had a secure base for gathering funds and followers. And he was seldom out of the headlines as a self-proclaimed "irritant" of local and national elites.

During the late 1930s and '40s, the handsome, elegantly dressed politician led protests against the exclusion of blacks from New York construction and sales jobs. Beginning in the early '50s, Powell annually introduced into Congress an amendment (drafted by the NAACP) that would have denied federal money to any segregated facility. In 1956, accusing his own party of taking a craven position on civil rights, he endorsed President Eisenhower for reelection. That stand, as well as a fondness for taking "official" trips abroad with women to whom he was not married, made Powell a notorious man in official Washington. But he refused to recant or apologize, and, around the country, most blacks applauded him as a hero.

Such acclaim did not flow from a grassroots insurgency. At a time when black southerners were mounting the greatest protest campaign in modern U.S. history, their brothers and sisters in the North were more involved in supporting those efforts than in challenging white power at home. The Chicago NAACP occasionally picketed City Hall to protest assaults on black housing tenants; rent strikes against slumlords periodically rocked black neighborhoods in New York. But the thousands of black Chicagoans who came, in 1955, to mourn Emmett Till and view his mutilated body dwarfed all demonstrations in that city until a decade later. And Congressman Powell was never more eloquent than when, at the beginning of the '60s, he urged Americans, black and white, to support the Woolworth sit-ins and the Freedom Ride.

Why was the civil rights movement fairly insignificant in the urban North, despite the growing black presence there? The torrent of new migrants was itself part of the answer: with the exception of some churches, older community networks fell apart or into irrelevance as tens of thousands moved up from the South, mushrooming what had been black enclaves with narrow geographic and cultural boundaries.

It was also more difficult to define the foe in the North than in segregationist Dixie. Illinois and New York already outlawed separate facilities, and most prominent downtown employers were hiring at least a few blacks to fill white-collar positions. Open housing remained the civil rights issue on which the least progress had been made. But pushing it, as William Dawson understood, meant splitting the Democratic base on which blacks otherwise depended. It also raised the question of whether, as James Baldwin bluntly stated, "A ghetto can be improved in one way only: out of existence."[37]

But the dispersal of the existing community, even as a distant prospect, filled few black hearts with joy. Integration had never been the sole aim of the freedom movement; access to jobs, houses, and commodities mattered far more than did the opportunity to mix with white folks. In postwar America, a growing minority of ghetto inhabitants turned to leaders who argued that the black community should shut itself off from the culture and religion of the white oppressors and erect its own Jerusalem—in Harlem, the Deep South, or in the original homeland of Africa. "The white man's heaven is the black man's hell," ran a popular lyric inspired by the Nation of Islam.[38]

Black nationalism was not a new idea. The philosophy of racial pride and self-reliance had always appealed more intensely to ordinary African Americans than the integrationist alternative—associated as it was with a small elite of educated professionals. The slave rebel Nat Turner, the Jamaican immigrant Marcus Garvey and his million-member United Negro Improvement Association of the 1920s, and the unemployed Detroit autoworker who changed his name to Elijah Muhammad and founded the Nation of Islam in the 1930s articulated a similar desire for black people to unite and gain power for their race. Full acceptance by white society might be desirable, they admitted, but it was utterly unrealistic.

In the 1950s and '60s, leaders of the Nation of Islam preached a flamboyant and controversial version of this ideology. Elijah Muhammad's worldview—which he learned from an immigrant Arab silk peddler named Wali Farrad—was rooted in a conspiratorial cosmology: black people had been the only human beings until an evil geneticist named Yacub bred a bleached race to do his bidding. Centuries of white supremacy followed. Christianity, charged Muhammad, was the biggest ruse in the devil's bag of tricks. Bible-spouting reverends fooled African Americans into worshiping a white God and longing for brotherhood with people who lynched and exploited them.

Despite its incredible myth of racial origins, the Nation gained widespread respect in the ghettos (although no more than 50,000 members). Part of the reason was its stern counsel that black people shed personal habits that chained them to unhealthy desires and loyalties: change your "slave" name to a Moslem one or simply to X (signifying one's ancestral African family, its name forever lost); renounce alcohol, drugs, tobacco, pork, fried foods, gaudy clothes, and processed hair; and form strict monogamous couples in which the husband rules. To keep black wages from going into white pockets, the Nation also sponsored a sprinkling of small businesses. Here was a teaching of self-improvement and self-love mixed with strong draughts of righteous hatred.

But Muhammad, a quiet man who spoke with a lisp, lacked a powerful platform presence. From the mid-'50s to 1963, Americans learned about the Nation of Islam (which an unfriendly press soon dubbed "the Black Muslims") from televised snippets of speeches by the minister of its Harlem mosque—the light-skinned former convict Malcolm X. After his death in 1965, Malcolm quickly became a black icon, a powerful symbol of racial redemption. But when he served as chief spokesman for the Nation of Islam, the man born Malcolm Little was most influential as a bold critic of what he saw as the dangerous integrationist illusions put forth by Martin Luther King, Jr. and his admirers. Such convictions ran strong in Malcolm's family. In the 1920s, his father, a Protestant minister, had been a Garveyite leader in Omaha and Milwaukee. The Reverend Little died in a suspicious accident, and Malcolm always believed his father's politics had gotten him killed.

There was really no difference, asserted Malcolm X, between liberals like Walter Reuther and the most stalwart defenders of Jim Crow. The latter were wolves, while the former were foxes: "The job of the civil rights leader is to make the Negro forget that the wolf and fox belong to the [same] family. Both are canines; and no matter which one of them the Negro places his trust in, he never ends up in the White House but always in the doghouse."

A devout Muslim, Malcolm nevertheless belonged, like his father, to the great tradition of black preaching. He charged the "white devils" with repudiating their own egalitarian creed and denied that Americanism had anything to offer the black masses: "We didn't land at Plymouth Rock. Plymouth Rock landed on us." When civil rights leaders called him an "extremist," Malcolm shot back, "You show me a black man who isn't an extremist and I'll show you one who needs psychiatric attention!" Even his many critics acknowledged the Muslim minister's oratorical powers. "He was a mesmerizing speaker, the toughest man in debate that I've ever seen," remembered NAACP head Roy Wilkins. "None of us could touch him, not even Dr. King."[39]

In 1963 Malcolm made his most important convert—the heavyweight boxer Cassius Clay. As a youth in Louisville, Clay had been vocal about his

Malcolm X, leading voice of black nationalism in the late 1950s and early 1960s. Source: *Express Newspapers/Archive Photos*

hatred for white power. He responded to the murder of Emmett Till by hurling stones at a U.S. Army recruiting poster. In 1960, Clay won a gold medal in the Olympic Games and then turned professional. He quickly added to his fame with brash claims of his "greatness" delivered in humorous rhyme. Quietly, he became close to Malcolm X; in February 1964, minutes after winning the world heavyweight championship, Clay proclaimed his membership in the Nation of Islam. He also announced he was shedding his "slave name" (which happened to be that of a nineteenth-century white abolitionist) and taking a new one: Muhammad Ali.

The conversion of the world's most famous athlete was a great boon to the cause of black nationalism. But the Nation of Islam had no larger strategy for change. Elijah Muhammad kept his group aloof from other organizations and ordered his disciples to abstain from politics; Malcolm X went along, despite increasing doubts, strengthened by learning that Muhammad had fathered several children by women other than his wife. In 1964 the spokesman left the Nation of Islam and ceased denouncing King and other civil rights activists. But without a mass movement led by him or anyone else, blacks in the northern ghettos could only nurture their anger and attempt to battle the mounting despair that accompanies blasted hopes.

Black Americans had awakened in the 1940s and '50s to the possibility that the mantra of "freedom"—universally invoked as the purpose of both World War II and the Cold War—might finally benefit them. But, by the beginning of the '60s, it had become obvious to black activists and their white allies that the authorities, both North and South, rarely aided the process of liberation unless—as during the Freedom Rides—the movement made it politically uncomfortable for them to stall.

CHAPTER 3

The New Frontier of American Liberalism

IT REALLY IS TRUE THAT FOREIGN AFFAIRS IS THE ONLY IMPORTANT ISSUE FOR A PRESIDENT TO HANDLE, ISN'T IT? I MEAN WHO GIVES A SHIT IF THE MINIMUM WAGE IS $1.15 OR $1.25 . . . ?

—President John F. Kennedy in conversation with Richard Nixon, 1961[1]

In American popular memory, the 1960s are regarded as years of ascendant liberalism. According to this view, liberals in Washington, D.C. and elsewhere had a more or less free hand in setting the political agenda for the decade. In domestic policy, they launched a "war on poverty" that raised unfulfillable expectations, squandered vast sums of money, and may even have been responsible for worsening the conditions prevailing in the nation's central cities. In the courts, they sponsored a "rights revolution" that led to noisy demands for special treatment by minorities, welfare recipients, homosexuals, criminal defendants, and others outside the mainstream of American society.

In the end, the liberals' overweening ambitions put them out of touch with the real values and best interests of the American middle class, bringing the liberal cause—along with the Democratic party—a well-justified repudiation at the polls. Thus stands the contemporary historical indictment of Sixties liberalism.[2]

While there are certainly elements of truth in this interpretation, it considerably overstates the power of liberals to shape events in the 1960s. Of the three branches of the federal government, liberals held the commanding heights through the decade in only one branch, the judiciary (and, ironically, several of the liberal lions of the U.S. Supreme Court in the 1960s, including Chief Justice Earl Warren, had been appointed by President Eisenhower). In the legislative branch, notwithstanding Democratic majorities in both houses of Congress, liberal Democrats were nearly always a minority. Every

Democratic congressional majority since the late 1930s had included a conservative Trojan horse: the 60 to 70 southern Democrats who were as likely to
ally themselves on any given issue with Republicans rather than with liberal
Democrats. As for the executive branch, neither of the two Democratic presidents who occupied the White House from 1961 through 1968 would, at the
moment of their rise to national power, have been the first choice of the party's
liberal wing. Particularly at the start of the 1960s, liberalism was neither sufficiently coherent as a political philosophy, nor sufficiently well organized as
a political movement, to realize many ambitions, overweening or otherwise.

In the late 1950s liberalism was a philosophy with a heroic past, and an
uncertain future. It was chiefly due to that past, embodied in the memory of
Franklin Delano Roosevelt and the legislative legacy of the New Deal, that
"liberal" was considered an honorable and even desirable political label to
wear within the Democratic Party. To be sure, not all Democrats, and few
indeed in the South, would use the word to describe themselves. But the
liberal designation remained a virtual prerequisite for a serious bid for the
Democratic presidential nomination.

In a very general sense, what liberalism meant to its adherents on the eve
of the 1960s was, first and foremost, the preservation of the "New Deal coalition," that politically winning alliance of organized labor, farmers, blacks, intellectuals, and southern whites established by Franklin Roosevelt and passed
on to Harry Truman. The term "liberalism" evoked 20 years of Democratic
leadership during which the nation had survived its worst economic depression, and then gone on to triumph in the most devastating war in history. It
stood for policies and laws that came out of Roosevelt's New Deal and Truman's Fair Deal, and that most American believed in, such as providing pensions to the elderly and relief to the unemployed. It expressed faith in the
wisdom and legitimacy of a strong federal government, and particularly in
the ability of a strong president to secure the greatest possible good for the
greatest possible number of Americans.[3]

But, except for Harry Truman's upset victory in 1948, liberal Democrats
did not fare well at the polls from the end of World War II to the late 1950s.
Senator Joseph McCarthy and other zealots on the Right accused them of being "soft on Communism" or of actively abetting the Soviet state. Their party
lost the presidency to the Republicans in the lopsided contests of 1952 and
1956. And a majority of Congress, even in the years when Democrats made
up a majority, was unsympathetic to most proposals for extending the New
Deal tradition of government activism into new programs, although President Eisenhower, a shrewd moderate leader, carefully refrained from undo-
ing the social welfare provisions that his Democratic predecessors had put in
place in the 1930s and 1940s.

Liberalism is a philosophy of change, and when Democratic electoral
prospects suffered in the aftermath of World War II, liberals were eager to

embrace new ideas, causes, and constituencies that would restore their political clout. But how much and what kind of change would be required?

One group of liberal intellectuals counseled a tough-minded approach to social ills. In his 1949 manifesto *The Vital Center*, Harvard historian Arthur Schlesinger, Jr. criticized his fellow liberals for cherishing a naive faith in the perfectability of mankind. He preached instead a militant opposition to visionary ideals, a chastened liberalism of restraint and limits. Citing William Butler Yeats' "terrible vision" of the "rough beast, its hour come round at last, . . . slouching toward Bethlehem," Schlesinger warned that there was to be found "a Hitler, a Stalin in every breast." Ideological mass movements, dreaming of establishing heavens on earth, were like lemming migrations, a "convulsive mass escape from freedom to totalitarianism," hurling nations "from the bleak and rocky cliffs into the deep, womb-dark sea below." Liberals needed to break with those he characterized as "the sentimentalists, the utopians, the wailers," and identify instead with "the politicians, the administrators, the doers."[4]

But what still needed "doing" in post–New Deal America? Schlesinger would make his reputation as a historian with biographies of Andrew Jackson and Franklin Delano Roosevelt, liberal presidents who had come to power during times of economic distress.[5] Thanks in part to what Schlesinger described as the "brilliant success" of the New Deal, the United States had put behind it the hard times of the 1930s, apparently forever. What then, if anything, would propel future liberal Democrats into the White House? The "quantitative liberalism" of the Roosevelt era, Schlesinger noted in an article published in the mid-1950s, had focused on "immediate problems of subsistence and survival." These were no longer of relevance in a prosperous postwar United States. It was time to move on to a "qualitative liberalism," that would be dedicated, in ways that Schlesinger left somewhat vague, "to bettering the quality of people's lives and opportunities."[6]

John Kenneth Galbraith, an economist and Schlesinger's colleague at Harvard, tried to fill in some of the programmatic details of this new "qualitative" liberalism. In a series of popular books and articles published in the 1950s, Galbraith argued that America's recent prosperity had not made its citizens truly secure. True, most working-class families were doing better than ever before, and big corporations were churning out a dazzling array of pleasing goods. The common welfare, however, was being neglected. At the civic core of what Galbraith dubbed "the affluent society," he glimpsed a growing rot. Schools were crowded, parks were dirty and sparse, urban transportation inefficient, and municipal workers underpaid. Galbraith offered a grim portrait of the pursuit of pleasure in Eisenhower's America:

The family which takes its . . . air-conditioned, power-steered, and power-braked automobile out for a tour passes through cities that are badly paved, made hideous by litter, blighted buildings, billboards. . . . They pass into a countryside that has been rendered largely invisible by commercial art. . . . They picnic on exquisitely packaged food from a portable icebox by a polluted stream and go on to spend the night at a park which is a menace to public health and morals. Just before dozing off . . . they may reflect vaguely on the curious unevenness of their blessings. Is this, indeed, the American genius?[7]

By the later 1950s a host of other liberal-minded authors had examined the current state of American society and found it wanting in all kinds of ways, most of them related to the stultifying and unaesthetic quality of daily life, as reflected in advertising, corporate culture, television, the suburbs, and the like. This critique, embodied in such popular works as John Keats's *The Crack in the Picture Window* (1956), William H. Whyte's *The Organization Man* (1956), and Vance Packard's *The Hidden Persuaders* (1957) and *The Status Seekers* (1959), testified to a growing unease, at least among the educated middle class, with the rewards offered by "the affluent society."[8] But taken in their entirety, these books hinted at few remedies beyond the hope that culturally sensitive readers might take a more enlightened approach in their consumer and career choices. No one was going to take to the political barricades solely on the basis of the tastelessness of contemporary bill-board advertising.

But along with such "qualitative" discontents, another issue was beginning to draw the attention of liberals—one that was at once more deadly serious and yet more amenable to political solutions. That was the issue of civil rights. For many white liberals, the inequality of black people was gradually becoming the prime symbol of what needed to be changed in American society. African Americans, in the liberal view, were the great exception to the postwar boom, a people whose plight embarrassed the nation abroad (where it became a staple of Soviet propaganda) and mocked the most cherished American ideals at home.

The most influential text on race relations in the postwar years was a thousand-plus-page book entitled *An American Dilemma* that had been published in 1944 by a Swedish social scientist named Gunnar Myrdal. The "dilemma" of Myrdal's title referred to the apparent contradiction between the "American Creed" of equality before the law and equal opportunity, and the actual treatment of the black "caste" at the bottom of American society. The "Negro problem," Myrdal insisted, was in reality a white problem. Like the Progressive Era social reformers, he believed that once an enlightened middle class had been confronted with the facts of injustice, they would act decisively to make amends. The role of blacks in this process of change was largely to demonstrate their own worthiness for full citizenship, abandoning the *"pathological condition"* of their communities (which, in Myrdal's view included not only crime and illegitimacy, but also "the emotionalism in the Negro church"), and go on *"to acquire the traits held in esteem by the dominant white Americans."*[9]

Many of Myrdal's assumptions would come to sound patronizing to later generations (although his book was hailed by black civil rights activists in the 1940s and remained popular reading among black college students up to the early 1960s).[10] Few white liberals in the 1950s were yet able to imagine a time in which black Americans would be able and willing to lead the fight for their own emancipation (relying heavily on the power of their "emotional" churches) or to define their own aspirations in ways that might diverge from being simply the dark shadow of middle-class white society. Myrdal's most lasting contribution to the future civil rights movement was to identify the struggle first and foremost as a moral struggle, and one that would become the defining issue for the nation's future. "Mankind is sick of fear and disbelief, of pessimism and cynicism," Myrdal wrote. "It needs the youthful moralistic optimism of America." Thus the "Negro problem" was not just "America's greatest failure" but also its "great opportunity for the future." If Americans embraced full racial equality, the United States would gain "a spiritual power many times stronger than all her financial and military resources—the power of the trust and support of all good people on earth."[11] A sympathetic foreigner was one of the first to argue that the best way to realize America's providential mission in the world was through ensuring racial justice at home.

Activists motivated by the ideas of Schlesinger and Galbraith, and the moral imperative of civil rights, felt most at home in the Democratic Party (although there were also a scattering of liberal activists in the Republican Party, particularly in the northeast). But the party itself, on the eve of the 1960s, was an unsteady colossus, one foot firmly resting on its achievement of the 1930s and 1940s, the other poised uncertainly in midair. Was it enough to be the party of the New Deal and the Fair Deal—as former president Truman, most of the urban political bosses, and many labor leaders believed? Or should Democrats focus on continuing problems that had not been adequately addressed by previous Democratic administrations, like racial discrimination and structural poverty?

The stakes were high. Polls taken at the turn of the decade indicated that the numbers of politically involved Americans who described themselves as either "liberal" or "conservative" were roughly equal. The outcome between the two camps would be decided when one side or the other found the issues and constituencies that would allow it to win over the uncommitted majority of voters. With the right choices, Democratic liberals believed, they could not only return to the White House but secure their control of the national government for the next generation.[12]

The Democratic party's organizational base was in flux. In most industrial cities the once powerful political machines were undermined by the postwar move to the suburbs by white working-class voters, as well as the dying off the older European immigrant generations. The continued migration of blacks to northern cities supplied new voters to Democratic Parties, but also raised tensions as newcomers and oldtimers competed for living space, jobs, and political patronage.[13]

In the Northeast, Midwest, and along the Pacific Coast, trade unions remained a powerful electoral force that could deliver campaign expertise, manpower (both in terms of paid staff and volunteers), and financial contributions, just as they had during the New Deal. Indeed, as the older forms of electoral party machinery decayed, labor's participation became even more important to Democratic strength—in some states, like Michigan, the unions virtually took over the party.

But even as official labor's importance within the Democratic Party electoral machinery increased, its ability to speak convincingly for the general welfare declined. Institutional stability brought many benefits to the unions and their members, but these came at the cost of a sense of social mission. Every year at annual conventions, delegates adopted resolutions pledging support for a wide range of ambitious social reforms, but few people in or out of the labor movement took them very seriously. Unions existed primarily to service the needs and represent the interests of their own members, not to

Mayor Richard Daley of Chicago, marching in a civil rights march, 1963. On his left is NAACP leader Roy Wilkins. Source: James Dugan, Chicago Historical Society

wage crusades on the behalf of non–dues payers, however just their cause or dire their plight. Established unions thus did little in the 1950s to help the most exploited workers in the land—migrant farm laborers up and down both coasts, and domestic workers all over. These groups were heavily black and Latino, and they had been left unprotected by the landmark labor laws of the 1930s. Neither did unions do much to appeal to the growing mass of service and clerical workers, heavily female, whose jobs still seemed ancillary to the manufacturing dynamo. Government workers, however, organized themselves and demanded changes in the law that would legitimize their new unions.[14]

Within the ranks of labor's leadership, conservatism and, on occasion, venality seemed to reign. George Meany, head of the AFL-CIO, boasted that he had never walked on a picket line. When the black trade unionist A. Philip Randolph spoke up at the 1959 AFL-CIO convention and challenged the lily-white composition of many of the nation's skilled craft unions, Meany angrily dismissed his concerns: "Who the hell appointed you as the guardian of all the Negroes in America?"[15] The presidency of the huge Teamsters Union was held by Jimmy Hoffa, who vigorously defended his members' economic interests but also flagrantly promoted his own, with the aid of the Mafia. Nationally televised hearings in 1957 of the Senate Committee on Improper Activities in the Labor or Management Field (popularly known as the McClellan hearings, after its chairman John McClellan of Arkansas), made Hoffa and his union synonymous in the public mind with corruption. The committee's aggressive chief counsel was Robert Kennedy, who would certainly never have taken on the position if he thought it would harm the presidential aspirations of his brother John. But there was little political cost, and much to be gained by bashing union bureaucrats, as many Americans came to view "big labor" as just one more selfish special interest, uninterested in the nation's general well-being.

Into the vacuum of power and ideas within the Democratic Party stepped a new generation of liberal activists. These earnest young men and women, who were overwhelmingly white and middle class, worked through advocacy groups like Americans for Democratic Action (ADA), campus organizations like the National Student Association (NSA), and reform-oriented groups like the Village Independent Democrats in New York City. They certainly wanted to be counted among Schlesinger's "doers." At gatherings of Reform Democrats, the rhetorical emphasis, wrote a political scientist, was "on fact-finding, *expertise*, research, background papers, and 'resource persons'" rather than "deductions from an a priori ideology."[16]

But beneath the surface sobriety of 1950s liberalism lurked fugitive traces of the idealistic, the visionary, and the romantic—all those qualities whose political utility Schlesinger had discounted. Like millions of their fellow Americans, the young liberal activists of the 1950s were living a great success story. The "bleak and rocky cliffs" of freedom to which they clung, came equipped with picture windows and two-car garages. Liberals might not have always enjoyed reading the daily newspapers in the 1950s, but they were, after all, living the American dream—enjoying the opportunity to pursue higher education in colleges and universities (institutions whose expansion was fueled by such Democratic legislative achievements as the GI Bill), along with the opportunity to move out of crowded, decaying urban neighborhoods to the sprawling and shiny new suburbs (financed by GI Bill loans, or the New Deal–initiated Federal Housing Administration), The many young liberals from Jewish or Roman Catholic backgrounds were coming of age during the first time in American history when non-Protestants were encouraged to think of themselves as full members of the national community.

Not only was postwar America prosperous, it was powerful. Liberals, for the most part, felt at ease with that power. It was part of the world they had inherited from Franklin Roosevelt. They saw in the Cold War a continuation of the liberal internationalism of the Second World War, a war of ideas as well as power blocs that Roosevelt had defined as a struggle for the "Four Freedoms"—freedom of speech, freedom of religion, freedom from want, and freedom from fear. The first two freedoms were the same as those sought by the classical liberalism of the nineteenth century—the absence of restraint. But the last two suggested the need for a strong, interventionist government, along the lines of Roosevelt's own New Deal, to redistribute resources or stimulate economic growth to do away with "want," and to protect the rights of political and racial minorities to do away with "fear." A foreign policy conducted for such goals implied commitment to improving the lives of other peoples, as well as securing the best interests of the United States.

The older generation of liberals, including some who had cut their political teeth in the bitter feuding between Communists and "anti-Stalinists" in the 1930s and 1940s, tended not to ask too many questions about the actual conduct of the Cold War by Washington policymakers. Outside of the tiny Communist and pacifist movements, few Americans in the 1950s of any political perspective argued that there were fundamental problems with America's chosen role in the world.

Still, liberals of the younger generation offered a more selective support to the Cold War than their elders. They found themselves uneasy with the "excesses" of American policy—the U.S. government's decision to develop and test hydrogen bombs, the State Department's cozying up with Generalissimo Franco in Spain, and the pretense that Chiang Kai-shek's exile regime in Taiwan was the real government of mainland China. These were merely cracks in the Cold War consensus, but in time they would widen.

In 1959 a recent graduate of Smith College named Gloria Steinem took a job organizing a delegation of young Americans to attend and disrupt a Communist-sponsored international youth festival in Vienna. The funding

Gloria Steinem, future feminist leader, as she appeared in her 1956 college yearbook. Source: *Sophia Smith Collection*

for the group, carefully hidden from the delegates but probably known to Steinem, came from the Central Intelligence Agency. Steinem, however, did not think of herself as the covert agent of a great power. Upon her return from Vienna in August 1959 she wrote to a relative: "I suppose this was my small world equivalent of going off to join the Spanish Revolution."[17]

Allard Lowenstein, a graduate of the University of North Carolina, served for a year as president of the National Student Association at a time when the CIA was secretly subsidizing the group. Yet in 1959, as a freelance journalist investigating the apartheid system in South Africa, Lowenstein risked his own freedom by smuggling an African dissident out of the country, hidden in the back of Lowenstein's Volkswagen Beetle. His friends jokingly referred to him as "U.S. undercover agent 1001"—although furthering the struggle against apartheid was far from official U.S. policy in 1959.[18]

In the 1950s Steinem and Lowenstein were patriotic young people, and committed cold warriors. But there was a streak of independence in that commitment—not so much "my country, right or wrong," but an attitude that might be described as "my country—just as long as *it is* right. . . . "

The new currents in American liberalism that began to emerge in the 1950s represented less a well-defined set of political doctrines, and more a kind of political sensibility reflecting a new social environment. Younger, middle-class liberals, many coming from "ethnic" and working-class backgrounds, and in many instances the first generation in their families to enjoy college educations, were now, in effect, laying claim to a political territory that had formerly belonged to socially prominent, old-line Protestant Republicans. They were becoming self-appointed spokesmen for the public interest in good government, civility, and social responsibility. Theirs was a vision that harkened back to Progressive Era notions of responsible citizenship, or what philosopher John Dewey had called, in the 1920s, the goal of creating a "Great Community," a society in which "an organized, articulate Public" was deeply and directly involved in every aspect of government decision making. At the same time, there was a new and more quixotic element within this liberalism, a kind of instinctive adversarial stance, a willingness to stand against the current, like Yossarian in *Catch-22*, if that's what conscience seemed to dictate.

To whom did such a mixed vision of community and individualism appeal? One of the leading liberal weekly journals of opinion, *The New Republic*, took a survey of its readers in the early 1960s. The magazine's "typical reader," it turned out, was about 35 years old, had completed college and at least one year of graduate school, was married to a college graduate and had one child.[19] Professionals, like lawyers, architects, and journalists, accounted for 35 percent of the readership, teachers 18 percent, and students 12 percent.[20]

Although the entire readership of *The New Republic* at the start of the 1960s could have been gathered together in one of the nation's larger football stadiums,[21] it represented a significant constituency just beginning to find its own voice in American politics. Younger Americans at the start of the 1960s were better educated than their parents and more apt to have careers requiring professional accreditation; and they were postponing marriage and child bearing (which would, in a few years, bring the postwar "baby boom" to its close). These were people who had the spare time, the financial wherewithal, the credentials, and the self-confidence to challenge conventional wisdom and take on established authorities.

They would, in the course of the 1960s, come to be referred to as "the conscience constituency," or "the new class."[22] They embraced new causes, or old causes that had gone out of fashion, like environmentalism and women's rights. They combined a passion for social change and social justice with the belief in the power of reasoned argument—which is why they so often came to a new cause by having read some seminal book on the topic. Jane Jacobs's *The Death and Life of Great American Cities*, published in 1961, sparked a movement in defense of livable urban neighborhoods. Rachel Carson's *Silent Spring*, published in 1962, made converts for a new environmental movement. Betty Friedan's *The Feminine Mystique*, published in 1963, contributed to the rebirth of American feminism. And Ralph Nader's *Unsafe at Any Speed*, published in 1965, did the same for a new anticorporate consumer movement.[23]

Tellingly, such books were often referred to by their admirers as "the bible" of this or that cause. Notwithstanding their commitment to rational debate, the outlook of the new liberalism also embodied a highly moralistic vision; political involvement became an extension of—or, increasingly, a substitute for—a personal quest for spiritual salvation.[24]

Many Democratic leaders were wary of the new missionaries of reform. Professional politicians like Harry Truman, hard-bitten labor leaders like George Meany, and old-line urban bosses like Mayor Daley scorned the reformers as "eggheads"—arrogant and impractical intellectuals. The new Reform Democrats admired a few labor leaders, particularly Walter Reuther of the United Auto Workers, who walked on civil rights marches and waxed idealistic about a broader welfare state. But Reform Democrats were not, on the whole, all that interested or well versed in the bread-and-butter economic issues that had been the mainstay of Democratic Party policy and political strategy during the New and Fair Deals. Despite the disdain of the old pros, however, the Reform Democrats gained significant influence in the mid- to late 1950s in Democratic parties in such key electoral states as New York, Michigan, Minnesota, Pennsylvania, and California. The enjoyed the patronage of Eleanor Roosevelt, the leading liberal icon of the Democratic Party, and they gained useful political experience and contacts in Adlai Stevenson's presidential campaigns of 1952 and 1956. But they remained, at the end of the 1950s, a movement without a clear leader.

Ironically, the man who became identified, for most Americans, with a new birth of liberalism was a thoroughly practical politician of the old school who tended to view idealists and moralists as sentimental fools.

John F. Kennedy was born in Brookline, Massachusetts, in 1917, the second of nine children fathered by Joseph P. Kennedy. The elder Kennedy was the grandson of impoverished Irish immigrants who had emigrated to the United States to escape the potato famine. The old Protestant elite in Boston looked on the arrival of Irish Catholics as a kind of barbarian invasion. Young Joe Kennedy, whose father was a prosperous Boston saloon keeper, grew up determined to beat the Protestants at their own game in both business and politics. Shrewd investments in the 1920s made him a millionaire. But although he enjoyed prominence in Democratic Party circles in the 1930s, and was awarded with political plums such as the chairmanship of the Securities and Exchange Commission and the ambassadorship to Great Britain, he would never realize his life's ambition of becoming president of the United States. That would be left to his sons, who were groomed from childhood for the run for the White House.

President John F. Kennedy. Source: *John F. Kennedy Library, photo number AR7018G 1 Feb. 1962*

Pride of place fell to John (nicknamed Jack) after his older brother, Joseph, Jr., died in a World War II plane crash. John suffered from a variety of physical ailments that frequently confined him to bed and plagued him throughout his life. But his father still demanded that the boy join his siblings in rigorous physical exercise, sailing races, and touch football games. His mother, Rose Kennedy, herself the daughter of a prominent Irish-American politician in Boston, pinned notes to his pillowcase urging him to memorize the presidents. Competition was the family creed. "Don't play unless you are captain," Joe Kennedy, Sr. advised his brood. "Second place is failure."[25]

John Kennedy enjoyed every advantage his father's money could buy him. His Harvard education culminated in the publication of his first book, *Why England Slept,* a study of British foreign policy in the late 1930s. It became a best-seller, in part because Joe Kennedy persuaded *New York Times* columnist Arthur Krock to revise it for his son, and in part because Joe Kennedy took the precaution of purchasing thirty thousand copies of it himself, most of which were relegated to the family attic.

After Pearl Harbor, Jack Kennedy enlisted in the navy, was commissioned an officer, and given command of a PT (patrol torpedo) boat in the South

Pacific. On an August night in 1943, near the Solomon Islands, a Japanese destroyer rammed Kennedy's PT boat, slicing it in half. Kennedy rallied his men, helping the survivors make it to a nearby island, and personally towing an injured sailor several miles to safety. Joe Kennedy induced the *Reader's Digest*, the highest circulation magazine in the country, to run excerpts from a laudatory account of his son's rescue of the crew of PT-109; when Jack Kennedy returned from the war and ran for Congress in 1946, thousands of reprints of the article appeared on subway and bus seats throughout the Boston-area congressional district he was seeking to represent. Kennedy won in a landslide, and six years later, again well financed by his father, he secured election to the United States Senate.

In the last half of the 1950s, Kennedy devoted himself single-mindedly to a new prize, the 1960 Democratic nomination for the presidency. The campaign included the publication of yet another ghost-written best-seller (*Profiles in Courage*, which appeared in 1957 and, once again through Joe Kennedy's intervention, was awarded a Pulitzer Prize). Kennedy's supporters stressed his intellectual attainments, and he himself preferred a style of cool rationality to any excessive display of sentiment or emotion.[26]

But the candidate's real appeal had little to do with intellect. By 1960 the Kennedy image of glamour, grace, and inspirational leadership was provoking the kind of adulation formerly associated with such male sex symbols as Frank Sinatra (who was a prominent Kennedy enthusiast in the 1960 campaign). After witnessing Kennedy speak that summer at the Democratic national convention, novelist Norman Mailer marveled that "the Democrats were going to nominate a man who, no matter how serious his political dedication might be, was indisputably and willy-nilly going to be seen as a great box-office actor." The consequences for American politics, Mailer mused, "were staggering and not at all easy to calculate."[27]

In his campaign for nomination, John Kennedy benefited from the support of prominent liberal activists such as Schlesinger and Galbraith. Most liberals, however, would have preferred any number of other candidates for the presidential nomination: Adlai Stevenson, not formally in the race, was backed by both Mrs. Roosevelt and Walter Reuther, while Minnesota senator Hubert Humphrey, Missouri senator Stuart Symington, and others actively pursuing the nomination had their partisans. Kennedy was regarded with suspicion by the Democratic Party's liberal wing because of his father's isolationism in the 1930s, his own lackluster congressional record, and his temporizing over the issue of McCarthyism in the early 1950s.[28]

Whatever reputation Kennedy had for liberal sympathies in 1960 was more a matter of a calculated style than of policies: the tousled hair, the fondness for touch football and windswept walks on the Hyannis beach, the Harvard affiliation, all seemed to imply a combination of youth and vigor and daring. His demurely beautiful wife, the former Jacqueline Bouvier, with her

family ties to genuine European aristocracy, her fondness for French de-
signers, and her stylish bouffant hairdo, only enhanced the Kennedy image.

Kennedy won the presidential nomination at the Democratic convention
on the first ballot. Liberals, by and large, swallowed their disappointment at
his nomination (although, as Schlesinger reported privately to Kennedy in
August, ADA was responding to his candidacy with "utmost tepidity").
Kennedy further dismayed liberals by choosing Texas senator Lyndon Johnson as his running mate. Johnson had begun his political career in the 1930s
as an outspokenly liberal congressman but had moved to the right in the
years since. Liberals viewed Johnson as an unprincipled wheeler-dealer, and
his nomination as vice president as a dangerous and unprincipled sop to conservative southern Democrats. ADA refused outright to endorse Johnson's
candidacy.[29]

In the fall campaign, Kennedy shored up his reputation with liberals by
hitting hard at the Eisenhower record on domestic policy. His opponent,
Richard Nixon, bore the burden of defending the record of the administration in which he had served eight years as vice president—and, unfortunately
for his cause, had to do so in the midst of an economic recession. Kennedy
declared that the "war against poverty and degradation is not yet over," citing statistics showing millions of American living in substandard homes, and
millions of elderly people living on inadequate assistance.[30] In response,
Nixon pointed to the growth of giant shopping centers as evidence of American well-being—the very sort of development that Galbraith, Packard, and
others had spent the past half-decade denouncing as a wasteful and frivolous
misuse of resources.

Kennedy's promise that he would "get the nation moving again," was as
vague about specifics as a good campaign slogan should be, but not so the
party platform, adopted by the delegates at the Democratic national convention in 1960. Kennedy ran for office committed to a liberal wish list of bold
initiatives; if elected, and true to these promises, he would raise the minimum wage, improve the conditions of farm workers, secure passage of national health insurance for the elderly, and launch a 10-year campaign to
eliminate urban slums.

The Democratic Party platform also pledged vigorous enforcement of existing civil rights legislation and praised the southern student sit-in movement. And in the waning days of the campaign, Kennedy was persuaded by
his liberal advisers to reach out to the civil rights movement in a direct and
dramatic fashion; when Martin Luther King was hustled off to a Georgia
prison in late October on a bogus charge of violating probation from an earlier traffic violation, Kennedy called up Coretta Scott King to offer the prisoner's wife his sympathy. His brother and campaign manager Bobby called a
Georgia judge, who arranged to get King released. The Kennedy campaign
heavily publicized these gestures in black communities. Although many white

voters in the South were put off by Kennedy's evident sympathy for King (and others could not, in any case, bring themselves to vote for a Catholic), Kennedy was the last Democratic candidate for president to win both a majority of the southern white vote and a majority of the national black vote.

The black ballots proved decisive. On election day a full 70 percent of black voters who went to the polls cast their ballot for Kennedy (up 10 percent from the black vote for Stevenson in 1956). Kennedy's narrow margin of victory (which also benefited from some creative vote counting in Democratic precincts in Illinois and Texas) lagged considerably behind the total popular vote for Democratic congressional candidates.[31]

Once in office Kennedy charmed liberals (and much of the country) with the dash he brought to public occasions, especially his frequent press conferences. He cultivated intellectuals and artists: Robert Frost read a poem at Kennedy's inauguration; Pablo Casals provided cello music at a White House reception. Jackie Kennedy was much in evidence at such affairs, chatting in French with novelist André Malraux, pointing out the works of art she had had installed in the White House in an effort to sweep away the dowdiness into which it had fallen in the Eisenhower years. Both Kennedys managed the daunting challenge of associating themselves with high intellectual life without appearing stuffy or snobbish themselves. At a dinner honoring Nobel Prize winners from throughout the Americas, Kennedy described them with characteristic sly wit as "the most extraordinary collection of talent, of human knowledge, that has ever been gathered together at the White House, with the possible exception of when Thomas Jefferson dined alone."[32]

But Kennedy style and the Kennedy substance remained separate categories. During the first two years of the New Frontier, the lights did not burn late in the White House while the president fretted over domestic issues. In his inaugural address, where he stirred the country with an idealistic appeal to "bear any burden, pay any price" in defending freedom abroad, the new president failed to mention domestic policy at all. The liberals in his campaign entourage found themselves confined to odd corners of the administration, far from domestic policymaking. Schlesinger crafted speeches, not policy, while Galbraith went off to India as U.S. ambassador. Kennedy brother-in-law Sargent Shriver (sometimes referred to by administration insiders as the "house Communist") was given the directorship of the newly created Peace Corps—a high-profile/low-influence position. Galbraith would later describe the role of the administration's liberals as resembling that of "Indians firing occasional arrows into the campsite from outside."[33] Not many arrows hit home: Kennedy regarded most of the domestic issues that concerned liberals as a distraction from the all-important military and diplomatic confrontation with the Soviet Union.

In the 1960 election Kennedy had managed to outflank Richard Nixon on the right when it came to the issue of American foreign policy, suggesting that the Eisenhower administration had carelessly allowed the Soviet Union to outpace the United States in the arms race, and in the struggle to influence developing nations around the world. While the charges were largely spurious (it was the United States in 1960 that enjoyed a substantial lead in nuclear weapons and the ability to deliver them against enemy targets), there is no question that Kennedy was a devout anti-communist who conceived of his role as commander-in-chief of the free world as the most important of his new responsibilities. He surrounded himself with a crew of foreign policy advisers who were, in the ironic description later provided by journalist David Halberstam, "the best and the brightest." They included the secretary of defense, Robert McNamara, the Harvard Business School-educated president of the Ford Motor Company, and national security adviser Mc-George Bundy, dean of the College of Arts and Sciences at Harvard. Bobby Kennedy, the new attorney general, also played a key role in the administration's foreign policy discussions.[34]

JFK and his advisers were prepared to wage the conflict with Communism on many fronts. First, they sought to contain the USSR, led by mercurial premier Nikita S. Khrushchev, inside its client bloc in eastern Europe, and to make sure that the Soviets gained no advantage in the nuclear arms race or the space race. Kennedy initiated the most dramatic peacetime military buildup in American history, spending more money on nuclear weapons, missile systems, and fallout shelters in three years than the Eisenhower administration had spent in eight. The total megatonnage of the American nuclear arsenal more than doubled in the three years Kennedy sat in the White House.[35] At the same time, Kennedy committed the United States to sending a man to the moon by the end of the decade; as he declared in a message on "urgent national needs" to a joint session of Congress in May 1961, it was "time for this nation to take a clearly leading role in space achievement, which in many ways may hold the key to our future on earth."[36]

Kennedy and his foreign policy advisers also committed themselves to reversing the gains made by Communists and other anti-American radicals in the Third World, where both the decay of the old colonial empires and extreme social and economic inequalities were generating what seemed in the early 1960s like a tidal wave of revolutionary activism. Asked by a reporter about a little-known conflict going on in South Vietnam in 1961, Bobby Kennedy spoke dismissively of its significance in the overall scheme of U.S. policymaking: "We've got twenty Vietnams a day to handle."[37]

Kennedy's first attempt to challenge Soviet influence in the Third World—an adventure initially planned by the Eisenhower administration but eagerly pursued by the new one—was a disaster. On April 17, 1961, a brigade of 1400 Cuban exiles, trained and armed by the United States, began an invasion of their homeland. The purpose of the landing at a beach called Playa Girón—better known as the Bay of Pigs—was to begin the overthrow of the government of Fidel Castro, which had in the past year openly allied itself with the USSR. But Castro's willingness to thumb his nose at Cuba's overbearing neighbor to the north was popular with many Cubans. Moreover, he had advance warning of the attack. It took Cuban planes and troops less than 24 hours to force the outmanned invaders to surrender. Just before the invasion, Kennedy called off a planned air strike on Playa Girón for fear it would reveal U.S. sponsorship of the whole affair. Such an attack would not have changed the outcome of the botched invasion, but Kennedy's belated caution created the suspicion in some quarters that he had "sold out" the anti-Castro cause.[38]

The embarrassing failure at the Bay of Pigs, for which Kennedy publicly assumed blame, strengthened the president's obsession with a regime he viewed as nothing more than a launching pad for Soviet aggression. Within six months, the administration had initiated Operation Mongoose, a secret program that did everything short of another invasion to destroy Castro's regime. Under Mongoose, hundreds of American and Cuban operatives, coordinated by the CIA, gathered intelligence, sabotaged the Cuban economy, and launched numerous assassination attempts against Castro, including one plot involving a poisoned cigar. Mongoose failed to topple Castro; instead it convinced the Cuban leader to seek ironclad protection from his Soviet allies against the Yankee behemoth to the north.[39]

That search helped set in motion events that nearly ended in nuclear war between the superpowers. Responding to Castro's entreaties, Nikita Khrushchev decided to base Soviet missiles in Cuba, missiles capable of carrying nuclear warheads to every major city on the east coast of the United States. The plans were kept secret, but in the fall of 1962 American spy planes flying over Cuba photographed feverish construction efforts on the ground. It did not take long for intelligence analysts to realize what was being built.

In the early 1960s it seemed that Berlin was the most dangerous flash point in East–West relations. In 1961 Kennedy and Khrushchev had faced off over the latter's threat to restrict Western access to Berlin, long a pawn in the Cold War. The Communists ended that crisis in brutal fashion when they erected a high concrete wall separating the two sectors of the city, gunning down any East Germans who tried to scale it. Kennedy knew there was not much he could actually do about the Berlin situation, except to make it clear to West Berliners that the United States would stick by them in any future conflict with the East. He was not, however, prepared to stand by idly at the expansion of Soviet power in his own backyard.

For nearly two weeks in October 1962, the president and the premier engaged in the most dangerous international confrontation in history. Each side gambled that the other would recoil from the prospect of nuclear confrontation. But it was a near thing. A number of Kennedy's top advisers urged him to take decisive actions against Cuba ranging from air strikes to a full scale invasion, each of which might have triggered a Soviet nuclear response. Kennedy, however, opted for a more cautious and flexible strategy, using U.S. naval strength to "quarantine" Soviet shipping to the island to prevent any missiles or warheads from getting through. In the end it was Khrushchev who relented, sobered by Kennedy's resolve and well aware that the U.S. nuclear arsenal was much larger than its Soviet counterpart. Soviet merchant vessels turned around in midvoyage to Cuba and returned to their home ports. In return for an agreement to dismantle the missile bases in Cuba, the Soviet leader demanded that the U.S. president promise not to invade the island, and to remove U.S. missiles stationed near the Soviet border in Turkey. Kennedy readily agreed, particularly since the United States had already planned to remove the increasingly obsolete missiles. The crisis was over.[40]

In the United States, the outcome of the Cuban missile crisis was seen as an unambiguous American victory—the two great powers went "eyeball to eyeball" as the saying went, and Khrushchev blinked. Kennedy's personal popularity soared. The president, however, was sobered by the affair, and for the first time began to rethink his reflexive Cold War militancy insofar as it involved the possibility of direct confrontation with the Soviet Union. Khrushchev too was eager to avoid any replay of the crisis. The expensive arms race between the superpowers continued, but both sides toned down their rhetoric and avoided making gestures that would set off the nuclear trip wire. Although the word "detente" was not yet in vogue, a new kind of confidence slowly grew between the two powers that a third and final world war was avoidable. Months after the crisis, the United States quietly removed its missiles from Turkey. The White House and the Kremlin installed a "hotline" to facilitate communication in the event of future crises. And negotiations began on a treaty to stop nuclear testing in the atmosphere, with ratification coming in the fall of 1963.

In the early 1960s protests against the nuclear arms race, and interventions in Third World countries, were restricted to small circles of radicals and pacifists. But by 1962 Kennedy's domestic priorities—or his apparent lack of such priorities—was creating discontent among his liberal supporters. Now that they actually had a decidedly unsentimental "administrator" in office, many liberals found that they didn't much like it. In 1962 John Roche, a political scientist at Brandeis University and national chairman of ADA, denounced Kennedy's "technocratic liberalism." Roche suggested his administration could benefit from an infusion "of good old-fashion crusading zeal."[41]

Kennedy wanted to be a great president, and in the scope and authority given him to conduct foreign policy, he felt he had an arena in which to make his mark. Domestic policy in contrast, seemed a terrain full of potential pitfalls. Kennedy was mindful of the narrow margin of his victory in 1960; he was mindful, too, of the likelihood of facing a strong Republican challenge, most likely from the conservative Arizona senator, Barry Goldwater, in the 1964 election. He also faced formidable legislative constraints. The Democrats had lost 22 seats in the House and 2 in the Senate in 1960, despite their success in taking back the White House. Congress was even more firmly under the control of a coalition of southern Democrats and conservative Republicans in Kennedy's first two years in office than it had been in the last two years of Eisenhower's administration.

Kennedy strategists calculated that fewer than 180 of the 435 members of the House of Representatives could be counted to regularly support liberal legislation. As a result, 16 of the 23 bills dealing with domestic matters that the president sent to Congress in 1961 were defeated.[42] And Kennedy wasn't asking for all that much, for he was eager to reassure a nervous business community that the return of the Democrats to power would not mean reckless spending or inflationary policies.

By 1962 the new administration's heavy spending on defense had pushed the federal budget into the red, but it had also given the sluggish economy a jump start. Kennedy gradually came to understand what liberal economists had believed for a generation, that there were worse things for the economy than having the federal government engage in deficit spending. Under the tutelage of Walter Heller, chairman of the Council of Economic Advisers, Kennedy became a convert to the "New Economics." Heller and others convinced the president that he had the power and the responsibility to shape the economy through the government's fiscal policies. The most useful weapon in his economic arsenal, they argued, would be a tax cut, which would stimulate economic growth. In January 1963 Kennedy proposed a $10 billion tax cut.[43]

To placate liberals, who noted that most of the benefits of Kennedy's economic policies would flow to those already well off, the president lent support to some limited initiatives in public welfare, including the Area Redevelopment Act, which provided loans to businesses willing to relocate to depressed regions like Appalachia, and the Manpower Development and Training Act, which created programs for the retraining of workers displaced by automation. Notwithstanding his skepticism about its worth, he secured an increase in the minimum wage, as well as a broadening of unemployment and Social Security benefits. But taken together, these measures fell far short of the glowing promises of the 1960 Democratic party platform.[44]

Quite unintentionally, Kennedy made an important contribution to one beleaguered liberal cause, and that was equal rights for women. He issued an executive order in 1961 establishing the President's Commission on the Status of Women, chaired by Eleanor Roosevelt until her death in November 1962. Kennedy had little if any interest in women's issues, but he saw the establishment of the commission as a gallant gesture to women in the Demo-

cratic Party, and also as a painless way to reward Eleanor Roosevelt for joining his campaign after he had won the Democratic nomination in 1960.

However limited the intent, the symbolism of his act had important consequences. Many states established their own status-of-women commissions,
whose representatives met periodically in Washington. In October 1963, the
President's Commission presented a report to Kennedy calling for equal employment and educational opportunities for women, and a wider role for
women in American political life. Like the reports of most presidential commissions, it was politely received by a president who had no serious intention of pursuing its recommendations. Still, the commission's report documented the discrimination women faced in the workplace and helped to
legitimize a public debate over women's roles and rights.[45]

Of all the domestic issues Kennedy had to deal with, civil rights was the
most politically problematic, since any gains made in pleasing black voters
in the North came at the likely expense of alienating white voters in the
South. Kennedy responded to the successive civil rights crises of 1961–1962
primarily in terms of crisis management, rather than the opportunity to provide political leadership. He angered civil rights supporters by appointing a
number of staunchly segregationist federal judges in the South and by backing away from his campaign pledge to end discrimination in public housing
"with a stroke of the pen" by means of executive order (he finally got around
to issuing such an order after the November 1962 midterm elections were
safely past). And the Justice Department, under Bobby Kennedy, did little to
protect the lives of civil rights workers in the dangerous work of voter registration in the Deep South.

Through 1962, Kennedy's liberalism remained for the most part a matter of style rather than substance. In terms of domestic policy, John F.
Kennedy became the liberal he is remembered as only in the last year of his
life. Meanwhile, the decisions he was making about American policy in distant Vietnam would soon split Democrats into warring camps, to the lasting
detriment of the liberal cause and agenda.

CHAPTER 4

Why Did the United States Fight in Vietnam?

NEITHER YOU NOR I KNOW THE AMERICANS WELL, BUT WHAT WE DO KNOW OF THEM . . . SUGGESTS THAT THEY ARE MORE PRACTICAL AND CLEAR-SIGHTED THAN OTHER CAPITALIST NATIONS. THEY WILL NOT POUR THEIR RESOURCES INTO VIETNAM ENDLESSLY.

—*Ho Chi Minh, in conversation with a Communist diplomat, autumn 1963*[1]

The Vietnam War was a war within a war. It was one battlefront in the nearly half century Cold War the United States fought globally against the Soviet Union and its allies. The Cold War ended in American triumph. The Vietnam War did not. And before it ran its course, the Vietnam War plunged the United States into its most bitter civil conflict in a century. Before the war ran its course, more than 58,000 Americans, and millions of Vietnamese, would die. Before the war ran its course, two American presidencies would be either directly or indirectly shattered by its consequences. Before the war ran its course, Americans would get used to thinking of each other as divided into polarized enemy camps: pro-war and antiwar, hawks and doves, and on from there to ever more scurrilous epithets. No legacy of the 1960s had as long and embittering an effect on the politics and culture of the United States as that left by the war in Vietnam.

The war in Vietnam differed from other American conflicts in which the United States had fought for clearly defined strategic or territorial goals. In Vietnam, the rationale for fighting the war, like the battlefront itself, was constantly shifting. The most consistent explanation for why Americans needed to fight in Vietnam was the defense of the Cold War "credibility" of the United States—in itself a murky, ambiguous goal.

Vietnam also differed from other American wars in which clearly defined lines divided peace and war, such as the Confederate firing on Fort Sumter in 1861. In Vietnam no single event or decision clearly marked the beginning of the war. Arguments could be made to date the real start of the conflict, or at least the point of no return, anytime from the mid-1950s until the mid-1960s. The roots of American involvement stretch back much further.[2]

Vietnam, a country that is roughly the size of New Mexico in square miles, stretches in an S-shaped curve along the eastern seaboard of Southeast Asia. Two fertile river deltas, the Red River in the north and the Mekong River in the south, fan out to the sea. A narrow coastal plain runs up the seacoast, while rugged mountain chains and high plateaus run north and south the length of the country's heavily forested interior.

When Americans first fought in Vietnam, they did so, ironically, as allies of Vietnamese Communist leader Ho Chi Minh. Indochina, which includes Laos and Cambodia as well as Vietnam, had been colonized by France since the late nineteenth century, the richest and most important colony in the French empire. For over a half century the French ruthlessly suppressed any challenge to their authority in the region. Then, in 1940, France was itself conquered by Nazi Germany. The following year, French Indochina was occupied by Japan. French colonialists offered little resistance to the Japanese invaders, but Ho Chi Minh and the Communists formed a national resistance movement, opposing both the Japanese occupation and French colonialism. Within four years the Viet Minh had a half million followers, and a 5000-man army.

In the closing days of the Second World War, a team of American intelligence agents parachuted behind Japanese lines in Vietnam to establish contact with Ho Chi Minh's forces. These troops, the Viet Minh, had proved themselves useful to the Americans by rescuing downed American fliers. In July 1945 the Americans brought medical supplies and small arms to Ho, and trained his Viet Minh fighters in guerrilla tactics. Two months later, following the Japanese surrender, American advisers were with Ho when his troops marched in to take control of Hanoi, the principal city of northern Vietnam. On September 2, 1945, Ho, a frail man with a wispy beard, whose bearing suggested more a scholar than a military commander or a politician, stood before a crowd of a half-million of his countrymen in a central square in Hanoi and declared Vietnamese independence. He chose to do so in words that sounded familiar to the American military men in attendance: "We hold truths that all men are created equal," Ho declared. "That they are endowed by their Creator with certain unalienable Rights: among these are Life, Liberty, and the pursuit of Happiness."[3]

Though he had borrowed freely from the American declaration of independence, Ho Chi Minh was by no means a Jeffersonian democrat. He was a hard-bitten revolutionary who had spent many years in exile from Vietnam in the service of the Communist movement. He was born as Nguyen Tat Thanh in 1890 in Nghe An Province in central coastal Vietnam. Though well educated, he signed onto a ship in 1912 as a common laborer and sailed over

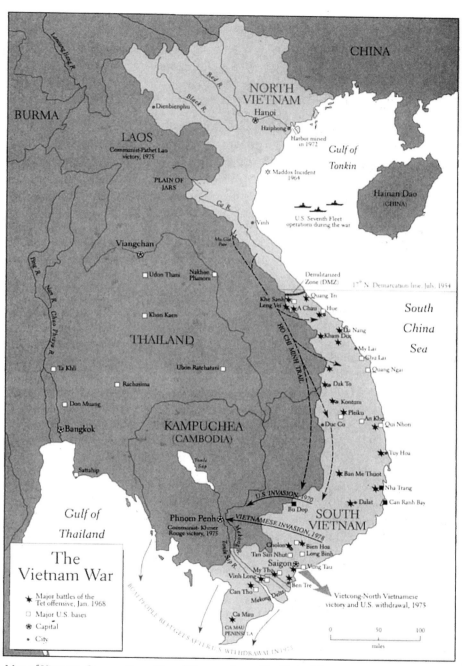

Map of Vietnam. Source: *From* Grand Expectations: The United States, 1945–1974 *by James T. Patterson. Copyright © 1996 by Oxford University Press, Inc. Used by permission of Oxford University Press, Inc.*

the next few years to Africa, Europe and North America. (During this period he lived for nearly a year in Brooklyn, New York.) His thoughts, however, remained anchored in his homeland, and it was during this period also that he took a new name, Nguyen Ai-Quoc, which means "Nguyen the Patriot" in Vietnamese. He would not become known by the name Ho Chi Minh ("He Who Enlightens" in Vietnamese) until 1944.

During the First World War and its immediate aftermath, Ho lived in Paris. There, in 1920, he joined the French Communist Party. Communist leaders in Moscow had issued a call for world revolution, including the overthrow of the colonial regimes of Asia and Africa. To Ho, the Communist movement represented a long-sought ally for Vietnamese independence. He rose quickly within the leadership of the international Communist movement, traveling to Moscow and China on its behalf.

In 1930 Ho held a secret meeting in Hong Kong to organize the Vietnamese Communist Party. However, the party could not function openly in Vietnam. The French regularly executed nationalist and Communist opponents in Vietnam; Ho knew he faced a death sentence if he was captured. In 1941 he slipped back into Vietnam to organize the Viet Minh to do battle with the Japanese and the French.

Ho was a Communist, which meant that he was a loyal supporter of the Soviet Union. In the context of the Cold War that would make him an enemy in the eyes of American policymakers. But Ho's first priority was attaining Vietnamese independence. During the Second World War, he came to hope that the United States, for reasons of its own, could be brought to support the cause of Vietnamese independence.

America's wartime leader, President Franklin Delano Roosevelt, was certainly no admirer of French colonialism. "[T]he case of Indochina is perfectly clear," he wrote to Secretary of State Cordell Hull in January 1944. "France has milked it for one hundred years. The people of Indochina are entitled to something better than that."[4] Beyond vague speculation about establishing an international "trusteeship" to govern Indochina after the war, however, Roosevelt never spelled out any definite alternatives to allowing the French to reestablish their control of the region.

The world changed swiftly in the months that followed Roosevelt's death in April 1945, with the unraveling of the wartime alliance of the United States, Britain, and the Soviet Union. In March 1947 President Harry Truman announced what became known as the Truman Doctrine, declaring it the policy of the United States "to support free peoples who are resisting attempted subjugation by armed minorities or by outside pressures."[5] Never before had an American president committed the nation to a foreign policy that, potentially, involved an unceasing series of military interventions throughout the world.

In Vietnam, in the year following the end of the Second World War, the contending French and Viet Minh forces faced each other in an uneasy stand-off. In February 1946 Ho wrote Truman and asked that the United States become the "guardian" of Vietnam. Noting that the United States had recently granted independence to its former protectorate in the Philippine islands, Ho declared: "Like the Philippines our goal is full independence and full cooperation with the UNITED STATES. We will do our best to make this independence and cooperation profitable to the whole world."[6]

In all, Ho addressed 11 such messages to the American government. His movement received no material aid from the Soviet Union, or any other Communist country in those years. Moscow ignored him, and his former comrades in the French Communist party disparaged him as politically unreliable. Some American intelligence officers who kept tabs on Indochina in the 1940s believed Ho had the potential to become the "Tito of Southeast Asia"—that is, like Marshal Tito of Yugoslavia, he would steer an independent course in foreign relations, not beholden to the Soviet Union.

Truman never responded to Ho's entreaties. Indochina was a minor concern to American policymakers. Their main concern was the defense of western Europe, where France was a valued American ally. The French, who had suffered a grave national humiliation with their defeat and occupation by the Nazis, had no intention of relinquishing control over their colonial empire. To Truman and his advisers, there seemed no alternative to backing the French in Indochina.

In November 1946 French forces went on the offensive against the Viet Minh. French warships bombarded the northern Vietnamese port of Haiphong, killing about 1,000 civilians. The Viet Minh abandoned the cities to the French and fought back from the countryside, using the classic guerrilla tactics of stealth and surprise.

Other armies were on the march in Asia. In October 1949 Chinese Communist forces led by Mao Zedong came to power on the Chinese mainland; afterward, arms and ammunition began to be smuggled to the Viet Minh across the Chinese–Vietnamese border. In June 1950 the armies of Communist North Korea swept over the border into South Korea. To American leaders, the events in China and Korea were ominously reminiscent of Hitler's aggression in Europe in the late 1930s; in 1950 President Truman believed that the Korean invasion represented the opening shots of a Third World War.

From the experience of dealing with the Nazis in the 1930s, American leaders concluded that appeasement only whetted the appetite of aggressors. The only way to deter an expansionist dictatorship, whether led by a Hitler or a Stalin, was the resolute application of counterforce. It was with this understanding that Truman in June 1950 committed America's military might to the aid of the beleaguered South Koreans. For the first time, American soldiers were engaged in a full-scale shooting war against a Communist foe. That same month, the United States began providing military supplies to the French forces in Indochina. By 1954 American aid had increased to the point where the United States was funding nearly 80 percent of the French war effort.

The Viet Minh proved a formidable enemy, and after a series of military setbacks, the French switched commanders in Indochina. In May 1953, the new French commander, General Henri Navarre, declared, "Now we can see [victory] clearly, like light at the end of a tunnel."[7] The phrase would come back to haunt him. Seeking a climactic showdown with the Viet Minh, the French commander sent 15,000 crack troops to a remote village in northwestern Vietnam called Dien Bien Phu. But in their overconfidence, the French neglected to occupy the heights surrounding their new base.

Viet Minh troops under the command of Vo Nguyen Giap cut roads through supposedly impassable terrain, and dragged artillery to those hilltops. On March 13, 1954, they launched their offensive, cutting off the French garrison from reinforcement or retreat. Americans took part in the attempted resupply of the garrison; two American pilots were shot down and killed in the effort. A crisis atmosphere prevailed in Washington as Admiral Arthur Radford, chairman of the Joint Chiefs of Staff, proposed to President Eisenhower that the United States relieve the defenders by means of air strikes, possibly including the use of tactical nuclear weapons.

Several influential lawmakers, including Senator John F. Kennedy and Senate majority leader Lyndon B. Johnson, warned against intervention, as did Army Chief of Staff General Matthew Ridgway. Kennedy had earlier criticized the Truman administration for its policies in Indochina, declaring in 1952, "we have allied ourselves to the desparate effort of a French regime to hang on to the remnants of Empire."[8] No one wanted another costly land war in Asia. Eisenhower, who had been elected in November 1952 in part because of his promise to a war-weary electorate to end the Korean war, held back. Surrounded and outnumbered, the battered survivors of the French garrison at Dien Bien Phu surrendered to the Viet Minh on May 7, 1954.

In the weeks that followed, a conference of western and Communist powers meeting in Geneva, Switzerland, drew up an agreement to end the conflict. The Geneva accords provided for the temporary division of Vietnam at the 17th parallel, with Viet Minh forces left in control of the northern half of the country and the Vietnamese emperor Bao Dai (an ally of the French) in control of the southern half. Nationwide elections were scheduled for 1956 to reunify the country. As President Eisenhower would later acknowledge, Ho Chi Minh was by far the most popular political figure in Vietnam during the war and would easily have won a free election for national leader.[9]

Shortly before the fall of Dien Bien Phu, President Eisenhower likened the loss of Vietnam to the Communists to a "falling domino": "You have a row of dominoes set up, you knock over the first one, and what will happen to the last one is the certainty that it will go over very quickly. . . . So, the possible consequences of the loss are just incalculable to the free world."[10] Over the next few years Eisenhower committed substantial economic and military aid to shoring up an independent anticommunist regime in southern Vietnam.

Ngo Dinh Diem, a conservative nationalist from a wealthy background, emerged as the new strong man in South Vietnamese politics. He returned from years of exile in the United States and Belgium in 1954 to become prime minister under Emperor Bao Dai. Diem, an ardent Catholic, enjoyed the patronage of influential American backers, including Senator Kennedy and New York City's Cardinal Spellman. In October 1955 Diem organized a national referendum that led to the creation of the new Republic of Vietnam (South Vietnam), with its capital in Saigon. Diem was elected the republic's first president by means of a blatantly rigged election. The following summer he refused to allow reunification elections with northern Vietnam to be held as scheduled by the Geneva accords. In the meantime, the Communists consolidated their own power in the Democratic Republic of Vietnam (North Vietnam), with its capital in Hanoi. When Diem visited the United States in May 1957, President Eisenhower hailed him as the "miracle man" of Asia, who had saved southern Vietnam from Communist enslavement. Without American aid, however, Diem could never have remained in power. In the mid-1960s the U.S. Defense Department undertook a top-secret study of the origins of American involvement the Vietnam war. The authors of what became known as the "Pentagon Papers" concluded, simply, that "South Vietnam was essentially the creation the United States."[11]

As fears of Soviet conquest of western Europe subsided in the later 1950s, the focus of Cold War competition shifted to what was beginning to be called the "Third World," the less developed nations of Asia, Africa, and Latin America. Since the end of the Second World War, the old European colonial empires had begun to collapse. Great Britain granted independence to India and Pakistan in 1947; the state of Israel was created out of the British protectorate in Palestine by a United Nations decision in 1948; in 1956, Britain ceded control of the Suez Canal to Egypt, and starting that same year began granting independence to its African colonies. By 1954, the French had been driven from Indochina, and would soon after lose their African colonies as well (with Algeria gaining independence in 1962, following a brutal and protracted armed struggle). The Dutch, Belgian, and Portuguese overseas empires were also in retreat. The United States, for its part, granted self-government to the Philippines in 1946. Decolonization produced some states sympathetic to the West (like Israel and the Philippines), but others (like India) sought neutrality in the Cold War. And some leaned toward the Soviet Union.

The Soviets regarded the struggle against the fading colonial empires as a great opportunity for shifting the balance of world power toward their own camp. Soviet premier Nikita Khrushchev pledged his country's support to "wars of national liberation," and many in the Third World, like Castro in

Cuba, looked to the Communist world for models of revolutionary struggle and economic development. But in South Vietnam, the march of Communism had apparently been stopped in its tracks. The country was emerging in the eyes of American policymakers as a "proving ground for democracy" as then-Senator Kennedy called it.[12]

Edward Lansdale (head of the CIA mission in Saigon), forged close relations with Ngo Dinh Diem. Diem owed a lot to Lansdale, who helped organize a mass exodus of hundreds of thousands of northern Vietnamese Catholics to South Vietnam in 1954. Catholic refugees became Diem's most reliable supporters—in a country with a large Buddhist majority. Lansdale also made generous use of CIA funds to buy off potential South Vietnamese rivals to Diem.

The early days of American involvement in Vietnam were almost like an adventure story. Ogden Williams, a CIA official who worked as an assistant to Colonel Lansdale in Saigon, would later recall his time in Vietnam with obvious nostalgia. First of all, there was a strong "sense of mission" shared by the military advisers and intelligence agents in the country:

> We were the nation that had won World War II and were honored throughout the world. To serve the United States overseas was a dream in those days, because you had very high standing—even low-level Americans did. We had enormous prestige in that period.

Americans had long cherished the belief that they had a special role to play in determining the future of Asia. Generations of religious missionaries had dedicated their lives to redeeming China from pagan superstition and barbaric custom. The Communist revolution in China had brought the expulsion of those missionaries. But some of the same impulse lived on, in more secular form, among the young men like Ogden Williams who were sent to Saigon in the 1950s with the goal of preserving the South Vietnamese from the political dangers that beset them from the north. And it didn't hurt that Vietnam was such an exotic destination:

> There was that sense of a young country, which was very inspiring. . . . There was a very graceful, traditional culture, an enormously pleasant way of life. Saigon was an elegant city. The beautiful tropical foliage, the flamboyant trees, the cabarets, the lovely slim women. . . . The whole thing was just elegant and romantic as hell. . . . It was always an enormous letdown to come back to the United States.[13]

Those who served in Vietnam in those years knew, of course, that the Diem regime's methods of governing were less than democratic. His American-trained police arrested tens of thousands of political opponents, many of whom were tortured and executed. His government reclaimed land that had been turned over to the peasants by the Viet Minh during the first Indochinese war and distributed it to wealthy landlords and Catholic refugees. But, in the name of shoring up an anti-Communist ally, Americans in Saigon and Washington were willing to overlook Diem's shortcomings. Certainly the North Vietnamese Communists, who executed thousands of peasant landowners during "land reform" campaigns in the mid-1950s, were no gentler or more democratic in their own methods of governing. Given the choice, Americans believed, no people would of their own volition choose communism over the political and material advantages offered by an alliance with the United States.

What American diplomatic and political strategists overlooked was that the Vietnamese had their own way of looking at the world, one that did not necessarily coincide with the assumptions guiding policymaking in Washington. American policymakers looked at Ho and saw a Communist; many Vietnamese peasants in both the southern and northern halves of Vietnam looked at Ho and saw a patriot. A thousand years before the start of the Second World War, a Vietnamese army had driven out Chinese invaders to establish an independent kingdom. Time and again in the centuries that followed, the Vietnamese fought would-be conquerors from China and other nations. Vietnamese history was filled with stories of heroes and martyrs in the cause of independence, and Ho Chi Minh and the Viet Minh inherited their prestige when they challenged and defeated the French in 1946–1954. Joseph Alsop, a prominent American journalist and ordinarily a staunch supporter of Cold War assumptions, toured Viet Minh–controlled areas of southern Vietnam in December 1954. He described it as an underground government (a "palm hut state") with a "loyal population" of nearly 2 million Vietnamese:

> At first, it was difficult for me, as it is for any Westerner, to conceive of a Communist government's genuinely "serving the people." I could hardly imagine a Communist government that was also a popular government and almost a democratic government. But this is just the sort of government the palm-hut state actually was.[14]

Few of Alsop's countrymen in the 1950s were prepared to look beyond the stereotypes of the Cold War in interpreting events in Southeast Asia (and Alsop himself would later become a firm supporter of the U.S. war effort in Vietnam).

In opposing Ho, Diem could count on the backing of most of the country's Catholic population. His other major source of support was the army, most of whose commanders had served the French in the war against the Viet Minh. Diem used the army, and his American-trained police force, to root out the vestiges of Viet Minh support in the south. Thousands of suspected Communists were killed or imprisoned. Starting in 1957, former Viet Minh soldiers still living in southern Vietnam countered with their own cam-

Ho Chi Minh. Source: *Archive Photos*

paign of assassination of Diem's police agents and village chiefs. With weapons left over from the First Indochina War, or captured from Diem's forces, they also launched small-scale attacks against government forces. Ho Chi Minh and other North Vietnamese Communist leaders were ambivalent about the campaign. They wanted to solve pressing political and economic problems in the north before being drawn into renewed military conflict. It was not until 1959 that Hanoi decided to lend its support to the spontaneously emerging guerrilla movement in South Vietnam.

Southern-born Viet Minh soldiers, who had moved to northern Vietnam after the partition of the country, returned to join the struggle. Some of them were regular soldiers in the North Vietnamese army; before they left for the south they exchanged their army uniforms for the black pajamas of the typical Vietnamese peasant. They made their way southward along a network of rough paths and dirt roads running through the border regions of eastern Laos and Cambodia, which came to be known as the Ho Chi Minh Trail. There they joined up with the existing guerrilla forces in the South. In December 1960, the revolutionary movement in South Vietnam officially established itself as the National Liberation Front (NLF). South Vietnamese and

American official called NLF fighters the Viet Cong, a derogatory phrase for "Vietnamese Communists." To the American soldiers who would soon be arriving by the thousands in South Vietnam, the enemy would become familiarly known as the "VC," or "Victor Charlie," or just "Charlie."[15]

When John F. Kennedy delivered his inaugural address pledging that the United States would "pay any price, bear any burden, [and] meet any hardship" in the defense of liberty around the world, there were about 800 American military advisers stationed in South Vietnam. The war was beginning to cost Americans lives as well as money; two U.S. advisers were killed in a guerrilla attack at Bienhoa in July 1959, the first Americans to die in the renewed warfare in Vietnam. But the U.S. commitment was still limited. Few Americans could find Vietnam on a map. Fewer still thought of that far-off and obscure land as a place that, in and of itself, would be worth the expenditure of tens of thousands of American lives to defend. If the United States was going to go to war, the likely place in 1961 seemed to be West Berlin, not South Vietnam.

Kennedy's first six months in office were filled with setbacks in foreign policy. In June 1961, when Kennedy met with Khrushchev in Vienna, the Soviet leader had attempted to intimidate the inexperienced American president. Shaken by Russian bullying, Kennedy remarked to a reporter afterwards: "Now we have a problem in making our power credible, and Vietnam is the place."[16]

But was Vietnam the right place to reestablish "credibility" with the Russians? Kennedy's top foreign policy advisers, almost to a man, agreed that it was. One of the trademarks of these men was their habitual reliance on argument by statistical analysis—although in reality the statistics they cited were often substantiated by little more than guesswork and wishful thinking. Thus acting Assistant Secretary of Defense William Bundy, a graduate of Harvard Law School and a former CIA agent, sent a memorandum to Robert McNamara in October 1961 outlining U.S. options in South Vietnam in the face of recent gains by the Viet Cong:

> An early and hard-hitting operation has a good chance (70% would be my guess) of arresting things and giving Diem a chance to do better and clean up. Even if we follow up hard . . . however, the chances are not much better that we will in fact be able to clean up the situation. It all depends on Diem's effectiveness, which is very problematical. The 30% chance is that we wind up like the French in 1954; white men can't win this kind of fight. On a 70–30 basis, I would myself favor going in.[17]

Kennedy was not as optimistic as his advisers about American military prospects in South Vietnam. He also felt that the really important struggle with the Soviets would come either in Berlin or in Cuba. For all his criticisms of Eisenhower's foreign policy, he was no more eager than his predecessor to involve the United States in a major land war in Asia. But he never seriously considered abandoning the American commitment to the preservation of a noncommunist South Vietnam. Like Eisenhower, he firmly believed in the domino theory. In early September of 1963, he was interviewed for CBS News by television correspondent Walter Cronkite. While telling Cronkite that "in the final analysis" the war was one that the South Vietnamese would have to win for themselves, he also warned of the consequences of defeat. Should the United States withdraw from South Vietnam and leave it to its fate, "pretty soon Thailand, Cambodia, Laos, Malaya would go and all of Southeast Asia would be under control of the Communists and under the domination of the Chinese."[18] And Kennedy was also haunted by the memory of how the last Democrat to sit in the White House, Harry Truman, had been attacked by Republicans for "losing" China. As he commented to an aide in 1963, "If I tried to pull out completely now from Vietnam we would have another Joe McCarthy red scare on our hands."[19]

The use of credibility as a rationale for American involvement had the quality of a self-fulfilling prophecy. The more the United States declared that Vietnam was the place where its credibility would be established, the more it seemed to policymakers in Washington that its credibility would suffer if things didn't work out as expected.

There is, however, no evidence that Communist leaders in Moscow or Beijing viewed the war as a test of U.S. resolve or military capability. They saw the weakness of the Saigon regime as the key to an eventual Communist triumph.

George Ball, who served as undersecretary of state in both the Kennedy and Johnson administrations, was one of the few dissenters from the pro-war consensus in the executive branch. Ball warned Kennedy in 1961 that deepening involvement in Vietnam could get out of hand, leading to the deployment of hundreds of thousands of American troops within a few years' time. Kennedy laughed and dismissed that possibility: "George, you're supposed to be one of the smartest guys in town, but you're crazier than hell. That will never happen."[20]

One of the reasons that Kennedy sought to engage the enemy in Vietnam was that it would give the United States an opportunity to test out a new political/military strategy known as "counterinsurgency." Chinese Communist leader Mao Zedong had taught his followers that in guerrilla war maintaining close relations with the local populace was all-important: the guerrillas were the fish swimming in the sea of the people. In the First Indochina War, the Viet Minh could depend on the peasants to warn them of the deployment and movement of French troops. American strategists in the early 1960s reasoned that the way to defeat a guerrilla insurgency was to dry up that sea of popular support for the guerrillas. That meant convincing Vietnamese peasants that they should give their allegiance to the government and not the guerrillas. Counterinsurgency, which made use of relatively small numbers of American military advisers and technicians, would supposedly forestall the necessity for a major commitment of American ground forces.

The men of the U.S. Army's Special Forces were assigned a key role in this strategy. The Special Forces had been established in 1952 with the mission of waging unconventional warfare: fighting behind enemy lines, living off the land, and enlisting and training local populations for guerrilla operations. No one ever thought they would be America's first line of defense in any future war: it was assumed by the military that they would be deployed behind the lines in eastern Europe in the event of an all-out war with the Soviet Union. The first Special Forces units had been sent to Vietnam in 1957 to train South Vietnamese troops (the Saigon government's military forces were, in official jargon, the Army of the Republic of Vietnam, or ARVN).

Until Kennedy came into office, the Special Forces enjoyed little prestige or attention. It was widely believed in the U.S. Army that for an officer to be assigned to Special Forces was a career-killing dead end. In case of war with the Communists, the place to be was in an armored division, battling it out with the Red Army in Germany. In such a war, the Special Forces would be only a sideshow. But Kennedy rescued the unit from obscurity, if not from the disdain of regular army officers. He believed that the Special Forces represented the kind of "flexible response" capability the United States needed to counter the Communists in limited wars. He ordered their expansion and authorized them to wear the distinctive headgear that gave them their popular nickname, the "Green Berets."

In the spring of 1961, Kennedy sent an additional 400 Green Berets to Vietnam. Their new mission was to train the hill tribes of South Vietnam, like the Montagnards who lived along the country's rugged western frontier, as a paramilitary force. The Green Berets specialized in raids and ambushes, designed to harass the Viet Cong with their own tactics on their own terrain. Special Forces advisers shared living quarters and food with the tribesmen and often forged close relationships with them. They now enjoyed flattering press coverage in the United States, where they were celebrated as a combination of James Bond and Daniel Boone (or, as one magazine article described them, the "Harvard PhDs of warfare"). They also were the subject of the only popular pro-war song to come out of the Vietnam era, Special Forces staff sergeant and Vietnam veteran Barry Sadler's 1966 hit "Ballad of the Green Berets," which in turn inspired the only profitable movie set in Vietnam in the 1960s, John Wayne's *The Green Berets*. Highly motivated, many Special Forces soldiers signed up for repeated tours of duty in Vietnam. But by the mid-1960s their efforts would be overshadowed by those of more conventional U.S. military units assigned to Vietnam.[21]

The enemy that the Green Berets were sent to fight was unlike any the American military had confronted in the twentieth century. If anything, in those first years of the conflict, the war in Vietnam most closely resembled the Indian wars of the American frontier in the nineteenth century. "Come on," an American infantry captain remarked to war correspondent Michael Herr inviting him to go along on a mission into Viet Cong–held territory, "we'll take you out to play Cowboys and Indians."[22]

The Viet Cong was not a conventional army; it had no tanks, no airplanes, no army bases or barracks. Its soldiers dressed in the same black pajamas as the local peasants; their footwear consisted of "Ho Chi Minh sandals," shoes cut out of rubber tires, held onto the foot by a strip of inner tube. The Viet Cong's strength was greatest in rural areas of South Vietnam, where four-fifths of the population lived. In Communist-controlled regions, the Viet Cong functioned as a combination military force, political movement, and government rolled into one. Part of its power was based on intimidation; officials and villagers who cooperated with the government were executed by Viet Cong death squads.

But there is no question that, in much of the countryside, the Viet Cong enjoyed genuine popular support. The guerrillas were often related to or neighbors of the villagers; they provided schooling and medical services and helped grow crops to feed both themselves and villagers. They also championed the cause of land reform. As *Washington Star* reporter Richard Critchfield wrote in the mid-1960s in a dispatch from rural Long An Province:

> [G]overnment and the mass of peasantry still seem to be on the opposing sides. Land is of such paramount importance here that the Viet Cong allow only the landless or very poor farmers to command guerrilla units or qualify as party members. The provincial government's social order is the exact reverse. Most of the military officers, civil servants, and community leaders come from the land-owing classes.[23]

Communist ideology was probably not much of a draw to the average peasant, but the Viet Cong's claim to represent both the cause of land reform and national sovereignty was a powerful one, a claim not easily countered by the corrupt, brutal, and ineffective government in Saigon.[24]

At the start of the 1960s, the Viet Cong could count about 15,000 fighters in its ranks. Most of them were natives of southern Vietnam, still living in or near the villages in which they had been raised, reinforced and often led by well-trained Viet Minh veterans returning from the North. Their numbers grew rapidly; by mid-decade there were an estimated 63,000 full-time guerrillas, and somewhere between 100,000 and 200,000 part-time local fighters. As late as 1963, according to U.S. intelligence estimates, less than 10 percent of their arms came from allied Communist nations; the remainder were captured from the French or the Americans, or were homemade. Although later in the decade they would acquire more sophisticated weapons from the Soviet Union and China, including the deadly AK-47 automatic rifle and the RPG (rocket propelled grenade) rocket launcher, the Viet Cong were always outgunned by the Americans and South Vietnamese government forces. But superior enemy gunfire, and the heavy casualties they often suffered, did not seem to faze the Viet Cong. As Kennedy military adviser Maxwell Taylor would note, with puzzled admiration: "The ability of the Viet Cong continuously to rebuild their units and to make good their losses is one of the mysteries of this guerrilla war. . . . Not only do the Viet Cong units have the recuperative powers of the phoenix, but they have an amazing ability to maintain morale."[25] In contrast, the U.S.-backed South Vietnamese military lost hundreds of men every month from desertion.

American military strategy in Vietnam in the early 1960s was two-pronged: while the Green Berets were out fighting an unconventional war in the bush, American advisers and technology would be employed to help the regular South Vietnamese army fight a more effective conventional war. In August 1961 U.S. advisers were authorized to accompany ARVN battalions and even company-sized units on field operations. Soon American pilots began bombing raids in support of South Vietnamese operations. By early 1962 American helicopters were ferrying ARVN soldiers into battle zones. Helicopter pilots and crew members saw some of the fiercest fighting in the early days of the war. Helicopters provided the Americans and their South Vietnamese allies the much-prized capacity for "air mobility." Troops could be moved swiftly from distant bases to reinforce an embattled outpost or attack an enemy stronghold. The rough terrain and thick jungle that made up so much of Vietnam's landscape posed no obstacle to the transport into battle of airborne troops.

Marine lieutenant Kenneth Babbs recalled that when he arrived in Vietnam, the U.S. military effort was still officially limited to advisory and technical support:

> Our job was to haul supplies in and out of outposts; evacuate wounded; and carry ARVN on heliborne operations. We weren't supposed to participate in the fighting. But when we started taking on fire, we knew we had to be ready to protect ourselves, and we started arming our choppers. . . . At first the VC were frightened by the choppers, but word must have gotten around quickly how vulnerable the machines were. . . . As our tour continued, instead of running the VC stayed and fired back.

Before long, marines in Babbs's squadron were getting involved in firefights with guerrillas. "We went in like Boy Scouts and came out like Hell's Angels," he concluded.[26] Despite public denials by President Kennedy that American troops were involved in combat in Vietnam, the death count began to climb. Army Specialist Fourth Class James Davis was killed in a Viet Cong ambush on December 22, 1961, the first "official" U.S. death in the Vietnam War.

A marine helicopter manned by an American advisor supplies South Vietnamese Army troops, 1964. Source: *Archive Photos*

To meet the requirements of a widening war, the American military command structure in Saigon was reorganized in February 1962 with the establishment of the U.S. Military Assistance Command, Vietnam (MACV). MACV was initially under the command of General Paul Harkins; in 1964 Harkins was replaced by his deputy, General William Westmoreland.

Military and political advisers provided Kennedy with a stream of optimistic reports on the prospects for victory in Vietnam. General Maxwell Taylor was Kennedy's most trusted military adviser (in 1962 Kennedy would appoint him as chairman of the Joint Chiefs of Staff, and he would also serve as the U.S. ambassador to South Vietnam in 1964–1965.) Following a visit to Saigon in November 1961, Taylor cabled the president with advice to expand U.S. forces in South Vietnam. "As an area for the operation of U.S. troops," he told Kennedy, the Vietnamese countryside was "not an excessively difficult or unpleasant place to operate." Taylor urged Kennedy to increase logistical support for the ARVN, and to dispatch 8000 U.S. combat troops to the country under the guise of providing "flood relief." He dismissed the possibility that the United States might be "backing into a major Asia war" as "not impressive."[27] Secretary of Defense McNamara, who formed a close working relationship with Taylor, concurred.

Although McNamara later claimed that he soon had second thoughts about the wisdom of Taylor's report, he could hardly rein in his own enthusiasm on many subsequent occasions, so much so that the the newspapers began to call the conflict in Vietnam "McNamara's War."[28] Returning from a whirlwind inspection tour of the American war effort in South Vietnam in 1962, McNamara briskly informed a skeptical reporter, "Every quantitative measure we have shows we're winning the war."[29]

Kennedy, publicly as optimistic as his advisers, gave vent to some doubts about the Vietnam enterprise in private. "The troops will march in; the bands will play; the crowd will cheer; and in four days everyone will have forgotten," he complained to speechwriter Arthur Schlesinger, Jr. in November 1961, while considering Taylor's proposal for increased military involvement in South Vietnam. "Then we will be told we have to send in more troops. It's like taking a drink. The effect wears off, and you have to take another."[30]

In 1961, Bobby Kennedy had downplayed the importance of the conflict in South Vietnam; that country was just one of a score of trouble spots around the world that the Cold War crisis managers in the White House, the State Department, and the Pentagon would be handling. Two years later, the war in South Vietnam had become John F. Kennedy's single most pressing international concern—a change due almost entirely to the decisions made by his administration in the interim. Looking back on those critical years three decades later, a chastened Robert McNamara traced the deepening American involvement in Vietnam to a myopic anti-Soviet zeal. "U.S. leaders" he wrote in a co-authored volume on the history of the war, "tended to see their interests in Vietnam in a larger context dominated by the Cold War struggle between the United States and the Soviet Union. The stakes for the United States, therefore, appeared to be extremely high." American anti-Communism may have been a legitimate response to Soviet expansionism since 1945, but the way it was applied in the Vietnamese conflict was tragically misguided: "The American obsession with the global chessboard of the Cold War blinded leaders in Washington to the decisive importance of Vietnamese nationalism and the desire of the Vietnamese people for reunification."[31]

As of January 1, 1963, John F. Kennedy had stationed 11,000 American "advisers" in South Vietnam. Seventy-seven had been killed to that date in the war. Many more would soon be on the way to defend the credibility of the United States.

CHAPTER 5

1963

THE POLICE CAN COME TO OUR MEETINGS, BRING THEIR GUNS AND THEIR BADGES
AND LITTLE MICROPHONES TO CHURCH, BUT IF YOU WANT TO BE FREE, THERE IS
NOTHING THEY CAN DO ABOUT IT.
> —*Civil rights organizer James Bevel during the 1963*
> *Birmingham campaign*[1]

As President John F. Kennedy celebrated Christmas of 1962 in Palm Beach, Florida, it looked like a very good year, even a triumphant one, could be in the offing. Unemployment was down, inflation was running at only 1 percent a year, and both business leaders and ordinary citizens were cheering the president's plan for a permanent cut in income tax rates. According to the Gallup poll, 76 percent of the public approved the way the president was handling his job; even a majority of Republicans in the survey agreed.[2]

Gone as well was the grim tension of the missile crisis of the previous fall. The president was about to order the Atomic Energy Commission to stop testing nuclear weapons, at least temporarily. He wanted to see if diplomats from the United States, Great Britain, and the Soviet Union—the only nations that possessed the bomb—could negotiate a treaty to ban the lethal experiments altogether. Perhaps the world could edge away from the threat of nuclear annihilation.

The midterm election results had also brightened the mood in the White House. The Democrats suffered the loss of only six seats in the House of Representatives, and they gained four in the Senate. Among the new Democratic faces in the upper chamber was the president's younger brother Edward (an athletic-looking 30-year-old whom everyone called Teddy) and a former history professor named George McGovern who hailed from South Dakota, a traditionally Republican state.

From California came the election's biggest surprise. In his bid for the governorship, Richard Nixon was buried at the polls by the liberal incumbent Pat Brown. The night of his defeat, the man who had almost been elected president just two years before seemed finished with campaigning forever.

"You won't have Nixon to kick around anymore," he spat out to reporters who, as a group, had always distrusted his motives and satirized his awkward style. "Just think how much you're going to be missing."[3]

Nixon wasn't the only Republican humbled by the party that controlled the White House and Congress. Twice as many Americans identified with the Democrats as with their opposition. And, in early opinion polls, John F. Kennedy was leading every likely GOP challenger by more than 30 points. The president was clearly enjoying himself in office. "Vaughan Meader was busy tonight," he told a fund-raising dinner at the end of January, referring to the comedian whose amicable satire, *The First Family*, had sold a million records, "so I came myself."[4]

Kennedy knew the movement for black rights could split the Democratic Party. So, exactly a century after the Emancipation Proclamation, he was not unhappy to learn that the freedom struggle was at low ebb, its leaders unable to build on the momentum provided by the sit-ins and Freedom Rides that had opened the decade. Lee White, the White House aide for civil rights, blithely reported to the president that Negroes were "pretty much at peace"; in a national poll, barely 4 percent of Americans thought "racial problems" were the country's biggest challenge. The president sympathized with the activists who were registering voters and challenging Jim Crow laws in a scattering of southern towns and cities. But, as a cautious politician, he felt no need to ask Congress to consider a civil rights bill. He didn't even mention the subject in his annual State of the Union address.

Prosperity at home, a glimmer of peace in the Cold War, and splendid political auguries—this seemed the best of times for the liberal state and the energetic men who ran it. Of course, harmony didn't exist in the poorer regions of the world. Eight thousand miles away in South Vietnam, Communist guerrillas were fighting to topple a regime the United States had financed since 1954, equipping its military with modern weapons and 11,000 American advisers. But, surely, victory for the free world could not be far away. The president himself had told reporters in mid-December, "we don't see the end of the tunnel, but I must say I don't think it is darker than it was a year ago, and in some ways lighter."[5] Then, from a hamlet in the Mekong Delta of Vietnam, came troubling news.

Winter: Ap Bac

On January 2, 1963, in a stand-up battle, a force of 350 Viet Cong thoroughly defeated a detachment of South Vietnamese army (ARVN) soldiers four times its size. Ordered by their American advisers to seize a Viet Cong radio in the village of Ap Bac, ARVN troops seemed to have every advantage: they were on the offensive, they alone had tanks, helicopters, and fighter-bombers, and only they could call in reserves to augment their already superior numbers. How could they lose?

In retrospect, this battle for a village located only 40 miles from the capital of Saigon illustrated why the entire U.S. mission in Vietnam was destined to fail. The ARVN commander in the province that contained Ap Bac was Major Lam Quang Tho, a wealthy landowner who held his position at the sufferance of the Saigon regime. The president of that regime, Ngo Dinh Diem, had risen to power with the backing of the United States. He disliked sending his troops into combat, fearing that defeat would undermine his already tenuous image as a powerful leader and encourage a coup d'état. Diem thought U.S. artillery and air power could keep the Viet Cong at bay. Knowing this, Major Lam took no part in the assault on Ap Bac himself, even though his headquarters was just 2 miles from the village.

Most ARVN troops saw little reason to fight aggressively. Few welcomed a Communist victory, but neither did they relish dying for a government run by men who were the political descendants of the French colonialists, who had been driven out of power less than a decade earlier—by the Viet Minh, forerunner of the Viet Cong. So the typical ARVN soldier, a peasant getting low but regular pay, happily assented to his commander's reluctance to do battle. When ordered into combat, he moved as slowly as possible, hoping his foes would vanish. Usually they did.

From the other side, the war looked quite different. General Paul Harkins, head of U.S. forces in the country, referred to the Viet Cong as "those raggedy-ass little bastards."[6] Neither he nor the American commanders who followed him ever understood why the enemy fought so well. Viet Cong soldiers were peasants too, but they were men—and sometimes women—who believed they were defending their homes, their villages, and their country from a foreign invader and a handful of traitorous Vietnamese allies. For the Viet Cong, this was a revolutionary war for independence. Most of their rifles and ammunition had been captured from the well-stocked ARVN and its American overlords.

The Viet Cong battalion that operated in and around Ap Bac relied on its 600 residents to help them prepare for battle. Troops and local peasants together dug foxholes after spies alerted them that an attack was coming. To avoid detection by aircraft, they were careful not to disturb the surrounding foliage and to cover the holes with branches when they finished. Most of the villagers then hurried to hide in swamps near the village, but some remained to assist the troops. It was a feat of cooperation repeated in numerous Vietnamese hamlets and one the ARVN could never achieve.

The plan developed by U.S. military headquarters was, first, to "soften up" the guerrillas with bombs from the air; then to assault Ap Bac from three sides, leaving the enemy an "escape" route that, in reality, led to certain doom. But the Viet Cong commander in Ap Bac recognized the trap and decided that he and his fellow guerrillas had only one choice. He wrote in his diary, "Better to fight and die than run and be slaughtered."[7]

The guerrillas' only chance was to neutralize the enemy's superior might. So they trained their rifles on the deadly machines bearing down on their trenches—helicopters manned by U.S. advisers and hulking armored personnel carriers (called M-113s) driven by ARVN troops. Shooting from camouflaged positions, experienced Viet Cong marksmen downed five of the helicopters. American flight crews exacerbated their losses by faithfully trying to rescue comrades shot out of the sky. Once on the ground, the saviors were as defenseless as those they were attempting to save.

Meanwhile, the Viet Cong's decision to stand and fight unnerved ARVN men inside the armored carriers, even though the latter had the advantage of deadlier fire power and the protection of bulletproof steel. The unfamiliar sound of bullets hitting his vehicle impelled one ARVN gunner to start shooting wildly at the sky; several frightened drivers fled the safety of the M-113s to hide behind ruined helicopters. But seven or eight of the machines kept rolling toward the trenches, where it seemed men armed only with carbines and hand grenades could not possibly stop them.

Then something remarkable occurred. A Viet Cong squad leader named Dung jumped up from his foxhole. He pulled a grenade from his belt and threw it toward an M-113, causing a loud but harmless explosion. Emboldened, Dung's comrades leapt from their trenches, hurling scores of grenades at the same target. This was enough to convince the ARVN crews, whose morale was never high to begin with, to give up the battle. They threw their M-113s into reverse gear and left the village. Fewer than 20 Viet Cong guerillas had been killed.

American advisers screamed at their Vietnamese charges to return and fight. Colonel John Paul Vann, a skillful combat veteran who was the leading U.S. officer at the scene, blasted his ARVN counterpart, "Goddamit, you want them to get away. You're afraid to fight. You know they'll sneak out this way and that's exactly what you want."[8] When night fell, the Viet Cong quietly departed Ap Bac and marched to a nearby canal where concealed sampans carried them to safety. "They were brave men," acknowledged Vann, "They gave a good account of themselves today."[9]

By conventional military standards, the battle meant little: neither side had wiped out the other or captured new territory. But a group of crack young journalists—including Neil Sheehan of United Press International and David Halberstam of the *New York Times*—reported at length on the events occurring so close to their Saigon hub. And television news, just then coming into prominence in the United States, brought the humiliating details to a wider audience back home. Official military spokesmen claimed the battle had ended indecisively, but they could not expunge the image of a disaster that was not supposed to happen.

The battle of Ap Bac demonstrated that ARVN soldiers, even when they took the offensive with all the material odds in their favor, could not be counted on to defeat their Communist-led countrymen and -women. It was the Viet Cong who kept their heads in the thick of battle, who had the motivation to fight courageously and to endure great punishment. If the men who ran the U.S. war effort hoped to defeat the "raggedy-ass little bastards," they would eventually have to send American troops to do the job.

Spring: Alabama

Meanwhile, in the heart of the American South, a different kind of insurgent force was preparing to go on the offensive. In 1963 Birmingham was the largest city in Alabama—and, in racial reputation, the meanest. Northern corporations held the economic whip hand in what was the steelmaking capital of the South. The local government had long been the property of tough white politicians. They erected and maintained an iron barrier against the hopes of black citizens, who numbered 40 percent of the population, for equal access to good jobs, housing, and commerce. Birmingham's most prominent office-holder was Eugene "Bull" Connor, the commissioner of public safety, who ran the all-white police force and the fire department. Connor firmly believed that the civil rights movement was a Communist plot and that stern, even brutal measures were needed to turn back the threat it posed to the traditional racial order.

Bull Connor and his men did little to stop white vigilantes, some of whom belonged to the Ku Klux Klan, from carrying on a terror campaign against local blacks who dared transgress the color line. Birmingham bombers frequently targeted African Americans who bought property in traditionally white neighborhoods; since 1947, more than 50 explosions had torn into black homes, businesses, and churches—far more than in any other southern city. After three churches identified with civil rights activism were bombed in the month of January alone, Connor told the press, "Negroes did it." After all a black worshiper had sounded an alarm after finding a burning fuse, and eyewitnesses "saw Negroes running from the churches."[10]

Such comments from the official guardian of "public safety" embarrassed the business elite of Birmingham, known as the "Big Mules," who were ever mindful of their city's image up north. Early in 1963, large employers had endorsed a city council form of government that would throw Bull Connor out of his job. But, for the moment, Connor was the law in Birmingham; and, besides the Ku Klux Klan, he had a powerful political ally: George C. Wallace, the newly elected governor of Alabama.

Wallace had begun his political career in the 1940s as something of a southern liberal. He supported higher taxes on corporations and did not at first indulge in the vicious race baiting that had been a staple of Deep South politics since the disenfranchisement of blacks at the turn of the century. After the Supreme Court's 1954 *Brown* ruling, however, Wallace resolved never again to be "soft on the nigger question."[11] In 1962, he won the race for governor by stoking the fear and anger of his fellow whites about the potential horrors of "race-mixing"—the integration of schools and workplaces. And on January 14, his inaugural address made Wallace the best-known defender of white supremacy in America. "In the name of the greatest people that have ever trod this earth," he announced, "I draw the line in the dust and toss the gauntlet before the feet of tyranny. And I say, segregation now! Segregation tomorrow! Segregation forever!"

Black freedom activists saw such ferocity as a challenge—and an opportunity. A major civil rights campaign in Birmingham could compel Bull Connor and his allies to respond with all the brutality of which they were capable. In so doing, it could force white people throughout the nation to confront the moral terms of the struggle. "[Connor] was a perfect adversary," recalled Wyatt Walker, a top aide to Martin Luther King, Jr. at the Southern Christian Leadership Conference. "He believed that he would be the state's most popular politician if he treated the black violently, bloodily, and sternly. We knew that the psyche of the white redneck was such that he would inevitably do something to help our cause."[12]

Early in 1963, Walker mapped out the strategy he dubbed "Project C"— for confrontation. The demands on city authorities were straightforward: desegregate the economic life of Birmingham—its restaurants, hotels, public toilets, and the unwritten policy of hiring blacks for menial jobs only. To press its demands, the SCLC would rely on parishioners of sympathetic black churches to fill Birmingham's streets and, if necessary, its jail cells. They would start with small sit-ins and a boycott of downtown businesses and end with mass marches designed to draw national attention. Walker and his fellow activists hoped the protests would exacerbate the split between the "Big Mules" and the ordinary whites Bull Connor represented. They also needed to put black freedom high on the national agenda again, and they hoped the campaign would rejuvenate their ranks and their spirits.

But there were no illusions about the human cost: during these peaceful demonstrations, black blood was going to flow. In January Dr. King told an SCLC leadership meeting, "I have to tell you that in my judgment, some of the people sitting here today will not come back alive from this campaign."[13]

Despite such forebodings, the Birmingham protests began quietly in early April. Bull Connor had just been defeated in a race for mayor, and this dissuaded some black residents from risking their health and livelihood on a picket line. The police did arrest scores of demonstrators who left the Sixteenth Street Baptist Church and marched into downtown Birmingham. But, on Connor's orders, they kept their nightsticks by their sides and their attack dogs in their kennels. Despite the boycott, thousands of blacks were still shopping in the big department stores where none could get a job. When a state court enjoined the SCLC from further actions, King defied the ruling and went to jail—on Good Friday. He was released on Easter Sunday, frowning that the expected resurrection of the black movement had not yet occurred. "Wyatt, you've got to find some way to make Bull Connor tip his hand," he told Walker.[14]

Within days, SCLC leaders decided on a new tactic: they would mobilize schoolchildren. Rev. James Bevel, a King aide, offered a "simple formula: any child old enough to belong to a church should be eligible to march to jail."[15] For Baptists, that meant the minimum age of qualification for protest was 6. So on May 2, a month after the Birmingham campaign began, a thousand children, most of them high school students, filed out of the big stone church on 16th Street. Singing "We Shall Overcome," they moved toward downtown, at first overwhelming Connor's police with the joyful intensity of the duty they were performing. "Hurry up Lucille," cried one young protester to a friend, "If you stay behind, you won't get arrested with our group."[16]

The new departure convinced Connor that intimidation would be necessary after all. The next day, when hundreds of children again took to the streets, city firemen turned on high-pressure hoses to drive them off. German shepherds from police K-9 squads tore into their flesh. That night, television viewers all across the nation saw the white South at its worst.

Images of young black people, neatly dressed, set upon by fierce dogs and pinned to the ground by jets of water strong enough to strip bark from trees provoked northern outrage. Bull Connor was, indeed, the best "organizer" the black freedom movement ever had, After that day in May, it was inevitable that President Kennedy would propose and that Congress would pass a major civil rights bill. And several weeks later, a committee of the "Big Mules" signed a desegregation agreement with the SCLC.

Nonviolent "direct action" could not, however, address the deeper sources of racial inequality. In an eloquent letter he wrote in jail, Martin Luther King, Jr. told white clergymen who had advised him to call off his "unwise and untimely" demonstrations:

> We have waited for more than 340 years for our constitutional and God-given rights. The nations of Asia and Africa are moving with jet-like speed toward gaining political independence, but we still creep at horse-and-buggy pace toward gaining a cup of coffee at a lunch counter. . . . There comes a time when the cup of endurance runs over, and men are no longer willing to be plunged into the abyss of despair. I hope, sirs, that you can understand our legitimate and unavoidable impatience.[17]

Most of the children who marched came from churchgoing families with steady incomes. But when they were attacked, hundreds of poorer black men and women made clear that the era of turning the other cheek was over. They hurled rocks, bottles, and epithets at the police, confronted white pedestrians on downtown sidewalks, and burned down some white-owned businesses. Meanwhile, the Imperial Wizard of the KKK, Robert Shelton, bristled that the SCLC "has not gained *one thing* in Birmingham, because the white people are not going to tolerate the meddlesome, conniving, manipulating moves of these *professional businessmen.*"[18] Men of Shelton's ilk continued to bomb black churches, political groups, and homes—including that of Rev. A. D. King, brother of the SCLC leader. It was going to take much more than one victorious campaign to dismantle the structures of white supremacy continually built and rebuilt during all the years since the first African slaves had disembarked at Jamestown, Virginia, one morning in 1619.

George Wallace soon gave defiant whites an opportunity to rail at their enemies, both in the federal government and in the civil rights movement. During his 1962 campaign for governor, Wallace had promised to "stand in the schoolhouse door" if courts ordered the integration of his alma mater, the University of Alabama. The following June, he got his chance. Two aspiring black students, Vivian Malone and James Hood, were scheduled to register in June for the summer session at the Tuscaloosa campus. Malone wanted to major in accounting; Hood favored clinical psychology. For several weeks, U.S. Attorney General Robert Kennedy and Nicholas Katzenbach, his deputy, tried to persuade Wallace to avoid a confrontation and the potential for more violence. The governor agreed to warn his angry white supporters to stay away from the campus. But he insisted on making a stand.

On the morning of June 11, Wallace stood at a podium placed in front of the auditorium where registration was under way. A thicket of journalists with microphones and cameras stood ready to record anything that transpired on this muggy, 95 degree day. An irritated Katzenbach got out of his car, strode up to the podium, and asked Wallace "for unequivocal assurance that you or anyone under your control will not bar these students . . . who, after all, merely want an education in the great University." In response, the governor, reading a four-page statement, vowed, "There can be no submission to the theory that the central government is anything but a servant of the people . . . [I] do hereby denounce and forbid this illegal and unwarranted action."[19] Then he retreated inside the air-conditioned auditorium and let Malone and Hood register, accompanied by federal officials.

On the surface and in the eyes of the Kennedy administration, the little ceremony was an awkward fig leaf for Wallace's surrender. But, in reality, it had confirmed their antagonist's reputation, in the eyes of many whites, as a courageous champion of the common man beset by a meddling government. Wallace's defiant posture, cleft chin and back straight, before the taller Katzenbach made him seem a plebeian descendant of Confederate heroes, doing battle again with the federal dragon. Slaying the beast might be impossible, but the pugnacious governor had set the terms for future combat. George Wallace had converted his failure to stop two black students from attending

George Wallace announcing his refusal to submit to a federal order to open the University of Alabama to black students, June 1963. Deputy Attorney General Nicholas Katzenbach glares at him from the right. Source: *Archive Photos*

a public university into a potent symbol of protest against a federal government toward which many white Americans felt uneasy. "Wallaceism is bigger than Wallace," Martin Luther King, Jr. told an interviewer soon after the drama in Tuscaloosa, " . . . I am not sure that he believes all the poison he preaches, but he is artful enough to convince others that he does."[20]

On the night of June 11, John Kennedy told the nation in a televised address that the time had finally come "to treat our fellow Americans as we want to be treated." A full century after the Emancipation Proclamation, black men and women were still not truly free. "We preach freedom around the world, and we mean it," said the president, referring to the Cold War which had always been his main concern. "But are we to say to the world—and much more importantly, to each other—that this is the land of the free, except for Negroes, that we have no second-class citizens, except Negroes, that we have no class or caste system, no ghettos, no master race, except with respect to Negroes?"[21] Then he outlined the most far-reaching civil rights law in the nation's history.

It was, agreed black leaders at the time and most historians since, John Kennedy's finest hour. But just after midnight, the white resistance claimed another victim. From a vacant lot in Jackson, Mississippi, Byron de la Beckwith, a fertilizer salesman with a maniacal hatred of blacks, shot a bullet into the back of Medgar Evers, militant leader of the Mississippi NAACP. An all-white jury found Beckwith not guilty. Later, he boasted to a KKK meeting, "Killing that nigger gave me no more inner discomfort than our wives endure when they give birth to our children. We ask them to do that for us. We should do just as much."[22]

It would be comforting to think that hostility to civil rights in the 1960s was restricted to diehard southern racists like Beckwith. The reality is more complicated. Even as President John Kennedy and his brother reached out politically to Martin Luther King, Jr., and proposed pathbreaking civil rights legislation, they continued to view the movement King led with suspicions left over from the 1950s.

By 1963, Federal Bureau of Investigation (FBI) director J. Edgar Hoover was providing the attorney general with a steady stream of derogatory reports about King, accusing him of falling under the influence of alleged Communist advisers. Hoover's antagonism to King reflected both ideological and racial preoccupations; Hoover preserved the FBI as a lily-white organization, and would privately refer to Martin Luther King as a "burrhead." In the summer of 1963, he successfully pressured Robert Kennedy into authorizing wiretaps on some of King's close political associates; in October 1963, the taps, with Kennedy's approval, would be extended to King's own telephones, both in his office and his home. In addition, Hoover's men began to put listening devices into King's hotel rooms when the civil rights leader was traveling.

Recording evidence of King's marital infidelities on the road, the FBI put together a "sex tape" of such episodes and in 1964, mailed it to King's home, where his wife Coretta Scott King discovered it and played it. The tape was accompanied by a crude anonymous letter, crafted by FBI agents as if it had come from a disillusioned black supporter, and implying that King could only avoid public exposure as an adulterer by killing himself.

This seamy FBI campaign against King was launched under the banner of a secret program known as COINTELPRO (or "counterintelligence program"), launched in the 1950s against the Communist Party and other radical groups, and intended to spread dissension and confusion among their ranks. Robert Kennedy, according to his friends, would later be conscience-stricken about his role in authorizing FBI harassment of King. He might have been more willing to stand up to the FBI director, had it not been for the fact that Hoover was in a position to reveal politically damaging information about John F. Kennedy's many extramarital affairs. Behind-the-scenes decision-making in the Kennedy White House seemed on occasion to be scripted by a team divided between the classical playwrights of Greek antiquity and contemporary writers of television soap operas.[23]

Summer: You've Really Got a Hold on Me

On June 23 the streets of downtown Detroit filled with purpose. Some 200,000 people, black and white, marched to protest the killing of Medgar Evers and to show that the civil rights movement could flourish in the industrial North.

The leading organizer of the march was the Reverend C. L. Franklin, a charismatic Baptist minister whose radio program of sermons and gospel music was heard in black homes all over the nation. Aretha, the minister's teenage daughter, sometimes lent her powerful voice to the broadcasts. The main speaker at the "Great March to Freedom" was Martin Luther King, Jr. "I have a dream this afternoon," he told the throng, "that the brotherhood of man will become a reality." Within weeks, a local record company named Motown released his speech as the centerpiece of an album commemorating the day.[24]

In 1963, popular music and the civil rights movement were often intertwined, each stimulating the growth and creativity of the other. One of the best-selling singles that year was "Blowin' in the Wind," a new folk song with lines like "How many years can some people exist before they're allowed to be free?" that evoked the demands of the black insurgency—although both its author, Bob Dylan, and the artists who recorded it—Peter, Paul, and Mary—were white. But rock and roll dominated the air waves and represented a break with the musical past.

When it emerged in the 1950s, rock frightened many older Americans, precisely because it refused to honor the separation between a mainstream pop style—designated as "white"—and the ghettoized category of "race" records. Rock shouted a joy of the sexy and the unpredictable; it invited everyone to dance. In 1955 some country-and-western musicians blasted Elvis Presley, who was then only 20, as a "white nigger" because he loved to play black spirituals and blues and moved on stage with sensual abandon—eliciting a cascade of passionate screams from female fans. To established pop singers, the new wave appeared barbaric. "Rock 'n' roll smells phony and false," snapped Frank Sinatra at a congressional hearing in 1957. "It is sung, played, and written for the most part by cretinous goons . . . the most brutal, ugly, desperate, vicious form of expression it has been my misfortune to hear."[25]

By 1963, such opinions were rarely heard, at least in public. Ever practical, the recording industry quickly learned to appreciate the market value of sounds that beguiled tens of millions of young people with billions of dollars to spend. Older white stars soon gave up the fight as well, consoling themselves with the knowledge that many Americans still adored their music. In January 1961 Frank Sinatra sang at the inaugural gala of his good friend, John F. Kennedy. But rock 'n' roll was here to stay.

Without conscious intention, young rock artists were subverting cultural and racial assumptions that Americans carried around in their heads. In 1963, hearing Smokey Robinson's love song "You've Really Got a Hold on Me" on the radio struck a white teenager from the Detroit area with the force of prophecy. "Before it was through," Dave Marsh wrote later, when he'd become a noted rock critic, "my world had changed, caught up in the magic of a sound which revealed to me . . . the falsity of the racism within which I'd been raised. Maybe it was just hearing the humanity in Smokey Robinson's voice, and finally putting it together with the knowledge that he was a black man."[26]

The company that produced "You've Really Got a Hold on Me" was distinctive in its own right. In 1963, only four years after its founding, Motown was already the most successful black-owned record company in U.S. history. Its 38-year-old president, Berry Gordy, Jr., had become a celebrity, a model for other black executives to follow. National hits by such artists as Martha and the Vandellas, Little Stevie Wonder, and Marvin Gaye, as well as Smokey Robinson and his group, the Miracles, rolled out of the firm's modest headquarters on West Grand Boulevard in the heart of black Detroit.

"Rolled" was a word Gordy himself might have used. Part of the inspiration to start Motown came from an unlikely source—a Ford factory where, as an assembly line worker, Gordy had fastened chrome and nailed upholstery. "At the plant cars started out as just a frame, pulled along on conveyor belts until they emerged at the end of the line [as] brand spanking new cars," Gordy recalled. "I wanted the same concept for my company . . . a place where a kid off the street could walk in one door an unknown and come out another a recording artist—a star."[27]

On the front of the Motown building, Gordy placed a huge sign reading "Hitsville, U.S.A." Inside, he assembled a team of crack songwriters, studio musicians, choreographers, and wily executives (including vice president Smokey Robinson). They instructed talented youngsters how to sing and perform for other kids of all races. The Motown way was slick and methodical: aspiring stars took dance lessons from a tap artist and smoothed the rough edges of their ghetto upbringing with lessons in elegant table manners, vocabulary, and even the proper way to hold a cigarette. To promote his new productions, Gordy sent his newly refined talent on the road as the Motortown Revue. But all the grace in the world could not cool the rage of the white South. Returning from performing before an integrated audience in Birmingham, troupe members found their bus pockmarked with bullet holes.

Motown became renowned for its tight orchestrations and catchy lyrics. The music also challenged listeners, offering something new and even revelatory, at the same time as it made them want to move their hips. "Heat Wave," sung by Martha and the Vandellas, made it to #4 on the pop music charts in the summer of 1963. Accompanied by the driving, lilting beat of a baritone saxophone and an electric organ, lead singer Martha Reeves (who had been "discovered" among Motown's corps of secretaries) asked, "Has high blood pressure got a hold on me or is this the way love's supposed to be?" Her response: "Can't explain it, don't understand it, ain't never felt like this before." Nearly every teenager and young adult could "second that emotion," as Smokey Robinson put it in one of his best songs.[28]

Stevie Wonder, one of Motown's most talented and popular artists. Source: *Archive Photos*

Little Stevie Wonder's "Fingertips, Part 2" held down the #1 spot in the nation for three weeks that year. Wonder was then only 12 years old, hence the diminutive nickname. Blind since birth, the boy christened Stevland Morris was indeed a musical *wunderkind*. He had signed a contract with Motown when he was only 8. By then, he was already active in his church choir and performing on a wide range of instruments.

Wonder's first big hit, however, was no spiritual. Recorded in a Chicago theater before an enthusiastic audience, "Fingertips, Part 2" showed off his virtuosity and revealed that the Motown way, slick as it was, still allowed for improvisation. Little Stevie moved between harmonica and organ, singing a few lines composed on the spot. The turbulent piece ended abruptly, with a drummer's smash. In the background, one can hear a confused bass guitarist asking, "What key? What key?" Like the best of rock music, "Fingertips, Part 2" defied convention, mingling spontaneity and smooth production values— and refused to take itself too seriously.

Meanwhile, Bob Dylan was busy creating his own brand of popular art in Greenwich Village—New York City's cradle of avant-garde artists with a leftish bent since early in the century. Folk music had been Dylan's escape from the staid provinciality of his hometown of Hibbing, located deep in the Iron Belt of northern Minnesota. The middle-class Jewish boy born Robert Allen Zimmerman remade himself in the image of the sensitive outlaw limned by such popular culture heroes as Elvis Presley, country singer Hank Williams, actor James Dean, and the '50s rhythm-and-blues artist Little Richard. He renamed himself after both the hard-drinking Welsh poet Dylan Thomas and Matt Dillon, manly protagonist of a popular TV western series.

No one, he hoped, would suspect anyone named Dylan of being either soft or Jewish. Postwar society bred legions of white kids longing, in similar ways, to reject and transcend their comfortable backgrounds. But no other wrote or sang with Dylan's painful eloquence.

The young artist had come to New York to meet Woody Guthrie, another paragon of authenticity. In the 1930s and 1940s, Guthrie became an emblem of exuberant rebellion. He left the Oklahoma Dust Bowl to ride the rails, write about migrant workers and union maids, and denounce stuffed shirts and hypocrites wherever he found them. Few who heard his best-known song, "This Land Is Your Land," knew that he was a member of the Communist Party. When Dylan met him, Guthrie was trapped in a hospital bed, slowly dying of a congenital nerve disease. But he was charmed by his 20-year-old admirer who sat by the bed, playing his guitar and singing both traditional folk tunes and his own protest lyrics.

Dylan's first album, issued in the spring of 1962, paid homage to the Guthrie tradition. Produced by the veteran folklorist John Hammond, it was filled with blues standards from the Deep South like "Gospel Plow" and "See That My Grave is Kept Clean"—although Dylan performed them with a gleeful ferocity of grunts, yelps, and chuckles that owed more to Elvis than to veteran black bluesmen like Blind Lemon Jefferson or Son House. One of the two original compositions on the album was "Song to Woody" which ended with the lines:

> I'm a-leavin' tomorrow, but I could leave today,
> Somewhere down the road someday.
> The very last thing that I'd want to do
> Is to say I've been hittin' some hard travellin' too.[29]

Indeed, Dylan would soon leave the emulation behind. His second album, *The Freewheelin' Bob Dylan,* released in May of 1963, contained almost no songs but his own. Some were clearly motivated by political outrage: particularly "Blowin' in the Wind," "Oxford Town" (about Mississippi whites who rioted to stop integration of the state university), and "Masters of War," an icicle-sharp polemic against generals, bomb makers, and nuclear strategists, whom the writer cannot wait to see entombed.

But equally vital were his lyrics, both bitter and wistful, about ex-lovers and ex-friends who wouldn't give up their independence or moderate their ego. Songs like "Don't Think Twice, It's All Right" and "Bob Dylan's Dream" revealed a performer with a self-knowledge rare for someone who had just entered adulthood. Influenced by such modern poets as Thomas and Rimbaud, Dylan created surreal, often brutal images of a world out of joint. In one song, a boy reports back from a landscape apparently devastated by nuclear weapons: "I saw a newborn baby with wild wolves all around it, I saw a highway of diamonds with nobody on it, I saw a black branch with blood that kept drippin', I saw a room full of men with their hammers a-bleedin'. . . . "[30]

By the end of the summer, *Freewheelin'* had sold 100,000 copies; Bob Dylan was a star. What is more, he was fast becoming a bigger culture hero than the folksingers he had idolized while conjuring himself out of the Iron Range. Young male and female admirers alike copied Dylan's signature outfit of unpressed jeans, motorcycle jacket and boots, and workman's cap over bushy

Part of the crowd of 250,000 at the August 1963 March on Washington for Jobs and Freedom. Source: *George Meany Memorial Archives*

long hair. Budding bohemians from the suburbs marveled at his poetic intensity and ironic manner. Joan Baez, fellow folksinger and Dylan's sometime
girlfriend, appealed to many of the same fans. Her long straight hair, lack of
makeup, and unaffected vocal style seemed to announce that she aimed to
please nobody but herself. Dylan, however, lived more on the edge. "My songs
speak for me," he wrote to a friend in the early '60s, "I write them in the
confinement of my own mind. If I didn't write I think I'd go insane."[31]

Through 1963, Dylan kept composing about and singing for the poor and
the underdog—though his appetite for "message songs" was fast diminish-
ing. In July he sang at a SNCC rally for voting rights in Greenwood, Mississippi. The following month, with a handful of other folk musicians, he performed at the huge demonstration for Jobs and Freedom in Washington, D.C.,
where Martin Luther King, Jr. gave a different version of the "I Have a Dream
Speech," which Motown had earlier recorded in Detroit. The integrated crowd
was in a hopeful mood; perhaps the nation was finally beginning to cleanse
itself of racism. But Dylan was characteristically dubious. Near the end of the
day, he looked over toward the Capitol and grumbled, "Think they're listening? No they ain't listening at all."[32]

Fall: Saigon and Dallas

Friday, November 1, was a holiday in Saigon. Most Vietnamese were Buddhists and thus did not celebrate All Saints Day, as the nation's former French
colonizers had done. But the leaders of South Vietnam were devout Catholics
and set the official calendar. That morning, President Ngo Dinh Diem held
a short meeting with the U.S. ambassador, Henry Cabot Lodge, a patrician
Republican who had assumed the post in August. "Tell President Kennedy
that I take all his suggestions very seriously and wish to carry them out but
it is a question of timing," Diem told the stern diplomat who towered over
him.[33]

Since the past winter's humiliation at Ap Bac, American policymakers
had become increasingly frustrated with the way Diem was running his country. Not only did he squander millions of dollars of aid without aggressively
challenging the enemy to battle. He rebuffed calls to hold free elections and
ordered troops to crush the regime's peaceful, non-Communist opponents,
which only kindled a larger movement to replace him. Diem's soldiers killed
Buddhist demonstrators for displaying traditional flags on Buddha's birthday,
broke into temples and arrested dissident *bonzes* (monks), and violently shut
down the nation's universities. The initiators of this tough, politically obtuse
policy were the president's younger brother, Ngo Dinh Nhu, who commanded
the secret police, and his wife, Madame Nhu. Both were infamous for their
sadism. When, in a grisly protest, the *bonze* Quang Duc committed suicide

by dousing himself with gasoline, Madame Nhu chortled about "Buddhist barbecues" and offered to buy fuel for anyone who chose to follow.

In the summer, dozens of young military officers began planning a coup d'etat under the leadership of General Duong Van Minh ("Big Minh"), a popular figure among rank-and-file soldiers. The plotters were anxious for U.S. support; without American backing, any new government would surely fail. But General Harkins preferred to keep bargaining with Diem, the devil he knew, and top officials in Washington, including President Kennedy, sharply criticized the South Vietnamese leader yet could not resolve to make him go.

Lodge, however, had made up his mind only days after arriving in Saigon. On August 29, he cabled his superiors, "We are launched on a course from which there is no respectable turning back: the overthrow of the Diem government . . . there is no possibility, in my view, that the war can be won under a Diem administration."[34] For the next two months, Diem continued to hold regular, cordial meetings with a diplomat who was firmly committed to his political demise. By the end of October, U.S. policymakers had arrived at the same conclusion.

The coup began on November 1, soon after Lodge departed the presidential palace for his midday nap. Rebel troops moved into the capital and, under the command of Colonel Nguyen Van Thieu, advanced toward Diem's stronghold. At 4:30 P.M., Diem telephoned Lodge, demanding to know, "What is the attitude of the United States?" Lodge lied, disdainfully: "I do not feel well enough informed to be able to tell you. . . . Also it is 4:30 A.M. in Washington and the U.S. government cannot possibly have a view."[35] Diem and his brother soon fled the palace to take refuge in the Chinese quarter of Cholon. When the sun rose the next morning, Thieu's forces had finished blasting their way into the seat of power.

Diem and Nhu expected to become exiles, living perhaps on some French-speaking island on the largesse of their former American patrons. But the U.S. embassy failed to dispatch a plane for them. And the most vengeful of the military plotters had a different idea. "To kill weeds, you must pull them up at the roots," vowed one rebel officer. About an hour after the Ngo brothers voluntarily surrendered to coup leaders on the morning of November 2, two experienced assassins shot and stabbed them to death. "A remarkably able performance in all respects," Lodge cabled the State Department the next day.

John Kennedy did not agree. "A look of shock and dismay" crossed his face, remembered Maxwell Taylor, then chairman of the Joint Chiefs of Staff. Days later, the president was still distressed about the affair. To a friend who called Diem and Nhu "tyrants," he responded, "No, they were in a difficult position. They did the best they could for their country."[36]

Later that month, the president traveled to Texas to heal a more benign sort of civil conflict. Democrats in the huge and swiftly growing state were split into two mutually suspicious factions. One, led by Governor John Connally, championed the needs of oil barons and the values of white farmers; its members tended to view civil rights bills and organized labor as obnoxious northern imports. The other camp of Democrats, led by Senator Ralph Yarborough, sought to renew the programs and spirit of the New Deal. The liberals represented embattled unionists, the interracial poor, and intellectuals. Kennedy had won Texas by only 46,000 votes in 1960, and if the Republicans nominated a conservative in 1964, a divided party would imperil his chances there.

On the morning of November 22, the president and his wife, Jacqueline, flew into Dallas. They were prepared for a cool, if not unfriendly, reception. The city, which had more than doubled in population since 1940, usually voted Republican, and local right-wing activists were aggressive both in word and deed. A month earlier, UN ambassador (and former presidential candidate) Adlai Stevenson had endured heckling, spittle, and a blow from an angry picketer. On November 22, as the president dressed for the day, he glanced at a full-page ad in the *Dallas Morning News* which demanded he answer such questions as "WHY have you approved the sale of wheat and corn to our enemies when . . . Communist soldiers are daily wounding and/or killing American soldiers in Vietnam?" and "WHY have you ordered or permitted your brother Bobby [the attorney general] . . . to go soft on Communists, fellow-travelers, and ultra-leftists in America, while permitting him to persecute loyal Americans?"[37]

By noon, no hostility was evident as the Kennedy motorcade glided slowly through downtown Dallas on the way to a lunch with businessmen. Newspapers had printed a map of the route the president and his party would take, and hundreds of thousands of people had left work or school to take a look. Seated in the back seat of an open Lincoln limousine behind Governor Connally and his wife, Nellie, the president and first lady were delighted with the large, friendly crowds. As the motorcade entered Dealey Plaza (named for the first publisher of the *Morning News*), Nellie Connally turned around and beamed, "Mr. President, you can't say that Dallas doesn't love you." He responded, "No, you certainly can't."[38]

Then, a few seconds after 12:30, three rifle shots tore all comfort to shreds. The first bullet missed the limousine and hit a curb nearby, spraying fragments on several spectators. The second struck the president in the back of the neck, exited through his throat, and then hit Governor Connally in the shoulder. The third blasted the president's skull from behind, blowing his head apart and splattering the first lady with blood and brain tissue. Connally survived and had a long political career, the last segment of it as a Republican. But for John Kennedy, the frenzied rush to the hospital was pointless. He had died, the fourth U.S. president to be assassinated but the first to be murdered in full view of thousands of his fellow citizens. Minutes later, the number of spectators expanded to include the entire nation and much of the world.

Newscasters in the United States talked about and showed pictures of little else until the president's funeral ended four days later. Certain images from those days became instantly famous, a collective album through which the assassination will long be remembered: Johnson grimly taking the oath of office as Jacqueline Kennedy stands beside him in shock, her pink suit soaked in gore; 3-year-old John Kennedy, Jr., in knee pants, saluting his father's casket; the riderless black horse that walked in the funeral procession, with empty black boots reversed in the stirrups; people of all races weeping openly and freely. Before the year was over, the dead president's name was affixed to countless schools, streets, buildings, New York City's largest airport, and the cape in Florida where scientists and astronauts were working to beat the Soviets to the moon.

At the time, the esteemed historian Bruce Catton struggled to sum up the meaning of this torrent of grief. "What John F. Kennedy left us was most of all an attitude. To put it in the simplest terms, he looked ahead. He knew no more than anyone else what the future was going to be like, but he did know that that was where we ought to be looking. . . . President Kennedy came to symbolize that moment of change, not because he caused it but because he fitted into it; not because of what he did but simply because of what he was."[39] Swiftly and without hindsight, a shrewd politician whose main preoccupation in office had been winning the Cold War was transmuted into an icon of strength and idealism, the selfless young reformer who died for all Americans.

The end of Kennedy's life also marked the beginning of one of the most furious—and longest-lived—controversies in American history. For almost four decades, who killed Kennedy and why are questions that have seldom lost their power to both haunt and fascinate.

Part of the reason is that Lee Harvey Oswald, who was quickly arrested and charged with the murder, was himself assassinated two days later by a strip-club owner named Jack Ruby, who was friendly with the Dallas police. Part is due to Oswald's earlier defection to and return from the Soviet Union and his subsequent passionate support of the Cuban revolution. Part can be blamed on a "rush to judgment" by the Warren Commission, which the new president, Lyndon Johnson, appointed to investigate the killings. The commission published its final report in September 1964, only 10 months after the events in Dallas. Even its defenders later acknowledged that President Johnson, the Kennedy family, and the FBI pressured the panel of jurists and politicians to confirm that both Oswald and Ruby had acted alone and lacked any motivation other than personal rage. The fact that Johnson expanded U.S.

At John F. Kennedy's funeral. His widow Jacqueline, stands with her children, Caroline and John. Flanking them are his brothers Edward and Robert. Source: *CNP/Archive Photos*

troop strength and firepower in Vietnam, with disastrous conclusions, also led to speculation that his beloved predecessor was killed because he had begun to doubt the wisdom of the war.

Over 500 books, several of which were best sellers, bear witness to the broad, fervent desire to discover that some group of conspirators killed the president. The suspects include nearly every locus, real or imagined, of national power in the mid-'60s: the CIA, the Mafia, the military–industrial complex, corrupt leaders of the Teamsters' Union (especially Jimmy Hoffa), wealthy Cuban exiles, oil magnates, and Lyndon Johnson himself. Cuban dictator Fidel Castro and the rulers of the USSR are also favorite culprits.[40] Each of the theories neglects or diligently minimizes details that might refute it. But, together, they have persuaded most Americans. As of 1994, more than 80 percent of the public believed in some kind of plot to kill Kennedy.[41]

Such pervasive suspicions are one measure of how little confidence Americans, since the assassination, have had in the goodwill of the authorities, elected and self-anointed, who shape their lives. The federal government, in particular, came to seem both mendacious and fragile. As the chief executives who followed Kennedy lied and blundered from crisis to crisis, cynicism, while morally regrettable, became a form of self-defense. If "they" could kill a president, anything was possible. Speak truth to the powers that be or, at least, give them hell. In a Dallas hospital, minutes after doctors confirmed the death of her husband, Jacqueline Kennedy was asked if she'd like to wash and change her clothes. "No," she replied. "I want them to see what they have done."[42]

CHAPTER 6

The Rise of the Great Society

KENNEDY COULDN'T HAVE GOTTEN THE TEN COMMANDMENTS THROUGH CON-
GRESS.

—President Lyndon Baines Johnson, in a private comment to
an aide, 1965[1]

For four days in November 1963 the country virtually shut down, as millions of Americans watched the events of that long weekend unfold on their television screens. From Dallas came endless reports on the assassination itself, on the nature of the president's fatal wounds, of the arrest and killing of Lee Harvey Oswald. From Washington came coverage of the new president's arrival at Andrews Air Force Base after having been sworn in on Air Force One on the somber return flight from Dallas, of his proclamation of a day of national mourning for the slain president, of Kennedy's lying in state in the Capitol rotunda, and then on Monday, November 25, of the funeral procession with the riderless horse, followed by the burial ceremony in Arlington National Cemetery.

Two days later the country watched again on television as a grim-faced Lyndon Baines Johnson delivered his first presidential address to a joint session of the Congress of the United States. Less than three years earlier, in his own inaugural address, John Kennedy had declared, "Let us begin." Now President Johnson added, humbly, "Let us continue."[2]

But continue what? According to public opinion polls taken days after the assassination, 70 percent of Americans were unsure how the country could "carry on without" Kennedy.[3] Even in the White House, Johnson couldn't escape the feeling of being an interloper. It wasn't until February that the White House staff got around to taking down the pictures of the late president from their offices and replacing them with pictures of his successor.[4]

It was bad enough that Kennedy had been murdered in Johnson's home state, tarring the new president by association with his state's virulent strain of political extremism. What Johnson also had to be aware of was that a small but influential circle of liberal insiders in his own party were meeting privately to discuss whether they could deny him the nomination at next summer's Democratic national convention. Johnson was determined to head off any potential movement to anoint Attorney General Robert Kennedy heir-apparent to his martyred brother.[5]

Johnson understood that he had to move swiftly to reassure the country as a whole, and the Democratic party in particular, that he was indeed a legitimate successor to John Kennedy. The best way to do so would be to show that he could be more successful than Kennedy himself in pushing "Kennedy programs" through Congress. Meeting with Walter Heller, chairman of the Council of Economic Advisers, shortly after taking office, Johnson asked him to "tell your friends—Arthur Schlesinger, Galbraith, and other liberals" that he had not the slightest intention of going back to the conservative policies of the 1950s. "To tell the truth," Johnson added, "John F. Kennedy was a little too conservative to suit my taste."[6]

The thirty-sixth president of the United States was born in 1908 in the hill country of central Texas, a brush-strewn highland whose soil had been ruined by too many generations of small farmers trying to get rich, or just get by, growing cotton. Lyndon Baines Johnson was the eldest of five children born to Sam and Rebekah Johnson. Although Johnson would later exaggerate his family's poverty for political purposes, they certainly lived close to the margin. Sam Johnson was a landowner and a six-term member of the Texas state legislature. But unlike many of his fellow lawmakers, he scorned the bribes that flowed freely from Texas business lobbyists eager to purchase legislative favors. A Democrat of populist sympathies, Sam Johnson believed that government should serve the interests of ordinary men, not the wealthy and big corporations. Young Lyndon admired the way his father stuck to his principles; he also couldn't help but notice that such idealism could be costly. After a disastrous collapse of cotton prices following the First World War, Sam Johnson wound up working on a road crew on some of the same state highways he had helped bring to his district.[7]

Lyndon Johnson was keenly aware of the differences between his own background and the "Harvards" in John Kennedy's administration. No one had handed him an Ivy League education, or anything else in life. He had worked his way through Southwest Texas State College in San Marcos (including a stint teaching poor Mexican-American children in a dusty border town, an experience that he would often refer back to), graduating in 1930. Then, after another year of teaching, he secured a position in Washington, D.C., as secretary to a Texas congressman. His public life had begun.

Johnson was not a handsome man; his manners were crude; he could be overbearing and a bully. But he was also intelligent, with a prodigious memory and, most importantly, a gift of keen political perception. He understood how to make use of the ambitions and anxieties of the people around him to accomplish his own aims. As a young man on the rise, he learned how to turn a calculated deference to his elders to his advantage. As one of his fellow congressional aides from the early 1930s would recall, "With men who had power, men who could help him, Lyndon Johnson was a professional son."[8] Ambition overrode ideology: in the company of conservative elders he was conservative; in the company of liberals, he was liberal. Coming to Washington on the eve of the New Deal, the prevailing winds were from the liberals, and he tacked accordingly.

Johnson formed one of his most rewarding relationships with fellow Texan Sam Rayburn, the House Democratic leader and later Speaker of the House. In 1935 Rayburn helped him secure appointment as Texas state director of the National Youth Administration (NYA), a New Deal agency that provided work grants to needy college students and public employment to other young people in need of jobs. In 1937 when the congressman from his home district in Texas suddenly died, Johnson declared himself a candidate. He ran a campaign designed to link himself in voters' minds with President Roosevelt and the New Deal: "Franklin D. and Lyndon B." read his campaign signs. After his election, he returned to Washington, where he met the president for the first time. Roosevelt wasn't taken in by Johnson's "professional son" routine, but he was impressed nonetheless. He remarked to political adviser Harry Hopkins, "this boy could well be the first Southern President."[9]

Johnson continued his climb to power with election to the U.S. Senate in 1948; having secured the Democratic nomination (tantamount to election in Texas in those years) by a scant and suspect majority of 87 votes, he also acquired the painful nickname of "Landslide Lyndon." In his years in the Senate he grew more conservative, reflecting both the mood of Texas voters and increasingly close ties with the oil and gas interests in his home state. (He also became a wealthy man in those years, building a financial empire in television stations—a field of enterprise in which his influence with the Federal Communications Commission did not hurt him in besting his commercial rivals.) In 1953 he was elected by his Democratic colleagues as Senate minority leader, and in 1955, after Democrats had regained control of the Senate, he was elevated to majority leader.

No longer the deferential youngster, Lyndon Johnson was now a towering presence in the Senate anterooms where deals were cut, a wheeler-dealer who poked his face within inches of his fellow senators, gripping their forearms with one hand, persuading, intimidating, and calling in his debts to secure the votes he needed for advancing his legislative and personal agenda.

In November 1960 Johnson advanced to within one heartbeat of the presidency. And for the next three years, it seemed to him that was as close as he was ever likely to get. The vice presidency was no place for a man with a Texas-sized ego. Johnson had served his purpose for the Kennedys in 1960 in helping his running mate secure the loyalty of southern Democrats; now the president and his brother Bobby had neither use nor respect for the talents of "Landslide Lyndon." "I cannot stand Johnson's damn long face," President Kennedy complained to a sympathetic listener. "He just comes in, sits at the Cabinet meetings with his face all screwed up, never says anything. He looks so sad."[10] Kennedy started sending the vice president on round-the-world goodwill trips, just to get him out of Washington and out of sight. And then came the trip to Dallas.

"Everything I had ever learned in the history books taught me that martyrs have to die for causes," Johnson would tell interviewer Doris Kearns after his own presidency had come to an end:

> John Kennedy had died. But his "cause" was not really clear. That was my job. I had to take the dead man's program and turn it into a martyr's cause.[11]

President Johnson's campaign to lay claim to Kennedy's legislative mantle began the night in November 1963 when he first addressed a joint session of Congress. There was, Johnson declared, "no memorial or eulogy [that] could more eloquently honor President Kennedy's memory than the earliest possible passage of the civil rights bill for which he fought."[12] It was not by accident that Johnson began his campaign for "Kennedy's program" with civil rights. As a southerner, he had a better-than-average record on civil rights, but he also had to contend with the suspicions of civil rights activists and northern liberals that he would seek to turn the clock back on race relations to the pre-Kennedy status quo. Johnson laid those doubts to rest as he brought all his formidable persuasive powers to bear to achieve passage of the Civil Rights Act, which until that point had been considered unlikely to pass anytime before the next presidential election. The proposed legislation would outlaw segregation in public facilities and racial discrimination in employment and education. On July 2, 1964, he was able to sign the bill into law. It was the most significant federal measure on behalf of equal rights for black Americans seen since the Reconstruction era. And, since a southern congressman had somewhat whimsically amended the act to ban gender as well as racial discrimination, the Civil Rights Act proved a turning point in the legal rights of women as well as blacks.[13]

Civil rights was just the beginning, as Johnson also turned his attention to the economy. By the end of February 1964, he had secured passage of Kennedy's proposal for a tax cut, a measure that had spent the last 10 months stalled in various congressional committees. To win support for the tax cut, he had pledged that he would hold the next year's federal budget to under $100 billion. The promise seemed to dictate cautious spending policies, with no dramatic new government programs.

But Johnson was not in the mood for caution. He had not spent a quarter-century climbing the rungs of power in Washington just to become a Democratic version of Dwight Eisenhower. He wanted to be the Franklin Delano Roosevelt of the 1960s; indeed, he dreamed of outdoing Roosevelt in the breadth and popularity of his programs and legacy. So Johnson was going to have his tax cut, and he was also going to have the kind of bold social programs that many people had by now persuaded themselves John Kennedy had stood for.[14]

Kennedy had, in fact, contemplated introducing some new liberal reform measures in the year leading up to the 1964 presidential election. In the spring of 1963, Kennedy's economic adviser Walter Heller had passed along to the president a copy of a recently published book entitled *The Other America* by the socialist activist and intellectual Michael Harrington. Despite the prevailing consensus about the arrival of the "affluent society," Harrington argued that there was "another America" of 40 to 50 million inhabitants living in the United States, "the unskilled workers, the migrant farm workers, the aged, the minorities, and all the others who live in the economic underworld of American life." This "invisible land" of the poor existed in rural isolation or in crowded urban slums where middle-class visitors seldom ventured. "That the poor are invisible," Harrington wrote, "is one of the most important things about them."

Harrington's other main point, for which he acknowledged his debt to anthropologist Oscar Lewis, was that "poverty is a culture." Poor Americans were not simply distinguishable by their lack of adequate income. Rather, they were "people who lack education and skill, who have bad health, poor housing, low levels of aspiration and high levels of mental distress." Each of these problems was "the more intense because it exists within a web of disabilities." The tenacity of the "culture of poverty," which was passed down from generation to generation of poor Americans, meant that it was a delusion to believe that poverty as an economic condition could be solved by exhortations to the poor to lift themselves up by their own bootstraps. "Society," Harrington concluded, "must help them before they can help themselves."[15]

Harrington's statistics and the case he presented for federal action on behalf of the "invisible poor" impressed Kennedy. He had not forgotten the scenes of economic destitution he had encountered while campaigning in the West Virginia primary in 1960. When the president conferred with Heller for what turned out to be the last time in November 1963, he told him that he definitely wanted to include some kind of antipoverty program in next year's legislative package.[16]

On the day after Kennedy's assassination, Heller briefed the new president on economic issues, mentioning Kennedy's interest in antipoverty legislation. "That's my kind of program," Johnson responded. "Move full speed ahead." A scant six weeks later, in his State of the Union address in January

Unemployed young men in West Virginia, c. 1961. The Great Society aimed to lift them out of poverty. Source: *George Meany Memorial Archives*

1964, Johnson announced that his administration, "today, here and now, declares unconditional war on poverty in America."

Johnson pushed the war on poverty as another tribute to John Kennedy. But unlike the civil rights act or the tax cut legislation, which had actually been drafted and submitted to Congress before Kennedy's assassination, the "war on poverty" was little more than a phrase and a file drawer full of position papers from obscure government functionaries and academic theorists. All Johnson knew for sure about the program when he gave told Walter Heller to go "full speed ahead" was that he wanted something big. When approached the following month with a proposal for a modest experimental antipoverty program, limited to five urban and five rural pilot projects, Johnson was not impressed. Congress didn't like to fund experiments, and neither did he. He wanted something he could sell to the country as the *solution* to poverty. "These boys are pretty theoretical down here," Johnson complained to civil rights leader Roy Wilkins in January, shortly before his declaration of the war on poverty, "and if I get it passed, I'm gonna have to have more practical plans."[18]

Johnson appointed Sargent Shriver to convene a task force to draw up antipoverty legislation. The appointment was a shrewd one. As Kennedy's brother-in-law, Shriver was a useful symbol of continuity with the past administration. He was also the founding director of the Peace Corps, one of the most politically popular of the Kennedy administration's initiatives. Johnson hoped that the Congress and the public would respond to the new call for a crusade to end poverty at home with the same enthusiasm they had shown for the idea of spreading American ideals and practical know-how to impoverished nations abroad. "The sky's the limit," Johnson told Shriver in persuading him to take on this new task. "You just make this thing work, period. I don't give a damn about the details."[19]

It turned out, however, that Johnson did give a damn about the details. There is one simple solution to poverty (technically simple, if politically complicated), and that is for government to take money from those who have it, through taxation, and pass it on to those who lack it. This is what economists call "income redistribution" or "transfer payments," and is more popularly known as "welfare" or "the dole." But Johnson, already committed to passing a tax cut that would benefit wealthy and middle-class voters, was unsympathetic to that approach. "You tell Shriver, no doles," was the message he gave to aide Bill Moyers to pass on to Shriver as planning for the war on poverty began.[20]

Another solution to poverty is to have government provide the poor with jobs. In part that was what Johnson's tax cut was designed to accomplish, if only indirectly: putting more money into the pockets of better-off consumers would in turn stimulate demand for goods and services from private industry, leading to increased production and, presumably, higher employment rates among the formerly jobless. If that process proved too slow, or was undermined by "automation" (business investment in labor-saving machinery and techniques), or simply failed to reach groups cut off from the benefits of an expanding economy, such as unemployed coal miners in isolated and depressed regions like Appalachia, the government might also step in directly as employer of last resort. That would mean launching the kind of federally sponsored public works projects undertaken by Roosevelt's New Deal during the Great Depression (building and maintaining roads, schools, airports, and so on) and/or the expansion of public services (hiring more teachers, social workers, firemen, and the like). This was, or had been since the 1930s, the classic liberal solution to economic difficulties (John Kenneth Galbraith had made an eloquent case for increased public services in *The Affluent Society*[21]). But such programs were expensive; President Roosevelt's Works Projects Administration (WPA) cost $5 billion in its first year of operation, an unprecedented federal expenditure for domestic welfare. They also carried political liabilities, with the business community tending to view them as wasteful subsidies to workers lacking the initiative or skill to find jobs on their own.

So, although Johnson had promised Shriver that "the sky's the limit," it turned out to be a low-ceilinged sky indeed. Johnson told Shriver he could have under a billion dollars for the first year's war on poverty programs—or less than one-fifth what Roosevelt had secured for the WPA in 1935 (more like one-tenth, taking into account the inflation of the preceding 30 years.) As members of Shriver's task force deliberated in the spring of 1964, they operated under planning constraints that led them to fashion a strategy for ending poverty that was quite different in scope and philosophy from that of the New Deal era.

The war on poverty, as it finally emerged from the planning process, was designed to be fought through government-sponsored programs that would help the poor to improve themselves—a "hand up, not a handout," as Shriver would put it. The war on poverty was not going to be a jobs program, and it was certainly not intended to be a welfare program. If anything, the war on poverty strategists believed that their efforts would lead to a vast reduction in existing government programs providing cash benefits to the poor, such as Aid to Families of Dependent Children (AFDC), a welfare program created in 1935 to help single-parent families with children. Under the war on poverty, poor Americans would be encouraged to take advantage of job-training programs and other forms of educational assistance that would allow them to benefit from the opportunities provided by an expanding national economy—hence the title given Shriver's package of legislative proposals, the Economic Opportunity Act of 1964. Only the truly unemployable—widows with small children at home, and people with severe disabilities such as blindness—would still have to turn to welfare agencies for assistance. The war on poverty would not seek to transfer income and would not seek to transform the economy. The only thing it sought to change was the worldview of the poor, the "culture of poverty" that Michael Harrington had discussed in *The Other America*.

The press coverage of the war on poverty that spring was extensive and, for the most part, sympathetic. Harrington's book became a best-seller in paperback, and his "invisible poor" were being sought out by an army of newspaper and television reporters. President Johnson did his part by making a well-orchestrated trip to eastern Kentucky in late April, where he visited with an unemployed coal miner named Tom Fletcher and his wife and children in their three-room, tarpaper-covered shack.[22] Harry Caudill's *Night Comes to the Cumberlands*, a portrait of life in southern Appalachia published in 1963, was also influential in shaping the emerging image of the newly visible poor. "This is Daniel Boone country," wrote Johnson's liberal Secretary of the Interior Stewart Udall in his foreword to Caudill's book. He further described the Cumberland Plateau of Kentucky as a region where once "fiercely independent frontiersmen found in these isolated valleys the elements that sustained vigorous life."[23]

As long as the poor continued to be thought of as the great, great grand-children of Daniel Boone—which is to say white and rural—the fortunes of the war on poverty would remain in the ascendant. And yet, even in the spring of 1964 when most Americans pronounced themselves in favor of Johnson's antipoverty efforts, public opinion polls nonetheless revealed that at the same time a plurality continued to believe that the poor were mainly to blame for their own condition. In March of that year the Gallup poll asked the following question: "Which is more often to blame if a person is poor—lack of effort on his own part, or circumstances beyond his control?" The re-sults were revealing: 33 percent of the sample responded "lack of effort," 29 percent blamed "circumstances," and 32 percent thought the two were equally important.[24]

Signed into law in August 1964, the Economic Opportunity Act estab-lished the Office of Economic Opportunity (OEO) as an independent federal agency under the directorship of Sargent Shriver, with an initial appropria-tion of $800 million. Most of OEO's limited funding would go toward pro-viding grants to locally organized community action agencies (CAAs) in poor neighborhoods across the country (over a thousand of them would be set up in the next year.) The CAAs were charged with determining what mix of gov-ernment programs would work best in combating poverty in their particular neighborhoods, and then setting up and administering those programs. (In a provision attracting little attention at the time, the CAAs were required to seek the "maximum feasible participation" of the poor themselves in their operations.)

Among the programs OEO would oversee was a Job Corps (providing vocational training to unemployed teenagers), several other work–training and work–study programs, and literacy and adult education programs. There were loan programs for struggling farmers and small businessmen. There were also provisions for various kinds of "in-kind assistance," such as food stamps, designed to improve the immediate health and circum-stances of the poor. Finally the war on poverty legislation established VISTA (Volunteers in Service to America) as a kind of domes-tic Peace Corps, enlisting volunteers for social service work in poor communities.

Johnson's legislative agenda for the spring of 1964 resembled a Christ-mas gift list. There was the civil rights act for blacks. There was a tax cut for the better-off. And there was a war on poverty for the poor. But Johnson did not want to simply provide services for this or that constituency. His vision of politics was much grander. He was after "consensus," the creation of a great and durable political majority who shared a common vision of an ideal America. And so in May, in preparation for the fall presidential campaign, Johnson set forth his political philosophy in a speech to a wildly enthusias-tic audience of students at the University of Michigan. What he hoped to accomplish as president, Johnson declared, was nothing less than the creation of a "Great Society":

> The Great Society . . . demands an end to poverty and racial injustice. . . . But that is just the beginning. The Great Society is a place where every child can find knowledge to enrich his mind and enlarge his talent . . . where leisure is a welcome chance to build and reflect, not a feared cause of boredom and restlessness . . . where the city of man serves not only the needs of the body and the demands of commerce but the desire for beauty and the hunger for community.[25]

This was Schlesinger's call for a new "qualitative liberalism" coming to fruition, but with an important difference. Johnson's speech was no cautious exercise in "fact-finding, *expertise,* and background papers." The rhetoric, crafted by former Kennedy speechwriter Richard Goodwin, was exalted, evangelical, and unabashedly utopian. "Will you join in the battle to give every citizen the full equality which God enjoins and the law requires?" Johnson called to the students. "Yes" they shouted back. "Will you join in the battle to build the Great Society, to prove that our material progress is only the foundation on which we will build a richer life of mind and spirit?" "Yes!", again, came the response. The speech was an enormous success. As Goodwin would note, it capped the process by which "the country witnessed, first with relief, then with gathering acclaim, the unexpected emergence of a new leader who seemed both formidable and benign."[26] Johnson was becoming the country's leader in his own right, no longer simply chief caretaker of the Kennedy shrine.

The next six months proved the high point of Lyndon Johnson's presidency and life. Though far ahead in the polls (and even further ahead after the Republicans, in a raucous and divisive national convention, nominated ultraconservative Arizonan Barry Goldwater as their standard-bearer), Johnson nonetheless kept up a campaign schedule that exhausted younger aides. Whenever his energy seemed to flag, all he had to do was come in contact with adoring voters. As reporter Mary McGrory noted, "What the cup of coffee or the hair of the dog are for some men, the sight of a throng is for Lyndon Johnson." Huge crowds turned out along the routes of his motorcades across the country; as he drove past, Johnson would shout to them as if he were campaigning with his father back in the Texan hill country, "Come down an' hear the speakin!" or "Bring your children and the family to hear the speakin'!"[27] In November Johnson swept past Goldwater with 61 percent of the popular vote, better than Franklin Roosevelt had managed in his great reelection victory in 1936. No one could ever again describe the president as "Landslide Lyndon" with ironic intent.

President Johnson had dealt with another Kennedy legacy in 1964, even as he was crafting his war on poverty, and that was the war in Vietnam. Johnson was every bit as determined as Kennedy had been to avoid a politically damaging debate ("Who lost Vietnam?"). Not only did he have to prove to the Republicans that he was tough on communism, he also had to prove to his own party that he was as strong a leader as the slain president. A masterful figure in domestic politics, Johnson had little experience in international affairs. Although often resentful of what he considered slights from the well-educated elitists in Kennedy's circle of advisers, he also was intimidated by them and deferred to what he regarded as their superior wisdom. This was particularly true in the case of Robert McNamara, whom Johnson called "the ablest man I've ever met."[28] Three days after Kennedy's assassination, Johnson issued secret instructions requiring "all senior officers of the government" to provide "full unity of support for established U.S. policy in South Vietnam."[29]

When Robert McNamara returned from a visit to Vietnam in December 1963, he again assured the press of the great progress being made there. Privately, he warned the new president that the "current trend" in Vietnam "will lead to neutralization at best or more likely to a Communist-controlled state."[30] On his next visit to Saigon, in March 1964, McNamara reported that things had "unquestionably been growing worse" since the previous fall.[31] The Communists were more numerous, better armed, and extending their control over much of the countryside, while the new South Vietnamese government was proving even more ineffective than the Diem regime. In fact, it was hard to tell who was in control in Saigon; over the next year, there would be a total of three coups and five governments briefly in power.

President Johnson was being told by McNamara and the other foreign policy advisers he had inherited from John Kennedy that, however unpromising the situation in South Vietnam appeared, the United States had to stay the course set by his slain predecessor. Johnson agreed. But every once in awhile he would turn to one of his older associates, Senior Richard Russell of Georgia, for an alternate opinion. Russell had been a good friend and loyal backer of Johnson for many years, and Johnson respected his political advice. Although a resolute conservative and anti-Communist, Russell was deadset against the deepening American involvement in the Vietnam War. "We should get out" of Vietnam, Russell told the new president in a telephone conversation (recorded by Johnson) on December 7, 1963, just two weeks after John F. Kennedy's assassination. Russell reminded Johnson of how the two of them had met with President Dwight Eisenhower in 1954, and urged him not to provide direct military assistance to the French in Indochina. "I tried my best to keep them from going into Laos and Vietnam. . . . Said we'd never get out, be in there fifty years from now."

Six months later, on May 27, 1964, Johnson called Russell again and plaintively asked him "What do you think of this Vietnam thing? I'd like to hear you talk a little." Russell leaped at the opportunity to save his old friend from what he saw as a disastrous policy and misguided advice. "It's the worst damn mess I ever saw . . . our position is deteriorating. . . . a tragic situation. It's just one of those place where you can't win. Anything that you do is wrong. . .." Russell had just gotten through listening to Robert McNamara's testimony on U.S. policy in Vietnam before the Senate Armed Services Committee, which Russell chaired. He had not been impressed: "I'm not sure he's as objective as he ought to be in surveying the conditions out there. He feels like it's sort of up to him personally to see that the thing goes through. And he's a can-do fellow. But I'm not too sure he understands the history and background of those people out there as fully as he should."

Russell was particularly scathing about those who were urging the president to launch air strikes against North Vietnam, a strategy he characterized as "Bomb the North, and kill old men, women and children." He had no faith in the ability of American air power to cut off North Vietnamese support for the insurgency in the South: "We tried it in Korea. We even got a lot of old B-29s to increase the bomb load and sent 'em over there and just dropped millions and millions of bombs, day and night, and in the morning, they would [fix] the road and in the morning, the damn people would be back traveling over it. . . . We never could actually interdict all their lines of communication although we had absolute control of the seas and the air, and we never did stop them. And you ain't gonna stop these people either." Johnson listened carefully to his old friend, agreed with him often, but concluded with a resigned sigh, "Well, they'd impeach a president though that would run out, wouldn't they?"[32]

Unable to do anything about the deteriorating political situation in South Vietnam, frustrated American policymakers concluded that the solution lay in carrying the war directly to North Vietnam. "We are swatting flies," Air Force Chief of Staff Curtis LeMay declared in December 1963, "when we should be going after the manure pile."[33] Over the next few months, Johnson's military and civilian advisers developed plans for a series of military escalations leading to a full-scale bombing campaign against North Vietnam. They drew up a draft of a congressional resolution of support for American policy in Vietnam, intending to introduce it at the right moment to secure bipartisan endorsement for the war. Johnson sought to postpone any decisive action in Vietnam until after the November election. But at summer's end Americans got a foretaste of the widened war to come.

On July 30, the U.S. destroyer *Maddox* entered the Gulf of Tonkin, the coastal waters that lie beside North Vietnam. The *Maddox* was monitoring North Vietnamese radio broadcasts, attempting to gauge the strength of the country's coastal defense. Ever since February, South Vietnamese PT boats had been raiding North Vietnamese coastal installations, as part of an American-designed operation code-named Operation Plan 34A. Now they struck again, raiding two North Vietnamese islands. The North Vietnamese were on edge, expecting further assaults at any moment. In the next few days the *Maddox* sailed as close as 8 miles to the North Vietnamese mainland and 4 miles to the islands attacked by the South Vietnamese.

On the night of August 2, three North Vietnamese torpedo boats sailed at high speed toward the *Maddox* (possibly believing it to be the South Vietnamese vessel involved in the July 30 raid). The Americans fired first; the North Vietnamese responded by launching two torpedoes. In the 37-minute battle that followed, two torpedo boats were damaged by American planes, and a third by shellfire from the *Maddox*. The *Maddox* itself was unscathed, and there were no U.S. casualties.

The Navy ordered another destroyer, the *C. Turner Joy*, to join the *Maddox* in the Gulf. The next night, August 3, South Vietnamese ships again raided the North Vietnamese coast. On the evening of August 4, sailors aboard the *Maddox* began to pick up radar and sonar readings indicating the presence of enemy ships. Although there were no visual sightings of North Vietnamese craft, several sailors claimed to have seen torpedo wakes heading toward the destroyers. Over the next 2 hours, seamen manning sonar equipment reported 22 torpedoes fired at the *Maddox*. The *Maddox* and the *Turner Joy* fired 400 shells in the direction from which the attack seemed to be coming.

They also called in air support. But the planes from the USS *Ticonderoga* could find no sign of the enemy. The captain of the *Maddox* finally called off his gunners and cabled his superiors: "Entire action leaves many doubts. Suggest complete evaluation before any further action."[34] Later it would be suggested that a jittery sonar man aboard the *Maddox* had mistaken the sound of his own ship's rudder for onrushing enemy torpedoes, while freak weather conditions led to a misinterpretation of radar readings. In retrospect, it seems likely that there were no North Vietnamese ships in the area that night.

Notwithstanding the murky circumstances surrounding the supposed attack, policymakers in Washington set in motion contingency plans developed the previous spring for military escalation. In a televised address shortly before midnight on August 4, President Johnson announced that in retaliation for an unprovoked attack on American ships on the high seas, U.S. bombers were already on their way to North Vietnam. Two U.S. planes were shot down in the attack, which struck at North Vietnamese fuel depots, PT boat bases, and antiaircraft installations. One pilot died, while the other, Lieutenant (j.g.) Everett Alvarez, was taken prisoner. He would remain a captive in North Vietnam until 1973.

According to public opinion polls, an overwhelming majority of Americans approved the raids against North Vietnam. With their servicemen under attack, Americans instinctively rallied around the flag and their president's policies. The Gulf of Tonkin events were seen as a kind of mini–Pearl Harbor, except this time it was the enemy that was sent away with a bloody nose. Television commentators and editorial writers hailed President John-son's cool-headed resolution in the crisis, and his standing in public opinion polls jumped.[35]

Privately, Johnson was skeptical about the August 4 incident, confiding to an aide, "Hell, those dumb stupid sailors were just shooting at flying fish."[36] But he was delighted by the chance to strike a blow at the Vietnamese Communists, boasting in his rough-hewn style, "I didn't just screw Ho Chi Minh. I cut his pecker off."[37] More importantly, following the script devised by his advisers that spring, Johnson was able to go before Congress to ask for a resolution authorizing him to "take all necessary measures to repel an armed attack against the forces of the United States and to prevent further aggression."[38] The resulting Gulf of Tonkin resolution passed the House of Representatives unanimously, and passed the Senate with only two dissenting votes, those of Ernest Gruening of Alaska and Wayne Morse of Oregon, and went on to serve as the legal justification for the war until its repeal in 1970.

The Gulf of Tonkin incident also served Johnson well in the fall presidential election. Having dispatched bombers to take what most Americans regarded as a just and measured retribution for Communist aggression on the high seas, Johnson was free thereafter to campaign as a man of peace. At a campaign rally near his Texas ranch on August 29, he declared unequivocally:

> I have had advice to load our planes with bombs and to drop them on certain areas that I think would enlarge the war and escalate the war, and result in our committing a good many American boys to fighting a war that I think ought to be fought by the boys of Asia to help protect their own land.[39]

With Barry Goldwater prone to loose speculation on how useful tactical nuclear weapons might prove in the jungles of Vietnam, most voters preferred to entrust the foreign policy of the United States and the fate of "American boys" in uniform to a moderate, reasonable, and seasoned commander-in-chief like Lyndon Johnson.

"Don't stay up late," the president admonished the celebrants as he left his inaugural ball in January 1965. "There's work to be done. We're on our way to the Great Society."[40] When the 89th Congress opened deliberations later that month, Johnson prepared to move swiftly on many fronts. He could call on the support of the strongest Democratic majority in the House and Senate since the heyday of the New Deal. The Democrats had picked up 2 seats in the Senate, and 37 more in the House of Representatives in the fall elections. Liberal Democrats, in alliance with the remaining liberal northern Republicans, could now construct a majority without having to depend on the votes of conservative southern Democrats. Yet Johnson still felt a sense of urgency. He knew how temporary even the most convincing electoral mandate could prove. "We've got to do this in a hurry," Johnson exhorted legislative aides. Banging his fist on the wall for emphasis, he added, "I want to see this coonskin on the wall."[41]

If President Johnson had done nothing else but preside over bill-signing ceremonies, he would have had a busy schedule in 1965. In the first six months of the year, the administration submitted 87 bills—"coonskins" in Johnson's terminology—to Congress. By October, when Congress recessed and Johnson entered the hospital for gall bladder surgery, he had nailed 84 of them to the White House wall. Johnson claimed that not even his old political hero Franklin Roosevelt in his first year in office had signed so many fundamental reforms into law.

Among the bills the president put his signature to in 1965 were social welfare measures providing federal health insurance for the aged (Medicare) and for poor families (Medicaid). Proposals for some sort of national health insurance had been a staple of the liberal agenda since Harry Truman's presidency, but had been stymied by the medical lobby, which denounced the specter of "socialized medicine." Even at this high point of liberal influence, Johnson did not feel he had the votes to deliver a program for universal health coverage. But he was able to bring a measure of protection to two of the most vulnerable groups in the country in terms of health problems.

Medicare turned out to be a very popular program. Far from being regarded by the public as an unwarranted intrusion of the government into a previously sacrosanct economic activity, it was seen as the natural extension of the already popular provisions for social security pensions; soon after its passage, over four out of five Americans proclaimed themselves backers of the measure. In fact, of all social groups in the country, the elderly may have benefited most from the liberal reforms of the 1960s. In addition to Medicare, elderly Americans also benefited from new policies tying social security payments to the cost of living. As a result, the poverty level among elderly Americans dropped precipitously by the mid-1970s. For those over the age of 65, the war on poverty proved an unqualified success. Senior citizens, known to politicians as reliable and knowledgeable voters, proved so highly effective in lobbying in their own interest that some commentators began to refer to the emergence of "Grey Power."[42]

In his 1965 State of the Union address, Johnson had committed himself to preserving a "green legacy" for future Americans. In line with that pledge, and reflecting the concerns of the "qualitative liberalism" of the 1950s as well as those of a newly emerging environmentalist movement, Johnson backed a measure proposed by Senator Edmund Muskie of Maine to establish federal regulations protecting the nation's water quality against industrial and other forms of pollution. In October Johnson signed the Water Quality Act of 1965, better known as the Clean Water Act, into law, proclaiming (in a perhaps deliberate echo of the themes of Galbraith's *Affluent Society*) the nation's "refusal to be strangled by the wastes of civilization."[43] Two weeks later he signed another bill, the Clean Air Act, also proposed by Muskie, establishing federal air quality regulations.

The 89th Congress passed, at the president's behest, measures establishing a new cabinet-level agency, the Department of Housing and Urban Development (HUD), as well as endowments providing federal grants to support scholarship and the arts. Congress also passed measures providing federal aid to elementary and secondary schools, as well as providing federal scholarships for low-income college students (and underwriting private education loans to better-off students).[44]

As important as Johnson's Great Society legislative initiatives were in realizing the liberal agenda in the mid-1960s, they were not the only force pushing for social reform. The federal judiciary and new social movements outside of government also played important roles in the decade's resurgent liberalism.

The mid-1960s were the third time in the twentieth century that reformers in the White House and Congress joined together in seeking fundamental changes in American society. In dramatic contrast to earlier periods of liberal ferment, like the Progressive Era and the New Deal, this time the reformers were joined, rather than being opposed, by a majority of justices of the Supreme Court. Indeed, the reformist mood of the Supreme Court preceded that in the other branches of the federal government by a decade.

In the 1950s and 1960s, the Supreme Court dramatically broadened the definition of constitutional rights guaranteed United States citizens. Under the direction of Earl Warren, the California Republican appointed by President Eisenhower in 1953, the Court's decisions encouraged and lent legitimacy to new social movements, particularly those concerned with the conditions of minority groups and women.[45]

The language of "rights" is central to the American experience, as a quick glance at the Declaration of Independence and the Constitution will confirm. But there never has been a consensus on exactly what and who was to be included in these broad assertions of natural and equal rights. Much of the history of the United States consists of a process by which more and more groups lay claim to more and more rights. However, until the 1960s, most of the excluded constituencies and insurgent movements seeking what they saw as their fair share of rights—blacks, women, working men and women, and others—focused their demands in terms of equal treatment before the law and equal ability to participate in the political process. They sought an extension of the franchise and the protection of rights of free speech, free assembly, and free association.

The 1960s and their aftermath led to an explosion of demands for new rights—such as rights to reproductive freedom—or by groups who had not been thought of as possessing any special rights of their own—such as homosexuals, criminal defendants, convicted prisoners, mental patients, the handicapped, and welfare recipients.[46]

In 1954, as the newly appointed chief justice, Earl Warren played a central role in persuading several wavering justices to sign on to the Court's unanimous decision in favor of the NAACP's position in *Brown*. Warren nursed a guilty conscience from his role in the incarceration of California's Japanese Americans in the Second World War; he had been state attorney general at the time and had provided legal justification for the decision. *Brown*, and subsequent Court decisions reinforcing civil rights and civil liberties, were at least in part his atonement for complicity in that earlier act of racial injustice.[47]

If the only Supreme Court ruling with which Earl Warren's name was associated was *Brown v. Board of Education*, he would still be remembered as one of the most influential chief justices in American legal history. But *Brown* was just the beginning of 15 years of landmark decisions. In the late 1950s, in a series of cases involving civil liberties of Communists, the Warren Court restricted the power of government to punish political dissenters. In the late 1950s and in the 1960s, the Court struck down censorship statutes banning pornography and made it more difficult for public officials to bring libel suits against media critics. In a series of decisions, starting with *Baker v. Carr* (1962) and concluding with *Reynolds v. Sims* (1964), the Court ordered that American electoral districts from the state to the federal levels be reapportioned according to the principle of equal legislative representation for equal numbers of people (more popularly known as "one man, one vote"). This overturned the excessive power that sparsely populated (and usually conservative) rural districts had long exercised in American politics.

In the 1960s the Court also rendered decisions in a series of cases involving the rights to due process for criminal defendants, excluding the use of improperly seized evidence in criminal trials and guaranteeing the right of indigents to an attorney in felony trials. Most famously, in *Miranda v. Arizona* (1966), the justices excluded the use of improperly obtained confessions from criminal trials.

Griswold v. Connecticut (1965) was an exceptionally important decision, although its full ramifications became clear only after Warren left the Court. The decision struck down a ban in the state of Connecticut on the dissemination of information about contraception. By this point the widespread availability of birth control pills had made the Connecticut statute seem like a relic of Victorian prudery (Justice Potter Stewart called it an "uncommonly silly law"). The real significance of the case lay in the Court's reasoning that the law was unconstitutional because it interfered with the "right to privacy"—a right nowhere mentioned in the Constitution, but that a majority of the justices now felt was "implied." This expansive definition of rights, which would survive Earl Warren's retirement as chief justice in 1969, lay at the base of the Court's ruling in *Roe v. Wade* (1973) which overturned state laws banning abortion.

Many of the Court's decisions involved it in controversial social issues. The Warren Court energized both the Left, in support, and the Right, in opposition. Liberals celebrated the Supreme Court's attempts to remedy injustice through "judicial activism"; conservatives, who had previously looked to the courts as a reliable bastion against liberal innovations in public policy, now condemned the Supreme Court for exercising "judicial tyranny." One of the legacies of the Warren Court was that future nominees for the bench would receive a thorough ideological scrutiny from liberal and conservative advocacy groups, and from Congress, unlike anything that had prevailed in the past.

The United States, as observers since the time of de Tocqueville have noted, is a society of joiners. Throughout the nineteenth and into the early twentieth century, Americans banded together around issues of moral and political reform, usually defined as doing away with one or another social evil, from the abolition of slavery to the abolition of saloons. That tradition seemed to languish in mid-twentieth century America. With the exception of the NAACP, with nearly 400,000 members in 1960, advocacy groups associated with liberal causes could count on, at most, a few tens of thousands of members: in 1960, for example, the American Civil Liberties Union (ACLU) had 52,000 members, the Committee for a Sane Nuclear Policy (SANE) fewer than 25,000, ADA about 20,000, the Sierra Club just over 16,000. [In contrast, in 1919, out of a much smaller population, the National American Women's Suffrage Association (NAWSA) counted over 2 million loosely affiliated members.[48]]

McCarthyism was among the reasons for this relatively low membership in liberal groups; years of seeing people hauled before congressional investigating committees for having joined the wrong group or signed the wrong petition certainly did not encourage political participation that extended beyond the anonymity of the voting booth. But the low enrollments were also the product of a lack of interest on the part of the advocacy groups themselves in expanding membership. For the most part, these were not organizations of activists. Members paid their dues, and perhaps attended an annual banquet (or, in the case of the Sierra Club, a hike), but otherwise let the leaders of these highly centralized groups do the advocating. It was a style of political organizing that assumed that a word from a prominent insider to a legislator or reporter carried more weight than any number of mass, public expressions of dissent or support. And for that, these groups didn't need a large or particularly active membership.[49]

But that would soon change, largely as a result of the influence of the civil rights movement, with its emphasis on local organizing and direct action. In the early 1960s, civil rights support activities gave large numbers of northern white liberals a crash course in the dynamics of mass organization. Consider the case of the ACLU. From the sit-ins in the spring of 1960 and on through the decade, the ACLU dispatched attorneys and raised funds to defend people arrested in civil rights protests. The ACLU also greatly expanded its notion of what constituted "civil liberties"—defining the protection of free speech and free association to include such new concerns as draft resistance, prisoners' rights, and reproductive rights. In line with its new activist policies, the organization actively recruited new members and opened new offices. By 1965 it was up to 80,000 members; by 1970, over 100,000. It also became a truly national organization in the same period, expanding from 7 state affiliates in 1960 to more than 40 a decade later.[50]

The Sierra Club went through a similar transition, growing to 29,000 members in 1965, and to over 100,000 in 1970. From its traditional base in California, it grew into a national movement and one that, notwithstanding battles between traditionalists and activists in its leadership, was far more combative vis à vis both industry and government than it had been in its early days. Increasingly, its focus was on fighting polluters, not simply on preserving wilderness. In addition to its handsome calendars and glossy picture books, the club was now issuing paperbacks with titles like *Ecotactics: The Sierra Club Handbook for Environmental Activists*.[51] Other long-established environmental groups like the National Audubon Society and the Wilderness Society would follow the Sierra Club's example in embracing an activist style and strategy. And across the country, local advocacy groups, focused on issues ranging from industrial pollution to nuclear safety sprang up—particularly after 1969 when a disastrous oil spill caused by offshore drilling operations polluted the beaches of prosperous communities in California like Santa Barbara.[52]

New departures in liberal activism were not confined to the white middle class. In the rich farming region of California's San Joaquin Valley, a group of activists, most of them Mexican American, created a labor movement dedicated to improving the lives of some of the most exploited workers in the land. Migrant farmworkers typically earned no more than the minimum wage and endured painful and often dangerous working conditions to plant and harvest the fruits and vegetables Americans consumed daily. Many workers spent their days bent over at the waist because employers furnished them only with short hoes; laborers risked their health picking crops sprayed with powerful disinfectants. Unprotected by federal or state labor laws and ignored by politicians, the farmworkers needed to find a way to wake up the nation.

In 1962 Cesar Chavez, a veteran community activist who had been a migrant laborer himself, spearheaded formation of the first union of farmworkers established since the Great Depression—and the only one ever controlled by the Mexican Americans who made up the majority of California field laborers. In 1965 the United Farm Workers threw its small membership into a

Cesar Chavez, leader of the United Farm Workers, during a rally to support the grape strike and boycott, 1965. Source: *George Meany Memorial Archives*

strike against the grape growers of the San Joaquin Valley. Rapidly, the work stoppage mushroomed into a peaceful uprising by an ethnic group the Anglo majority had long disparaged. In mass demonstrations, including a 300-mile march to the state capital, union workers held aloft banners emblazoned with a black Aztec eagle on a bright-red background and others adorned with the image of Our Lady of Guadalupe, the patron saint of Mexico. Chavez called the movement "both a religious pilgrimage and a plea for social change," and, throughout the Southwest, "La Causa" sparked a political awakening among Mexican Americans who had been relatively quiescent before.[53]

But Chavez and his fellow organizers knew that only massive pressure would force the growers to abandon the use of nonunion workers. So the United Farm Workers broadened their movement into a national civil rights cause. Beginning in 1966, the union drew on thousands of middle-class liberal allies, most of them Anglo, to mobilize a national boycott of table grapes. Prominent supporters like Senator Robert F. Kennedy, UAW president Walter Reuther, Catholic bishops, and actor Paul Newman helped publicize the boycott and raise funds. And the boycotters became a sophisticated team. "We got to the point where we could track a grape shipment from California to Appleton, Wisconsin, and have pickets waiting for them at the loading docks at two o'clock in the morning," recalled one organizer.[54] In 1970, after an arduous five years of struggle, most grape growers in the San Joaquin agreed to recognize the union.

Perhaps the most significant new social movement to emerge in the 1960s was the movement for the equality of women. Unlike the first women's rights movement, which had required nearly three-quarters of a century to achieve the right to vote, the revived movement for women's rights in the 1960s realized many of its goals with astonishing rapidity. Not that scoffers and opponents were absent; feminists were derided in many quarters in the 1960s, on the left as well as the right, as unattractive, extremists. Still, within a decade of what has been called the "second wave" of American feminism, public opinion polls showed that most women and many men embraced proposals that, when advanced in the 1960s, had been confined to the margins of American political and social discourse: equal pay for equal work, equal responsibility of men and women for housework and child rearing, an end to domestic violence, an end to the "glass ceiling" that kept women out of managerial positions, an end to sexual harassment in the workplace—even if those who came to espouse such views often prefaced their beliefs with the disclaimer, "I'm no women's libber, but. . . . "

Betty Friedan played a key role in the revival of the movement. A 1942 graduate of Smith College, Friedan retired from a decade-long career as a labor journalist to concentrate on raising her three children in the 1950s. But she kept up her writing on a freelance basis, mostly contributing to large-circulation women's magazines. At the end of the 1950s, on the occasion of the fifteenth reunion of her graduating class, she took a survey of her Smith classmates, measuring how they felt about their life's achievements. Nearly 90 percent of those who responded were housewives, and many confessed to feeling dissatisfied with their failure to make better use of their education. Few of them would have described themselves as feminists, but Friedan argued that their unhappiness stemmed from the unequal relations of men and women in American society. She began writing about these issues for women's magazines, and then in 1963 presented her conclusions in a book. *The Feminist Mystique* presented Friedan's life as representative of the unfair choices forced upon educated women in American society (to further her presentation of herself as a typical housewife, she downplayed her past history as a political radical).[55] Friedan argued that "a sexual counterrevolution" had taken place in the 1950s, "a moratorium during which many millions of women put themselves on ice and stopped growing." They accepted the notion—or "mystique"—that the true glory of womanhood lay in the role of wife and mother, and nowhere else. The personal dissatisfaction she found so prevalent among women her own age, and younger women as well, she called "the problem with no name," and argued its solution lay in allowing women the opportunity to find satisfying careers outside the home. The vision of the future that Friedan put forth in the conclusion of *The Feminine Mystique* was not, however, one of a victory of women over men in some eternal battle of the sexes. Rather, just as in that same year Martin Luther King would call on white and black Americans alike to join together in harmonious re-creation of the American dream, so Friedan imagined the mutually enhanced lives of men and women in a new world of genuine sexual equality:

> Who knows of the possibilities of love when men and women share not only children, home, and garden, not only the fulfillment of their biological roles, but the responsibilities and passions of the work that creates the human future and the full human knowledge of who they are?[56]

Friedan's feminist egalitarianism, like King's racial egalitarianism, struck a responsive chord among many Americans in the 1960s; *The Feminine Mystique* would go on to sell a million copies.

Thanks to the passage of the Civil Rights Act of 1964, sexual discrimination in employment was now against federal law. The newly created Equal

Betty Friedan, at center, and other founders of the National Organization for Women, 1966.
Source: *Schlesinger Library, Radcliffe College*

Employment Opportunity Commission (EEOC) was instructed to enforce the provisions against both sexual and racial discrimination. For a time, however, EEOC commissioners proved reluctant enforcers of the new rules as they applied to women. The notion of sexual discrimination in the workplace struck them, as it did most employers at the time, as trivial if not ludicrous. Were they supposed to be upset if a man couldn't find employment as a Playboy bunny? Newspapers began referring to the anti–sexual discrimination provisions of Title VII as the "bunny law."[57]

But the women who had been involved in the work of the President's Commission and various state commissions on the status of women were not amused. And they drew an important lesson from the recent history of the civil rights movement. Blacks had the NAACP and other groups to lobby for their interests; if American women expected the same respect and results, they clearly needed to develop equivalent organizational clout. Thus in 1966 a small group of female activists formed a new organization which, at Betty Friedan's suggestion, took the name National Organization for Women (NOW). Most of the women initially involved were established professionals and, in the beginning, NOW's preferred approach to women's rights issues was through a combination of litigation and high-level insider lobbying. But younger women, many of them veterans of the civil rights or campus radical movements, soon joined up and pushed the organization leftward in political tactics, style, and issues.[58]

During the 1960s, Richard Goodwin would write, "men and women [lived] as if their world was malleable to their grasp."[59] Goodwin's experience of the decade mirrored that of many of the "Reform Democrats" who came out of the 1950s. By decade's end, he had been both a liberal insider and a liberal outsider: a member of government and a member of a social movement outside of government. A speechwriter first for Kennedy and then for Johnson, he coined the phrase "Great Society" for which the Johnson administration would be most fondly remembered by subsequent generations of liberals. But in the later 1960s, Goodwin moved into opposition to the president he once served, joining the antiwar Democrats who sought to bring Johnson's political career to an end.

Liberals helped change America in the 1960s, and during those years enjoyed the heady feeling of living in a world "malleable to their grasp." But eras of reform and social change in American history are judged not simply by the achievements of their own time, but also by their political legacies. The legacy of Franklin Roosevelt's years in office included a newly powerful trade union movement, representing the interests of millions of members in the halls of legislative power as well as in the workplace.

The political legacy of Lyndon Johnson's years in office was more ambiguous. Liberalism, and with it, much of the Democratic Party, had been transformed by decade's end. Although unions remained a powerful force in the Democratic party (if less so every year in the workplace), they were no longer the source of the party's sense of its social mission. Liberals no longer shied away from the idea of crusades and mass movements, as they had in the late 1940s and early 1950s. Nor was there any shortage of new movements with which they could ally themselves: powerful organizations promoting civil rights, civil liberties, environmentalism, and feminism, and a host of other worthy causes competed for their attention. If the stereotype of the typical liberal in the 1950s had been one of a tweedy, middle-aged male intellectual poring over the latest issue of *The New Republic* in a university library, by the late 1960s it had been replaced by that of an youthful and energetic man or woman, knocking on doors or buttonholing strangers on a street corner to collect signatures on a petition for the burning liberal cause of the moment. The egghead was dead; the activist triumphant.

Michael Harrington was one of the few activist intellectuals of the 1960s who sought to link the institutional legacies of the New Deal with the new social movements emerging in the era of the Great Society. He welcomed the advent of what he called the "conscience constituency" of middle-class liberal activists. But he did not think that the new liberals could change America by themselves. The "daily concerns of working people and the poor," he wrote in the waning days of the Johnson administration, "must merge with the values of the college educated and the religiously inspired in a new majority party."[60]

That merger Harrington called for never took place. To a large extent, it was never attempted, save briefly in such campaigns as the one in support of California farmworkers. The new liberalism remained a movement of, by, and for the educated middle classes. The consequences of that fact, for the future of the Great Society and for the future of American politics, would be profound. Within a very few years, the world would seem a much less "malleable" place to American liberals.

CHAPTER 7

1965

MR. JOHNSON IS ALMOST UNIVERSALLY LIKED. . . .
—*Editorial in* The Nation, *January 11, 1965*[1]

Presiding over the annual tree-lighting ceremony at the White House shortly before Christmas 1964, Lyndon Johnson was in a triumphant mood. "These are the most hopeful times," he proclaimed with characteristic expansiveness, "since Christ was born in Bethlehem." Veteran political reporter Kenneth Crawford tweaked the president a few weeks later in *Newsweek* for his fondness for hyperbole, but conceded there was ample cause for his optimism. Lyndon Johnson, Crawford wrote, was leader of "the most powerful, most prosperous, and most lavishly endowed nation not only of these times but of any times."[2]

A month earlier Johnson had been elected to the presidency by the largest plurality the American electorate had ever given any candidate for the White House. Johnson was given to insecurity, and in the first months after inheriting his office from Kennedy, he later confessed, he felt "illegitimate, a naked man with no presidential covering, a pretender to the throne, an illegal usurper."[3] But after November 1964 his power was, in his own eyes, complete and legitimate; no longer need he sustain even the rhetorical pretense ("Let us continue") of merely being the humble successor to his martyred predecessor.

The nation that President Johnson had been chosen to lead was itself at a peak of self-confidence. When asked if they were "satisfied or dissatisfied with [their] family income," 64 percent of white respondents answered in the affirmative (compared, however, to only 30 percent of nonwhites).[4] It seemed, at least to the white majority, that the country had arrived at a permanent plateau of prosperity. Since 1961 the volume of economic activity in the United States had increased by $100 billion, or over 25 percent. In May 1965 the United States would break the peacetime record for a business upswing. By year's end, the unemployment rate would drop below 4 percent, with no significant inflationary pressures yet visible on the economic horizon.[5]

Americans also felt confident about the role their nation played in the world. The United States, in the popular saying, had "never lost a war" (the ambiguous outcome of the war in Korea, a decade earlier, was generally passed over in silence). In the aftermath of the Cuban missile crisis, when Khrushchev, not Kennedy, had been the first to blink at the prospect of nuclear apocalypse, earlier fears that the United States had fallen behind its Communist rival in military strength had faded away. In 1965 Johnson was commander-in-chief of armed forces that, in destructive power if not sheer numbers, dwarfed those of the Soviet Union, or for that matter, any force ever before assembled on the globe. Over 800 intercontinental ballistic missiles, 31 Polaris submarines, and nearly 1000 strategic bombers were available to deliver America's nuclear arsenal in case of an all-out war. Fifteen attack carriers, and over 900 other U.S. naval vessels ceaselessly crisscrossed the world's oceans. Nearly a million American soldiers and 200,000 Marines patrolled the front lines of potential battlegrounds from Germany to Korea (including about 23,000 "military advisers" in South Vietnam), or were held in reserve for rapid deployment from bases in the United States and its allies.[6] In the heavens as on earth, American will power and technology were prevailing. Beginning with astronaut John Glenn's orbital flight in February 1962, the United States had matched Soviet space achievements step by step.

Lyndon Johnson, Hubert Humphrey, and their families celebrate their inauguration, January 20, 1965. Source: *George Meany Memorial Archives*

The Mercury space program, designed to put Americans in space, concluded after six successful launches; in the spring of 1965 the Gemini program began, featuring flights of longer duration, space walks, and docking maneuvers in space. Project Apollo, manned exploration of the moon, was soon to follow. The United States was well on its way to achieving Kennedy's promise of placing an American on the moon by the end of the decade.

The world was still seen as a dangerous place, full of snares for the unwary. But surely America's leaders, tested in decades of crisis and confrontation, could be relied upon to steer a steady course both abroad and at home. In a Gallup poll taken in February 1965, 64 percent of respondents agreed with the statement that this would prove a year when "America will increase her world power."[7] Johnson campaigned in 1964 as the candidate of national prosperity and international peace, and American voters had taken him at his word on both counts. Walter Lippmann, the dean of Washington newspaper columnists, and a frequent critic of the government's Cold War policies, wrote on the occasion of Johnson's inaugural in January that, for the first time since the start of the Second World War, the United States had a president whose attention was "not fixed upon the danger abroad, but on the problems and prospects at home."[8]

Winter: Vietnam

Meanwhile, Americans continued to die in Vietnam. Five days before Lyndon Johnson's election victory, five Americans were killed and six B-57 bombers were destroyed in a Viet Cong mortar attack on Bienhoa Air Base, 20 miles northeast of Saigon. On the day before Christmas, two Americans were killed and 37 wounded when the Viet Cong dynamited a U.S. officers' billet in Saigon itself. By the end of 1964, 267 Americans had been killed in action in South Vietnam, well over half of them in the 13 months since Johnson took office.

Throughout the fall, Johnson pondered his options in Vietnam. The consensus among his advisers was that once the election was safely decided, the United States would need to act decisively to save the faltering Saigon regime from collapsing to the Communist onslaught. In early September Assistant Secretary of Defense John McNaughton sent a memorandum to his boss, Robert McNamara, outlining a "scenario" for future U.S. actions in Vietnam. "[N]ew initiatives" should include a series of provocative actions against North Vietnam similar to those leading up to the Gulf of Tonkin incident. Assuming the North Vietnamese responded with new attacks of their own, the results would "provide good grounds for us to escalate if we wish" with a bombing campaign.[9]

In the Gulf of Tonkin incident, where no American lives had been lost, Johnson had hastily ordered retaliatory strikes. But as 1964 drew to a close, with more Americans dying every day in the war, the president hesitated on the brink of decisive action. When Maxwell Taylor, the American ambassador to South Vietnam, urged Johnson to hit back at North Vietnam for the bombing of the officers' billet in Saigon, he refused. "Every time I get a military recommendation," the president complained in a cable to Taylor, "it seems to me that it calls for a large-scale bombing. I have never felt this war would be won from the air."[10]

The one usually reliable dissenter from the pro-escalation consensus in Johnson's inner circle had been Undersecretary of State George Ball. Ball drafted a memorandum in October challenging the basic assumptions of American policy. American international credibility would suffer more for the irresponsible escalation of the war than from possible Communist gains in Southeast Asia. If the United States upped the ante in Vietnam, the Communists could respond by increasing their own attacks, which would require a still greater American commitment, with no end in sight. "Once on the tiger's back," Ball prophesied famously, "we cannot be sure of picking the place to dismount."[11]

Despite Ball's prophecy, and Johnson's end-of-the-year misgivings, the momentum for launching an air war against North Vietnam was proving irresistible in Washington. On January 14, Ambassador Taylor was instructed by the White House to be on the alert for any plausible excuse for the United States to step up military activity: "immediately following the occurrence of a spectacular enemy action," he should "propose to us what reprisal action you considered desirable."[12] The necessary "spectacle" came along three weeks later at Pleiku, the site of a U.S. air base in the central highlands of South Vietnam, its airstrip crowded with military planes and helicopters. At 2 A.M. on February 7, the airstrip and a barracks a few miles away were hit simultaneously by Viet Cong mortar and ground attacks. In 15 minutes, eight Americans were killed, and more than a hundred wounded. "I've had enough of this," Johnson declared in a meeting of his National Security Council.

Time was running out for any option short of a vastly expanded war. But even at this late hour, Johnson was hearing from other voices, urging caution. In a memo to the President in mid-February, Vice President Hubert Humphrey pointed out that most opposition to the war was coming from within the ranks of the Democratic Party, that there was no widespread public support for escalating the war, and that a wider war would undercut the chances for achieving the domestic goals of the Great Society. Johnson's landslide victory the previous November had given him the political capital he needed to get out of Vietnam. "Politically, it is always hard to cut losses," Humphrey wrote to his boss. "But the Johnson Administration is in a stronger position to do so than any Administration in this century. 1965 is the year of minimum political risk for the Johnson Administration. Indeed it is the first year when we can face the Vietnam problem without being preoccupied with the political repercussions from the Republican right." Johnson turned a deaf ear to Humphrey's plea; in fact, it would be another year before he would allow the Vice President to take part in deliberations over policy in Vietnam.[13]

A few hours later, fighter-bombers from the U.S. aircraft carriers *Ranger*, *Coral Sea*, and *Hancock*, stationed in the South China Sea, were attacking military bases in North Vietnam. Unlike the Gulf of Tonkin incident, this was not going to be just a tit-for-tat reprisal. On February 13, the president authorized the start of Operation Rolling Thunder, a sustained bombing campaign of North Vietnam that was to last for almost three years. Later President Richard Nixon would resume where Johnson had left off; before the Vietnam War ended, the United States would drop triple the amount of bombs on North Vietnam than were dropped by all sides in Europe, Asia, and Africa in the Second World War.[14]

"Wars generate their own momentum," former defense secretary McNamara would reflect with hindsight, "and follow the law of unanticipated consequences."[15] As the winter of 1965 turned to spring and then summer, events in Vietnam bore out the wisdom of McNamara's maxim. At the start of the New Year, there may still have been time to turn back from a major war in Vietnam, but that time was fast running out. Johnson had been skeptical about the effects of bombing North Vietnam as he weighed his options in 1964. At best, he had hoped that attacking North Vietnam would give South Vietnamese forces a "breathing spell." But by the spring of 1965 he had persuaded himself that those attacks would be the solution to the war. He predicted to one associate in March that the bombing would force the North Vietnamese to settle the conflict within a year to 18 months.[16] Bombing appealed to Johnson as a factor he could control, unlike, say, the battle-readiness of ARVN troops, or the stability of the coup-prone South Vietnamese government. He devoted many hours to fine-tuning the bombing campaign, deciding just which targets should be hit, how hard, and how often.

Escalation in the air was followed soon after by escalation on the ground. By the beginning of March Johnson agreed to the request from General William Westmoreland, commander of American forces in South Vietnam, for the dispatch of two battalions of U.S. Marines to protect the air base at Da Nang. On March 8, at 9:03 in the morning Vietnamese time, the Ninth Marine Expeditionary Brigade began wading ashore on the beaches north of Da Nang. Pentagon spokesman declared that the marines had been sent to South Vietnam with a strictly "limited mission" to relieve government forces guarding American air bases, thus allowing the South Vietnamese to carry the fight to the enemy.

Such talk may have briefly reassured anxious American civilians, but it was not taken seriously by anyone who knew President Johnson's thinking on the war. The previous December, when Johnson expressed doubts over the efficacy of air strikes, he was already leaning toward committing U.S. ground forces to combat. "It seems to me," he told Ambassador Taylor, that what was needed was "a larger and stronger use of rangers and special forces and marines, or other, appropriate military strength on the ground and on the scene. . . . Any recommendation that you or General Westmoreland take in this sense will have immediate attention from me, although I know that it may involve the acceptance of larger American sacrifices."[17]

Five days after the marines landed at Da Nang, General Westmoreland asked for an additional 40,000 troops. Johnson, as he had earlier signaled, was eager to fulfill such requests. By early April, Johnson had quietly authorized use of the marines for combat patrols. In late June Westmoreland received an open-ended authorization to commit American forces to battle whenever he deemed it necessary.

The days of Green Beret–style "counterinsurgency" were clearly waning, as main line army and marine combat units arrived in force, with their full accoutrement of tanks, trucks, helicopters, and heavy weapons. But just how these forces were going to be used remained uncertain at first. It was mid-1965 before military strategists developed the plan for fighting the ground war that became known as "search and destroy."

In past wars, American troops had always seized territory and then held it. In this war, rather than attempting to secure particular areas of countryside, General Westmoreland kept his troops continually on the move, seeking out the Viet Cong in South Vietnam's forests, jungles, and mountain ranges. Sometimes intelligence reports pinpointed the exact location of an enemy unit. Then the fighter-bombers, helicopters gunships, and the big B-52s from Guam or Thailand could pile on the enemy with bombs, rockets, and napalm, followed by ground troops delivered by helicopter to landing zones (LZs) nearby. But more often, soldiers and marines had to pull on their packs and "hump the boonies," seeking out contact with the enemy in the back country. That was the "searching" part of search-and-destroy. When contact was made, the troops could call in artillery, napalm strikes, and helicopter gunships. Afterward, the enemy bodies would be counted up and compared to American casualties; if there were many of the former and few of the latter, military dispatches would boast of a favorable "kill ratio," and another victory would be chalked up. Killing the enemy was not the means to tactical or strategic gain such as taking back this or that village or hilltop from the enemy. Killing the enemy was an end in itself in a war of attrition.[18]

Vietnam was a war fought by young men. The average American infantryman in Vietnam was just 19 years old (some were as young as 17), compared to an average age of 26 for his Second World War counterpart. The "baby boom" provided an abundant pool of new 18-year-olds to meet the stepped-up monthly draft calls. And by relying on the younger draftees,

President Johnson could avoid calling up either the National Guard or military reserve units, potentially controversial steps that could raise further questions about the necessity of the war.[19]

Search-and-destroy operations left many American soldiers and marines—the "grunts" as they called themselves—feeling that their role in the war had been reduced to the unheroic one of serving as bait for enemy attack. In a day of patrolling, an American unit might never actually sight an enemy soldier, and yet still suffer casualties from booby traps and snipers. Even if they found and engaged the enemy, they would have nothing to show at the end of the day except, perhaps, a favorable "kill ratio"—meaning that more Viet Cong and North Vietnamese were killed than Americans. When a firefight was over, the grunts returned to their base camps, and there was nothing to prevent the remaining enemy soldiers from moving right back up the mountain or into the jungle abandoned by the Americans.

In March 1965, as Johnson was taking the decisive steps to escalate the war in Vietnam, Assistant Secretary of Defense John McNaughton, the principal civilian war planner in the Defense Department, set down a list of "U.S. aims" to guide fellow policymakers in Washington. It is a revealing document, both for the reliance on statistical format favored by the "the best and the brightest" and because of the relative weights assigned to each war aim. The reason the United States had to stay the course in Vietnam, McNaughton argued was:

70%—To avoid a humiliating U.S. defeat (to our reputation as guarantor)
20%—To keep SVN [South Vietnam] . . . from Chinese hands.
10%—To permit the people of SVN to enjoy a better freer way of life.[20]

The fate of South Vietnam, in other words, was unimportant in and of itself, except as the forum in which the United States would establish its credibility in international affairs, its "reputation as guarantor." How great a price the United States was prepared to pay to that end would become the most important question in American politics for the remainder of the decade.

Spring: Selma

On the afternoon of March 7, the day before the marines waded ashore at Da Nang, another force was gathering for a battle of another sort halfway around the world in Selma, Alabama. Six hundred civil rights demonstrators, most of them local black citizens, assembled at Selma's Brown Chapel African Methodist-Episcopal Church. Late that afternoon they set out, arrayed in a long line two by two, following SCLC organizer Hosea Williams and SNCC's

Demonstration at Selma, March 1965. Source: *Corbis/Flip Schulke*

national chairman, John Lewis, down Selma's main street to the Edmund Pettus Bridge, which spans the Alabama River. Their intention was to march across the bridge and from there on to the state capitol of Montgomery, 50 miles away. In Montgomery, they intended to protest the denial of voting rights to blacks in the South, as well as the violence that had been directed against civil rights demonstrators in Alabama since the start of SCLC's voting rights campaign in January.

Across the Edmund Pettus bridge, the would-be marchers were met by a force of Alabama state troopers, backed up by Dallas County Sheriff Jim Clark's mounted posse. Ordered to disperse, they silently held their ground, some kneeling to pray. Scarcely a minute after the order had been given, a phalanx of club-swinging and yelling troopers and posse members slammed into the column. As tear gas billowed across the scene, newspaper photographers and television news cameramen recorded the ensuing chaos. Men, women, and children were beaten to the ground with billy clubs, cattle prods, and bull whips; one posseman beat retreating marchers with a rubber hose wrapped with barbed wire. Some marchers were ridden down by horses; others jumped or were pushed from the bridge to the water below. John Lewis was struck on the side of the head with a billy club; he remembered thinking as he fell to the ground, "People are going to die here. I'm going to die here." Rebel yells could be heard over the screams of the beaten, as well as the voice of Sheriff Clark yelling "Get those god-damned niggers!"[21] Dozens of marchers, including Lewis, required hospitalization for concussions, lacerations, and broken bones. In the spring of 1965 the voting rights struggle in Selma provided the nation a tableau of violent conflict and redemptive suffering that would move President Johnson to compare its historical significance to the battles of Lexington and Concord.

Southern blacks had been kept from the voting booth since the late nineteenth century through a combination of legal subterfuge and open terror. In Alabama in 1965, fewer than one in five eligible blacks were registered to vote. In Dallas County, Alabama, where Selma was the county seat, the figures were even more dismal: of the 15,000 blacks of voting age (potentially half the county's total electorate), just over 300 were registered to vote.[22]

In his State of the Union address in January, Johnson had called on the South to eliminate obstacles to black voting. However, he had no immediate plans to seek federal legislation guaranteeing voting rights. He had devoted the full force of his legendary political skills and energy to secure passage of the Civil Rights Act in 1964. But he feared that other legislative priorities, like Medicare and Medicaid, would be damaged by a divisive debate over a voting rights bill in 1965. According to Johnson's own political calculations, would-be black voters in the South were just going to have to wait—perhaps months, perhaps a year or longer—to gain access to the ballot box. As late as mid-February, the Justice Department's preferred remedy for voting rights abuses was to seek a constitutional amendment—a process requiring the ratification of two-thirds of the states as well as a two-thirds majority in both houses of Congress, something that could have taken years to achieve.[23]

Martin Luther King, Jr., and other senior civil rights leaders were just as much political realists as Lyndon Johnson. They wanted Johnson to win a decisive victory over Barry Goldwater in the presidential election (since Goldwater had been one of only eight Republican senators to vote against the 1964 Civil Rights Act). The major civil rights organizations maintained an informal moratorium on demonstrations in the fall of 1964 to avoid any incident that might embarrass the president.

But civil rights leaders had their own priorities independent of Johnson's and made their own calculations. And in 1965, they felt the time for caution was over. King and other movement leaders needed to create the circumstances that would allow Johnson to transform his rhetorical commitment to their cause into legislative deeds. As they had learned in earlier civil rights campaigns, that meant creating a crisis that would dramatize the issue for a national audience.

Activists from the Student Non-Violent Coordinating Committee had been trying to register voters in the city of Selma for several years, but despite mass arrests of would-be registrants, SNCC's efforts had gained little attention. Selma's prosperous years had come and gone a century earlier, when it had been an important cotton and slave trading center. Now, its 30,000 black and white residents lived in a political and economic backwater that one civil rights activist described as looking as if "a movie producer had re-constructed a pre–Civil War Southern town," complete with muddy streets and decaying buildings.[24] Selma was significant only because the civil rights movement decided to make it so. As Martin Luther King explained when the SCLC launched its own voter registration campaign in early January 1965, the city had been chosen because it was "a symbol of bitter-end resistance to the civil rights movement in the Deep South."[25]

The personification of that bitter-end resistance was Sheriff Jim Clark: short-tempered, profane, and swaggering, he was every northern liberal's worst nightmare of southern law enforcement. Selma's more moderately in-clined police chief, Wilson Baker, who hoped to contain the protests with-out violence, referred to the members of Clark's posse as "Ku-Klux-Klan type."[26] Not even the most optimistic of SCLC's strategists believed that they would be able to persuade someone like Sheriff Clark of the righteousness of their cause. But if nonviolent *persuasion* was a lost cause in Selma, nonvio-lent *provocation* had real potential for a movement heavily dependent on me-dia coverage to get its message out to a wider audience. The denial of voting rights was undramatic; no one would pay attention to pictures of people *not* voting. When Sheriff Clark and his deputies laid into the ranks of would-be voters with nightsticks and cattle prods, they turned abstract constitutional injustice into easily grasped moral outrage.[27]

On the evening of January 2, SCLC opened its campaign in Selma with a mass rally at Brown Chapel. King was there to inspire the audience, and then flew off to other speaking engagements. He returned on January 18 to lead the first march of voting rights supporters to the Dallas County Court-house in downtown Selma. That day's march passed peacefully. But the next day, as 50 would-be registrants again lined up outside the courthouse, Sher-iff Clark lost his cool—just as SCLC strategists had hoped he would. He roughly arrested one of the local protest leaders, Mrs. Amelia Boynton, while photographers recorded the scene for the national press. In the weeks that followed, the volatile Clark repeatedly managed to get his face on the front page of northern newspapers and on evening television broadcasts, as he beat protesters into submission with his nightstick and punched black ministers in the face. King himself was arrested in a mass demonstration on Monday, February 1; by the end of the week when he was bailed out, more than 3000 demonstrators were being held in jails in Dallas County.[28]

On February 18, the violence escalated in neighboring Lowndes County, where SNCC and SCLC were also conducting protests, as a young black man named Jimmie Lee Jackson was mortally wounded by a state trooper for try-ing to shield his mother from being beaten at a voting rights rally. SCLC strategists decided, in response, to escalate their own campaign by marching from Selma to Montgomery. They sought to lay responsibility for the violence in Dallas and Lowndes counties at the doorstep of Alabama governor George Wallace.

Sheriff Clark and his troopers easily won the resulting battle of "Bloody Sunday," March 7, but, in doing so, lost the war. ABC News interrupted the network's Sunday night movie, the premiere showing on television of *Judgement at Nuremburg* (a movie about bringing to justice the Nazis guilty of war crimes in World War II), to show 15 minutes of raw and dramatic footage from the attack on the Edmund Pettus Bridge. In the days that followed, fresh volunteers poured into Selma to join the struggle. A new march, this time led by Martin Luther King, headed down to cross the now-famous bridge over the Alabama River on March 9; but King turned the marchers around when they reached it, unwilling to defy a federal court order temporarily banning the attempt. One of the newly arrived volunteers who marched that day was a white Unitarian minister from Boston named James Reeb. That evening, after eating a meal in a black restaurant in Selma, he and two other white ministers were set upon by four local whites, who called out at them "Hey, you niggers!" Reeb was struck in the back of the head with a wooden club, and he fell senseless to the ground. He died the next day of his injuries. (His accused assailant was acquitted by an all-white jury nine months later.)

This new martyrdom further inflamed northern opinion. As the president sent flowers to Reeb's widow and four children, picketers marched outside the White House and in dozens of northern cities demanding federal action. On the floor of Congress, speakers compared Alabama governor George Wallace to Hitler, and Sheriff Clark's posse to Nazi storm troopers. President Johnson met with Wallace in the White House on March 13, urging the Alabama governor to protect the civil rights protesters from further attack. Johnson pleaded with Wallace to stop "looking back to 1865." And then, in his thickest southern accent and with calculated eloquence, the president demanded of the governor:

> What do you want left after you when you die? Do you want a Great . . . Big . . . Marble monument that reads, "George Wallace—He Built"? . . . Or do you want a little piece of scrawny pine board lying across that harsh, caliche soil, that reads, "George Wallace—He Hated"?

Three hours later, having been given the full Johnson treatment, an unusually subdued Wallace confided to an aide, "Hell, if I'd stayed there much longer, he'd have had me coming out for civil rights."[29]

On the evening of March 15, Johnson went on television to address the nation. To an audience estimated at 70 million, the president declared that the events in Selma were not a "Negro problem" or even a "southern problem" but an "American problem." It was "deadly wrong," he said, for "any of your fellow Americans" to be denied the right to vote. He announced his intention to bring a voting rights bill to Congress in the next 48 hours. Martin Luther King, who was in Selma watching the speech on television in the home of a movement sympathizer, wept when he heard Johnson's concluding line, with its deliberate echo of the civil rights movement's anthem, "And . . . we . . . shall . . . overcome."[30]

With legal obstacles swept aside, and with President Johnson federalizing the Alabama National Guard to provide protection from further attack, SCLC again prepared to march on Montgomery. On Sunday, March 21, King led 3000 marchers across the Edmund Pettus Bridge. By prearrangement with the authorities, 300 marchers made the entire 54-mile march through Lowndes County to Montgomery County, their numbers swelled upon arrival in Montgomery by thousands of other supporters.

The SCLC rally in Montgomery on March 25 was, in many ways, the culmination of the civil rights movement. Ten years earlier, Montgomery had witnessed the birth of the movement when Rosa Parks refused to give up her seat on one of the city buses. Martin Luther King had risen to national leadership as a result of the ensuing bus boycott. When the movement set out, 10 years earlier, few Americans outside the black community were concerned with the century-long denial of equal rights to black citizens. But by the spring of 1965 Gallup polls showed that 52 percent of American identified civil rights as the "most important problem" confronting the nation, and an astonishing 75 percent of respondents favored federal voting rights legislation.[31]

Montgomery had served as the Confederacy's first capital in 1861. The Confederate battle flag was displayed more prominently in the city than the American flag; even the Alabama national guardsmen who were there to protect the marchers wore metallic badges on their uniforms displaying the emblem of the southern rebellion.[32]

Not since Reconstruction a century earlier had so many northern civilians, white and black, set off as volunteers in the effort to remake southern society. They came by car and plane to Montgomery, to join with thousands of black Alabamians. Twenty-five thousand people in all marched through Montgomery that day, passing Martin Luther King's old church on Dexter Avenue en route. "Keep your eyes on the prize, hold on," they sang as they marched. Montgomery's black citizens lined the streets and cheered or joined the march themselves; Montgomery's white citizens were nowhere to be seen.

The marchers gathered for their rally before the steps of the state capitol building, the same site where just over two years earlier Governor Wallace, in his inaugural address, had vowed "Segregation now! Segregation tomorrow! Segregation forever!"[33] But on this day in Montgomery Wallace was nowhere to be seen; he peeped out at the crowd from behind closed shades in his office. This was Martin Luther King's day, and in his speech to the gathered throng, he predicted that the sacrifices of civil rights activists would lead the nation to redemption, and in the not so distant future. "How long?" he asked. "Not long. Because the arm of the moral universe is long, but it bends towards justice." And then he ended with the words of the Civil War anthem, The Battle Hymn of the Republic:

> How long? Not long, because mine eyes have seen the glory of the coming of the Lord, trampling out the vintage where the grapes of wrath are stored. He has loosed the faithful lighting of his terrible swift sword. His truth is marching on. Glory hallelujah! *Glory hallelujah!*[34]

Michael Harrington, author of *The Other America,* was one of the northerners who had traveled to Montgomery for the rally. He reported afterwards how stirring it had felt to stand before the capitol building, where the Confederate stars and bars flapped in the breeze, while the U.S. flag was nowhere to be seen. When the crowd began to sing "The Star Spangled Banner," he said, it sounded "like a revolutionary anthem."[35]

Congressional passage of the Voting Rights Act was now a certainty, but not before its opponents claimed one more victim. Mrs. Viola Liuzzo, a Detroit housewife, had been helping to shuttle demonstrators back to Selma from Montgomery after the rally, when she was killed by Klansmen who fired into her car on Highway 80. On August 6, President Johnson signed the Voting Rights Act into law in the room adjoining the Senate chamber where President Lincoln had signed the Emancipation Proclamation in 1863. Within days, the first of the South's 2.5 million previously disenfranchised eligible blacks were lining up to register to vote under the watchful eyes of federal officials at county courthouses in Alabama and five other states in the Deep South. In two months the number of black voters in Dallas County, Alabama, jumped from barely 300 to nearly 7000. By the next presidential election, over half of Alabama blacks were on the voting lists.[36]

Summer: Watts

Johnson understood that there were political risks involved in linking his administration and the Democratic Party to the cause of equal rights for black Americans. After signing the civil rights act of 1964, he reportedly remarked to aide Bill Moyers that he had just "delivered the South to the Republican Party for a long time to come."[37] And, in the election that followed, he did lose five previously loyal southern states to the Republicans. There had also been glimmers of what was coming to be called in the north "white backlash," in the votes that Governor George Wallace attracted in the Democratic presidential primaries in states like Wisconsin and Indiana. But in the end those voters, most of them working-class whites and longtime Democrats, had cast their ballots for Johnson rather than Goldwater in November, and the Democrats had strengthened, not weakened their hold on Congress. Not a single congressman who had voted in favor of the civil rights bill was defeated in his bid for reelection; on the other hand, half of the 22 northern Congressmen who voted against it had gone down to defeat in November 1964.[38] So there was hope as well as risk in the Democratic Party's new commitment to securing civil rights for southern blacks. *If* large numbers of blacks were enabled to vote in the South, and *if* the Democrats could retain their support among whites in the rest of the country (as they had in 1964), and *if* a certain percentage of southern whites (particularly those in lower income groups) could be persuaded that they had interests in common with newly enfranchised southern blacks, then the result would be a strengthened Democratic majority coalition. When Michael Harrington returned from Montgomery in March, he predicted that the coalition of civil rights supporters, clergy of all religions, liberals, and trade unionists who had assembled there to challenge white supremacy represented "a new Populism," and "the human potential for a new American majority."[39]

It was a political gamble, but it seemed a reasonable one, until August 11, just five days after the signing of the Voting Rights Act, when rioting broke out in the black community of Watts in Los Angeles. Watts was a

LBJ engaged in one of his favorite activities—signing a bill passed by the Democratic Congress. He is handing a pen to Senator Paul Douglas (D-Ill.). Source: Chicago Historical Society

neighborhood of single-family detached houses that to many outsiders did not look like a "slum" at all. But it had all the problems of more congested urban neighborhoods, including poor schools, high unemployment, and a high crime rate that included a growing drug-abuse problem. When a white California highway patrol officer arrested a drunk black driver who resisted arrest, the incident sparked rumors in the black community that police had also, and without provocation, beaten a black taxi driver and a pregnant woman. Bands of teenagers, chanting "Burn, baby, burn!" began to throw stones at police, and at cars driven by whites. When the police failed to re-store order that night, looting and arson followed. There was an air of des-peration but also insurrectionary bravado in the disorders. "These fucking cops," one of the young rioters declared, "have been pushin' me 'round all my life. Kickin' my ass and things like that. Whitey ain't no good. He talked 'bout law and order, it's his law and his order, it ain't mine."[40] Five days later, when a force of 16,000 police, highway patrol officers, and National Guards-men had managed to bring the riot to an end, 34 people were dead, a thou-sand injured, and four thousand in jail. Property damage was estimated at $40 million, with over 250 buildings burned down.[41] *Time* magazine com-pared the scenes in Los Angeles streets that week to those in "embattled Saigon."[42] President Johnson was so appalled by the political implications of the rioting for his party's political future that, according to political aide Joseph Califano, "he refused to look at the cables from Los Angeles."[43]

Martin Luther King, Jr. was also horrified. He flew to Los Angeles soon after the rioting ended and walked through the smoldering ruins of Watts. Less than three months earlier he had marched in triumph through the streets of Montgomery. Now he found himself heckled by young black militants, who accused him of being a sell-out "Uncle Tom" for suggesting that they had anything to atone for in taking on the police in the streets of Watts. For the younger generation in the black community, Watts was something of which they were proud. As political scientist Edward Banfield noted a few years later with dismay, they regarded it as "a kind of black Bunker Hill."[44] As one young veteran of that summer's fighting in Watts proclaimed, "if I've got to die, I ain't dying in Vietnam, I'm going to die here."[45]

Fall: Liberty Island

The escalation of the war in Vietnam in the spring of 1965 and the outbreak of racial warfare in America's central cities in the summer, dimmed the prospects for President Johnson's Great Society but did not immediately halt the momentum for legislative reform. On a bright windy day in early Octo-ber in New York harbor, President Johnson stood before the Statue of Liberty and explained his reasons for signing the most significant immigration law to be passed since the 1920s. The act, Johnson declared, "repairs a deep and painful flaw in the fabric of American justice. It will make us truer to ourselves as a country and as a people."[46] Cheers rang out from an audience made up of powerful politicians as well as hundreds of ordinary New Yorkers, transported to Liberty Island for the day to symbolize and celebrate the city's ethnic potpourri.

The 1965 Immigration Act reversed a policy that intentionally discriminated against people who harked from anywhere in the world other than western and northern Europe. In the mid-1920s, Congress had established a quota system for prospective newcomers with the candid purpose of fixing the ethnic composition of the nation at its current percentages, lest white Protestants suffer what some alarmists were calling "race suicide." Among those applauding the passage of the discriminatory legislation was the Ku Klux Klan, which then boasted millions of members in the North and Midwest as well as in the South.

Under the 1924 quotas, a few nations—Germany, England, and Ireland in particular—could send generous numbers of immigrants, while only a trickle of people from eastern and southern Europe could enter. Asians were almost completely barred. Most members of Congress believed that racial and ethnic background was the best predictor of who would make a good citizen. Doctor Harry N. Laughlin, a prominent spokesman for immigration restriction, criticized Americans for being "so imbued with the idea of democracy . . . that we have left out of consideration the matter of blood or natural born hereditary and moral differences." No one who understood the value of "pedigreed plants and animals" would neglect the importance of the right sort of heredity in breeding future Americans.[47]

Emmanuel Celler, then a freshman congressman from a Brooklyn district full of immigrants and their offspring, found such reasoning repugnant. A Jewish graduate of Columbia Law School, Celler spoke out against theories of ethnic and racial supremacy, insisting that one's national origins had nothing to do with the making of a good American. Routinely reelected over the next 40 years, he kept fighting to repeal the quotas, but complained that his efforts "were about as useless as trying to make a tiger eat grass or a cow eat meat."[48]

Finally, in 1965, during his fifth decade as a congressman, the 75-year-old Celler was able to do something about it. As chair of the House Judiciary Committee in a congress dominated by liberal Democrats, Celler oversaw the drafting of the new law and helped win big margins for it in both houses.

Not by accident did Celler manage to achieve his decades-old goal in the same year that Congress passed the Voting Rights Act. The framers of the new act sought to extend the principles of equal rights to immigration policy. Henceforth, first preference in admitting new immigrants would be given to the immediate relatives of American citizens, without regard to race or ethnicity. Then foreigners who possessed desirable skills—professionals, artists, and scientists—moved to the front of the list. Celler's bill was not strictly egalitarian (poor and uneducated applicants without family ties lost out), but it did abolish the quota system with its implied hierarchy of racial and ethnic desirability. The entire Eastern Hemisphere—Europe, Africa, and Asia included—could now send 170,000 persons a year as immigrants, with no more than 20,000 coming from any single country. A qualified Nigerian was now, officially, just as welcome in the United States as an equally qualified Norwegian. Western Hemisphere countries could send an additional 120,000 people a year. Future bills adjusted these numbers in minor ways but did not alter the essential handiwork of the Great Society Congress.

At its signing, the Immigration Act provoked surprisingly little controversy for such a dramatic shift in policy. Outside the Deep South, few politicians would now go on record espousing the view that any nation or race's heredity was inferior to any other's. And it was even less appealing to lawmakers to stand up in opposition to the principle that parents should have the right to join their children and wives to live with their husbands in America. President Johnson shrewdly capitalized on this aspect of the immigration act by presenting it as the fulfillment of, rather than a challenge to, America's best traditions. In his speech at the Statue of Liberty, President Johnson extended a special invitation to Cubans with family members in the United States to emigrate to Miami, where a large number of their compatriots, refugees from Castro's revolution, already resided. "I declare to the people of Cuba that those who seek refuge here will find it," Johnson announced. "The dedication of America to our traditions as an asylum for the oppressed will be upheld."[49]

But the legislation signed at Liberty Island that day would change the nation more than its supporters imagined. Within a few years, the number of newcomers from Asia skyrocketed, with Chinese, Koreans, Indians, and Vietnamese leading the way. Millions more came from Central and South America—many of them openly, but just as many taking advantage of the country's porous borders to enter as "illegals." By 1990, more than four out of five immigrants to the United States began their journeys in Asia or Latin America.

Just like nineteenth-century immigrants, the new immigrants came for a variety of reasons, from economic opportunity to religious and political freedom to consumer bounty. But the new immigrants were often less likely than the old to pay even lip service to the once-cherished ideal of America as "melting pot." In the 1800s and early 1900s, despite the arrival of millions of immigrants, the cultural dominance of white Protestants of Anglo-Saxon descent was never in serious jeopardy, whatever hysterical nativists might have chosen to believe. A rapid assimilation into American society was widely if not universally assumed by newcomers and old-line Americans alike to offer the shortest and most appropriate route to success and security in the New World. While remaining faithful to traditional religious beliefs and familiar cuisines, most immigrants proved eager to learn English, to put aside those customs, costumes, and behaviors that marked them off as exotic strangers (except perhaps on ceremonial occasions), to have their children and grandchildren be accepted as "one hundred percent Americans." But the new immigrants who arrived after 1965 found themselves in a country where long-established but still marginal groups like blacks and Hispanics were questioning the values and superiority of the "dominant culture," and asserting the right to redefine American identity to fit more comfortably with their own customs, beliefs, and past histories. In the decades that followed the passage of the 1965 Immigration Act, the United States became the most ethnically diverse society in the world. But the 1965 act also planted the seeds of future conflicts over what it meant to be an American.

Christmas: Homecomings

As the holidays approached in the late fall of 1965, Americans got their first inklings of the true costs of the war in Vietnam. A week before Thanksgiving several hundred soldiers from the American First Cavalry were surrounded and for a time cut off by North Vietnamese regulars in a place called the Ia Drang Valley in the central highlands of South Vietnam.[50] Over the next few days 234 Americans were killed in the battle, often in hand-to-hand combat. Enemy dead were estimated at over 1300, leading General Westmoreland to hail this first major encounter between Americans and North Vietnamese as an unqualified victory. He then promptly cabled Washington, asking that an additional 200,000 American troops be sent to Vietnam in 1966.

The North Vietnamese also counted the battle of the Ia Drang as a victory. They had chosen where, when, and how long to fight, and they had held their own on the battlefield, notwithstanding the superior firepower of the Americans. If their casualties were high, they had learned invaluable tactical lessons, particularly the importance of what they called "clinging to the belt" of the Americans—fighting at such close quarters that it made it difficult for U.S. artillery and aircraft to provide effective tactical support (several of the American soldiers who died in the battle were burned to death by U.S. Air Force napalm drops). Secretary of Defense McNamara came to Vietnam on one of his fact-finding missions in late November and was briefed by Colonel Hal Moore, the American battlefield commander in the Ia Drang. He listened in silence and asked no questions. Shortly afterward, as he prepared to return to the United States, he told reporters, "It will be a long war."[51]

Most Americans still described themselves in public opinion polls as optimistic about eventual victory in Vietnam. But few could have believed that "the boys" were coming home anytime soon, and certainly not by Christmas. As the year drew to an end, the American press and television news were filled with stories of how the troops would be celebrating the season in Vietnam. Planeloads of celebrities, entertainers, and clergy descended upon Tan Son Nhut airport in Saigon to spend the holidays with them. Bob Hope told jokes and Cardinal Spellman said prayers. Every American serviceman in South Vietnam was promised a hot turkey dinner on Christmas Day, even if he was serving in the most isolated and dangerous outpost.

In Washington, D.C., as befitted a wartime Christmas, the annual White House tree-lighting ceremony in mid-December was kept low key. The president had spent much of the fall convalescing in Texas after his gall-bladder operation. The incision from the surgery continued to cause him discomfort, and he was eager to return home to the comforts of his ranch in Johnson City.

There was another Texas homecoming of a different sort that Christmas for Sergeant First Class L.C. Block of the U.S. Army's famed First Infantry Division (the "Big Red One"). Block, 35 years old, a 17-year veteran of the military, and the father of six, had shipped out for Vietnam with his unit in September. He died in action on November 23, one of the first of the over 20,000 casualties that the First Division would suffer in Vietnam over the next five years. By the time Sergeant Block's body was shipped home to Texas for his funeral, it was already mid-December. Sergeant Block was an African American, and although the U.S. military was now largely integrated, the funeral parlor in his hometown of Hemphill, Texas, was not. His wake had to be held at another undertaking establishment 20 miles away from the cemetery where he was finally laid to rest. On the day after the funeral the widow sat at home with her youngest child on her lap, reading and rereading the last letter Sergeant Block had sent home from Vietnam. "People wonder and ponder what the war is for," Mrs. Block remarked quietly and thoughtfully to a reporter. "They wonder what does it mean. I don't know. I guess it's necessary. L.C. died for his country, I guess."[52]

CHAPTER 8

The Making of a Youth Culture

I HAVE MY FREEDOM, BUT I DON'T HAVE MUCH TIME.
—*The Rolling Stones*

In October 1955, an announcement of a poetry reading circulated around the North Beach neighborhood of San Francisco. "Remarkable collection of angels all gathered at once in the same spot," it promised. "Wine, music, dancing girls, serious poetry, free satori. Small collection for wine and postcards. Charming event." The venue was the Six Gallery, a converted auto-repair shop.

The reading and the whimsical notice were the creation of 29-year-old writer Allen Ginsberg. During the previous decade, Ginsberg's life had wildly diverged from values most Americans held dear. A Jew and a homosexual, he entered Columbia University in 1944 on scholarship. Within months, he was suspended for writing an obscenity on his dirty dormitory window to irk a careless cleaning lady. Then he got arrested for letting a poetic drifter named Herbert Huncke hide stolen goods in his apartment. To avoid jail, Ginsberg agreed to spend several months in a psychiatric hospital. There, he and a fellow patient feigned insanity by smashing down on the keys of a piano while screaming at the top of their lungs.

Ginsberg was an exceedingly generous soul. He delighted in sharing his poetic visions, his semen, and a variety of mind-altering drugs with an ever expanding number of male writers—including erstwhile college football player Jack Kerouac, who later published the autobiographical novel *On the Road*. Ginsberg also read deeply in the sacred texts of Zen Buddhism and became a lifelong devotee (which explains his reference to satori—Japanese for "a state of enlightenment").

With little money, the young poet worked at odd jobs and slept on borrowed beds in various Manhattan apartments belonging to his friends. Ginsberg also found time to travel around the continent. In Mexico, he marveled at intricate temple ruins, took long hikes wearing nothing but shoes, built a

Allen Ginsberg, c. 1970. Source: *Russell Reif/Archive Photos*

set of wooden drums that he played at all hours, and harvested cocoa beans alongside Mayan Indians. He hitchhiked to Florida, flew to Cuba in expectation of orgies that did not occur, and then returned to Greenwich Village.

By the time he arrived in the San Francisco Bay Area in the mid-'50s, Ginsberg was at the center of a small but growing band of young artists and erotic adventurers one of them dubbed the Beat Generation. "Beat" was Jack Kerouac's term; in half-serious tribute to his Catholic upbringing, he claimed it was short for "beatitude." By 1955 a few articles about the group had appeared in newspapers and small magazines. But most Americans were quite unaware of their outrageous escapades and unorthodox spiritual quests. That would change after Ginsberg's performance at the Six Gallery.

Ginsberg was nervous as he stepped to the front of the small stage to recite a long poem entitled, simply, "Howl." He had never read poetry in public before and had bolstered himself with many glasses of cheap wine. But almost immediately, his exuberance began to flow:

"I saw the best minds of my generation destroyed by madness,
starving hysterical naked,
dragging themselves through negro streets at dawn looking for an
angry fix,
angelheaded hipsters burning for the ancient heavenly connection
to the starry dynamo in the machinery of light . . . [2]

From that opening to the poem's last lines—"in my dreams you walk
dripping from a sea-journey on the highway across America in tears to the
door of my cottage in the Western night"—Ginsberg swirled together candid glimpses of his own life with laments about the damage American culture had done to maverick souls. Ginsberg's name for that culture was
"Moloch," a Semitic deity who gobbled up children. As the crowd whooped
and Kerouac yelled "Go" from a corner of the stage, Ginsberg chanted a
series of rapid portraits of the (mostly unnamed) "best minds" on their
wild ride of the past decade: "who got busted in their pubic beards returning through Laredo with a belt of marijuana for New York . . . or pur-
gatoried their torsos night after night with dreams, with drugs, with waking nightmares, alcohol and cock and endless balls." In the face of sexual
repression and Cold War hysteria, he and his friends had emerged,
strangely triumphant.

That evening at the Six Gallery was a declaration of independence from
the rigid, authoritarian order the Beats believed was throttling the nation. It
enabled the Beats to create themselves as an icon-smashing legend. Rebel
dramatist Michael McClure later wrote, "In all our memories no one had been
so outspoken in poetry before—we had gone beyond a point of no return—
and we were ready for it. . . . None of us wanted to go back to the gray, chill,
militaristic silence . . . to the spiritual drabness."[3] "Howl" was indeed a protest
against social evils. But Ginsberg drew no distinction between those who resisted Moloch by letting "themselves be fucked in the ass by saintly motor-
cyclists" and other sorts of heretics who handed out "Supercommunist pamphlets in Union Square," mecca of a once-influential American left. Surviving
on one's own terms was rebellion enough.

Some powerful San Franciscans clearly agreed. In May 1957, vice-
seeking local police arrested Lawrence Ferlinghetti, the publisher of *Howl and
Other Poems,* at his North Beach bookstore where the book was sold. The
trial was reported around the world; it ended in acquittal. In his decision,
the presiding judge hewed to the standard for obscenity recently laid down
by the Supreme Court; "Howl," ruled the judge, was *not* "entirely lacking in
social importance."[4]

Sexual controversy proved a splendid form of advertising. Ginsberg's brief
volume sold well over 100,000 copies during the next few years. In 1966, the

Supreme Court, in the case of *Redrup v. New York*, essentially abandoned its role as a moral guardian of the arts. Liberal intellectuals argued that censorship could backfire, encouraging the victims of repression to seek "unhealthy" sexual outlets.[5]

The Beats helped to plant seeds that would sprout, luxuriantly, during the 1960s and after—particularly among white people in their teens and twenties. One was a desire for sexual adventure, untethered to the values of monogamy and heterosexuality that had reigned supreme in the Western world since the dawn of Christianity. Another was glorification of the outlaw spirit, as embodied in men and women who viewed conventional jobs and sanitized entertainment as akin to a living death. Millions of young people would act out such beliefs with the aid of illegal drugs like marijuana, peyote, and especially LSD. The Beats also generated a romantic yearning for "authentic" experiences, which they associated with poor and working-class people, black and white and Latino. The cultural downscaling of middle-class white youths would take place most energetically through the mushrooming medium of rock 'n' roll. In 1960 an obscure English band paid tribute to Ginsberg and friends by changing their name to the Beatles.[6]

The congregation of Beats also helped generate a new burst of spirituality—at once more personal, eclectic, and fervent than the kind found in most churches and synagogues. Seeking alternative routes to the transcendent, many Americans explored aspects of the Buddhist and Hindu traditions, and invented their own recombinant faiths. Finally, "Howl" proclaimed the perilous beauty of small, beloved communities composed of rebels loyal to no one but each other and bound by a common vision of hedonistic liberation. To belong to such a fellowship was to believe that one grasped the cause of all contemporary miseries and, perhaps, possessed the key to healing them.

Such notions flowered among members of a generation whose dreams seemed unlimited. Familiar with a world of mass consumption, many middle-class white baby boomers believed that an era of perpetual affluence and total freedom of choice was at hand. They were eager, at least for a few years, to forego the quest for economic security and its material tokens that had driven their elders. By the early '60s, youth communities had sprung up on the outskirts of college campuses, often in cheap housing available near black or Latino ghettos. South Campus in Berkeley, Mifflin Street in Madison, Wisconsin, and the neighborhood behind the Drag in Austin, Texas, were among the more famous of such venues. Surrounded by one's peers and largely free from the responsibilities of career, family, and mortgage, young people could experiment with their bodies and minds in ways that usually shocked and enraged older people raised amid the constricted horizons of the Great Depression and World War II.

At the same time, the "generation gap" was often a matter of differences more stylistic than ideological. Cultural rebels were acting out a vision of individual fulfillment as old as the free market and the Protestant Reformation. "To dance beneath the diamond sky with one hand waving free," sang Bob Dylan who, as a teenager, read Ginsberg's poetry and later became his friend.[7] Young people who consumed psychedelic ("mind-revealing") drugs and attended rock concerts grumbled about big corporations and the warfare/welfare state, but had little notion of what might replace them.

Meanwhile, some of the nation's biggest corporations quickly learned to tap the generation gap with slogans like Pepsi's ("For those who think young") and low-slung, fast cars like the Ford Mustang. "To be young is to be with it," remarked a business journalist in 1968. "Youth is getting the hard sell." Advertising agencies, filled with people who considered themselves hip and creative, churned out commercials that made fun of conformity, snobs, and the very products they were selling.[8] "Moloch" proved to be a most accommodating fellow.

Still, there was a rebellious edge to the youth culture of the 1960s that retains its capacity to fascinate some Americans and to repel others. What was fresh and daring about the phenomenon always intermingled with its tendency to equate freedom with bigger and better thrills. Many young people combined the breaking of taboos with an effortless shift in consumer habits. Others followed the Beats in exalting the former and scorning the latter. Inevitably, the persistent hierarchy of wealth, race, and status framed one's opinions and cultural options. The lifestyle of a white suburbanite who attended Harvard or MIT mixed uneasily with that of a black youth from across the river in Roxbury who, after a few years of high school and a few weeks of boot camp, was likely to end up in Vietnam.

One way to understand this complex, but seldom boring, phenomenon is to focus on sex, drugs, and rock 'n' roll—the triad that became a clichéed marker for the entire popular culture of the young. That daring experiences could so rapidly turn into commonplace ones helps reveal how much changed during those years—and why many Americans feared and resisted the cultural transformation.

What *was* the "sexual revolution" of the 1960s? Most significantly, it was an insurgency rooted in the conviction that the erotic should be celebrated as an utterly normal part of life. Thus, Hugh Hefner's *Playboy* magazine helped legitimate the mass marketing of female nudity—by coupling abundant photos of young women (accompanying text stressed their wholesome values and career ambitions) to a "philosophy" that equated multiple sex partners with the drinking of good liquor and the wearing of sleek clothes. Thus, popular comedian Lenny Bruce mocked censors who had no problem with violence in films but forbid any depiction of sexual intercourse (which Bruce, a Jew, called *schtupping*—Yiddish slang—to avoid trouble with the police): "Well, for kids to watch killing—Yes; but *schtupping*—No! Cause if they watch *schtup* pictures, they may do it some day."[9] Thus, high school girls screamed orgasmically at the very sight of Elvis Presley and the Beatles. Some ran *en masse* after their idols and tore away bits of their clothing. Thus, Helen Gurley Brown, in her 1962 best-seller *Sex and the Single Girl*, encouraged her typical reader to have sex whenever "her body wants to" and then turned *Cosmopolitan* magazine into a vigorously irreverent manual for "swinging chicks."[10] Thus, many gay men and lesbians rejected their burdens of self-hatred and "came out" to friends, families, and coworkers.

The most avid participants in all this were in their teens and twenties, the age of sexual awakening. Millions of the young abandoned old strictures against premarital intercourse, oral sex, and candid public discussion of all aspects of lovemaking. In the "underground" newspapers that proliferated in youth communities, one could find guilt-free narratives of erotic experiences and personal ads that either offered or requested partners of every conceivable persuasion. Sweeping changes in technology and the law lessened the fear of pregnancy. The birth control pill, first available in 1960, and the spread of legal abortions in a number of states, gave young women, for the first time, options they themselves could control.

Higher education was in the front line of the sexual "revolution." Gradually over the course of the '60s, students pressured college authorities, who had traditionally acted as surrogate parents, to stop policing their carnal lives. Attacked first and most successfully were "parietal" rules that strictly limited the hours when men could visit women in their dormitory rooms and vice versa. Administrators were more reluctant to acquiesce to off-campus cohabitation. In 1968 Barnard College disciplined a student named Linda LeClair for lying about the fact that she was living with her boyfriend. Hundreds of her fellow students, as well as many faculty members, protested the decision. In the end, college officials meted out a rather strange "punishment": LeClair was barred from the Barnard cafeteria.[11]

Those who argued the cause of sexual liberty in the 60s could cite some well-known studies in their defense. The most prominent of these was the Kinsey Report, two thick volumes of interviews with some 18,000 white adults about their sexual practices. The report—a volume on men published in 1948 and one on women in 1953—exploded the myth of a puritanical America. Over a third of the men told biologist Alfred Kinsey and his team of researchers that they had achieved orgasm via a homosexual act, while a large majority admitted to premarital intercourse, often with a prostitute. Over half the women confessed to sexual activity before marriage; most, like the men, said they masturbated regularly when no partner was available. The gulf between the public morality of Americans and their private pleasures was hard to ignore. In a golden age of social science, the Kinsey Report set a new standard for sexual realism.

But critics quickly pointed out that Kinsey and his associates were trafficking in secondhand knowledge. The researchers made no attempt to judge whether people had told them the truth. That was not a problem for Dr.

William Masters and his coworker (and future wife) Virginia Johnson. In a laboratory on the campus of Washington University in St. Louis, the couple observed hundreds of men and women having orgasms, some with a partner and others through masturbation.

Masters and Johnson shared a mission—to help every adult achieve maximum sexual pleasure. In 1966 huge sales of their first book, *Human Sexual Response*, seemed to further that goal. Readers who managed to slog through the couple's often obscure prose (and millions of others who read or heard their findings distilled in the media) learned one critical fact: the clitoris, not the vagina, was the site of female orgasm. Masters and Johnson also discovered that women could have multiple orgasms in rapid order; thus, the female of the species was sexually superior to the male. The couple also recommended various methods, based on their research, for curing impotence and premature ejaculation. Despite or perhaps because of their assumption that good sex was merely a matter of correct technique, Masters and Johnson seemed to many Americans like liberators. One newspaper headlined a glowing review of their work, "A Short Course in How to Be Happy."[12]

Homosexuals probably benefited most from the new tolerance toward sexual matters. Until the 1960s, with few exceptions, their intimate lives had to be kept hidden. Exposure stripped uncounted numbers of men and women of their children, jobs, military careers, and reputations. Every authority—from churches to the federal government to the American Psychiatric Association—agreed that homosexuality was a form of "perversion" whose victims had to be cured, lest their depravity spread to others. Metropolises harbored a homosexual underground of bars, restaurants, and pornographic movie theaters. But such institutions were always fair game for police raids. In the early 1950s, police in the District of Columbia arrested over a thousand adults a year for homosexual activity, and comparable totals were registered in other big cities.[13] Guilt and self-hatred drove many homosexuals to alcoholism and others to suicide.

In the '50s, the Kinsey Report and the ribald candor of the Beats cracked open the wall of fear and loathing. In the '60s, the youth culture's embrace of open and promiscuous sexuality dismantled it. By the end of the decade, a growing number of homosexuals were proudly calling themselves "gay" and celebrating behavior they had once felt forced to conceal. Some gay activists even advised "straights" to learn from their example. The essayist Paul Goodman wrote in 1969:

> queer life . . . can be profoundly democratizing, throwing together every class and group more than heterosexuality does. . . . I myself have cruised rich, poor, middle class, and petit bourgeois; black, white, yellow and brown; scholars, jocks and dropouts; farmers, seamen, railroad men, heavy industry, light manufacturing, communications, business and finance, civilians, soldiers and sailors, and once or twice cops. There is a kind of political meaning, I guess, in the fact that there are so many types of attractive human beings.[14]

Nearly all the ardent champions of the new sexuality, whether straight or gay, were male. Young women could applaud the "discovery" of clitoral orgasms and the loosening of restrictions on where they could live and with whom. But it was men who produced the words and pictures that challenged obscenity statutes. And only men equated personal liberation with the desire, even the right to have sex with a diversity of partners, regardless of emotional commitment. This conviction united Hugh Hefner, a mansion-dwelling millionaire, with the working-class revolutionary John Sinclair, flamboyant leader of a popular Detroit rock band, the MC-5, and of the White Panther Party, a radical youth group briefly active in the Midwest. "We have found," asserted Sinclair, "that there are three essential human activities of the greatest importance to all persons, and that people are . . . healthy in proportion to their involvement in these activities: rock and roll, dope, and fucking in the streets. . . . We suggest the three in combination, all the time."[15]

For biological and cultural reasons, few women had ever embraced such a raging vision. The male libido, when unrestrained by custom or law, often led to rape, unwanted pregnancy, and/or abandonment. In 1968 the White Panthers slipped into their manifesto the line, "Fuck your woman so hard . . . she can't stand up."[16] Some men reading that cringed, but, for women, it confirmed the link between sex and subordination that all the glee about "liberation" had neglected. This became a major theme of the thousands of "consciousness-raising" groups that sprang up by the end of the decade— free spaces where women spoke honestly about the pain that inequality and a lack of both respect and self-respect had caused.

Budding feminists angrily rejected the countercultural image of the bra-less madonna, content merely to bake bread and have sex with her "old man." The male hippie became a figure to condemn. "Here they come," mocked writer Leni Wildflower at the end of the '60s, "Those strutting roosters, those pathetic male chauvinists. . . . Here come the freaks in those tight bell-bottoms, tie-dyed T-shirts which their 'old lady' . . . made for them. . . . Male liberators, *you* are stepping on my neck."[17] The flowering of a new "sisterhood" fused intimacy with a wariness toward men, nudged some heterosexual women into experimenting with lesbian relationships, and encouraged life-long lesbians to speak their minds. Could any man, trained as he was to dominate the other gender, really make a woman happy? In the erotic realm, at a time when porno theater marquees were pitching "THE INCREDIBLE SEX REVOLUTION," feminists may have been asking the most radical question of all.[18]

Were any revelations to be found in drugs? Since the '60s, it has been risky to offer even the most qualified assent. Parents and teachers, government officials and journalists condemn the chemicals most identified with the bygone youth culture—marijuana, LSD, peyote, and psilocybin—as nothing but instruments of self-destruction, for both individuals and society. Slogans like "Just say no" substitute for reasoned debate about the motivations of drug users and the effect of the chemicals on mind and body. Members of new generations consume the substances anyway, although few expect more than a short-lived thrill. It is difficult to capture a time when many young people, and not a few of their elders, believed the ingestion of certain substances was the pivot of a cultural renaissance. "Drugs were the fundamental text," remembered critic Geoffrey O'Brien, "If you had not read the book, you couldn't participate in the discussion that followed."[19] Or as rock icon Jimi Hendrix sang, "'Scuse me, while I kiss the sky."

The most common drug in the '60s was marijuana, nearly as ubiquitous in youth communities as was bottled beer everywhere else in America. The potency of the "grass" smoked or swallowed varied widely—from the hallucinogenic to the mildly intoxicating. As with many consumer products, so did the price. Marijuana had been illegal since 1937 (simple possession was a felony in many states), but that did little to slow the commerce. It may even have increased it, as young people bonded against what seemed an irrational, vindictive prohibition. Few restrictions were placed on sales of alcohol and tobacco products, despite the obvious risks to public health. So why were America's rulers and many conservative citizens so frightened by the dreamy, often erotic qualities of marijuana? The answers only heightened the cultural conflict that Allen Ginsberg and his friends had declared in the mid-'50s.

But it was LSD, the acronym for lysergic acid diethylamide #25, that occasioned the greatest claims and the greatest censure. Ginsberg journeyed to Auschwitz in 1967 and, standing before the entrance to the camp where Nazis had slaughtered millions of Jews and other victims, glibly recommended "that everybody who hears my voice, directly or indirectly, try the chemical LSD at least once, every man and woman and child in good health over the age of 14." Fellow poet Gary Snyder commented, more prosaically, "Acid just happened to turn up as the product of this particular society, to correct its own excesses."[20]

Such statements appalled Theodore Roszak, a professor in the San Francisco Bay area, who popularized the term "the counter-culture." "The gadget-happy American has always been a figure of fun," wrote Roszak in 1969, "because of his facile assumption that there exists a technological solution to every human problem. It only took the great psychedelic crusade to perfect the absurdity by proclaiming that personal salvation and the social revolution can be packed in a capsule."[21]

Ironically, the object of so much promise and dread was discovered by accident. One April day in 1943, Swiss chemist Albert Hofmann was at work near Geneva at the sprawling complex of Sandoz Laboratories. Hofmann decided to synthesize a fresh batch of a compound made from rye fungi that he had created five years earlier and put away. In the process of mixing the chemicals, Hofmann spilled a small amount on his fingertips. Quite soon, his diary notes, the scientist was overcome by "a remarkable but not unpleasant state of intoxication, characterized by an intense stimulation of the imagination and an altered state of awareness of the world." He closed his eyes and "there surged before me a succession of fantastic, rapidly changing image[s] of a striking reality and depth, alternating with a vivid, kaleidoscopic play of colors." This continued for almost three hours. Albert Hofmann had taken the world's first acid trip.[22]

After World War II, Sandoz quietly began marketing LSD to psychiatrists and other scientific researchers in Europe and North America. But, in the United States, two quite different sorts of client latched onto the amazing compound. One, predictably, was the bohemian artist who sought to test and broaden the imagination. Early trippers included jazz musicians Thelonious Monk and Dizzy Gillespie, as well as British novelist Aldous Huxley, then a resident of southern California. But an equally keen customer was the Central Intelligence Agency.

Hofmann's invention seemed, at first, to be a spymaster's dream come true. Under its influence, an enemy agent might divulge secrets lodged deep in his or her unconscious. LSD had neither odor, color, nor taste. Small quantities sprayed into a room or diluted in a water supply could, it was hoped, defeat one's foes humanely. Disoriented and frightened, they would simply surrender.

During the 1950s, the agency spent millions of dollars to test the miracle drug. One group, working out of CIA headquarters in Langley, Virginia, did some self-experimentation. A staff member would dose his morning coffee with LSD and then become subject for a day. One man wept after tripping and refused "to go back to a place where I wouldn't be able to hold on to this kind of beauty."[23] Another ran across a bridge over the Potomac River and went temporarily mad before his colleagues rescued him. Every automobile, he swore, looked like a bloodthirsty monster.

The CIA and the Army's Chemical Corps also tested LSD on hundreds of unwitting subjects, despite a provision of the Nuremberg Code, signed in the wake of the Holocaust, that forbade such experiments. Some of the victims were government scientists, others were prisoners, mental patients, and clients of prostitutes—all coerced into doing their bit for national security. A handful of suicides resulted, and a larger number of severe psychoses. And the CIA gained nothing. By the end of the '50s, those in charge abandoned research on the "magic" drug. Under its influence, subjects had failed to give accurate information and often failed to concentrate on the interrogation process itself.

In the meantime, however, word of the drug's existence had reached the Ivy League. At Harvard's Department of Psychology, junior professors Timothy Leary and Richard Alpert began in 1960 to give psilocybin mushrooms to selected students and other curious guests—including Allen Ginsberg. Within two years, the pair had graduated, enthusiastically, to LSD. They dutifully published scientific papers on their research in respected academic journals. But fellow professors criticized them for indulging freely in the drugs under study, and parents complained when, according to Leary, "bright youths phoned home to announce that they'd found God and discovered the secret of the universe."[24] In 1963 Leary left Harvard and became a relentless promoter of LSD consciousness. After Congress outlawed the drug in 1966, a series of arrests only added to his fame. Alpert began a personal voyage that

LSD as liberator, according to underground cartoonist Gilbert Shelton, c. 1969. Source: *Connections*

resulted in his conversion to Hinduism and a change of name to Baba Ram Dass.

As with marijuana, the ban on LSD only enhanced its luster. By the late '60s, one could buy the drug in most college towns and big cities. The greatest supplies and lowest prices could be found on both coasts. In Berkeley, a young chemist known as Owsley (short for Augustus Owsley Stanley III) got rich producing some 12 million high-quality doses from his own underground laboratory and distributing them throughout northern California.[25]

A certain lore grew up around the potent liquid. Which form of it was purest and strongest—on a square of blotter paper, on a slab of clear gelatin, or on a multicolored tablet? The drug's allure was enhanced by learning that many of the world's most prominent rock musicians were using and writing songs about it—the Beatles, Bob Dylan, the Rolling Stones, Jimi Hendrix, the Grateful Dead, and Jefferson Airplane. LSD never achieved the popularity—or cultural acceptance—of marijuana, which was ubiquitous in mass gatherings of the college-aged young by the late 1960s. But "tripping" had become an indispensable rite of initiation; one emerged from the experience with matchless stories to tell.

One set of these tales brimmed with oracular glory, while another set warned against the equation of self-knowledge with getting high. It was safest to take LSD with a band of friends, at least one of whom had tripped before. Such an environment could help create an experience of intense pleasure and emotional catharsis. A group of trippers might begin by talking quietly and listening to music; then one person would notice an object in the room, on the grass, or just focus on a stray remark and mention it to the others—and the whole gathering would break into wild laughter.

Many spoke of feeling saner and more aware of their thoughts while "on acid" than during normal life. The chemical laid bare one's obsessions and focused the mind on what seemed the greater spiritual unity present in the natural world—a common theme of mystics in a variety of cultures. As Aldous Huxley wrote about a trip on mescaline, whose effects mirrored those of LSD: "what Adam had seen on the morning of creation—the miracle, moment by moment, of naked existence . . . flowers shining within their own inner light and all but quivering under the pressure of the significance with which they were charged."[26] In mundane terms, LSD made it possible to have a decent conversation with a tree.

But if LSD opened a portal to the extraordinary, it also screened out the rational. Trippers mistook the obvious for great insight; acid wisdom often reduced itself to disjointed rambling about the wonders of a drink of water or the setting sun. The day after he first took LSD, the writer Arthur Koestler told Timothy Leary, "This is wonderful no doubt. But it is fake. . . . I solved the secret of the universe last night, but this morning I forgot what it was."[27]

The belief that acid was a magic potion that would change one's life—or the arrangements of society—was a terrible delusion. Serious depression struck many a persistent tripper, and some turned to drugs like heroin to soothe a mind jarred and jazzed instead of opened. To parry "straight" critics, acid devotees routinely cited all the legal chemicals—caffeine, nicotine, tranquilizers, barbiturates—that Americans consumed in huge quantities. By what right, they asked, do you condemn *our* choice of drugs? But the question negated the claim that psychedelics were a force for liberation. In the '60s, the Du Pont company began to advertise itself as providing "Better Living through Chemistry." Hippie street merchants sold buttons and multicolored posters emblazoned with the same words.

The bond of drugs also produced some horrific consequences. Thousands of young people moved to San Francisco's Haight–Ashbury neighborhood ("the Haight") in the mid-'60s seeking, as had the Beats a decade earlier, both sensual thrills and spiritual enlightenment. Such brilliant local bands as the Grateful Dead and Jefferson Airplane catered to the new bohemians. Soon the lush green hills of Golden Gate Park, adjacent to the Haight, were packed with barefooted adolescents and young adults getting high on marijuana and LSD. Many of these people had little or no money and no plans to get a job. So they lived off the generosity of relatives, local businesses and, for several months, a group of anarchists called the Diggers who distributed free food and used clothing.

The Haight was an instant village with no moral center, where drugged-out vapidity passed for self-knowledge. Writer Joan Didion spent several weeks there in the spring of 1967 and dispatched numbing reports from the new cultural front: young people shifting to hard drugs like heroin and amphetamine after a spate of "bad" acid trips, adopting new lovers and new "organic" diets with the same mercurial bemusement. Didion met one 5-year old girl who remarked, quite matter-of-factly, that she was "in High Kindergarten"; her mother routinely dosed her with LSD and peyote. What she had witnessed, remarked Didion, was "the desperate attempt of a handful of pathetically unequipped children to create a community in a social vacuum."[28] The Haight was clearly a village without a future.

In contrast, rock and roll was definitely here to stay. The music rapidly conquered the tastes and swayed the emotions of people whom other aspects of the youth culture had only grazed. LSD and sexual liberty were repellent to most churchgoing whites and blacks in the South. But they generally adored both Chuck Berry and Elvis Presley; soul singers like Aretha Franklin and Otis Redding also claimed fervent fans on both sides of the color line. By the mid-'70s, Americans were spending more on rock tapes and records than on movies and sports events—and four-fifths of all recordings were rock. All over the globe, young people who could buy or borrow a guitar were trying to emulate the musical avatars whose sounds filled the air and their imaginations.

The diffusion of rock and roll was one of the wonders of the postwar world. Emerging in the early '50s from the urban black music called rhythm and blues, rock quickly revealed its protean nature, altering every species of popular music—folk, country and western, jazz, romantic pop, Mexican ballads, even Christian hymns. Cheap, portable devices—the transistor radio and the 45 rpm recording—as well as high-quality car radios helped weld rock fans to their music in a way no earlier style had matched. The pioneers of rock seldom paused to reflect upon the cultural sea change they had initiated; they were content to reap the rewards of fame, monetary and otherwise. Still, as critic Greil Marcus wrote, "they delivered a new version of America with their music, and more people than anyone can count are still trying to figure out how to live in it."[29]

The newness began with a critical truth: the roots of rock and roll were mainly black. The term itself derives from services held in rural Holiness churches in the Deep South during the '20s and '30s. There, congregations of African-American laborers and domestics "rocked and reeled" to fast, bluesy rhythms played on guitars, horns, and drums. Since the days of slavery, the black church had been developing a style of singing—the call-and-response pattern and percussive accents that artists like Ray Charles and James Brown adapted to secular purposes in the 1950s. At the same time, the creators of rock freely borrowed whatever they needed—melodies, chord progressions, lyrics—from other musical traditions; particularly significant were the ballads and twangy guitar sounds of Scotch-Irish Protestants whose ancestors had settled in the foothills and mountains of the South. But rock and roll always remained a hybrid grafted from a robust black stock.

Ironically, that helps to explain why rock had such enormous appeal to young Americans who knew nothing of gospel music and didn't suffer from Jim Crow. Like the Beats, many whites in high school and college viewed black popular culture as a vibrant, emotionally honest alternative to a dominant culture they experienced as safe, boring, and hypocritical. In his 1957 essay "The White Negro," Norman Mailer had made clear that "in this wedding of the white and the black it was the Negro who brought the cultural dowry."[30]

Mailer's own examples were jazz and marijuana, but rock music provided more salient and infinitely more profitable ones. Elvis Presley modeled himself on black bluesmen like Arthur Crudup, and one of his first hits was a cover of Crudup's "That's All Right." In 1956 Elvis said of his music, "The colored folks been singing it and playing it . . . for more years than I know. . . . I used to hear old Arthur Crudup bang his box the way I do now, and I said if I ever got to the place where I could feel all old Arthur felt, I'd be a music man like nobody ever saw."[31] Across the Atlantic, white British groups like the Beatles and the Rolling Stones started out playing blues for youths like themselves who longed for the raw authenticity symbolized by such black artists as Muddy Waters and Howlin' Wolf.

The emerging demigods and demigoddesses of rock and roll were hardly the first young whites to adopt black styles. In the nineteenth century, minstrel shows featuring white actors pretending to be slaves were the nation's most popular form of entertainment. In the 1920s, white performers stirred by the rich Creole musical traditions of New Orleans, created jazz bands that, along with the black combos of Duke Ellington and Count Basie, dominated the airwaves and record charts through the 1940s.

Rock, however, carried a generational charge whose power transcended the sphere of racial borrowing. Spurred by wartime migrations and the virtual end of child labor, teenagers from diverse class backgrounds began flooding into high schools that once had been the nearly exclusive province of affluent whites. Old barriers between musical styles fell quickly too, as young bands scavenged through a cornucopia of ethnic traditions.

Social mingling spawned a taste for rebellion. During the mid-'50s, George "Hound Dog" Lorenz, a white disk jockey broadcasting from Buffalo, gained a huge following among young people of all races. Lorenz sported a goatee and purple trousers, used the "jive" lingo then associated with black musicians, and was a hero to working-class kids who chafed at the self-disciplined lives their parents had led. Meanwhile, in East Los Angeles, Mexican-American teenagers like Ritchie Valens were writing and playing rhythm and blues songs with bilingual lyrics.

But rock was not a political insurgency. Cultural leftists like John Sinclair and Abbie Hoffman, a former civil rights organizer, certainly tried to harness the music to their ideological purposes. The White Panthers were an outgrowth of Sinclair's rock band, and Hoffman hailed the birth of a quasi-revolutionary "Woodstock Nation" after the music festival held in a pasture north of New York City in the late summer of 1969 that attracted half a million people who got stoned and frolicked in the mud.

Such efforts to hitch the culture of rock and roll to political rebellion invariably flopped. The crowd at Woodstock booed the flamboyant Hoffman, when, high on LSD, he began denouncing the arrest of Sinclair for possession of marijuana. Peter Townshend, leader of the Who, promptly whacked Hoffman off the stage with his guitar. Rock musicians, even more than most artists, mistrusted political figures who wanted them to articulate a certain message they themselves had not conceived. "Won't get fooled again," chanted the Who in one of their more memorable songs.[32] For reasons of ego or creativity, few rock and rollers joined any contingent of the radical movement. "My music isn't supposed to make you riot," explained Janis Joplin, "It's supposed to make you fuck."[33]

Joplin's own life demonstrated rock's power to reinvent the individual—and its limits as liberation. Growing up with bad skin and a weight problem in the working-class town of Port Arthur, Texas, Joplin had few friends and little prospect of a brighter future. She spent a good deal of time in her room—listening to and writing music, making her own clothes, and taking drugs. A

Janis Joplin with Big Brother and the Holding Company, 1968. Source: *Archive Photos*

few years after high school, Joplin moved to San Francisco when the Haight–Ashbury scene was in full flower. There, backed by the band Big Brother and the Holding Company, she began to sing the blues in a most arresting fashion.

To hear Joplin's renditions of such blues standards as "Ball and Chain" and "Piece of My Heart" (originally recorded by black artists) was to glimpse a woman in the throes of shredding her inhibitions by displaying her pain. Joplin alternately moaned, screeched, and purred the lyrics—evoking agony and ecstasy in equal measure. She lured hordes of both male and female fans; the latter copied her wardrobe (feather boas, flowered shifts, and strand upon strand of costume jewelry) and a bit of her bawdy toughness. "It was seeing Janis Joplin that made me resolve, once and for all, not to get my hair straightened," recalled critic Ellen Willis.[34]

But adulation did not make Joplin happy. "Onstage I make love to 25,000 people," she told a reporter, "then I go home alone."[35] After a half-decade of performing, her voice was reduced to a rasp, and she was punctuating road trips with frequent shots of heroin and hard liquor. Once famous for a manner both brash and gentle, Joplin had turned into a bitter and desperate woman. In 1970, she died from an overdose of heroin. Like other rock stars who killed themselves in similar accidents (Elvis Presley and Jimi Hendrix, most prominently), she could not bear the thought of living in the twilight after her surge into the spotlight was spent.

Yet millions of young rock fans experienced rock and roll not as romantic tragedy but as a series of tiny discoveries. They quoted and sang scraps of lyrics at school, work, and in bed; melodies, rhythms, and chord changes became elements of a secret language that lost everything in the translation.

Consider the tangled history of "Louie Louie," a song written and first recorded in 1956 by Richard Berry, a black musician from Los Angeles, with his band, the Pharoahs. At home in LA's multiracial potpourri, Berry heard a local Filipino group that sang mostly in Spanish play a version of the tune. He reworked the melody into a mixture of calypso (a popular craze at the time) and a cha-cha, then added new lyrics. A Jamaican sailor tells a sympathetic bartender named Louie about the love who waits for him at home: "Three nights and days we sailed the sea. Me think of girl constantly. On the ship, I dream she there. I smell the rose in her hair. Louie, Louie, me gotta go."[36]

The song had a catchy Caribbean beat, the meld of Latin and African styles. But it was heard mainly on the West Coast and sold a modest 40,000 copies. Berry, who received just two cents per record, moved on to other projects. But, near Seattle, a young white singer named Rockin' Robin Roberts found a copy of "Louie, Louie" in a remainder bin and decided to make the tune his own. Roberts wailed the lyrics instead of crooning them and added the phrase, "Let's give it to 'em, right now!" which turned the song into a sexual anthem of sorts. In the Pacific Northwest, his version became a regional hit.

One spring morning in 1963, the Kingsmen cut another recording of "Louie, Louie" in their hometown of Portland, Oregon, and unintentionally created a rock legend. While rehearsing the tune, Jack Ely, the band's lead singer, had to strain to reach the microphone above him; fatigue and the braces on his teeth caused him to slur the lyrics even more. The drummer and lead guitarist were nervous and so performed more crudely than in their many live gigs. Having finished the unpolished run-through, the Kingsmen were amazed to hear their manager rave, "That was *great*, man, you never did that song better."[37] Disk jockeys were soon playing the song as a novelty.

Through a manic whim of fortune, the Kingsmen's version of "Louie Louie" rapidly shed its status as a joke recording and became the second-best-selling single in the country. The rough instrumental was, no doubt, part of the reason; it made the Kingsmen sound like a bar band at the climax of a long night—careening somewhere between ecstasy and exhaustion. But what made the song unforgettable was Ely's incomprehensible vocal. What *was* that guy singing? Mythical lyrics proliferated. Most were pornographic, transforming the lovesick sailor into an emblem of every teenaged boy's lust-filled fantasies. Parents and ministers protested, and J. Edgar Hoover's FBI soon took up the case. Following more than two years of an investigation that employed the latest in audio technology, the bureau concluded that the lyrics were "unintelligible at any speed."[38] Remarkably, no agent ever questioned Jack Ely.

Such stupidity helped ensure "Louie Louie" a long and prosperous life. If the raunchy-sounding song was officially deemed a cultural menace, then it *had* to be good. In decades to come, over 200 different versions were recorded—by punk bands, surf bands, swing bands, Latin bands, Russian bands, French bands, two college marching bands, and the comedian John Belushi for the soundtrack of the movie *Animal House*. When Richard Berry died in 1997, the *New York Times* graced him with a lengthy obituary, solely because of his creation of a sea chantey then more than four decades old. Berry had lived to see "Louie Louie" enshrined in the cultural pantheon of the '60s—a mediocre song that became an underground phenomenon and grew over time into a quirky kind of generational statement. Therein lay the beauty of rock and roll; anyone of a certain age could appreciate the joke.

* * *

But a more serious cultural insurgency gradually sprouted alongside the ephemeral variety. Some young rebels aspired to build self-regulating *communities* that would show both their myopic elders and their timid peers the glories of an authentic existence—free of an addiction to the mass market and the quiet desperation of individuals floundering in a harshly competitive society. Toward the end of the 1960s and into the next decade, new ways of living, dressing, working, celebrating, and organizing a family flourished in dozens of urban neighborhoods and a scattering of rural communities.

In such experimental gestures, the youth culture articulated what Herman Marcuse—a German émigré philosopher whose writings were then popular—called "the Great Refusal—the protest against that which is."[39] In an economy whose abundance should be equally shared, millions might cooperate to construct a more soulful, more sensual world. In 1968, the French radical Daniel Cohn-Bendit put it well, "I am a revolutionary because it is the best way of living."[40]

Many Americans who were young and black revolted by proudly asserting their identity as *Africans*. "The way we talk, the way we walk, sing, dance, pray, laugh, eat, make love, and finally, most important, the way we look make up our cultural heritage," wrote Harlem actress Barbara Ann Teer.[41] Unlike the conservative clothing and close-cropped hair styles long favored by the Nation of Islam, the new black style was innovative and flamboyant. Men and women grew long, bushy Afros or "naturals" and donned dashikis, caftans, turbans, and jewelry made from such materials as ivory and cowrie shells that evoked the continent of their ancestors. Urban radio stations played soul tunes that sang the praises of "blackness," and the tricolor of red-black-

and-green (created in the 1920s by pan-Africanist Marcus Garvey) appeared on countless medallions and banners. Small community businesses sprang up to sell these products—and helped seed the dream of a separate economy that might link up with the independent nations of Africa. In black neighborhoods, "brother" and "sister" became the common form of greeting, as if all black Americans were members of the same, close-knit congregation.

Meanwhile, a new breed of artists built institutions they hoped would stir racial pride and train cultural militants. The erstwhile beat playwright/poet Le Roi Jones changed his name to Amiri Baraka ("blessed prince") and founded a black theater, an African Free School, a literary magazine, and a publishing company—all dedicated to what he called "a radical reordering of the Western cultural aesthetic." In Baraka's own writing, that "reordering" sometimes veered into anti-Semitism and rhetorical posturing. The poet Sonia Sanchez helped to launch Black Studies programs at several colleges, where her limpid, passionate verses became a staple of the curriculum: "We are sudden stars you and i exploding in our blue black skins."[42]

The most popular creation of black cultural radicals may have been a new holiday. In 1966, Maulana Ron Karenga, an activist from Los Angeles, created Kwanzaa to replace the "alienated gift-giving" that, in his view, corrupted the observance of Christmas in many black families. Inspired by African harvest festivals, celebrants of Kwanzaa (which derives from a Swahili phrase meaning "first fruits") practiced a week-long set of rituals—including the lighting of black, red, and green candles; drinking from a Unity Cup; and the exchange of hand-made gifts at a feast of foods drawn from different regions of the African diaspora. Karenga hoped the holiday would foster a separate African identity unmoored to the traditions of white America. But Kwanzaa caught on in numerous black families who attended Christian churches and continued to give out Christmas presents.[43]

Thousands of young whites who rejected the norms of "straight America" found their own path to a separate identity—by living together in communes. The phenomenon mirrored the whimsical diversity of the youth culture itself. Individual bands of communards lived in teepees, geodesic domes, ramshackle and sometimes hand-made farmhouses, buses, and in crowded urban apartments. Some supported themselves through subsistence farming or selling marijuana; others published newspapers, operated medical clinics, ran health-food restaurants, bookstores, garages, or day-care centers. The settlements were motivated by a wealth of inspirations and ideologies: Christian, Buddhist, the spiritual beliefs of Native American tribes, anarchism, pacifism, feminism, and a ferocious desire to end the war in Vietnam. By the early 1970s, some 30,000 communes—large and small, rural and urban—served as home and, often, workplace for over three-quarters of a million people.[44]

Despite its miscellany, this was a movement of shared impulses. Radical equality headed the list. Nearly all communards believed that men and women should share the work—whether building houses, feeding babies, or recruiting new members. Often, child-rearing too became a collective responsibility, and kids were encouraged to speak up about their grievances and to take on any chores they could handle. At one commune near Boston, a seven-year-old girl complained at the weekly meeting that adults were gobbling up all the ice cream. To a man who protested he didn't have a sweet tooth, the child responded, "But that's not the issue. There is never enough . . . Don't be defensive with me!" Some communes were steered by a charismatic individual, but virtually all of them defied outside authorities—governments, corporations, established churches—when they could get away with it. On the 1970 U.S. Census form, one group named its cat as "head of household."[45]

In certain ways, the communes of the 1960s and early '70s belonged to a long tradition of utopian settlements in America, stretching back before the Civil War. Residents sought to practice the ideal ends they preached: to produce much of what one consumed, to gain a living from the land without destroying it, to enjoy sex without "owning" one's lover, to demonstrate that the cooperative ethic could gradually usher in a future of familial bliss, to be true to one's own natural instincts. However, the pioneers of most earlier "intentional communities" had envisioned a logically planned, neatly ordered society that would prohibit antisocial behavior. In a best-selling novel published in 1888, Edward Bellamy described the citizens of his imagined utopia, "Ceasing to be predatory in their habits, they became coworkers, and found in fraternity, at once, the science of wealth and happiness."[46]

In contrast, the young commune dwellers of the 1960s and after saw the squelching of individual desires as a major reason to condemn "straight" America and escape its clutches. The freedom to take drugs and have guilt-free sex with one's fellow communards often rivaled the attraction of sharing one's labor and resources equally. Stephen Gaskin, leader of The Farm, a large settlement in rural Tennessee, viewed the smoking of marijuana as a sacred right: "We believe that if a vegetable and an animal want to get together and can be heavier together than either one of them alone, it shouldn't be anyone's business."[47] For both genders and all ages, nudity, even while working in the collective garden, was accepted as "natural" and thus virtuous. Most communes aspired more to reclaiming Eden than to perfecting the social order. If alternative arrangements didn't liberate the senses, they were hardly worth the effort.[48]

The tension between personal freedom and the collective ideal helped doom most communes to a short, if compelling, existence. Some settlements found it hard to draw a line between eccentricity and mental illness; Morning Star East, a community in the mountains of New Mexico, was home to a man "who lived in a hole in the ground and ate nothing but dry pancake mix with syrup."[49] The lack of privacy in urban communes increasingly rankled residents who had grown up in middle-class homes where they could shut others out of a room of their own. So did the hardships of rural living without the benefits of modern technology. In Morning Star East, it froze in winter and the main source of firewood lay thirty miles away over a bad road. And monogamy usually triumphed over the doctrine of free love, particularly for women and the parents of small children.

By the late 1970s, a majority of communes had dissolved, while others survived only by filling a small niche in the market economy. Residents of The Farm, for example, manufactured tie-dyed garments, practiced midwifery, and sold books and pamphlets on ecological farming. Typically, communal property reverted to private uses; the New Buffalo commune, located on picturesque land near Taos, New Mexico, became a bed-and-breakfast inn, catering to hip tourists.

But the import of such places stretched beyond their settings—whether wood-heated mountain A-frames or aging, big-city apartments reeking with the smell of organic herbs and musty carpets. Communards believed they could set up a household and earn a living without compromising their ideals. As with all such yearnings, their desire was imbued with childish naïvete—and could only have taken flight at a time of unprecedented prosperity. Yet, it could also be breathtakingly seductive. Cultural rebels, from the Beats to Afrocentrists, refused to wait for most Americans to see the necessity and joy of personal emancipation, as they defined it. Their determination to create exemplars of what early civil rights organizers had called a "beloved community" reflected aspirations common to every religion and to most new nations. Their failure was unsurprising. But the desire endures.

CHAPTER 9

The New Left

AS EASY IT WAS TO TELL BLACK FROM WHITE/IT WAS ALL THAT EASY TO TELL
WRONG FROM RIGHT. . . .
—Bob Dylan, 1963[1]

In his inaugural address in 1961, President John F. Kennedy sounded a call
for selfless dedication to national renewal—posed significantly in terms of
generational mission. "Let the word go forth," the new president declared,
that "the torch has been passed to a new generation." And then, in the best-
remembered line of the entire speech, he proclaimed: "Ask not what your
country can do for you, ask what you can do for your country."

This summons to self-sacrificing idealism appealed to many young Americans coming of age in the 1960s, though the forms in which their response
was expressed would vary widely. Some joined the newly established Peace
Corps, and worked for low pay and in primitive conditions in "developing
countries" abroad. Others, later in the decade, would join VISTA, the domestic equivalent of the Peace Corps launched as part of the war on poverty,
and headed off to do good works in Appalachia and urban ghettos. The Peace
Corps and VISTA tended to draw the most recruits from the same campuses
as did the early New Left: the University of California at Berkeley, for example, was the single most important source of volunteers for the Peace Corps
in the early 1960s.[2]

The same impulse that led some to volunteer for government-sponsored
experiments in social service and community organizing led others to join
insurgent movements for civil rights and peace. Many young volunteers in
the civil rights movement felt, at least in the first flush of activism, that their
efforts were welcomed by the new administration in Washington. Even some
who protested against the Kennedy administration's bellicose foreign policy
in those years, demanding instead an end to the nuclear arms race, were encouraged to believe that the president, somewhere in his heart, sympathized
with them. When several hundred protesters from the Student Peace Union
(SPU) picketed the White House on a wintry day in February 1962, the pres-

ident told his kitchen staff to send out of an urn full of hot coffee to sustain their spirits. The SPU reprinted and sent out to supporters an article from the *New York Times* about antinuclear protests that claimed that "President Kennedy is listening at least."[3]

One of the more enduring historical clichés about the 1960s concerns the "alienation" of young radical activists from their elders and from mainstream American values and goals. Although young Americans in the 1960s were not the first generation in history to feel that they were more sensitive to hypocrisy and injustice than their elders, they were certainly unique in the degree to which they expressed their newly awakened political aspirations in terms of generational identity. It is easy to assume that the New Left's political outlook was rooted in a rebellion against familial or even all adult authority. "Don't trust anyone over 30" is, after all, one of the best-remembered slogans that came out of the New Left—specifically, the Free Speech Movement (FSM) protests at Berkeley in the fall of 1964. The Free Speech Movement grew, in significant measure, out of the civil rights movement; several of its leading figures, including undergraduate Mario Savio, had spent the previous summer in Mississippi in SNCC's "Freedom Summer" voter registration campaign. Most of the FSM's tactics, rhetoric, and songs, came out of the civil rights struggle. At a climactic moment in the FSM's confrontation with the Berkeley administration, as students sat in at a university administration building, Joan Baez stood outside on the steps encouraging them with a rendition of Bob Dylan's civil rights anthem "The Times They Are a-Changin'":

> Come mothers and fathers
> Throughout the land
> And don't criticize
> What you can't understand
> Your sons and your daughters
> Are beyond your command
> Your old road is rapidly aging
> Please get out of the new one
> If you can't lend your hand
> For the times they are a-changin'[4]

In the early 1960s, student activists were brash and impatient, and possessed a collective sense of self-assurance that could shade easily into self-righteousness. The songs they listened to often bristled with youthful bravado and defiance ("Your sons and your daughters/are beyond your command"). But the sense that some bitter, absolute, and unbridgeable political gap divided the generations was, in fact, not evident in those first years of the decade. It took a succession of emotional and political blows in the early to mid-1960s to redirect the youthful spirit of idealistic commitment

Mario Savio, leader of the Free Speech Movement at the University of California, Berkeley.
Source: *Archive Photos*

away from the official agendas of the "liberal establishment" in Washington and elsewhere.

To return to the example of Berkeley in 1964, slogans and songs aside, FSM activists actually *did* trust a good number of people over 30, and also expected them to lend a hand in the struggle for social change. And in this sense of connection with their elders, the FSM activists were quite typical of the New Left. Yale Medical School psychologist Kenneth Keniston undertook a study of young radicals in the mid-1960s, and concluded that most came out of close, achievement-oriented families of liberal or, in some instances, radical political persuasion. Typically, the children in such families wholeheartedly identified with their parents' values, though they sometimes felt their parents had not put those values to consistent or effective use. In adolescence, Keniston noted, "their rebellion characteristically consisted in using against their parents the parents' own principles, and inspiring *their* guilt."[5]

That also serves as a good description of the FSM's strategy against the administration at UC Berkeley. The students rose up because they felt that the university, in seeking to restrict political advocacy on campus, had fallen short of their high expectations of its purposes. They were offended when university president Clark Kerr described the modern university as part of the "knowledge industry." Kerr's choice of imagery was a rather accurate description of the institution he led, with its increasingly close ties to California business interests and federal defense contractors. But it rankled those students who assumed that their purpose in attending the university had something to do with acquiring wisdom and finding personal meaning in life. Notwithstanding the already prevalent beards-and-sandals media stereotype of protesting students, in their attitudes toward the purpose of higher education they were the traditionalists, while the button-down Clark Kerr was the radical innovator. Students at Berkeley, FSM leader Mario Savio declared in an impassioned speech on the steps of Sproul Hall, "don't mean to be bought by some clients of the university. . . . We're human beings."[6] Human beings, in Savio's view, sought knowledge for its own sake, not as a commodity to peddle in the corporate marketplace (as a study of students arrested in the FSM protests showed, they had higher grades, on average, than nonprotesting students). The FSM's attitudes were shared by many of their teachers. Indeed, a central element of the FSM strategy against the Berkeley administration was to win support from UC professors; when the faculty senate voted overwhelmingly toward the end of the fall 1964 semester to endorse the FSM demands for free speech on campus, they were greeted as they left their meeting by 5000 applauding students.[7]

But by the later 1960s, the times *were* "a-changin" in ways that would make the FSM protest seem tame and naive in contrast. The sense of the legitimacy and permanence of the old political and intellectual order gave way rapidly in the minds of tens of thousands of young people. Within the New Left, the chief organizational expression and beneficiary of this trend would be Students for a Democratic Society (SDS).

When SDS was created in 1960, few people took notice, even on the Left, and even fewer expected that it would have much of a future. Al Haber, an undergraduate at the University of Michigan, had joined a tiny group of campus leftists called the Student League for Industrial Democracy (SLID) a few years earlier. SLID was subsidized by the League for Industrial Democracy, a pro-labor advocacy group that was funded by some of the more liberal trade unions. Haber was frustrated by SLID's inaction and lack of vision, and one of his first acts upon taking over as the group's director in 1960 was to rename it SDS. For the public debut of SDS, Haber organized a conference in Ann Arbor in the spring of 1960 that drew together white northern students and some of the black students who had been leading the sit-in movement in the South. Among those attending the conference was the student editor of the *Michigan Daily*, a thoughtful and ambitious junior named Tom Hayden. Hayden joined SDS soon afterward. The following year he went South to do what he could in the name of the group to support the black student movement. Over the course of the following year, SDS remained a very small and obscure organization, but it began to attract a talented circle of activists, drawn by the leaders' open and nondogmatic commitment to rebuilding a radical presence on the campuses.

In the spring of 1962 several dozen student delegates met at a United Auto Workers educational camp in Port Huron, Michigan, to debate a proposed program for SDS, largely authored by Tom Hayden, who by this point had become the group's president. After several days of debate, the young radicals arrived at consensus, adopting what became known as the Port Huron Statement. Over the next few years, tens of thousands of mimeographed copies of the statement were circulated on college campuses, and, as much as any single document, it defined the politics of the emerging New Left.[8]

It began with a statement of generational identity: "We are people of this generation," Hayden wrote, "bred in at least modest comfort, housed in the universities, looking uncomfortably to the world we inherit." Part of what followed consisted of a rather unsurprising political wish list for a group on the Left: the delegates endorsed increased spending on social welfare, decreased spending on the military, and civil rights legislation. What would later attract attention to the statement was not the programmatic details, but the emphasis on "values." "Men have unrealized potential for self-cultivation, self-direction, self-understanding, and creativity. . . . The goal of man and society should be human independence. . . . finding a meaning in life that is personally authentic." After reviewing the inadequacy of the "old slogans" left over from the communist and socialist movements of the 1930s, the statement called for the creation of a new kind of radical movement dedicated to creating a genuinely "participatory democracy" in which individual citizens could help make "those social decisions determining the quality and direction" of their lives. Colleges and universities, SDSers argued in the Port Huron Statement, had a vitally important role in creating such a movement, since "[a]ny new left in America must be, in large measure, a left with real intellectual skills, committed to deliberativeness, honesty, reflection as working tools. The university permits the political life to be an adjunct to the academic one, and action to be informed by reason."[9]

Over the next several years, SDS grew slowly, as its founders experimented with various political strategies. Many SDSers, including Hayden, moved into poverty-stricken neighborhoods in northern cities, in an attempt to create "an interracial movement of the poor" that was modeled on SNCC's community-organizing efforts in the South. Relations with the parent organization, the League for Industrial Democracy, were strained because SDS seemed insufficiently anticommunist to the LID elders (many of whom had cut their ideological teeth in battles between Communist and Socialist groups in the 1930s). By 1965 the two had parted ways. But up through that spring, SDS enjoyed increasing visibility and respect in the liberal community. UAW president Walter Reuther helped fund its community-organizing projects; and in the pages of *The Nation*, SDS was described, along with SNCC, as a collection of "thoroughly indigenous radicals: tough, democratic, independent, creative, activist, unsentimental."[10]

The New Left was, of course, always much larger than SDS; indeed, one of the defining characteristics of student radicalism in the 1960s was its high degree of decentralization and spontaneity (SDSers played very little role, for example, in the Berkeley Free Speech Movement, or in subsequent protests on the Berkeley campus). Bearing that qualification in mind, SDS's history still provides useful guidelines in charting the growth and development of the broader movement.

The events in Vietnam in the spring of 1965 proved a turning point for SDS and the New Left as a whole. As the war escalated, so did debate at home over its wisdom. The events of recent years had contributed to a new willingness among many Americans, and especially among the young, to challenge established authority, and to scrutinize political decisions in moral terms. Some of those who spoke out against the war in Vietnam were pacifists, who opposed all wars; others felt that United States policy in Vietnam was a reversion to big power bullying tactics and the worst excesses of Cold War paranoia. Johnson's decision to dispatch 15,000 marines to the Dominican Republic in April to quell domestic disturbances in that small Caribbean nation only added to the suspicion in antiwar circles that the U.S. government was bent on throwing its weight around as a kind of self-appointed policeman to the world. (Arkansas Senator J. William Fulbright, chairman of the Senate Foreign Relations Committee, and soon to become an important critic of the war in Vietnam, first broke with Johnson over the Dominican Republic intervention, calling it a "tragedy" that had been sold to the country "by a lack of candor and by misinformation."[11])

In late March, 3000 students turned out for a "teach-in" on the Vietnam war at the University of Michigan. Although supporters as well as opponents of the administration's policies were welcome to make their views known at the event, the overwhelming sentiment was against the war. The teach-in movement soon spread to over a hundred other campuses across the country. In April SDS sponsored an antiwar march in Washington, D.C. that attracted 20,000 participants, the largest antiwar demonstration in the nation's history until that point. The early anti-war protests were greatly influenced by the civil rights movement. "What kind of America is it whose response to poverty and oppression in South Vietnam is napalm and defoliation," the official "Call" for the SDS march on Washington asked, while its "response to poverty and oppression in Mississippi is . . . silence?" SNCC's Bob Moses was one of the speakers at the April rally, and SDS president Paul Potter told the crowd that "the reason there are twenty thousand people here today and not a hundred or none at all is because five years ago in the South students began to build a social movement to change the system."[12]

SDS was now the best-known radical group in the country. In the 1965–1966 school year, its national office in Chicago received a flood of letters from across the country from individuals and groups eager to join. A typical letter came from an Illinois high school student, who wrote in early 1966 asking for information about SDS. "I feel so strongly about civil rights, the war on poverty, etc.," she explained, "but I do so little for them . . . ":

> I listen to Pete Seeger's "We Shall Overcome" album, deck my bedroom with freedom posters and buttons, and argue in my English class. (I am one of two out of twenty-five who is pro-Civil Rights.) . . . My mind is torn as to whether we should be in Viet Nam. But I do feel that war is outdated and morally wrong. Knowing that it is my duty to form my opinion, I would like and appreciate your help.[13]

The national membership of SDS grew to about 15,000 that year, perhaps triple the membership of a year earlier.[14] And the organization became significantly more diverse, in the location and the kinds of school where its chapters took root. Early on, most SDS chapters were to be found in places like the University of Michigan, which had long histories of left-wing student activism. Now, students at schools like Dodge City Community College in Kansas and Ventura College in southern California were also forming SDS chapters. As a Ventura student wrote to the SDS national office that fall: "What I have read and heard of your group leads me to to believe we think much in the same direction." On their own, students at Ventura had formed a group called "Free Students for America," and now they wanted to affiliate with SDS. "The basic aims of [the Ventura group] are the removal of all American troops from Viet Nam, the use of aid rather than soldiers to combat the growth of totalitarian governments throughout the world, the affirmation of the right of any individual not to kill and not to be forced to serve in any military organization." In sum, the Ventura "Free Students" wanted to join SDS because "we feel there is considerably more creative power in the unity of many groups than there is in many separate groups."[15]

Thus, for the most part, SDS didn't have to send out organizers to recruit new members; the new members came to SDS on their own. These new recruits (dubbed the "prairie power" contingent because so many of them came from places other than the usual centers of radical strength) were less likely to share the theoretical sophistication or intellectual ambitions of the group's founding generation. The new breed tended to be unschooled in and impatient with radical doctrine, intensely moralistic, suspicious of "elitism" and "bureaucracy", and immersed in what was just starting to be referred to as the "counterculture" of casual drug use, sexual experimentation, and rock music. In contrast to the left-wing movements of the 1930s, where young radicals prided themselves on their analytic abilities and command of the intricacies of Marxist theory, a kind of emotional and moral plain-speaking was the preferred rhetorical style among SDSers.

SDS was changing, but chapter reports that flowed into the national office from around the country in 1965–1966 suggested that in most places, its members still thought of their role on campus more in terms of education

than confrontation. The student organizer for the University of Rhode Island
SDS chapter wrote in February 1966, outlining the group's activities since
the start of the new school year:

October [1965]: Folk concert and food sale to support member now working with MFDP [Mississippi Freedom Democratic Party]. Silent vigil (in
coordination with nationwide protest) to end the war in Vietnam.

November: Sponsor Rev. Arthur Lawson, Fellowship of Reconciliation,
speaking on visit to Vietnam. Eleven go to Washington to participate in
the SANE [National Committee for a Sane Nuclear Policy] demonstration.

December: Organized open discussion on the war in Vietnam.

January [1966]: Sponsored a . . . discussion on conscientious objection. . . .

February 15: Tom Cornell, Catholic Worker (burned draft card) to
speak.[16]

If SDS had ceased to exist in the spring of 1966, historians looking back
through its archives might well have concluded that the organization functioned primarily as a youth affiliate and support group for the pacifist and
civil rights movements, rather than any kind of self-consciously revolutionary, let alone violence-prone organization.

That was to change within the next year. In a short time, the very language of rational persuasion and nonviolence came to be regarded with suspicion by many in SDS, as it did throughout much of the New Left. The Port
Huron Statement had called in 1962 for the creation of "a left with real intellectual skills, committed to deliberativeness, honesty, reflection as working tools." But five years later, such sentiments had gone out of style. One
of the new leaders of SDS, Carl Davidson, declared in 1967 that radical students had come to understand "the impossibility of freedom in the university so long as it remained tied to the interests of America's corporate and
military ruling elite." Abandoning the early SDS vision, Davidson now called
for a strategy of "common struggle with the liberation movements of the
world" by means of "the disruption, dislocation and destruction of the military's access to the manpower, intelligence, or resources of our universities."[17]

Throughout the 1960s the fate of the white New Left was closely bound
to that of the struggle for black equality. Without the sit-ins of 1960, SDS
would likely have died a-borning. Without the Freedom Summer of 1964,
there probably would have been no Free Speech Movement at Berkeley. Writing in 1966, white radical journalist Jack Newfield argued that within the
New Left "one word, above all others, has the magic to inspire blind loyalty
and epic myth. SNCC."[18] However much changed in the politics of the white
New Leftists from the early to the late 1960s, the one constant was their im-

pulse to look to their black counterparts for direction and validation. Students willing to follow SNCC organizer Stokely Carmichael into nonviolent battle with the forces of white supremacy in Mississippi continued to follow his lead, at least rhetorically, when he espoused a strategy of armed self-defense in the urban ghettos of the North.

After the summer of 1964, SNCC veterans began to turn against the principles of interracialism and integration that had guided them since the group's founding in 1960. During Freedom Summer, whites actually outnumbered blacks in SNCC's voter registration projects in Mississippi; as a result, the campaign attracted the fulsome attention of the national media, as well as the support of many prominent white politicians in the north. That had been foreseen by SNCC's leaders, and was in fact the point of inviting white volunteers to Mississippi in the first place. But the very success of the strategy prompted some SNCC leaders to ask why it required placing middle-class whites in harm's way to prick the national conscience. Where had all those television news cameramen been when only blacks were being beaten, incarcerated, and murdered in Mississippi? Stokely Carmichael concluded that depending on sympathetic whites for political cover was, in itself, a concession to racism.[19]

Stokely Carmichael of SNCC (left) and Bobby Seale of the Black Panther Party (right), prominent black revolutionaries, 1967. Source: Jeffrey Blankfort

The last real opportunity for damping down the fires of racial separatism in SNCC came at the Democratic convention in Atlantic City at the end of the summer of 1964. SNCC activists had helped organize the Mississippi Freedom Democratic Party (MDFP) to challenge the credentials of the regular Mississippi Democrats who had been chosen in the customary all-white state primary election. Johnson, fearing the defection of southern white voters, saw to it that the MDFP's challenge was quashed, although he did offer them two at-large delegate seats at the convention, an offer the activists indignantly refused. After Atlantic City, black and white radicals alike were quick to condemn liberal Democrats as hypocrites whose commitment to genuine racial equality extended only to the symbolic. If moral persuasion had no effect, SNCC leaders concluded, they were going to have turn to other means. "We want more than 'token' positions," declared SNCC's Charles Sherrod. "We want power for our people."[20]

SNCC was also coming under the influence of the charismatic black nationalist leader Malcolm X. On a goodwill tour of independent black nations in Africa in the fall of 1964, SNCC leaders had a chance encounter with Malcolm, who was there on a tour of his own. Although often bitterly critical of the civil rights movement's adult leadership, Malcolm courted the young SNCC leaders. Just days before his assassination in February 1965, Malcolm made a rare appearance in the South, speaking at a rally in Selma at SNCC's invitation. Malcolm's militancy, including the advocacy of armed self-defense, and his pan-Africanism (the belief that all Africans shared a common destiny and should be linked politically) greatly appealed to SNCC's young black activists. In the last year of his life, Malcolm abandoned many of the antiwhite sentiments he had espoused before his expulsion from Elijah Muhammad's Nation of Islam organization. But he had not changed his mind on the question of whether blacks and whites should work together in the same groups. "I know," he declared in his autobiography, "that every time that whites join a black organization, you watch, pretty soon the blacks will be leaning on the whites to support it, and before you know it a black may be up front with a title, but the whites, because of their money, are the real controllers."[21] Malcolm's violent death only added to his political luster. John Lewis, who remained one of the more moderate voices within SNCC in 1965, commented after Malcolm's death that, "more than any other single personality," he had been "able to articulate the aspirations, bitterness, and frustrations of the Negro people," as well as representing "a living link between Africa and the civil rights movement in this country."[22]

SNCC's political outlook and its public image changed dramatically in the summer of 1966. Stokely Carmichael had defeated John Lewis that spring to become SNCC's new chairman. Lewis, southern-born, soft-spoken, and a firm believer in nonviolence had come to be seen by many in SNCC as the symbol of a passing age; Carmichael, urban, northern, fast-talking, and fed up with both nonviolence and interracialism, was now the man of the hour.[23] In late May, in one of his first official acts, Carmichael withdrew SNCC from the planning sessions for a White House conference on civil rights. To movement insiders and the media, that decision underlined the growing differences between SNCC and more mainstream civil rights organizations, but outside the movement relatively few Americans noticed. Something more dramatic was needed to get the message out that SNCC was no longer the same organization it had been in the days of "We Shall Overcome" idealism.

Carmichael found the moment he was waiting for when James Meredith, a black Air Force veteran whose enrollment at the University of Mississippi in 1962 had provoked a violent white riot on the campus, decided on his own to stage a "March Against Fear" across Mississippi. Meredith hoped to encourage the blacks he encountered along his route from Memphis, Tennessee, to Jackson, Mississippi, to register to vote. But he was only in the second day of his trek when he was wounded by a white gunman on a lonely stretch of Mississippi highway. Meredith, regarded by many in the civil rights movement as an eccentric loner, had undertaken his journey without any organizational backing. Now SCLC's Martin Luther King, Jr., CORE's Floyd McKissick, and SNCC's Stokely Carmichael pledged to carry out his mission, and march on to Jackson, Mississippi.

For the next 10 days the marchers, whose numbers ranged day to day from a few dozen to several hundred, made their way toward Jackson without further incident. The reporters covering the march at first assumed this would be simply a reprise of the previous year's Selma-to-Montgomery march, its larger purposes to be defined, as in the earlier event, by Martin Luther King's oratory. But Carmichael had other ideas. A SNCC activist named Willie Ricks had already been firing up crowds along the route by shouting the slogan "Black Power!" When Carmichael was arrested and briefly incarcerated in Greenwood, Mississippi, he decided to follow Ricks's example. That night, at a rally in Greenwood, he electrified a crowd of hundreds of black supporters by announcing "What we are gonna start saying now is Black Power." For the remainder of the march, it was Carmichael, not King, who set the tone. "What do you want?" SNCC organizers would shout at rallies during the rest of the march. "Black Power!" the crowds would roar back.[24]

The Black Power slogan, soon echoed by other groups on the militant wing of the movement such as CORE, terrified whites who associated it with violent urban outbreaks like the 1965 riot in Watts, and took it as the prophecy of full-scale race war. But the meaning of the term was not nearly as well defined in the minds of its supporters as the fearful reaction it inspired would suggest. To some advocates, Black Power meant little more than "black pride." This definition of black power could be satisfied by defining an identity around a distinctive African-American sense of history and culture. Others saw in Black Power the same tradition of ethnic cohesion and mutual aid that had been of such help to groups like the Irish and the Jews in their earlier breakthroughs to social mobility. None of this required a revolutionary transformation of American society; in the 1968 presidential election, Republican candidate Richard Nixon found it politically expedient to advocate his own version of "black power," which he defined as "an expansion of black ownership" of businesses, or "black capitalism."[25]

Black capitalism was not what Stokely Carmichael had in mind when he called for Black Power. But what he did mean by the slogan seemed to change month by month, and audience by audience. In July 1967 Carmichael traveled to Havana, Cuba, where, along with representatives of revolutionary groups from Central and South America, he was seated as an honorary delegate to the meetings of the Organization of Latin American Solidarity (OLAS). In Havana, Carmichael expressed his sympathy for Cuban-style communism and described the movement for Black Power in the United States as part of a worldwide struggle against "white Western imperialist society."[26]

Carmichael had not talked with anyone else in SNCC's leadership about his trip to Havana, or the positions he intended to take there. Julius Lester, who acted as Carmichael's press spokesman in Havana, was privately appalled by the SNCC leader's ideological posturing. As he confided to his diary: "I sit here with the Mick Jagger of revolution and think about all the people who believe in him, and I am frightened. . . . "[27] Leaving Havana, Carmichael moved on to Communist China and North Vietnam, before returning, after a stopover in Africa, to the United States. There, again without prior signal to or consultation with his increasingly bewildered followers, he changed course again. At a rally in Oakland, California, the following February, Carmichael announced that "Communism is not an ideology suited for black people, period, period. Socialism is not an ideology suited for black people, period, period." Instead, he advocated "an African ideology which speaks to our blackness—nothing else. It's not a question of right or left, it's a question of black."[28]

The swing to Black Power in the civil rights movement was as much a product of generational as racial conflict. Older and more established black leaders, like Martin Luther King, Jr. remained committed to an integrationist vision. This was true even within SNCC itself; Fannie Lou Hamer, 48 years old the summer of the "Black Power" march, resolutely opposed the ouster of SNCC's white staff, a position that led some younger SNCC activists to deride her as "no longer relevant" to the movement.[29] Public opinion polls taken at the height of the Black Power movement revealed that an overwhelming majority of African Americans still believed in integration as the best solution for ending racial inequality.[30] But despite that sentiment, and despite the ideological vagueness of the call for Black Power, the bloody rioting in the "long hot summers" of 1966 and 1967 led many Americans to believe that a deliberately fomented urban guerrilla war was indeed in the offing.

White liberals, many of whom were also offended by SNCC's new identification with the cause of Palestinian nationalists in the Middle East, severed their remaining ties with the group (a financial disaster for SNCC, hastening its demise). But those on the white New Left, for whom SNCC had functioned as "epic myth," were confronted with a more difficult choice. They (or people they knew or knew about) had been sufficiently committed to risk their lives in Mississippi when the call came from SNCC for Freedom Summer volunteers; was SNCC's advocacy of revolutionary violence now enough to scare them off?

By the summer of 1967, most white New Leftists would probably have agreed that the old interracial and nonviolent civil rights movement was not only over, but also had proven a failure. In the early 1960s, the inspirational language of the civil rights movement encouraged the belief that once the institutional barriers to racial equality had fallen, racism itself would rapidly wither and disappear. "All God's children," King had promised in his "I have a dream" speech in 1963, would be able to unite in singing the words of the old Negro spiritual, "Free at last! Free at last! Thank God Almighty, I'm free at last!" But racism had not disappeared with the subsequent passage of the Civil Rights Act of 1964 and the Voting Rights Act of 1965; instead it seemed to be growing stronger and more widespread. No longer was racism seen by New Leftists as merely a regional problem to be dealt with in the South, but as central to the identity and values of the nation as a whole. Mobs of angry whites had jeered at and stoned Dr. King during his Chicago "open housing" campaign in 1966—were they any different from the Ku Klux Klansmen who had beaten and murdered civil rights activists in Mississippi and Alabama? New Leftists might not have had the presumption of their counterparts in SNCC, who had, for some time, referred derisively to Martin Luther King as "de Lawd," but they no longer looked to him for leadership or inspiration.

Instead, like SNCC activists, SDSers and other New Leftists found it psychologically bracing to imagine themselves in alliance with the revolutionary forces of the Third World. Those who were a minority in their own country, were thus, looked at from the proper political perspective, actually moving in the same direction as the overwhelming majority of the world's population. Red plastic-bound copies of *Quotations from Chairman Mao Tse-tung*, published in English translation in Communist China, began to circulate in New Left circles in 1967, especially on the West Coast. In January 1967, Huey Newton and Bobby Seale, two black militants who had just formed an obscure local group in Oakland, California, called the Black Panther Party for Self-Defense, raised money to buy guns and ammunition by peddling copies of Mao's "little red book" to Berkeley students.[31] There was sometimes a trace of self-mockery among the would-be American Red Guards who carried the Little

Red Book around in their hip pockets; it served more as a curiosity or a fashion statement than as a frequently consulted source of political wisdom. But its appearance was significant nonetheless as a symbol of the New Left's desire to link up with distant and exotic battalions of revolutionary allies.

For all the talk that began to be heard of "picking up the gun," few white radicals were actually prepared to do so. But if black militants were now prepared to arm themselves in earnest, they weren't going to be second-guessed by their white comrades. Steve Halliwell, a graduate student in history and assistant national secretary of SDS, spent the summer of 1967 working with the SDS National Office in Chicago. Halliwell had been carrying on a running argument with one of his old professors at Columbia, Leo Haimson, a distinguished historian of the Russian Revolution. Haimson was considerably more skeptical about the prospects for revolution in the United States than his young student. But Halliwell urged the professor to consider the vulnerability of the system to acts of exemplary violence:

> The USA cannot continue to send black men overseas to learn how to fight in jungles and then bring them home to kill their brothers in the ghettoes—they just won't have an army. . . . Three guys with rifles could stop the Lake Street el [Chicago's elevated train system] every night at rush hour. I'm not suggesting that this is the substance of a revolutionary movement, but it is important that there is a growing reservoir of very militant people that can have real debilitating consequences even in small numbers.[32]

As Halliwell's comments suggest, the war in Vietnam was also much on his mind that summer. In fact, for many on the Left—and not just disciples of Mao—the struggle against the war and the struggle for black liberation had effectively merged.

As the New Left grew larger, it also grew more internally divided. The early 1960s vision of the movement as a "beloved community" in which all those committed to social change could join together in common effort and fellowship had come apart at the seams by mid-decade. Whites were no longer welcome in the black movement, save as outside supporters. And, within the white New Left, there were increasing tensions, if not yet any absolute division, between men and women.

When Tom Hayden sat down to write the Port Huron Statement in 1962 he had, without reflection, used a language of gender exclusivity. "Men," he wrote, "have unrealized potential for self-cultivation, self-direction. . . . " In using the term "men," he did not consciously intend to exclude women, but merely applied the then all-but-universal convention of having masculine designations serve as synonyms for "human beings." The same was true of other phrases in the statement, and commonly used in the movement, like "brotherhood." If any of the women at Port Huron noticed, they raised no objections at the time.

Within a few years, however, many women in the New Left would ask if there was any necessary connection between the "self-cultivation" and "self-definition . . . " of men and the aspirations of women for an equal measure of freedom and autonomy. Mary King and Casey Hayden (the latter Tom Hayden's wife) both worked on staff for the Student Non-Violent Coordinating Committee. "Why is it in SNCC," they asked in a position paper they circulated anonymously (fearing ridicule) at a SNCC conference in the fall of 1964, "that women who are competent, qualified, and experienced are automatically assigned to the 'female' kinds of jobs such as: typing, desk work, telephone work, filing, library work, cooking . . . but rarely the 'executive' "? The answer, they suggested, was "the assumption of male superiority."[33]

A year later, this time writing in their own names, they circulated what they called "a kind of memo" among women in the civil rights and antiwar movements. "Having learned from the movement to think radically about the personal worth and abilities of people whose role in society had gone unchallenged before," King and Hayden wrote, "a lot of women in the movement have begun trying to apply those lessons to their own relations with men." Although in 1965 they considered the chances as "nil" that "we could start a movement based on anything as distant to general American thought as a sex-caste system," they nonetheless wanted to "open up a dialogue" with other women who felt as they did.[34]

King and Hayden were wrong in their limited expectations. Their observations struck a chord with many young women, and not a few older ones. Women's caucuses and workshops sprang up in SDS and other movement groups in 1966–1967, and by the fall of 1967 independently organized women's groups were meeting in Chicago, New York, and a few other cities. Very often, the early groups consisted of small circles of friends and acquaintances who would gather at one or another's home to talk about their experiences as women in the movement and the broader American society in what became known as "consciousness-raising groups."[35]

Some men in the civil rights movement and the New Left were sympathetic to the the call for what began to be known as "women's liberation." Others saw the new movement as a trivial distraction from more serious issues of racism and war. And not a few felt personally threatened, since the "dialogue" begun by women in the movement often raised intimate questions about sexual behavior and privilege. "What is the position of women in SNCC?" Stokely Carmichael joked in response to the initial Hayden–King paper. "The position of women in SNCC is prone!" And, according to Mary King, his was one of the more sympathetic responses.[36]

Male hostility, along with the example set by the rise of Black Power, led many of the new feminists to adopt their own separatist stance in regard to men. "I once thought that all that was necessary was to make men understand that they would achieve their own liberation, too, by joining in the struggle for women's liberation," poet and activist Marge Piercy wrote in the late 1960s, "but it has come to me to seem a little too much like the chickens trying to educate the chicken farmer."[37] By the late 1960s, locally organized "women's liberation" groups could be found in virtually every major city and on every college campus, sponsoring a wide range of activities, from consciousness-raising discussion groups to women's health clinics, bookstores, coffeehouses, newspapers, battered women's shelters, and more. These were evidence both of the success of the women's movement—and of the failure of the New Left to provide a welcoming environment for feminist concerns. In 1962 Tom Hayden had suggested that the quest for a sense of "personal authenticity" could be part of the glue holding together a movement for social change. But by the later 1960s, competing visions of authentic and meaningful personal existence were instead pulling the movement apart.

As black and whites and men and women in the movement went their own ways, they were still bound together in common opposition to the war in Vietnam. Just how best to oppose the war was, however, often a divisive issue. Some sought to use the traditional methods of political canvassing, petitioning, and electoral politics. An organization called "Vietnam Summer" sent tens of thousands of volunteers door to door in the summer of 1967 to spread the antiwar message. That fall, voters in Cambridge, Massachusetts, and San Francisco were asked in ballot referendums whether the war should continue, and roughly 40 percent of them in both cities supported American withdrawal.[38]

Building an antiwar majority was a painfully slow process, and gathering signatures on petitions seemed a tepid response to the ongoing carnage in Vietnam. And, even if the majority of voters in liberal bastions like Cambridge came out in opposition to the war, it seemed unlikely to have much effect on American policy. Searching for alternatives, antiwar radicals increasingly sought to emulate the tactics that had been employed so successfully by the civil rights movement. The struggle against Jim Crow in the South had relied upon the willingness of civil rights workers to "speak truth to power," by violating unjust laws—"putting your body on the line" in acts of courageous personal and collective confrontation of illegitimate authority.

The southern example was compelling—but misleading. In the civil rights movement, confrontation (at the lunch counter in Greensboro, on the Freedom Rides, on the streets of Birmingham and Selma) had served strategic ends. Such confrontations often capped years of patient, grassroots organizing (SNCC had spent two years in Selma, preparing the ground for the dramatic events of the spring of 1965). In the New Left and the campus antiwar movement, in contrast, media-oriented confrontation increasingly took the place of the long-term strategy and commitment displayed by the civil rights organizers.

The longer the war continued, the higher the draft calls, and the greater the number of flag-covered coffins returning to the United States from Vietnam, the more the conflict bred an atmosphere of frustration and extremism within the New Left. Vietnam was a particularly volatile issue around which to attempt to build a mass movement. Unlike the civil rights movement, which until 1965 was organized to achieve a series of concrete political and legislative goals, the antiwar movement could measure success only by one all-encompassing aim, the end of the killing in Vietnam. No partial victories were available: the movement would either force the United States government to end the war, or it would fail. As a result, the New Left wing of the peace movement swung back and forth between near-millennial expectations, and an ever darker and angrier despair. As historian Thomas Powers commented, "The violence in Vietnam seemed to elicit a similar air of violence in the United States, an appetite for extremes: people felt that history was accelerating, time was running out, great issues were reaching a point of final decision."[39]

For some on the New Left, their newly acquired revolutionary convictions argued against devoting too much energy to antiwar protest, which was seen as a problem for liberals to settle; instead, they thought, revolutionaries should focus on stopping "the seventh Vietnam from now" by organizing the poor to overthrow capitalism. But others saw in the antiwar cause, or as

A demonstrator arrested during Stop the Draft Week, Oakland, California, October 1967.
Source: *Jeffrey Blankfort*

they began to call it, "anti-imperialism," a way to confront both the war and the social and economic system that had spawned it. Those who were "radicalized" in the struggle against the war, so the theory went, would go on to become the shock troops of the coming final struggle against capitalism. Young revolutionaries paid little attention to more experienced leftists, like the radical journalist I. F. Stone, who had been around long enough to appreciate the resilience of American capitalism. ("If the cause of world peace depends on the overthrow of American capitalism," Stone noted drily in 1965, "there isn't much hope for the world."[40])

The trend toward ever more theatrical confrontations was already visible in the first summer of antiwar protest in 1965. After a spring of teach-ins, vigils, and peaceful marches against the war, student protesters began to look for ways to "put their bodies on the line." As before, Berkeley pointed the way. In August 1965 several hundred protesters from the University of California had stood on railroad tracks to block oncoming troop trains rolling into the Oakland Army Base. They didn't stop the trains, but they did create a dramatic tableau, with an element of genuine personal risk of dismemberment or death, should either a train engineer or a protester miscalculate. Steve Weissman, a veteran of Freedom Summer and one of the organizers of the train blockade, described the demonstration as a tremendous success and drew from it the following lesson:

> Civil disobedience is good when it feels good—not only at the point of disruption, but also as one looks back after the euphoria and the crowds have dispersed. . . . [C]ivil disobedience is more than self-indulgence: creative social dislocation that feels good will enlarge participation and limit the disillusionment and depoliticization that often follows those grueling days in court.[41]

The standard of political effectiveness used to measure and justify the campus antiwar movement's embrace of ever more militant tactics increasingly became the sense of gratification and commitment such tactics provided to participants, combined with the amount of coverage it guaranteed on the evening television news. There was a seductive exhilaration to feeling oneself part of a redemptive minority in the United States, allied in some intangible yet deeply felt way to that irresistible majority of peasant revolutionaries abroad who were rising up against the American empire. Some SDS leaders, like Tom Hayden, traveled to Hanoi and came back enthralled by the "fearlessness, calm determination, pride, even serenity" displayed by the Vietnamese revolutionaries confronting the world's greatest superpower.[42] Viet Cong flags began to dot the ranks of antiwar demonstrations, and young marchers provocatively chanted slogans like "Ho, Ho, Ho Chi Minh/The NLF is gonna win." SDS publications began to fill up with imagery of heroic guerrillas brandishing automatic weapons.

The antiwar movement, which was far broader than the New Left, included people with many different political views. There were groups of veterans, and clergy, and trade unionists, and businessmen, and many others who had no use for the extravagant rhetoric of revolutionary cultism. Even New Leftists were not universally enthralled by the romance of violent revolution. The draft resistance movement, which drew on support of religious radical groups like the Catholic Worker movement, as well as SDS and SNCC, coordinated campaigns of young men to turn in or burn their draft cards, and to refuse induction into the armed forces even at the risk of imprisonment. Draft resisters, by and large, remained true to nonviolent principles. But they too were attracted to a politics of "creative social dislocation." Many resisters were drawn to the movement precisely because of its emphasis on total commitment and an exclusive form of risk taking (only young men of draft age, after all, could join). As one draft resister described the outlook of his fellow resisters at the time, they shared "a profound suspicion and distrust of most of the usual political organizations and their analyses which so often lead to endless meetings and little or no action."[43]

The dangers involved in the politics of confrontation were not lost on some veteran leaders of the New Left, although they found themselves powerless to reverse the trend. Lee Webb, a former SDS national secretary, complained in an internal document in the fall of 1965 that "SDS influences its membership to become more militant rather than more radical. . . . Calls to fight the draft, stop a troop train, burn a draft card, avoid all forms of liberalism, have become . . . the substitute for intellectual analysis and understanding."[44]

But it was hard to argue with success, and confrontational politics were successful—at least on college campuses. Notwithstanding the loathing with which many Americans regarded the campus revolutionaries, SDS continued to double its membership with each new school year. By the end of 1967 SDS had grown to nearly 30,000 loosely affiliated members. And antiwar demonstrations grew larger as they grew more militant.[45]

In the spring of 1967, the National Mobilization Committee Against the War, a broad coalition of radicals, liberals, and pacifists, sponsored marches against the war in New York City and San Francisco. These were well-attended and peaceful affairs. Several hundred thousand marchers followed Martin Luther King and other notables from New York City's Central Park to the United Nations to demand the immediate withdrawal of U.S. forces from Vietnam. Antiwar leaders decided to follow up their success with another march in the fall, this time in Washington, D.C. The October march, Mobilization leaders declared, would mark the peace movement's transition "from protest to resistance." Meanwhile, other groups around the country laid plans for local demonstrations in October to "confront the warmakers."

The antiwar offensive started with "Stop the Draft Week" in Oakland, California, protests designed to shut down the functioning of the Oakland induction center. Pacifists sat in nonviolently early in the week, and several hundred allowed themselves to be peacefully carted off by police. Draft resisters turned in 400 draft cards to the federal attorney in San Francisco, in another peaceful protest. But as the week wore on, the crowds grew larger and the tactics more violent. By Friday, October 20, 10,000 young protesters were engaged in a massive street battle with Oakland police. There was no more sitting down waiting passively for arrest: the protesters charged police lines, built barricades in the streets, and in general tied up downtown Oakland in a chaotic scene that resembled a scene from the French Revolution. That same week, several hundred students at the University of Wisconsin sat in at a university building to block recruiting by the Dow Chemical Company (Dow was reviled by antiwar protesters for producing napalm for the war in Vietnam). Local police easily routed the sit-inners from the building with nightsticks and Mace, but they had more trouble outside controlling a crowd of several thousand onlookers, enraged at the sight of the bloodied heads of their fellow students. Eventually police used tear gas and dogs to break up the protest.[46]

The climax to the week's protests came in Washington on Saturday, October 21. Antiwar organizers had set up a two-part event: a "traditional" gathering for a rally and speeches at the Lincoln Memorial, followed, for the more adventurously inclined, by a march that crossed the Potomac River to the Pentagon building, headquarters to Secretary of Defense Robert McNamara. Jerry Rubin, who had won his spurs as an antiwar organizer in Berkeley, coordinated the event. Rubin had a taste for the dramatic that was matched by his associate, Abbie Hoffman, a veteran organizer for the northern support group, Friends of SNCC. Both Rubin and Hoffman were deeply attracted to the youthful counterculture that was emerging in places like Haight–Ashbury in San Francisco and the East Village of New York, which was evident in the spirit of whimsical militance they brought to the antiwar movement. Hoffman's promise to "levitate" the Pentagon and then spin it in midair in a ritual exorcism to drive out its "evil spirits," irritated some of the more sober-minded leaders of the antiwar movement, but succeeded in attracting hundreds of colorfully garbed hippies to join the march. (They looked "like the legions of Sgt. Pepper's Band," novelist Norman Mailer would write in *The Armies of the Night*, his celebrated account of the day's events. In their multihued and multithemed costumes, the protesters seemed to Mailer to be "assembled from all the intersections between history and the comic books, between legend and television, the Biblical archetypes and the movies."[47])

The Pentagon did not levitate, but 30,000 marchers did bring the antiwar message to within shouting distance of the building. Several thousand of

March on the Pentagon, October 1967. Source: *Minora Aoki, War Resisters League*

the most militant broke through lines of federal marshals, soldiers, and National Guardsmen and reached the side of the building. A few carried Viet Cong flags; others put flowers in the gun barrels of the young soldiers who surrounded their encampment. There they sat and sang and yelled "Join us!" to the soldiers. Some urinated on the side of the building; a few threw rocks at the military police. As dusk arrived, the marshals moved in with clubs and tear gas, and nearly 700 were arrested.[48]

Robert McNamara watched the protest from the roof of the Pentagon. Ironically, the experience filled him with nostalgia for the early innocent days of Sixties protest. Privately disillusioned with the war he had done so much to create, he found himself plotting strategy for the antiwar movement: "I could not help but think that had the protesters been more disciplined— Gandhi-like—they could have achieved their objective of shutting us down." McNamara's son Craig, a prep school student at the time, was already so dismayed by his father's responsibility for American policies in Vietnam that he had pinned a Viet Cong flag on his bedroom wall; later, as a college student, he would take part in violent antiwar protests. "I remember the rage setting in on me, and the frustration that we all felt because we couldn't stop the war," he would tell an interviewer years later. "What was in my mind . . . was rage, pure rage."[49]

As Norman Mailer walked toward the crowd before the Lincoln Memorial that October day, he heard the peal of a trumpet in distance, which seemed to him to "go all the way back through a galaxy of bugles to the cries of the Civil War. . . . The ghosts of old battles were wheeling like clouds over Washington."[50] The clouds continued to hover, the drums to beat on, the trumpets to sound. The war was truly coming home.

CHAPTER 10

The Fall of the Great Society

IT'S A TERRIBLE THING FOR ME TO SIT BY AND WATCH SOMEONE ELSE STARVE MY
GREAT SOCIETY TO DEATH. . . . SOON SHE'LL BE SO UGLY THAT THE AMERICAN
PEOPLE WILL REFUSE TO TOOK AT HER; THEY'LL STICK HER IN A CLOSET TO HIDE
HER AWAY AND THERE SHE'LL DIE. AND WHEN SHE DIES, I, TOO WILL DIE.
—*Former president Lyndon Johnson, 1971*[1]

In an issue of the *Village Voice* published late in 1966, cartoonist Jules Feiffer offered a wry analysis of the state of domestic politics in his weekly cartoon. "Big Daddy," a young girl in western dress asks a stricken-looking, cowboy-garbed Lyndon Johnson in the cartoon's first panel, "That look on your face—yer hidin' somethin'." "Sit down, child," Johnson replies gravely. "Yew gonna have t'be brave. . . . Great Society has had an accident, child." She begs reassurance that it's only a "li'l bitty accident," but Johnson tells her not to get her hopes up. Then, in the final panel, the child looks up at Johnson with suddenly dawning suspicion: "This accident o' Great Society's, Big Daddy. Has it already happened—or are yew about t'have it happen?" "Naow," Johnson responds slyly, "We don't want t'grow up too fast, child."[2]

By this time *Village Voice* readers, like many of Johnson's former supporters, had come to regard the president as a habitual liar. The man who, seemingly, had no enemies at the start of 1965, had fallen below a 50 percent approval rating by the spring of 1966. The term "credibility gap" was by now in wide circulation to describe Johnson's penchant for deceiving the public.[3] Feiffer probably did Johnson an injustice in suggesting willing complicity on his part in the demise of the bright hopes of the early Great Society. In retirement, Johnson would speak with obvious anguish of the fate of his social programs, about the ill luck and difficult political choices that hampered them while he was in office, and about their cruel dismembering at the hands of his Republican successor. "[N]ow Nixon has come along and everything I've worked for is ruined," he complained to interviewer Doris Kearns in 1971. "There's a story in the paper every day about him slashing another one of my

195

Great Society programs. I can just see him waking up in the morning, making that victory sign of his and deciding which program to kill."[4]

LBJ's self-exculpating account of the death of the Great Society cannot, however, be taken as the whole truth. The bold vision of social transformation that he had announced with such enthusiasm during the presidential campaign of 1964 would wither long before Richard Nixon was in the position to wield an executioner's ax. In the course of 1966, with overwhelming Democratic majorities still in control of both houses of Congress, Johnson could persuade Congress to pass only a single significant Great Society proposal, the Model Cities Act providing federal funding for the redesign and reconstruction of America's inner cities. And even that measure passed with greatly reduced majorities compared to those enjoyed by previous Great Society legislation. Johnson's real goal in 1966 was to hold down spending on existing Great Society programs rather than passing new measures. As domestic policy adviser Joseph Califano would recall, "Johnson's extravagant rhetoric announcing new programs belied the modest funds he requested to begin them."[5] Political reversals in the 1966 midterm elections reinforced Johnson's caution.

Lyndon Johnson could read election returns as well as any man who had ever sat in the Oval Office. Although he continued to propose new social programs in the years remaining in his presidency, they were in scale and ambition nothing like those he had put forward in 1964–1965. There was no more talk of unconditional war against poverty; now it was simply a "poverty program." By 1968, when he delivered his final State of the Union address, Johnson used the term "Great Society" in only a single passing reference.[6]

Johnson bore significant, though not exclusive, responsibility for blighting the promise of liberal reform in the 1960s. His responsibility lay first and foremost in the fact that after 1965 his first priority as president no longer concerned the Great Society or domestic policy in general, but winning the war in Vietnam. The war not only diverted Johnson's attention from domestic policy, but also drained billions of dollars in federal funding, some portion of which might otherwise have gone to the Great Society. The war also undermined Johnson's authority, divided Democrats into feuding camps, and emboldened his conservative opponents. But even without the war, the Great Society would likely have come to grief in the later 1960s, as it ran afoul of other conflicts breaking out between Americans over issues such as racial justice, crime, personal morality, and economic security.

By January 1966, when President Johnson delivered his third State of the Union address, there was no question that the United States was deeply involved in a war that was not destined to end any time soon. The president vowed in his address that the country would prove "strong enough to pursue our goals in the rest of the world while still building a Great Society at home."[7] But as the war in Vietnam escalated, so did its costs, in dollars as well as in lives. The $5 billion the United States spent in Vietnam in 1965 doubled the following year; by 1968 direct costs of running the war (excluding veterans benefits and related expenses) increased to $33 billion.

"Nothing I had read, no photographs I had seen prepared me for the immensity of the American effort," veteran correspondent Robert Sherrod reported from Vietnam in *Life* Magazine early in 1967. The "fantastic expense of the war," he argued, "can only be comprehended in the viewing."[8]

There was the new "Pentagon West" building in Saigon, providing offices for the 68 American generals stationed in the city, constructed at a cost of $25 million. There were nine new jet landing fields constructed between Da Nang and Saigon, each of them a 10,000 foot-long strip of aluminum or concrete, costing at least $5 million. There were three new deep-water piers in Saigon to handle incoming cargo from U.S. merchant ships, and three more in Da Nang. The new harbor at Cam Ranh Bay would by itself cost American taxpayers $110 million. And all that was just infrastructure. There was also the daily cost of fighting a war in which the United States relied heavily on superior firepower. One evening, Sherrod reported:

> I flew from the demilitarized zone down to Saigon, about three quarters of the length of this 900-mile string bean of a country. Much of the coast was lit up by flares; artillery shells twinkled in 40 or 50 different spots. No battles were being fought that night but the Viet Cong, if present, presumably were being kept awake and the interdicting fire prevented them from traveling certain routes in case they intended going that way. This lavish use of firepower, whether effective or not, contributes to the cost of killing the enemy, which is calculated at $400,000 per soldier—including 75 bombs and 150 artillery shells for each corpse.[9]

Johnson was reluctant to admit the actual costs of the war, not wanting to do anything that would make an already unpopular conflict even more so, or to hand enemies of his domestic policies a reason to demand fiscal austerity at home. Although short-term bookkeeping devices allowed Johnson to fudge the true costs for awhile, the bill would soon come due in the form of mounting government deficits as well as the beginnings of an inflationary spiral in the American economy. (Defense spending increases personal income but not the amount of consumer goods on which such income can be spent—a classic formula for inflation.) In the summer of 1967 Johnson finally bit the bullet and asked Congress for a 10 percent income tax surcharge to pay for the war.

Johnson was being hit from both the Right and the Left on the issue of spending in Vietnam. The Right demanded that Johnson cut domestic spending as the price for increased taxes (a dispute that delayed the actual passage of the income tax surcharge for nearly a year). "We are trying to get this message across," declared Wilbur Mills, the conservative chairman of the House Ways and Means Committee, in which the surtax bill was bottled up. "We want a pause in this headlong rush toward ever bigger government."[10] The

Left, on the other hand—at least that portion of the Left that still thought it shared any common political ground with Johnson—intended to hold the president to his pledge to provide guns *and* butter to the American people. Bobby Kennedy, now ensconced in Congress as a senator from New York State, and still officially a supporter of the war, challenged Johnson in the spring of 1966 when the administration proposed a lower than expected funding request for aid to disadvantaged schools. The "200 million dollars that is being cut [from the original request]," Kennedy declared, "is what it costs to send the B-52s over Vietnam for perhaps a week."[11]

"I knew from the start," Johnson told Doris Kearns:

> that I was bound to be crucified either way I moved. If I left the woman I really loved—the Great Society—in order to get involved with that bitch of a war on the other side of the world, then I would lose everything at home. . . . But if I left that war and let the Communists take over South Vietnam, then I would be seen as a coward and my nation would be seen as an appeaser.[12]

Johnson's only hope for salvaging his dream of being remembered in history as a great liberal reformer was to get "that bitch of a war" over with in a hurry, and then return to be faithful to "the woman I really loved—the Great Society." And so, like a gambler on a losing streak throwing good money after bad, he constantly upped the ante. As of December 31, 1965, there were 184,300 American troops stationed in Vietnam. Thus far, 636 had died in combat. Two years later Johnson had raised the number of American troops in South Vietnam to 485,600; 19,562 had died.

Johnson and his military commanders counted on search-and-destroy operations to bring victory in Vietnam. Every day thousands of American troops were out on patrol, humping the boonies, in search of the enemy. Often they found no trace of the enemy except well-concealed and deadly booby traps. Sometimes they got lucky and stumbled across an arms cache, or managed to flush out a squad of Viet Cong. Some of these operations went on for months, delivering large cumulative numbers of dead enemies to be tallied into "body counts" and "kill ratios" by the Pentagon's computers. Operation Masher, which ran from January through March 1966 on the Bong Son Plain in central Vietnam, provided a body count of 2389 enemy dead. Operation Junction City, a year later in War Zone C, northwest of Saigon along the Cambodian border, produced a body count of nearly 3000 enemy dead.

Some search-and-destroy operations were joint South Vietnamese–American efforts, but for the most part, the Americans were taking the place of their allies in combat. With the exceptions of some elite South Vietnamese battalions of airborne troops and marines, ARVN earned a reputation for its preference for engaging in what skeptical American observers dubbed "search-and-evade" missions. Reviewing the statistical performance of the Eighteenth

ARVN Division, which claimed to have conducted over 5000 patrols in one week in 1966, during which they made a total of only thirteen contacts with the enemy, U.S. military adviser John Paul Vann wrote disgustedly, "I can easily establish more enemy contacts on a daily basis myself."[13] The Saigon government, now jointly run by two former generals, Prime Minister Nguyen Cao Ky and chief of state Nguyen Van Thieu, did not inspire enthusiasm either in the civilian population or in the military. In 1965 alone, 113,000 South Vietnamese soldiers and militiamen deserted, a figure that nearly equaled the number of additional Americans sent that year to fight in Vietnam.[14]

As the French had learned in the First Indochina War, Communist guerrilla fighters were hard to find—unless they wanted to be found. The Communists were often tipped off in advance of American plans, either through the elaborate systems of spies they maintained on and near U.S. bases, or by preliminary air and artillery strikes. A study by the U.S. Army showed that from 1966 to 1967 the overwhelming majority of all battles in South Vietnam were started not by American forces, but by the Communists, usually by ambushing American units in the countryside.

Meanwhile the air war over North Vietnam continued and expanded. This too proved a costly enterprise. The North Vietnamese defended their air space with a sophisticated system of antiaircraft defense provided to them by the Soviets, including radar, antiaircraft weapons, SAM [surface-to-air missile] batteries, and MiG-17 and MiG-21 fighters. From 1965 through 1968 the United States lost over 900 aircraft over North Vietnam, with over 800 pilots and crewmen killed, and over 500 captured.

The costs were heavy but the results meager. A government-sponsored study of the effects of Operation Rolling Thunder concluded soberly that as of July 1966 "the U.S. bombing of North Vietnam had had no measurable direct effect on Hanoi's ability to mount and support military operations in the South at the current level." North Vietnam's agricultural economy could not be significantly damaged by air attack; its transportation system could be easily rebuilt after attacks; and because most of the weapons being funneled down the Ho Chi Minh Trail were imported by North Vietnam, it made little difference how many North Vietnamese factories were destroyed. Infiltration of men and supplies down the Ho Chi Minh Trail increased steadily during the years of the heaviest bombing. It was estimated that it took an average of a hundred tons of bombs dropped along the trail to kill a single North Vietnamese soldier.

When Defense Secretary Robert McNamara read this report in the fall of 1966, it furthered his growing personal disillusionment with the war. In a memorandum to President Johnson in May 1967, McNamara warned:

There may be a limit beyond which many Americans and much of the world will not permit the United States to go. The picture of the world's greatest superpower killing or seriously injuring 1,000 non-combatants a week, while trying to pound a tiny backward nation into submission on an issue whose merits are hotly disputed, is not a pretty one.[15]

McNamara kept his doubts to himself. Others did not. Perhaps the most eloquent dissent from the war came, not surprisingly, from Martin Luther King, Jr., who in a speech in New York City in April 1967 issued what he called a "declaration of independence" from the war in Vietnam. As a dedicated pacifist, King was first and foremost opposed to the war because of his moral objections to the use of violence. But he also challenged Lyndon Johnson's claim that Americans could enjoy both guns and butter. That issue had already been decided in favor of the former: "A few years there was a shining moment," King declared, when it seemed "as if there was a real promise of hope for the poor":

> Then came the build-up in Vietnam, and I watched the program broken and eviscerated as if it were some idle political plaything of a society gone mad on war. . . . So I was increasingly compelled to see the war an an enemy of the poor and to attack it as such.[16]

The war that President Johnson had proposed fighting against poverty was intended as only one part of the much more ambitious project of building the Great Society. But in historical memory the former has all but subsumed the latter; few people today remember how much of the Great Society, from Medicare to highway beautification to endowments for the humanities and arts, was designed primarily to benefit the middle class. Similarly, the costs of the war on poverty have been greatly exaggerated. Even at their height, Johnson's poverty programs never represented the "unconditional war" that he declared in his first State of the Union address. Daniel Patrick Moynihan, who as assistant secretary of labor in charge of the Office of Policy Planning and Research in 1964 had been present at the launching of the war on poverty, would later declare that it had been "oversold and underfinanced to the point that its failure was almost a matter of design."[17] The Office of Economic Opportunity, the agency overseeing the poverty program, received only 1.5 percent of the federal budget for all its programs in the years from 1965 to 1970. Had the money spent on poverty programs simply been parceled out in cash grants to every American whose income fell below the poverty line in those years, each poor person would have received a grand total of about $70 a year.[18]

The war on poverty had scarcely gotten off the ground when it ran into sustained political opposition. Conservative Republicans viewed the whole thing as an expensive government boondoggle. Many Democrats, particularly those in city government, came to oppose its provisions for "maximum feasible participation" of the poor in directing poverty programs, particularly

White construction workers react to an antiwar demonstration, Portland, Oregon, 1971.
Source: *David Weintraub*

through the community action agencies. Sargent Shriver had initially expected those agencies to function in ways similar to a board of education, formally independent of local government as school boards generally were, but certainly not in an adversarial position.[19] Instead, many of the agencies launched voter registration drives to oust incumbent politicians or sponsored marches on city halls to demand improved services for poor neighborhoods.

The backlash from urban Democratic leaders was immediate and intense. Two Democratic mayors, Sam Yorty of Los Angeles and John Shelley of San Francisco, offered a resolution to the 1965 meeting of the U.S. Conference of Mayors condemning the war on poverty for "fostering class struggle" in American cities. (Yorty had been a long-time conservative gadfly within the Democratic Party. Shelley, on the other hand, was a former trade unionist who had headed up the San Francisco Labor Council before becoming mayor—his disaffection had ominous implications for the future of urban Democratic politics.[20]) When Congress passed the Model Cities Act in 1966, it directed that the program be administered by the Department of Housing and Urban Development rather than the now-suspect OEO, and the provisions for "maximum feasible participation" of the poor were eliminated. Unlike the programs established in 1964–1965, Model Cities would be a program controlled by big city mayors, not by people in poor neighborhoods and ghettos.

By 1966 even the poor were complaining about the war on poverty, a war that had been launched on their behalf, but not at their behest. One of the defining characteristics of the "culture of poverty" that Michael Harrington had described in *The Other America* was a sense of fatalism, at odds with any kind of sustained political involvement. But the war on poverty created a sense of rising expectations among the poor that the antipoverty programs could do little to assuage. In April 1966, at a Washington, D.C. conference of the Citizen's Crusade Against Poverty (a private advocacy group set up at the behest of the United Auto Workers union to lobby on behalf of the poverty program), Sargent Shriver was booed and jostled by a dissident group of community activists when he attempted to address the group. Shriver was driven from the stage by chants of "You're lying!" and "Stop listening to him!" Afterward UAW official Jack Conway despaired that the poor "have turned on the people who wanted to help them."[21]

For all its limited scope, and for all the controversy it created, the war on poverty was not without its successes. The number of people in the United States whose annual income fell beneath the poverty line declined from 32 million (or 17 percent of the population) in 1965 to 23 million (or 11 percent of the population in 1973). To be sure, poverty had been declining in the 1950s even before there was a war on poverty, and the general prosperity and low unemployment rates of the mid-to-late 1960s certainly accounted for some of the decline. But save for the period of the Second World War, which brought the Great Depression to a sudden end, there was no other period in American history when poverty rates declined as rapidly as they did during the years of Johnson's presidency and its immediate aftermath.[22]

Nonetheless, by the later 1960s, Americans who disagreed on just about everything else were united in judging the war on poverty an abject failure. Government programs had clearly failed to eliminate poverty as either an economic category or as a "culture." If anything, the remaining urban poor (whose numbers began to increase again during the economic hard times of the later 1970s) seemed even more permanently mired in their condition than they had been before the federal government interested itself in their plight.

The conservative argument that the very programs liberals had foisted upon the country in the 1960s kept the poor bound to a "cycle of dependency" would become conventional wisdom within a very few years. While the number of poor people declined in the later 1960s, the number of AFDC recipients mounted at an even more precipitous rate. In 1960 fewer than three-quarters of a million families were receiving aid through AFDC at a cost to the federal and state governments of under a billion dollars; by 1972 there were 3 million families receiving AFDC, at an annual cost of $6 billion.[23] The swelling welfare rolls were accompanied by rising rates of illegitimacy, teenage pregnancies, single-parent families, violent crime, substance abuse, and a host of other ills that came to be laid at the feet of the liberal social engineers of the Great Society.[24]

In a curious way, the problem with the war on poverty was not that it failed, but that it succeeded—perhaps too well for its own political survival. The intent of the war, after all, was to lessen the distance between the "other America" and the mainstream. One of the characteristic elements of American national identity is the belief that citizenship, and personal security and dignity, are grounded in "rights." The war on poverty, through its rhetoric, and through the legal services it provided poor communities, reinforced the idea that the poor as well as the affluent should enjoy these rights. And one of the expressions of this new sensibility was the belief that those who received government aid in the form of welfare payments did so not as a matter of charity, but of right.

Since the start of the twentieth century, the term "welfare" had changed in American political discourse from a term with positive associations of health and well-being to one implying malingering incapacity and the waste of taxpayers' hard-earned money. At best, welfare tended to be viewed as a kind of gift that the better-off, through the government, offered to the less fortunate and deserving poor. Those who received it were expected to be appropriately grateful and as unobtrusive as possible.[25]

At the start of the 1960s only about a third of the families eligible to participate in the AFDC program were actually receiving benefits. AFDC was a program funded jointly by the federal government and the states, and administered at the state level. Many state legislatures did their best to discourage new applicants. Benefit levels were usually set below the states' own official guidelines for the minimum income necessary to support a family at a decent standard of living, and strict residency requirements prevented newcomers from claiming even these meager benefits. The welfare system was set up so that normal presumptions about prying into personal affairs did not apply to recipients. Since welfare was a "means-tested" program, every scrap of household income had to be reported to social workers: concealed earnings from a child's paper route could result in charges of "welfare fraud." Evidence of a "man in the house" would also result in AFDC recipients (most of them single women) being dumped from the program; social workers sometimes staged midnight raids on the homes of recipients to make sure that they remained as single as they claimed to have been when applying for benefits. All of this worked to reinforce the stigmatizing image of welfare and discouraged would-be recipients from even applying.[26]

In the course of the 1960s an alliance of poor people, middle-class advocates, and lawyers specializing in the new field of poverty law argued that welfare was not a gift, and certainly not stigmatizing, but rather a legally guaranteed entitlement. Local groups of welfare mothers began to coalesce in the mid-1960s, some of them brought together by Community Action Programs, others by independent community organizers.[27]

In 1966 George Wiley, a former chemistry professor and associate national director of CORE, helped pull together local welfare rights groups from across the country into a national organization, which took the name of the National Welfare Rights Organization (NWRO) the following year. Although its membership peaked at little over 20,000 members at the end of the decade, NWRO became a highly visible and, for a time, effective organization. While lawyers argued the case for welfare rights in the courts, welfare recipients took their demands into the public assistance offices, with marches and sit-ins. William Ryan, a white liberal psychologist, described such tactics as "the plain old-fashioned American practice of demanding and getting one's rights."[28] In a statement outlining its goals, NWRO declared in 1966:

> As members of a National Welfare Rights Movement . . . we are are not willing to exchange our rights as American citizens
> —our rights to dignity
> —our rights to justice
> —our rights to democratic participation
> in order to obtain the physical necessities for our families. . . . [29]

NWRO tactics led to many tangible benefits, both for its own members and for millions of other people on welfare. The level of AFDC benefits increased, and restrictions on eligibility were lessened. By the end of the 1960s nearly 90 percent of those eligible for AFDC benefits were receiving them.[30]

But practical success did not guarantee political success. The NWRO suffered the inevitable problems of organizations based on low-income members—high turnover and uncertain finances—and fell apart by the mid-1970s. More importantly, the goal of "welfare rights" never acquired the patina of legitimacy that came to be associated with the idea of equal rights for blacks and women. The more that welfare recipients exercised the "old-fashioned American practice" of a vocal assertion of rights, the less they seemed entitled to the status of the "deserving poor." When NWRO members conducted a sit-in during a Senate hearing on punitive welfare regulations, Russell Long of Louisiana declared, "If they can find the time to march in the streets, picket, and sit all day in committee hearing rooms, they can find the time to do some useful work."[31]

The hostility to welfare recipients was part of larger shift of sentiment against the poor in the later 1960s. The piety with which poverty had been spoken of in the early days of the Johnson administration gave way by the mid-1960s to a more astringent rhetoric. The vision of the poor as latter-day Daniel Boones perched up high on some West Virginia mountainside disappeared from the media and popular consciousness, to be replaced by the more durable and menacing image of a black urban underclass.[32]

In 1965 Daniel Patrick Moynihan unintentionally dealt the earlier idealized vision of the poor a fatal blow. Moynihan had come to Washington in 1961 with both political and academic credentials; he had been an assistant to New York governor Averell Harriman in the late 1950s, during which time he also managed to complete a Ph.D. in political science. He was committed to two goals during his years with the Labor Department, bringing the insights of contemporary social science to bear in the design of public policy, and making a name for himself. He succeeded in both endeavors when he oversaw the writing of a memorandum entitled *The Negro Family: The Case for National Action*, which became better known as the Moynihan Report.[33]

Moynihan described what he called a "tangle of pathology" that had undermined the urban black family in recent years. Moynihan's intention in analyzing black family structure was fully in conformity with the reformist goals of the war on poverty, and drew heavily on studies of ghetto life by black social scientists like E. Franklin Frazier and Kenneth Clark. There were also echoes of Gunnar Myrdal's *An American Dilemma*, including the phrase about "pathology." The instability of many black families, as measured in rates of divorce or abandonment, illegitimacy, female-headed families, and welfare dependency, was as Moynihan described it, a historical legacy of slavery, reinforced by the continuing high rates of black male unemployment, and the fact that AFDC payments were available only to households without an adult

Warding off looters during the riot in Newark, July 1967. Source: *Express Newspapers/F373/ Archive Photos*

male in residence. (Moynihan noted that this description did not apply to all black families, and that a large and increasingly successful black middle class was also emerging in American society.)

The solution for those who were trapped in the social tangle of ghetto ills, Moynihan thought, would be more jobs for black men, who would then be able to take their rightful place in society and in their families as bread-winners. However, Moynihan chose not to include that recommendation in the final version of the paper, a fateful omission.

The Moynihan Report was released in March, initially restricted in circulation to a small circle of top policymakers. Lyndon Johnson was among its readers, and its impact was seen in an address he gave at Howard University in June of 1965. It was, in one sense, the most radical speech of his presidency. Johnson declared that it was not enough for Americans to commit themselves to seeking "equality as a right and a theory" for black Americans; they should press on to achieve "equality as a fact." He went on to argue that black poverty differed in important ways from that experienced by whites: there were, he averred, "differences—deep, corrosive, obstinate differences—radiating painful roots into the community, and into the family, and the nature of the individual."[34] The previous year, when he sought passage of the war on poverty, Johnson deliberately downplayed black poverty, visiting Kentucky rather than Harlem to draw attention to the plight of the poor. Now, with a different purpose in mind, he was arguing that black poverty was even more devastating than that suffered by whites. The policy implications of that observation were not as clear as Johnson assumed.

The Moynihan Report was leaked to the press that summer (some suspected that Moynihan, not exactly averse to publicity, was the responsible party). The fact that the report's existence became known almost simultaneously with the outbreak of the Watts riot ensured that its conclusion would receive considerable attention—though not of the kind that liberals would welcome. Although there was nothing startling new or particularly original in Moynihan's observations about the black family, the word "pathology" leapt off the page of his report, infuriating black readers, who took it as an insult, and persuading many white readers that the problems of the black community were so intractable as to be impervious to government social welfare programs (the fact that Moynihan himself would later drift toward this position, at least temporarily, reinforced the belief that he had always intended the report as an attack on the war on poverty). In any event, after the summer of 1965 the behavior of the poor—and most particularly of the black poor—rather than any privations or injustices they endured, came to the fore in the minds of many Americans when they thought about the issue of poverty.

The war on poverty was founded on the assumption that the United States had entered upon an era of permanent abundance. The Economic Opportunity Act of 1964 declared its goal to be the elimination of the paradox of poverty in the midst of plenty. But even in the go-go years of the 1960s economy "plenty" was unevenly distributed in the United States, in ways that left a majority of American families vulnerable to any downturn. Workers' real wages and median family income increased dramatically in the postwar era, but income share remained virtually unchanged (the top fifth of the population received 43 percent of income in 1947, 41.2 percent in 1968).[35] The median family income for 1968, which stood at $8632, was still about a thousand dollars less than what the Bureau of Labor Statistics defined as "modest but adequate" income for an urban family of four. That meant that many working-class families had to scramble to stay ahead, either by going into debt or by fielding additional breadwinners, usually by means of sending wives into the workforce. (In 1960, 37.8 percent of women were in labor force; by 1970 that number had increased to 43.4 percent—and would jump to over 50 percent before the end of the next decade.[36]) Rising wages also began to erode as inflation picked up later in the decade and as taxpayers found themselves bumped upward into higher tax brackets.

White working-class taxpayers and property owners, already fearful about blacks moving into their neighborhoods, resented the war on poverty as a payoff to rioters, "welfare queens," and "poverty pimps." In a nation long obsessed with the automobile, it was only fitting that the earliest and pithiest statements of new political trends were to be found attached to rear fenders: when "I Fight Poverty, I Work" bumper stickers began appearing in the mid-1960s, it was clear that the nation's brief honeymoon of concern and goodwill with the poor was coming to an end.

The prospects for liberal reform were worsened by declining white support for the civil rights struggle. In 1964, 68 percent of northern whites supported the Johnson's administration's civil rights initiatives. That was before Watts and the riots that followed. Throughout the country, there were 11 major riots (defined as civil disturbances lasting two days or more) in the summer of 1966, and 32 minor riots; the following summer, the number jumped to 25 major and 30 minor riots, including the bloodiest outburst of the decade in Detroit, where 43 people died in the rioting in July 1967.[37]

By 1966, 52 percent of northern whites believed the government was pushing too fast for integration.[38] As long as "civil rights" had been seen as a regional problem, a battle fought between white and black citizens of distant states like Alabama and Mississippi, white ethnic voters in northern cities were prone to support or at least tolerate the liberal politicians who voted for legislation banning racial discrimination. But when confrontations broke out in northern cities between whites and blacks over issues of immediate local concern—housing, jobs, schools, political clout—and when nonviolent demonstrations gave way to or were accompanied by black rioting the equation changed.

When Martin Luther King, Jr. had somberly surveyed the ruins of Watts in August 1965, he remarked to Bayard Rustin, who accompanied him on the trip, "I worked to get these people the right to eat hamburgers, and now I've got to do something . . . to help them get the money to buy it."[39] Accordingly, in 1966, King led the SCLC into its first northern urban campaign, on behalf of the 700,000 black residents of Chicago. Building on years of patient organizing by an interracial coalition, King and lieutenants like Jesse Jackson aimed to expose and eradicate the de facto segregation of jobs, schools, and neighborhoods in the North. The SCLC decided to open its ambitious effort with a push for open housing, hoping to bring to bear the same combination of moral and political pressure that had succeeded in opening to black citizens the voting booths and the public schools of the South. SCLC imported rhetoric, songs, and tactics from the South to the North. One movement activist charged, in language intended to invoke the image of George Wallace in the school doorway, that Chicago realtors were "standing in the doorway of thousands of homes being offered for sale or rent."[40] SCLC organizers marshaled their followers to march into all-white neighborhoods, just as they had previously marched on segregated businesses and courthouses.

The reaction was not what King or his aides had intended. Instead of shaming the North, they succeeded instead in convincing many northern whites that southern whites may have had a point in their resistance to civil rights. In neighborhoods like Gage Park and Marquette Park on the southern edge of Chicago, thousands of white residents turned out to jeer and throw rocks at the SCLC marchers. Young males took the lead; one group of boys brandished a noose and sang to the tune of a popular commercial jingle, "I'd love to be an Alabama trooper/That is what I'd really like to be/For if I were an Alabama trooper/Then I could hang a nigger legally."[41] Martin Luther King was among those struck by a flying brick; only a massive police presence allowed the demonstrators to escape serious injury.

Newspaper editorials condemned the violence of word and deed, yet civil rights groups and liberal lawmakers were unable to push an open-housing bill through Congress. More support was expressed for the "overworked and overcriticized" Chicago police than for the marchers; pollsters and journalists found that white Americans tended to blame SCLC for provoking white rage. A man from Maryland wrote to King, "The results [of the marches] were predictable . . . hatred has been built up which it will take a generation to overcome."[42]

By the mid-1960s, the rhetoric and imagery of the civil rights movement was being appropriated by whites for their own purposes. As one Michigan woman wrote to her congressman, "These white people [in Chicago] wish to be left alone and should be allowed to live with their own kind of people, or is the white not supposed to have any freedom?"[43] Open housing proved to be an issue very different from the question of whether blacks should vote or be able to eat in any restaurant they could afford to patronize. Residents of places like Marquette Park had saved for years to buy their own homes in a secure, comfortable neighborhood. For them, black migration spelled a sharp increase in crime and social tensions; the value of their property and the quality of their children's educations, they feared, would decline rapidly.

The conflict in Chicago in the summer of 1966, and similar ones in other northern locales, revealed large numbers of whites now ready to stand up in the name of their own rights and grievances, in ways that did not bode well either for the civil rights movement or for any other part of the liberal reform agenda. Liberal politicians were held accountable for rising racial animosity, and a host of related evils. A resident of Marquette Park complained to Senator Paul Douglas, a longtime champion of such liberal causes as antipoverty programs and civil rights: "We work hard, pay our taxes, improve ourselves, only to find the more we improve ourselves and our property the more we are taxed and told what we can and cannot do with it."[44] Property, taxes, self-improvement, and self-rule—this was economic and cultural terrain perfectly suited for nurturing a new conservative political coalition. Senator Douglas would find that out in a hurry as he went down to defeat in November 1966 in his bid for reelection to what would have been his fourth term in office.

As Americans were becoming more mistrustful of liberal leaders, many also wished that traditional sources of authority could be restored to the role they had played (or were imagined to have played) in earlier days, as enforcers of a common morality and social harmony. "We are becoming cannibalized," a working-class Italian American from Brooklyn complained. "We didn't sass the policeman when he told us to move. Now in school they call teachers 'motherfucker.' "[45]

Cultural backlash intersected with the racial backlash and also with class resentments. Although many of the youthful denizens of places like Haight–Ashbury were in reality runaways or "throwaways" from poor and working-class families, the image of the counterculture became synonymous in the minds of many Americans with the privileged existence enjoyed by well-off students at the nation's best-known colleges and universities. The long-haired hippie/student aroused a curious mixture of antagonism and envy. "When I hear a college kid say, 'I'm oppressed,' I don't believe him," a 37-year-old white steel worker from Cicero, Illinois, told radio interviewer Studs Terkel:

> You know what I'd like to do for one year? Living like a college kid. Just for one year, I'd love to. Wow! (Whispers) Wow! Sports car! Marijuana! (Laughs) Wild, sexy broads. I'd love that, hell yes, I would.[46]

But his counterpart in Brooklyn, quoted earlier, regarded the same behavior as uncivilized and impermissible: "This sexual permissiveness is disgraceful, it's like dogs in the street. The way of living today, there are no values."[47] It was bad enough that the privileged young ignored traditional authority and morality; worse, they actually celebrated the resulting chaos: "We are out-laws!," the *Berkeley Barb*, a leading underground newspaper exulted: "We defy law and order with our bricks bottles garbage long hair filth obscenity drugs games guns bikes fire fun & fucking—the future of our struggle is the future of crime in the streets."[48]

There was a certain amount of deliberately provocative hyperbole in such editorial broadsides, and in rock anthems like Jefferson Airplane's "Volun-teers" ("We are all outlaws in the eyes of Amerika!"). But for urban Ameri-cans, both black and white, crime was no joking matter in the 1960s. After having declined steadily since the Second World War, rates of serious crime, including murder, rape, robbery, and auto theft shot up dramatically in the mid-1960s.[49]

There were many explanations put forward for this disastrous trend. Lib-erals favored explanations emphasizing environmental "root causes"—un-employment, poor schools, and the like. Conservatives, on the other hand, blamed permissive child-rearing practices, lax law enforcement, and crimi-nal-coddling courts. Criminologists pointed to additional factors that were beyond the control of public policy, either liberal or conservative. Young peo-ple in their teens and early twenties are always the group most likely to find themselves in trouble with the law. The fact that the growth in crime in the 1960s began when the first wave of baby boomers turned 16 certainly ac-counted for some, if not all, of the increase.[50]

Conservative politicians quickly recognized the political importance of the crime statistics. "[We] have heard of and seen many wars in the time of the present administration," Barry Goldwater declared in a campaign speech in mid-September 1964 in St. Petersburg, Florida. "But have we yet heard of the only needed war—the war against crime?" Johnson responded a month later in a campaign speech in Dayton, Ohio, avowing that his war on poverty "is a war against crime and a war against disorder."[51] The following March, in a message to Congress, Johnson declared a "war on crime," while still maintaining that "the long-run solution to crime is jobs, education, and hope."[52]

But the liberal emphasis on combating the "root causes" of crime, instead of just locking up criminals, was easily parodied by conservatives. "How long are we going to abdicate law and order . . . " House minority leader Gerald Ford asked rhetorically in 1966, "in favor of a soft social theory that the man who heaves a brick through your window or tosses a firebomb into your car is simply the misunderstood and underprivileged product of a broken home?"[53]

For millions of white Americans of middling income, "law and order" became both a cry of outrage at the political, cultural, and social upheavals of the 1960s, and the crux of the solution to them. The phrase conveyed the sense that the hard-won upward mobility of the postwar era was a fragile achievement, prey to the taunts of Ivy League radicals and ghetto rioters alike. The demand for "law and order" asserted the common grievances of ordinary people against the perversely misplaced sympathies of liberal politicians and intellectuals, a group who had come to seem contemptuous of the way normal Americans lived their lives.

In the course of the 1960s, the imagery of class conflict in America was turned on its head. Liberals—who had been thought of as defenders of the interests of the working classes in the 1930s, and who in the early 1960s embraced the cause of the most downtrodden of Americans, southern blacks and the poor—by the mid-1960s were viewed by many as an arrogant elite of "limousine liberals." And conservatives—those "economic royalists" denounced by FDR in the 1930s as the aristocratic defenders of privilege and power—were emerging in the 1960s as the new populists, speaking for the common man and woman. A liberal government that seemed more interested in protecting esoteric and expansive notions of "rights" for marginal groups than in protecting the lives and property of the vast majority was rapidly losing legitimacy. With the nation's financial resources engaged in the war in Vietnam, and its emotional resources engaged in the war on crime, there was precious little of either left over for a war on poverty. And if, as it seemed by 1966–1967, that the real political choice the United States faced was between constructing a Great Society or maintaining an orderly one, it is not surprising that so many would choose the latter over the former.

CHAPTER 11

The Conservative Revival

YOU WALK AROUND WITH YOUR GOLDWATER BUTTON, AND YOU FEEL THE THRILL OF TREASON.
—*Robert Claus, student activist at the University of Wisconsin, 1961*[1]

"I find that America is fundamentally a conservative nation," wrote Senator Barry Goldwater, Republican from Arizona, in a short, provocative book, published in 1960, that set forth his political creed. "The preponderant judgment of the American people, especially of the young people, is that the radical, or Liberal, approach has not worked and is not working. They yearn for a return to Conservative principles."[2]

At the time, most commentators found Goldwater's judgment in *The Conscience of a Conservative* to be both inaccurate and old-fashioned. Didn't most Americans endorse the central tenets and programs of modern liberalism? Didn't they welcome government's role in financing education, public housing, and insurance for the elderly and the unemployed? Hadn't strong unions made working-class Americans prosperous? Wasn't the liberal ethic of racial integration and cultural tolerance growing in popularity? Wasn't it sensible to coexist peacefully with the Soviet Union, a nation whose hydrogen bombs could destroy every major U.S. city? A popular study of American conservatism, published in 1962, was subtitled *The Thankless Persuasion*. In the Senate, Goldwater had sponsored no major piece of legislation. "His main business there," commented historian Richard Hofstadter at the time, "was simply to vote No." Did the Right have anything meaningful to say to Americans in the 1960s?[3]

Goldwater curtly dismissed that line of argument: "Conservatism, we are told, is out-of-date. The charge is preposterous. . . . The laws of God, and of nature have no dateline." Then the former World War II pilot went on the attack: against the welfare state ("My aim is not to pass laws, but to repeal them"); against forced integration, even though he personally favored biracial schools ("I am not prepared . . . to impose that judgment of mine . . .

213

on the people of Mississippi and South Carolina"); and against a foreign policy geared to "containing" the Soviet bloc instead of defeating "the Communist empire."[4]

In 1964 an unprecedented grassroots effort won Barry Goldwater the Republican nomination for president. By then, *Conscience of a Conservative* had sold over 3 million copies.

Much attention was paid, during the 1960s and after, to powerful liberals who molded social policy and to the flamboyant movements—black, antiwar, feminist, countercultural—that challenged liberal ideas and actions from the Left. But the dominance of liberalism was attacked just as loudly and strongly from the Right. A growing social movement of conservatives—active on campuses, in business circles, inside Protestant and Catholic churches, and among Republican party activists—tried to reverse much of what the New Deal and subsequent administrations in Washington had wrought. Although conservatives did not capture the highest offices in the land until 1980—when Ronald Reagan was elected president and Republicans won control of the U.S. Senate—they had become a major political and cultural force more than a decade before.

Blessed with hindsight, we can better appreciate the significance of the '60s Right. Conservatives began building a mass movement earlier than did the New Left. And they sustained morale and kept expanding their numbers for years after the young radicals had splintered in various directions. The Left blazed through the '60s like a meteor, reshaping the cultural landscape, particularly in the areas of gender and race. The Right established itself as a unified and potent political movement during the same decade. And, at the end of the twentieth century, its fire was not yet extinguished.

Sixties conservatism had deep roots in the American past. Goldwater's call to preserve social and moral order and to practice self-reliance echoed the sentiments of many a Puritan minister, slave-holding planter, and self-made industrialist. And, like such forerunners, modern conservatives mixed their idealism with a loathing of anyone deemed to be ruining what they held dear. The men and women of the 1960s Right were strongly motivated by a vision of the good society, as elaborated by conservative thinkers as well as the Scriptures. But their appeals to meaner sentiments, particularly white racism, helped the movement grow among groups the Right had never attracted before.

The intellectual revival began at the end of World War II. In 1945 the future seemed to belong to the Left. Liberal Democrats then governed in Washington and in most of the big states, and the membership and economic clout of unions was expanding. The federal bureaucracy had flourished during the war and might soon take on the tasks of economic planning and providing health care to all citizens—much as the new Labor government in Great Britain was doing. Conservatives quarreled among themselves about issues like the size of the postwar military and feared for their future. No wonder essayist Albert Jay Nock, near the war's end, dubbed "the Remnant" those like himself who continued to keep the traditional mode of conservatism alive.

At that melancholy moment, a new generation of thinkers was already crafting works that gave the Right a storehouse of concepts which activists would refine and draw upon during the ensuing decades. Some of these writers were libertarian philosophers and economists, like Friedrich von Hayek and Milton Friedman, who argued that liberty in the marketplace was the key to a free society. Others were apostates from Marxism, fierce anticommunists like James Burnham and Will Herberg, who warned that the West must cling to its religious and moral values if it hoped to prevail against Soviet power and pro-Soviet subversion. Others, like the historian Russell Kirk and the sociologist Robert Nisbet, drew inspiration from traditional concepts like natural law and denied that a "meddling state" could or should dissolve natural differences between human beings. All these intellectuals were cosmopolitan in background and eager to debate the ideas of Marx, Nietzsche, and Freud with their present-day admirers.[5]

At the core of the new conservatives' worldview lay two profound, if somewhat antithetical, concepts. The first, derived from the eighteenth-century British writer Adam Smith, was that human freedom required government to stay out of economic life. This stemmed as much from moral conviction as from a calculation of how to produce goods and services most efficiently. As von Hayek wrote in *The Road to Serfdom*:

> Economic control is not merely control of a sector of human life which can be separated from the rest. It is the control of the means of all our ends. And whoever has sole control of the means must also determine which ends are to be served, which values are to be rated higher and which lower—in short, what men should believe and strive for.[6]

For von Hayek, an Austrian emigré, liberal planners differed only in degree from their Nazi or Stalinist counterparts. All sought to coerce individuals to behave in ways the planners deemed most useful to society as a whole. All were "collectivists" who wanted to substitute a strong state for the spontaneous energies of citizens. As Milton Friedman, a disciple of von Hayek's who would later win the Nobel Prize in economics, argued in 1962, "The great advances of civilization, whether in architecture or painting, in science or literature, in industry or agriculture, have never come from centralized government."[7] Friedman advocated the end of any state agency or program—including the post office, the minimum wage, public housing, and national parks—that impeded or substituted for the marketplace.

The second big idea on the Right, inspired particularly by Adam Smith's contemporary Edmund Burke, was the superiority of stable structures of authority governed by a strict moral code. "Political problems," wrote Russell Kirk in 1953, "at bottom, are religious and moral problems. . . . Custom, convention, and old prescription are checks both upon man's anarchic impulse and upon the innovator's lust for power."[8] Liberalism, according to this view, was both foolish and dangerous: the impulse to perfect the world through the state would surely fail. But the effort to do so was tearing apart the traditional culture—rooted in the Bible—that had nurtured thriving families and local institutions from schools to churches to businesses. Will Herberg charged, " 'Modern man' . . . has disencumbered himself of his historic faith, Jewish or Christian, . . . [but] has opened himself up to the incursion of a host of devils . . . the most deceptive of pseudo-religions (Communism, Nazis, the Liberal cult of Progress)."[9] Herberg was a Jew, but the most prominent traditionalists tended to have been raised as Catholics or, like Kirk, later converted to that faith.

In the abstract, the viewpoint of a fierce economic libertarian was not congenial with that of a cultural conservative. Success in the marketplace required constant innovation: the ethic of newer and better clashed with the desire to preserve traditional values of thrift and sobriety.[10] For Milton Friedman, any restriction on individual rights was suspect, whereas thinkers like Kirk and Herberg worried that only communal pressure to act responsibly kept America from descending into chaos.

However, there were pressing reasons for conservative intellectuals to join forces in the late '40s and the '50s. Above all, they shared a hatred of Soviet communism and its mammoth new ally, the People's Republic of China—which they regarded as a puppet state of the Kremlin. Libertarians indicted the "Reds" for practicing collectivism at its most evil and for relentlessly spreading their false gospel to other lands. "Stalinism is worse than fascism," wrote former leftist Max Eastman, "more ruthless, barbarous, unjust, immoral, anti-democratic, unredeemed by any hope or scruple."[11] Traditionalists were equally repulsed by a revolutionary order that persecuted the pious and declared its hostility to classes and property rights. For Communists, nothing was sacred, save their own rigid dogma.

At home, the liberal "establishment" provided another incentive to intellectual fusion on the Right. New Deal reformers and left-leaning academics both promoted what conservatives called "creeping socialism." State regulatory agencies, strong labor unions, progressive income taxes, and civil rights laws all wrested control from employers, property owners, and local authorities. They implicitly punished anyone who had achieved worldly success and forced a redistribution of income. "Separate property from private possession," wrote Russell Kirk, "and Leviathan [the powerful state] becomes master of all. Economic leveling . . . is not economic progress."[12]

Conservatives of both persuasions were also unhappy with what they believed was an erosion of the spiritual values that, in their view, undergirded the republic and motivated the battle against "Godless communism." Although about half of Americans regularly attended a house of worship, religious instruction was waning in the schools. And mainstream Protestant denominations affiliated with the National Council of Churches seemed more concerned with teaching cultural tolerance than in saving souls for Christ.

In 1962 the Supreme Court turned conservative discontent into outrage when it decided, in the case of *Engel v. Vitale*, that no state could require schoolchildren to pray. The specific prayer in question, written by the New York Regents (the state board of education), was rather prosaic. It read, "Almighty God, we acknowledge our dependence upon Thee, and we beg thy blessings upon us, our parents, our teachers and our country."[13] But Jewish groups and the American Civil Liberties Union argued that the prayer violated the First Amendment's ban against establishing a religion, and a majority of justices agreed. One year later, the high court (in the *Schempp* and *Murray* cases) also ruled against mandatory Bible readings and recitations of the Lord's Prayer.

"The ruling could put the United States schools on the same basis as Russian schools," charged a Democratic congressman about *Engel v. Vitale*. His comment was among the more moderate ones uttered by critics of the Court. Billy Graham, the nation's most popular preacher, called the rulings part of a "diabolical scheme" that was "taking God and moral teaching from the schools" and ushering in a "deluge of juvenile delinquency." George Wallace, always eager to defy a federal mandate, vowed, "I don't care what they say in Washington, we are going to keep right on praying and reading the Bible in the public schools of Alabama."[14] Veterans' groups called for a constitutional amendment to reverse the Court, and congressmen from both parties scheduled hearings into the matter. For intellectuals on the Right, the judicial decisions confirmed a belief that liberals were bereft of moral principle; they were heartened to learn that, on this issue at least, most Americans concurred.

Thus, despite lingering differences about their ultimate ends, libertarians and traditionalists were drawn together by their antipathies. Both wrote for the same magazines—*The Freeman, Human Events*, and *National Review*—and promoted the political fortunes of such men as retired army general Douglas MacArthur and Barry Goldwater. Gradually, their ideas became well known among journalists and literate Americans.

The most influential meeting point for conservative intellectuals and budding activists alike was *National Review*, which began publishing in the fall of 1955. Founder and editor William F. Buckley, Jr., though only 30 at the time, was already a famous and controversial writer. His books wittily condemned the secular, liberal cast of teaching at Yale, his alma mater, and defended the anticommunist purposes of Senator Joseph McCarthy, if not every charge the reckless inquisitor had flung. Buckley intended *National Review* to be the beguiling standard-bearer for a new, fusionist Right. He and his fellow editors (including Brent Bozell, ghostwriter of *Conscience of a Conservative*) stood for an aggressive anticommunism and the unstinting defense of both the free market and traditional Christian virtues. But Buckley preferred writers who, like himself, hit their mark with an ironic foil instead of a polemical broadsword. His jaunty style demonstrated confidence in his opinions as well as the depth of his learning.

One 1962 column by Russell Kirk bemoaned the intellectual content of high school textbooks. Kirk ridiculed Wisconsin officials for censoring the old-style McGuffey Readers being used in one of the state's elementary schools. "You really *can't* allow ethical principles to take root in young heads, you know," mimicked Kirk. "The authorities discovered that the Readers actually contained quotations from the Sermon on the Mount. . . . Somewhat intimidated, the school board agreed to snip out or cover with strips of brown paper the offending quotations from that old discriminationist, Jesus Christ."[15]

National Review never let readers forget that it was a journal of combat against the Left. Buckley and his colleagues considered the black freedom movement as sure a foe as any liberal president or secular academic. In this stance, the editors of *National Review* revealed both the depth and callousness of their principles. Through the late '50s and early '60s, the magazine consistently sided with the white South. At first, while echoing the argument for "state's rights," *National Review* did not flinch from publishing candidly racist views. Were white southerners justified in resisting civil rights laws and demonstrators? "The shocking answer is Yes," the editors wrote in 1957, "the white community is so entitled, because, for the time being, it is the advanced race."[16]

A few years later, when Bull Connor became the poster boy of white supremacy, *National Review* backed away from such pronouncements. But, like George Wallace, the magazine continued to thunder against the federal courts for trampling over "the principle of home rule" and depicted liberal politicians cravenly giving in to "rioting mobs, intemperate demagogues and rampant ideology." "We are . . . depriving private citizens of the protection of their property; of enjoining, under threat of federal armed power, the police power from preserving order in our communities," warned Frank Meyer in the late spring of 1963.[17] Armed with the fusion of old ideals and even older prejudices, conservatives emerged from their intellectual subculture to build a movement.

They were not creating something entirely new. Anticommunists had been active on the Right for years and, during the early years of the Cold War, had mounted a furious campaign against movie stars and State Department officials whom they judged to be pro-Soviet "subversives." In 1954 the political humiliation of Joseph McCarthy, prime symbol of the crusade, made

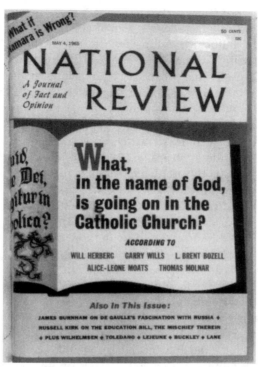

The leading conservative magazine's response to the liberal turn in Catholicism, 1965. Source: *National Review.*

Americans wary of the more lurid charges. But the imperative to fight communism remained the primary spur for many conservative activists.

Some groups determined to carry on McCarthy's work. They insisted that the Red enemy was lurking within the gates of national power, quietly bending the state to its will. A greater number of conservatives followed the lead of *National Review* and embedded their anticommunism within a broader, less alarmist critique of modern liberalism. Their discontent was channeled into building a strong network that could take over the Republican Party and transform the national political dialogue. By temperament and doctrine, the two groups were destined to clash.

The John Birch Society (JBS) was the largest organization on the militant Right. Founded in 1958, the JBS disdained ironic subtleties of the Buckley style. The United States, alerted Birch Society founder Robert Welch, heir to a candy company fortune, was at war with "a gigantic conspiracy to enslave mankind; . . . [one] controlled by determined, cunning, and utterly ruthless gangsters, willing to use any means to achieve its end."[18] Even President Dwight D. Eisenhower was, according to Welch, complicit in the grand plot, along with nearly every prominent advocate of nuclear disarmament and black rights, including the justices of the Supreme Court. Given the immensity of the threat, the JBS counterattacked in remarkably pacific ways: letter writing, radio commentary, billboards calling for the impeachment of Chief Justice Earl Warren, and selling alarmist literature through its own American Opinion bookstores. The obvious prosperity of most JBS members may have argued against more forceful means. But smaller groups like the Ku Klux Klan and the Minutemen who held a similar worldview did commit bombings and other acts of violence.

The 1960 election of John Kennedy, an avowed liberal, heightened the distress of dedicated anticommunists, and the Birch Society boomed. By 1963, the JBS had close to 100,000 members, and its bookstores proliferated in Sunbelt suburbs. Mainstream journalists and scholars labeled the JBS and such kindred groups as the Christian Anti-Communist Crusade "radical," "paranoid," and "extremist." But militant rightists dismissed the charges as enemy propaganda; they would persevere in telling uncomfortable truths.

In large parts of the South and West, the core of their gospel was quite popular. Conservative activists could deny or ignore Welch's wilder accusations but still affirm that the nation faced a dire challenge from a hydra-headed "collectivist" beast. In booming Orange County, California, the JBS boasted 38 chapters full of white doctors and dentists, engineers, small business people, middle-class housewives—and several congressmen. Ad hoc local groups with names like Citizens for Fundamental Education and the Californians' Committee to Combat Communism attracted thousands of other citizens.

These conservatives regarded the national Democratic Party and its union and civil rights allies as dedicated enemies of freedom. Moderate Republicans, in their view, were no better. Phyllis Schlafly, leader of GOP women's clubs, wrote a popular book charging that "a small group of secret king makers, using hidden persuaders and psychological warfare techniques" had "manipulated" the GOP "to nominate candidates who had sidestepped or suppressed the key issues." The grassroots Right demanded that the party stop behaving as a "dime-store New Deal" (Goldwater's pithy dig at the Eisenhower administration). Only the nomination of a presidential candidate sworn to protect individual and business freedom at home and take the offensive against communism abroad would do.[19]

Why did the Right gain so much support in Orange County? Since the beginning of World War II, the county had changed from a fruit-growing center into a beehive of military and aerospace production. New residents tended to be culturally conservative Protestants or Catholics who were ideologically committed to the same Cold War that guaranteed their prosperity. They saw no contradiction between damning "big government" and living well thanks to increasing federal outlays for the military and aerospace industries. Encouragement and funds came from such local businessmen as Walter Knott of Knott's Berry Farm and Patrick Frawley of the Schick Razor

Company, who had long resented moderate Republicans based in the East for compromising with the liberal enemy. In addition, Cardinal Francis McIntyre, head of the Roman Catholic Church in southern California, sent his priests to JBS forums to educate themselves about communism. In Orange County, the militant Right was not "extreme" at all. Indeed, it was a logical place to belong if one were a middle-class white Christian who believed that his or her values were under siege.[20]

The Right also established an energetic movement on college campuses. In the 1950s, the small Intercollegiate Society of Individualists experimented with tactics the New Left would later make commonplace. ISI members published newspapers that challenged liberal opinion, wrote sharp critiques of liberal textbooks used in their economics and political science classes, and mounted street demonstrations in favor of the House Un-American Activities Committee while their left-wing counterparts protested against it. Then, in the fall of 1960, young admirers of Barry Goldwater, who had given a graceful address to that year's Republican convention, created Young Americans for Freedom. From the first, YAF, unlike the more scholarly ISI, was enmeshed in political battles within the Republican Party and against powerful liberals, and it rapidly signed up some 25,000 members.

YAF set down its creed at its founding conference held in 1960 at William F. Buckley's family estate in Sharon, Connecticut. The Sharon Statement, largely written by 26-year-old journalist M. Stanton Evans, was a crisp synopsis of conservative principles. "In this time of moral and political crisis," it vowed to preserve "freedom" and defined that ubiquitous term as encompassing the market economy, victory over communism, and limited powers for government. The first issue of YAF's official journal, *The New Guard*, stated, "Ten years ago this magazine would not have been possible. Twenty years ago it would not have been dreamed of. Thirty-five years ago it would not have been necessary."[21]

Here was a rebellion that sought not to transform society but to revive the spirit of an earlier and presumably better order, free from the benighted "isms which have poisoned the minds, weakened the wills and smothered the spirits of Americans for three decades and more," as YAF phrased it. Like members of the burgeoning New Left, young rightists railed against the sway of liberal professors and administrators. "A conscious effort is constantly being made by instructors to liberalize the thinking of their students," complained one University of Minnesota undergraduate.[22] YAF members were sometimes accused (by their adversaries) of "arrogance" and bad manners.

But such qualities drove campus conservatives to the lectern and the party caucus rather than into the streets. During its heyday in the early '60s, YAF was mainly composed of young people from pious backgrounds who sought out elders to lionize not condemn. The strongest chapters tended to be located at Catholic colleges like Fordham and Notre Dame, and most activists followed the lead of *National Review* and looked forward to a career in electoral politics. Annual YAF conventions typically ended with a formal banquet, at which men in suits and women in cocktail dresses gathered to hear speeches by the likes of William F. Buckley and to give awards to such heroes as Russell Kirk and Herbert Kohler, a toilet manufacturer who was an inveterate foe of labor unions.

The first effort that united all contingents of the New Right was the campaign to elect Barry Goldwater president in 1964. The campaign, conducted with crusading fervor, did more than anything else to make American conservatism a mass phenomenon. In 1963 an avid circle of boosters organized themselves into a secret Draft Goldwater Committee headquartered in midtown New York City. Led by the veteran Republican strategist F. Clifton "Clif" White, they fanned out around the country, recruiting activists (many from YAF) and converting likely GOP convention delegates. On July 4 of that year, a rally to boost support for Goldwater drew almost 9000 people. In the crowd, remembered one organizer, were

> truck drivers with tattoos, . . . right-wingers convinced that Wall Street and the Kremlin were conspiring to run the world, Southern whites who had faith in the Cross and the Flag, retired people on Social Security worried about inflation, Westerners tired of catering to Easterners, anticommunists demanding action against Cuba and Khrushchev, small business-men fighting a losing battle against government rules and regulations, readers of *The Conscience of a Conservative*, high school and college rebels looking for a cause.[23]

By the time Goldwater agreed to be a candidate, he already had a huge advantage over any other hopeful.

In 1964 the organization mobilized a movement. In the weeks before the California primary, 8000 members of YAF, the Birch Society, and the Young Republicans visited over 600,000 households in the state. A nationwide direct mail campaign netted far more money than any other presidential candidate had received in that way. Most contributors gave $100 or less, unlike the Democrats, who relied on wealthier donors. Goldwater's new breed overwhelmed the rather staid GOP officials in many areas. "I was plagued by zealots who flocked to the cause," remembered a more orthodox Republican, "They were uncontrollable. They cared nothing about the Republican Party, only about their hero."[24]

Once nominated, Goldwater determined that Americans would hear the conservative verities, blunt and undiluted. During his acceptance speech, he proclaimed, "Extremism in the defense of liberty is no vice. Moderation in the pursuit of justice is no virtue." The candidate favored making Social Security a voluntary program and selling off the network of dams and utilities known as the Tennessee Valley Authority that had brought cheap electric power to millions of homes. He also opposed the nuclear test ban treaty and

"In Your Heart, You Know He's Right"—The 1964 Republican candidate. Source: *Author's collection*

favored allowing NATO commanders to use nuclear weapons against the Soviets, if they decided that were necessary. "In Your Heart, You Know He's Right," read his billboards and bumper stickers. A pro-Johnson wag changed the GOP slogan to read, "In Your Guts, You Know He's Nuts."

Goldwater also continued to denounce the Civil Rights Act that Congress had passed the previous June. The legislation, he charged (erroneously), "would force you to admit drunks, a known murderer, or an insane person into your place of business" and to hire "incompetent" workers.[25] Laws, he protested, could never change the way white racists felt about blacks.

Lyndon Johnson's landslide victory that November surprised no one save the most myopic Goldwater disciples, who thought that millions of "hidden conservatives" would miraculously surface to rescue the GOP. Only in the South did the Goldwater campaign live up to its hopes. A few years before, the senator had essentially written off the black vote when he advised "hunting where the ducks are" to build support below the Mason–Dixon line. Now, for the first time since Reconstruction, a Republican won a majority in Mississippi and Alabama, South Carolina, Georgia, and Louisiana. Goldwater ran close in every other southern state, except for the president's native Texas. Across Dixie, whites split their vote about equally between the two candidates. The hostility to black rights and to the "outsiders" who supported them had found a home in the party of Abraham Lincoln.

The Goldwater campaign had another consequence: it transformed the Right from a small, largely intellectual phenomenon into a huge grassroots force. Many future conservative leaders first threw themselves into national politics during this seemingly hopeless effort: William Rehnquist, Michael Deaver, Jesse Helms, Phyllis Schlafly, George Will, and Patrick Buchanan, among others. Years later, Buchanan rhapsodized, "Like a first love, the Goldwater campaign was, for thousands of men and women now well into middle age, an experience that will never recede from memory." Then he invoked Shakespeare's *Henry V:* "We were there on St. Crispin's Day."[26]

The conservatives who had flooded into the GOP were not about to cede it back to the hated "Eastern Establishment." Across the broad Sunbelt stretching from the beaches of Virginia to the jet factories of Orange County, conservatives increased their numbers and their influence in local politics. And the Republican Party was utterly changed; since the early '60s, the Right has exercised great, usually decisive, influence over the GOP's platform and choice of national candidates. No Republican has been elected president without strong conservative backing. Just after the 1964 election, an editorial cartoonist depicted Goldwater and a woman, dressed as the parents of a new bride, waving goodbye to their daughter. The politician consoled his "wife," "Look at it this way. . . . We haven't lost a presidency; we've gained a party!"[27]

Now conservatives had to persuade Democratic voters to look past the "extremist" label. In 1966 a 55-year-old actor making his first run for public office showed them how. Ronald Reagan had been a liberal Democrat for most of his adult life; during the 1940s, he served as president of the film actor's union and campaigned actively for both Franklin Roosevelt and Harry Truman. A growing dislike for government regulation of business and a deep-seated hatred of communism drew him rightward during the 1950s. In 1964, near the end of the fall campaign, the retired actor delivered a televised speech for Goldwater that was more impressive than any address the nominee himself had delivered.

Reagan adeptly turned the rhetoric of the New Deal on its head. He spoke with the same reassuring empathy and scorn for unearned favors from government that had once helped liberals gain the allegiance of working-class whites, both North and South. Reagan simply replaced older stories of workers abused by corporate power with fresh anecdotes about women leaving their husbands so they could be eligible to receive big welfare checks.

In 1966 Reagan ran for the governorship of California as a "citizen-politician." He declared himself free of entanglements to any existing structure of power—despite close ties to the Goldwater wing of the GOP and the financial backing of a ring of wealthy businessmen from the Los Angeles basin. His campaign zeroed in on the kinds of outrages "law and order" was intended to remedy: the Watts riot, the radical student movement at the University of California, and the mounting rate of violent crime. Reagan also trumpeted his opposition to open housing laws—and to the state supreme court's attempt to override the public will on that volatile issue. In 1964 California voters, by a 2–1 margin, had turned down the Rumford Act, which sought to make discrimination in real estate transactions illegal. When the court declared the results of that vote invalid, it allowed Reagan to wave the banner of democracy and to claim "infringement of one of our basic individual rights" by a clique of unelected judges.[28]

Still, California Democrats were not overly concerned. Reagan's opponent was Edmund "Pat" Brown, the two-term incumbent governor whose last opponent had been Richard Nixon. Brown had dedicated his administration to promoting the growth and prestige of his state. During his eight years in office, the freeway system was completed, an ultramodern water system perfected, and the state university expanded and elevated into one of the finest in the world. Brown's fervent endorsement of the war in Vietnam shielded him from the wrath of all but the most eccentric anticommunists. In fact, angry left-wing opponents of the war saw no difference between Brown and Reagan. How could this confident chief executive of the nation's most populous state lose to an actor who had supported the "extremist" Barry Goldwater?

Reagan, however, was a skillful campaigner who united the Republican Party and ensured that groups like the Birch Society would not tarnish his mainstream image. He told reporters who grilled him about the Birchers, "Any members of the society who support me will be buying my philosophy. I won't be buying theirs."[29] The same advertising firm that had worked for Nelson Rockefeller in 1964 crafted Reagan's television messages. Brown's campaign manager later praised the GOP candidate for using an inviting, even humorous tone when he attacked welfare mothers and student protesters. "Most of the cracks aren't very fair, and some of them aren't very nice. But they work off the predictable resentments and emotions of his audiences, without requiring him to be harsh or abrasive."[30]

Against an opponent who was riding a wave of popular disgust, Brown continued to bash Reagan's former profession—forgetting how many residents had been attracted to the state because of the imagery and industry that was Hollywood. One of Brown's most frequently televised ads showed the governor addressing an integrated class of schoolchildren. "I'm running against an actor, and you know who shot Lincoln, don't cha?"[31] Reagan won by just short of a million votes.

Republicans got good news outside California in 1966 as well. The party gained 47 seats in the House of Representatives and 3 in the Senate, virtually ensuring that Lyndon Johnson would get no more sweeping social programs through Congress. Seven other governorships fell to the GOP, including that of Florida, which had not elected a Republican to the statehouse for almost a century.

Animus against liberals and their causes was growing inside the other party as well. In Boston, Louise Day Hicks, an Irish-Catholic Democrat on the elected School Committee, became a heroine to many whites when she resisted state-mandated integration plans. "A small band of racial agitators, non-native to Boston, and a few college radicals," charged Hicks, were engaged in a "conspiracy to tell the people of Boston how to run their schools, their city, and their lives."[32] The rejection of racial liberalism also boosted the national hopes of a southern Democrat who was the very symbol of white resistance—George Wallace.

The events of 1963—in the streets of Birmingham and at the University of Alabama—had made the governor something of a celebrity. TV interviewers courted him, and students at northern colleges enjoyed jousting with him. A former amateur boxing champion, Wallace reveled in the rhetorical combat. On national television, reporter Anthony Lewis from the liberal *New York Times* accused Wallace of preventing black citizens from voting in his state. "We don't have any utopia in Alabama," the governor acknowledged, "But neither do you have one here in New York City where you can't walk in Central Park at night without fear of being raped, or mugged, or shot." Thousands of favorable letters soon arrived at his Montgomery office from all over the nation.[33]

Wallace entered three state presidential primaries in 1964 and did surprisingly well. Against stand-ins for President Johnson, he gained 45 percent in Maryland, 34 percent in Wisconsin, and 30 percent in Indiana. Small farmers and blue-collar workers, both those of eastern European ancestry and southern migrants who had started coming North during World War II, were his strongest supporters. They brandished law and order like a club against local blacks. At one Wallace rally in South Milwaukee attended mostly by Polish Americans, the local sponsor, a tavern keeper and ex-marine named Bronko Gruber, ordered two African Americans who refused to stand for the Star-Spangled Banner to leave. Then he asked, "Who is it that beats up our newsboys, rapes our women, attacks old women? You know who it is—it's your colored brothers. How long can we tolerate this?"

In this and later elections, George Wallace always denied that either he or his supporters were motivated by racism. Ever the adroit counterpuncher, he even charged that "the biggest bigots in the world are . . . the ones who call others bigots," because they—liberal journalists and radical protesters—dismissed, as a smokescreen for prejudice, the concerns of ordinary whites about job security and safe streets. But, fueled partly by the national media that wished him no good, the impression persisted that Wallace's political strength was the direct product of antiblack feelings that he skillfully whipped up with the use of "code words" like "law and order" and "neighborhood schools."[34]

But Wallace also used the racial crisis of the 1960s to draw a class line between two different groups of *white* people. He would needle liberal congressmen for sending their own children to private schools and insist that all he wanted was for parents to have a *choice* about where their children would be educated. "We're not talking about race," he protested, "we're talking about local democratic institutions."[35] His favorite targets were powerful judges, "bureaucrats," and "theoreticians" (their whiteness assumed) who wanted to foist "absurd" blueprints for change on average men and women. That many of those blueprints were attempts to aid black people was an essential element in the resistance mounted against them. But so was a widening cultural gulf between European Americans that had as much to do with differences of class and with moral judgments as it did with their opinions about the rights of African Americans.

As a populist spokesman on the right, Wallace accomplished something unique. He managed to look and sound more like an ordinary, working American than did anyone of prominence on the contemporary white Left, dominated as it was by activists bred in at least modest comfort. In his personal style as well as in his words, Wallace exuded a feisty self-confidence, a combative defensiveness, a pride in his background that appealed to millions of white Americans (more of them male than female) who worked with their hands or felt close to those who did.

The Alabamian had a canny regard for the particulars of wage-earning, small-property-holding white society. Unlike conventional politicians, Wallace fondly *named* the specific kinds of (white) Americans for whom he claimed to speak, thereby dignifying their occupations and honoring their anonymous lives: "the bus driver, the truck driver, the beautician, the firemen, the policeman, and the steelworker, the plumber, and the communications worker, and the oil worker and the little businessman."[36]

Wallace's tastes and bearing amplified his words. He had a common, rough quality that fascinated and/or repelled observers who expected aspirants for the presidency to carry themselves with relaxed dignity and to dress like big-city bankers. The governor slicked back his hair, wore inexpensive suits, and unapologetically admitted that he "put ketchup on everything." Moreover, his performance before crowds was designed not to inspire but to incite; he told hecklers to cut off their beards, dared "anarchists" to lie down in front of his car, and mused about how "mean" a steelworker in the White House would be. One conservative writer compared him to "Edward G. Robinson in the days of Little Caesar" and quipped, "he can strut sitting down."[37]

Blue-collar belligerence was a major element in Wallace's appeal. But his authenticity did have a softer side. A son of the plebeian South, he declared his adherence to evangelical Protestantism and his love for country music. The former allowed him to scorn "the liberal circles" for thinking "their minds are the greatest things in the universe and denying that "there is a God Who made all of us." The latter, aided by endorsements from such popular recording artists as Marty Robbins and Hank Snow, gave him a connection to a musical style whose popularity was exploding: by 1970, there were over 650 AM radio stations exclusively broadcasting country songs; a decade earlier, fewer than 100 had existed. "People that listen to the kind of music you are playing tonight," Wallace said on a TV show in Oklahoma City, "are the people that are going to save this country."[38]

Such calls for the common folk to make other Americans live right—or else—did not gladden many of the conservatives who had toiled in the Goldwater campaign. Writers like William F. Buckley, Jr. cherished the calm defense of laissez-faire economics and spiritual order. Wallace's constant jibes at "pseudo-intellectuals," his support of welfare programs in his own state, and his appeal to racial prejudice struck them as the acts of a demagogue willing to shout anything to win votes. Several *National Review* contributors argued vehemently that, as Frank Meyer wrote, Wallace's populism was "the radical opposite of conservatism" and would "poison the moral source of its strength." Buckley himself privately referred to the Alabamian as "Mr. Evil" and, in a televised debate, branded him a racist and a would-be dictator.

The geographic spread and obvious power of the white backlash required conservatives like Buckley to perform a difficult balancing act. On the one hand, they cheered the assertion of community and local rights against the liberal "establishment." Finally, ordinary Americans were rebelling against politicians, judges, and intellectuals in thrall to "social engineering." On the other hand, few of the voters who rallied to Hicks, Wallace, or Ronald Reagan were disenchanted with government largesse. They demanded that the state stop favoring blacks and the poor; they had little quarrel with such favorite targets of the Right as Social Security, the minimum wage, or the new Medicare program. And the rough, sometimes violent cast of places like South Milwaukee and Marquette Park gave pause to conservatives who revered the life of the mind and the lifestyle of benevolent aristocrats. If "the people" were suddenly veering rightward, could veterans of the Right control them?

The upcoming presidential election lent some urgency to the question. Conservatives of all stripes had gained strength since the debacle of 1964. Now they had to decide how to wield that influence, both to gain the White House and to promote their larger ideological agenda. Of one thing they were sure: less than a decade after he'd written it, Barry Goldwater's brazen assertion of 1960 sounded almost like common sense. Perhaps America was a conservative nation after all.

CHAPTER 12

1968

YOU'RE EITHER PART OF THE SOLUTION OR PART OF THE PROBLEM.
—*Eldridge Cleaver, black revolutionary*[1]

Significant change seldom respects the calendar. But, on occasion, a single year fills up with revolutions—attempted and dreaded, imagined and repressed. In 1848 the common people of every major nation in western and central Europe revolted against their hereditary monarchs and landlords. In 1919 mass uprisings led by radical socialists erupted in Italy, Germany, and Hungary. In China, the Communist Party was born amid a nationalist uprising. That same year, one-fifth of all U.S. workers went out on strike, and many Americans feared (while a few hoped) that the Bolshevik victory in Russia was about to be repeated on their side of the Atlantic. Then, in 1989, citizen movements helped bring about the collapse of European communism in a heap of debased ideals, authoritarian governments, and falling walls. Many of the revolutions launched in those years failed or took decades more to triumph. But, in each case, what had occurred transformed utterly what was to come.

1968 was that kind of year. Insurgencies against the dominant political and economic order broke out in every industrial nation, nearly always led by men and women under the age of 25. In the streets of Paris, university radicals erected barricades to fight police and touched off both a national student strike and a walkout by 10 million workers. Similar, if less massive, events occurred in Turin and Rome, Madrid and West Berlin, Rio de Janeiro and Tokyo. In Mexico City, soldiers and police massacred hundreds of students who had shut down their universities to protest earlier acts of repression. During the spring in Czechoslovakia, democratic-minded Communists led by Alexander Dubcek began to build "socialism with a human face." In August they learned, with the rumble of invading armor and troops, the high price of departing from Kremlin rules.

Nothing quite so dramatic took place in the United States. Still, 1968 was the pivot of the American decade. Young radicals emerged from events tinged

with violence to proclaim that a revolution was in the making. But politicians tested the waters of public opinion and quickly learned that most voters craved order and thought the nation had already undergone all the change
it could handle. Every season of the year shook with that conflict—between
an increasingly daring and insurrectionary "Movement" and the forces, elite
and popular, who were eager to put it down.

Winter: Tet

Early in the morning of January 31, the revolution came to Saigon. The capital city of South Vietnam, bloated with war refugees to a population of nearly
4 million, was slumbering through a cease-fire to mark the lunar new year,
the Tet holiday in which Vietnamese traditionally pay homage to their ancestors. Remains of firecrackers littered the quiet streets.

Then, just before 3 A.M., nineteen Viet Cong commandos drove up to the
U.S. embassy and began a bold attempt to capture the prime symbol of American power in their country. They blew a hole in the wall and began advancing, weapons blazing, on the compound itself. Thus began the "general
offensive and uprising" the Communists hoped would bring a rapid end to
the Saigon regime and force its American protectors to withdraw. On the
same day, 80,000 Viet Cong guerrillas launched assaults on every significant
city in South Vietnam, risking their lives to bring about what Communist
leader Ho Chi Minh predicted would be "total victory."

The war lasted another seven gory years before that outcome came to
pass. The raid on the American embassy was a virtual suicide mission, which
U.S. forces were able to crush before noon. The Viet Cong failed to hold any
city for more than a few weeks; fully half their fighters died in the offensive.
And their vaunted uprising never occurred; most urban dwellers ran for safety
instead of rallying to "liberation" as the guerrillas had expected. Thousands
of South Vietnamese soldiers did throw down their arms and desert, but the
Viet Cong emerged from the offensive a much weaker fighting force than at
its outset. For the remainder of the war, troops from the regular North Vietnamese army did most of the fighting on the Communist side.

But the Tet offensive succeeded in a manner its planners had not antic-
ipated. It ended a grand American illusion and altered the course of the conflict: before Tet, U.S. officials, from President Lyndon Johnson on down, had
assured the public the war was gradually but surely being won; what General William Westmoreland, commander of U.S. forces in South Vietnam,
called "the light at the end of the tunnel" seemed to be glowing more brightly.
After the offensive, no one was foolish enough to make such statements. At
the end of February, respected TV broadcaster Walter Cronkite, who to that

American marines prepare to take back the U.S. embassy from Viet Cong commandos, January 31, 1968. Source: *Texas Tech University*

point had been uncritical of the war effort, spoke for many Americans when he intoned on the evening news that it was "more certain than ever that the bloody experience of Vietnam is to end in stalemate." Clark Clifford, then the new secretary of defense, later confessed, "Tet, to me, was the roof falling in."[2]

Suddenly, the war had moved from the jungle into the city, heightening its visibility in new and uncomfortable ways. In Saigon, two cameramen filmed the chief of the national police executing a captured Viet Cong guerrilla with a pistol at point-blank range; fragments of the prisoner's brain spurted from his head as he fell. In the Mekong Delta, U.S. planes drove enemy forces out of the city of Ben Tre by reducing the provincial capital of 140,000 inhabitants to rubble. The major in charge explained, without a hint of irony, "It became necessary to destroy the town to save it."[3]

For American GIs, Tet touched off the bloodiest and most frustrating year of the war. Battles with North Vietnamese troops claimed thousands of casualties on both sides, with neither able to win a clear victory. Racial hostilities escalated within U.S. ranks, mirroring the riots and backlash back home. At rear echelon camps in South Vietnam, black and white GIs argued, sometimes violently, when Confederate flags were flown or enlisted men's clubs played country and western tunes instead of soul music.[4] Soldiers out in the bush were filled with tension, more unsure than ever about which Vietnamese to treat as enemies and which to regard as friends.

On March 16 the members of one infantry company snapped. On patrol in Quang Ngai Province, soldiers from the Americal Division entered the hamlet of My Lai, looking for Viet Cong guerrillas. Finding the villagers un-cooperative, the GIs savagely murdered at least 347 of them with grenades, bayonets, bullets, and fire, then hurled most of the bodies into a shallow ditch. Army officials covered up the story for 20 months, before it spilled out into the American press. But they could not stem the mounting rage of GIs who, whether or not they committed atrocities, had been sent to fight a war they could neither understand nor win.

For the warmakers in Washington, Tet made a painful decision un-avoidable. Most Americans, according to opinion polls, no longer believed the conflict would end in a U.S. victory, short of using nuclear weapons that risked touching off World War III. Four days before the My Lai massacre, the *New York Times* headlined a request by top army brass to send 206,000 more GIs to Vietnam, and an immediate public outcry resulted. Worse still, the long, expensive war had touched off an inflationary spiral that was jeop-ardizing the postwar boom. In February speculators in Europe began to bid up the price of gold and to sell off dollars, signaling their lack of faith in the future of the U.S. economy. The Johnson administration managed to end the crisis but not before the president warned western Europe's prime ministers that "these financial disorders can . . . set in motion forces like those which disintegrated the Western world" during the Great Depression of the 1930s.[5]

Lyndon Johnson, once considered the master politician of his era, was now in danger of losing the nomination of his own party. Before Tet, Eugene McCarthy, a bookish and rather obscure anti-war senator from Minnesota, announced he would take on the president in a string of primaries. After the Tet offensive, McCarthy remarked, "Only a few months ago we were told that 65 per cent of the [South Vietnamese] population was secure. Now we know that even the American embassy is not secure."[6] On March 12 McCarthy came within a few thousand votes of winning the New Hampshire primary. The stunning result convinced New York senator Robert Kennedy, charis-matic brother of the late president, to throw his own hat into the ring. Polls showed that either he or Richard Nixon, the expected Republican nominee, would draw more votes than the president.

In late March the political costs of the Tet offensive came due. President Johnson called together an eminent group of past and present makers of for-eign policy to help him decide what to do about Vietnam. Many of these "Wise Men" were key architects of the Cold War and had close ties to Wall Street and big industrial corporations.[7] They fretted that escalating the war would mean more civil unrest, in the ghettos and on campuses, as domestic ills were neglected; it might also touch off a more severe financial crisis. Soberly, they advised the president that it was time to stop. As former secretary of state Dean Acheson put it, "We can no longer do the job we set out to do in the time we have left and we must begin to take steps to disengage."[8]

On March 31 the president heeded their words. He had already decided against ordering a major increase in U.S. troops. Now, in a televised address, he announced a halt to the bombing of most of North Vietnam and a willingness to begin peace talks with the enemy. Then, at the end of the speech, Johnson, usually a plodding and undramatic speaker, shocked the nation: "I have concluded that I should not permit the presidency to become involved in the partisan divisions that are developing in this political year. Accordingly, I shall not seek and I will not accept the nomination of my party for another term as your president." Withdrawing from the race was the most popular thing LBJ had done in years; within a week, the president's job approval rating jumped 13 points. Antiwar protesters were jubilant, although few expected the war to end soon.

Spring: Memphis and Morningside Heights

Johnson's impending retirement from politics also lifted the hopes of America's most celebrated activist for peace and human rights. The year had not been going well for the Reverend Martin Luther King, Jr. and his great crusade. In January he had launched a Poor People's Campaign to mount "massive, active, non-violent resistance to the evils" of an economic system that seemed to reward the selfish and to punish the unfortunate. In private, King even advocated "a democratic form of socialism."[9] But organizing for the new campaign sputtered as some of his closest advisers doubted the wisdom of a plan to fill downtown Washington with "waves of the nation's poor and disinherited" until Congress funded either a jobs program or a guaranteed annual income.[10]

At the same time, King feared that white resistance, and the tough rhetoric of some Black Power advocates, would ignite another round of big city violence. "We cannot stand two more summers like last summer," he told a mostly white audience on March 31, "without leading inevitably to a rightwing takeover and a fascist state."[11] On top of such public woes, King's constant travel and frequent sexual liaisons were gradually destroying his marriage.

But his energy seldom flagged, and he kept looking for opportunities to link the causes of racial equality and economic justice. Since February, King had been traveling periodically to Memphis to support a strike by black sanitation workers. He viewed the garbagemen's ordeal as a microcosm of the problems faced by millions of the working poor in a land of plenty. The Memphis workers, who belonged to a segregated workforce, earned just a bit more than minimum wage (with no vacations or pensions) for cleaning the streets of a city renowned for its blues clubs and the palatial home of Elvis Presley.

Memphis officials, unlike many of their counterparts across the river in Mississippi, did not snarl at any mention of civil rights. But neither were they concerned with the troubles of their black constituents, half of whom lived below the poverty line. When 1300 sanitation men went on strike, Mayor Henry Loeb ordered them to return to work and announced he would never recognize their union. The workers took to the streets, wearing sandwich boards reading simply "I AM A MAN."

By early spring, the mayor had not changed his mind. Frustrated young activists were on the verge of tearing their own movement apart. On March 28, King walked at the head of a mass march by sanitation workers and their supporters and watched in horror as militants smashed store windows and battled with police. The renowned symbol of nonviolent resistance was rushed away by the authorities, as the mêlée raged. "Maybe we just have to give up and let violence take its course," King lamented that night to Rev. Ralph Abernathy, his best friend and coworker. "Ralph, we live in a sick nation."[12]

Rev. James Lawson, a local Methodist pastor and a founder of SNCC, attacked the young militants, who called themselves the Invaders, for chanting Black Power slogans and abandoning the cause of nonviolence. They demanded a role in planning demonstrations and suggested that Lawson and King were out of touch with an angry black community. The split mirrored one developing among African Americans nationwide: older activists wanted to keep trying to influence powerful whites through peaceful protest, while younger ones declared that nothing short of a black-led revolution would cleanse the nation of its racial sins.

As King's ability to control events diminished, the peril to himself seemed to grow. Every day he received multiple death threats; routinely, he rejected advice that he hire bodyguards. "I can't lead that kind of life," King told a Georgia newspaper editor, "There's no way in the world you can keep somebody from killing you if they really want to kill you." On April 3, King was back in Memphis to help the battling factions organize another march. That evening, he showed up at a half-filled auditorium and told the crowd not to worry about him. "I've seen the promised land," he declared. "I may not get there with you. But I want you to know tonight, that we, as a people, will get to the promised land. And so I'm happy tonight . . . I'm not fearing any man. Mine eyes have seen the glory of the coming of the Lord."[13]

The next day was filled with meetings. Just after 6 P.M., King took a break, relaxing on a motel balcony and bantering with aides, among them Jesse Jackson. King asked the leader of a band close to Jackson to play a favorite gospel song that night. "Ben, make sure you play 'Precious Lord, Take My Hand,'

Martin Luther King, Jr., giving one of his last speeches, 1968. Source: *Archive Photos*

. . . Sing it real pretty!" Moments later, a rifle bullet tore into the right side of King's face, and the great orator never spoke again. Earlier that day, King had called to arrange the Sunday sermon at his own Ebenezer Baptist Church back in Atlanta. The title he gave was "Why America May Go to Hell."[14]

News of the murder, committed by an escaped white convict named James Earl Ray, convinced thousands of black people that the present was damnable enough. They poured into the streets of over 120 cities to express grief and rage in a spasm of collective violence. In San Francisco, every store window was broken along Haight Street, recently mecca for those seeking "peace and love" in a psychedelic haze. In Baltimore and Kansas City, the National Guard patrolled black neighborhoods to stop looting and burning. In Chicago, Mayor Richard Daley gave police orders to "shoot to kill" any arsonists, after a large swath of the city's impoverished West Side went up in flames.

One of the most devastating riots, and certainly the most visible one, erupted in Washington, D.C. "Now that they've taken Dr. King off, it's time to end this non-violence bullshit," vowed Stokely Carmichael, the SNCC organizer who had persevered through brutal days in the Deep South when movement activists suffered beatings and murder without fighting back. Just hours after getting the grim news from Memphis, members of Congress could look out their office windows and see flames and hear breaking glass. Soldiers even set up machine guns on the steps of the Capitol.

By any material reckoning, the riot was an irrational act. Twelve black Washingtonians died, and the $25 million in damage was concentrated along 14th Street, NW, home to theaters and other businesses where local residents had long worked and played. But the violence was also a carnival of the oppressed; euphoric crowds looted fancy clothes and liquor stores and, laughing, ran away from police. "The Black people in this city were really happy for three days," reported a government worker, "They have been kicked so long, and this is the one high spot in their life."[15]

Martin Luther King, Jr. occupied a unique place in American political life. As Stokely Carmichael remembered, the inspiring preacher "was the one man of our race that this country's older generations, the militants and the revolutionaries and the masses of black people would still listen to."[16] King's funeral symbolized that status. So many national politicians and celebrities such as Jacqueline Kennedy and Diana Ross attended that little room was left in Ebenezer Baptist for its parishioners. But then some 50,000 mourners, representing a cross section of black America and white liberalism, followed King's mule-driven casket on a five-mile march to his alma mater, Morehouse College. It was probably the saddest demonstration of their lives.

King's murder and the riots that followed confirmed that what the black leader had feared was coming to pass: the shattering of his fragile, radical dream of a nonviolent, integrated society. The intransigence of most whites and black anger at the slow pace of change were creating a vicious cycle that would be difficult to reverse. If King had lived, his influence might only have continued to wane.

The fate of the Poor People's Campaign was instructive. In May a few thousand people traveled to Washington to embody King's vision of an interracial movement that would pry open federal coffers to help the jobless and destitute. On the Mall, participants erected a shantytown of tents called Resurrection City from which they planned to picket and sit in at government buildings. But heavy rains, violence among participants, and an increasingly conservative Congress soon put SCLC organizers on the defensive. At the end of June, police arrested the fewer than 200 protesters still camped out on the Mall. Without a dynamic movement behind him, one man, alive or martyred, could not alter the course of history.

At the same time, in New York City, a spirit of rebellion was seizing white and black student radicals at Columbia University, which borders on Harlem. Some students disrupted an official memorial meeting for Dr. King with charges that the school administration was "completely racist toward the community and toward its employees."[17] On April 23 a biracial group of radicals began a campus sit-in at Hamilton Hall. The next morning, the black protesters, un-

easy partners of the mostly white activists from Students for a Democratic Society, asked the SDS contingent to find their own building to occupy.

The protest soon expanded; two days later, hundreds of students and
other young people were living inside five barricaded university buildings.
Inside cavernous Low Library, protesters slept in the president's office,
smoked his cigars, drank his sherry, and rifled through his files for politically incriminating documents.

Life inside the "liberated" buildings was tense but passionate, sleepless
yet amusing. Constant meetings took place but so did a marriage. "We went
out on the balcony," remembered Richard Eagan and Andrea Boroff, "and the
[university] chaplain proclaimed us children of a new age. There were flowers. There was cake. They took us out and marched us around campus with
people banging on pots and pans. . . . Someone had keys to a faculty office
and they gave us a honeymoon suite."[18]

The rebels pressed specific demands on the Columbia administration,
whose main response to months of student organizing had been to ban
protests inside campus buildings. Radicals insisted that the university stop
building a gymnasium in a nearby park, which would have excluded local
black residents, and that Columbia sever all ties to an institute that conducted
military research for the government.

But, as SDS firebrand Mark Rudd admitted, "the issue is not the issue." For
black and white radicals alike, the gym and the defense institute were merely
good examples of what needed to be changed; battling against them was but
one step along the road to revolution. The young occupiers viewed Columbia
as a pillar of the system responsible for ghettoizing the residents of Harlem, exploiting the garbage workers of Memphis, and raining death on the peasants of
Vietnam. Their movement aimed to expose campus "complicity" with evil and,
somehow, to transform Columbia from a training ground of the elite into a
place dedicated to serving poor and working-class New Yorkers. And, being
normal 20-year-olds, most also meant to have some fun in the process.

Eight days after the occupations began, Columbia authorities decided to
end them. Police entered the buildings and arrested almost 600 students. The
black students marched out of Hamilton Hall in disciplined ranks and were
arrested peacefully—police feared setting off the wrath of Harlem. But the
white students refused to dismantle their barricades; in one building, protesters soaped down the stairs to slow the inevitable. With clubs, blackjacks,
and fists, the police returned the university to its legal owners. The bloody
conclusion provoked a student strike far more popular than the building
takeovers themselves. "This was unlike a labor dispute," observed a veteran
mediator after failing to resolve the crisis, "in that it was in the interests of
one of the disputants, SDS, *not* to settle."[19]

The student rebellion at Columbia was, at the time, the most prolonged
of its kind at a major university—and the first at an Ivy League school. As

hundreds of journalists recorded the events, radicals flocked to applaud and participate in what they believed was a tactical breakthrough for their developing struggle. Black Power spokesmen Stokely Carmichael and H. Rap Brown came from Harlem to confer with the students inside Hamilton Hall. "If the university doesn't deal with our brothers in there," Brown announced, "they're going to have to deal with the brothers out on the streets." SDS founder Tom Hayden helped occupy a building and was soon calling for "two, three many Columbias" to force U.S. leaders to choose between radical change and the military occupation of American campuses.[20]

But the Columbia rebels proved more successful at stirring up their opponents than in advancing their ultimate goals. Most politicians were outraged and blamed administrators for not calling in the cops sooner. "SDS tactics have succeeded in crippling a great university," charged a Republican congressman, "the next target can be City Hall, the State Capitol, or even the White House."[21] A minority of faculty members made common cause with SDS and the black occupiers. Others agreed with Columbia historian Richard Hofstadter who accused student radicals of threatening the university's commitment to "certain basic values of freedom, rationality, inquiry, [and] discussion" in the name of a dogma called "liberation."[22] SDS members and their black allies countered that universities like Columbia were training grounds for an elite that was exploiting ghetto dwellers and slaughtering Vietnamese. What was so rational about that?

Away from the campuses, student revolution usually seemed a contradiction in terms. Most ordinary white Americans felt they had more in common with working-class policemen than with the idealistic Ivy League students the officers had routed. In the two years after the Columbia events, similar confrontations occurred on hundreds of campuses. But, with each takeover, the prospect of building a movement as socially broad as it was tactically daring receded further into the realm of wishful thinking.

Summer: Chicago and Atlantic City

In late August, a larger battle between the Movement and its sworn adversaries took place on a grander stage: the downtown streets of the nation's second largest city. Chicago officials had lobbied hard to win the contract to host the quadrennial Democratic convention. Mayor Richard Daley raised a war chest from local hotel owners and reminded President Johnson of his loyalty and long service to the party. "He's been a great president. All you have to do is look at his record," affirmed the mayor. Daley also made clear that, unlike some of his counterparts in other metropolises, he knew how to stop civil unrest before it got out of hand. When Chicago was selected in October, 1967, the mayor declared it "a great honor [which] gives the people of Chicago another opportunity to show why it is the finest and friendliest convention city in the nation."[23]

Only 10 months later, an amicable gathering was quite impossible. By then, the Democratic Party had split into two warring camps—regulars like Daley who vowed to support the President and clamp down on protest at home versus insurgent liberals who carried the hopes of those who detested the war but still had faith in constitutional remedies. Since elected officials and other party insiders chose most of the delegates, Vice President Hubert Humphrey was almost certain to be the Democratic presidential nominee.

But the primaries, which Humphrey avoided, still featured a lively contest between Eugene McCarthy and Robert Kennedy. Both "Gene" and "Bobby" wanted to rescue the Democrats from the swamp of Johnson's war. But they had quite different strengths and weaknesses. McCarthy inspired thousands of fervent antiwar youths to knock on doors and pass out literature; by entering the race when LBJ still appeared strong, he seemed the candidate of principle. But the erudite senator had little rapport with blue-collar workers and the black and Latino poor who were among the Democrats' bedrock supporters—and hardly any respect from party bosses.

Kennedy, on the other hand, was a hero in the ghettos and barrios; on the night of King's assassination, he had gone to the heart of black Indianapolis (where he was contesting the Indiana primary) to communicate his rage and sorrow. Earlier, he had walked with Cesar Chavez in support of the grape strikers. Kennedy's opposition to welfare payments and his stalwart anticommunism also made him acceptable to white workers. But many liberal activists mistrusted Kennedy's motives: to them, his late entrance into the race smacked of opportunism and was splitting the ranks of reform. They knew President Johnson could be counted on to block his nomination; the two men had long despised one another.

After Kennedy entered the race in mid-March, he defeated McCarthy in all but one primary (in Oregon). On the night of June 5, Bobby was celebrating a narrow victory in the California race when a psychotic Palestinian nationalist named Sirhan Sirhan took his life. The public's grief was nearly as massive as that which had followed his brother's murder less than five years earlier. In the wake of another Kennedy martyrdom, McCarthy seemed the Democrats' only alternative to four more years of bloodletting and rancor, at home and in Southeast Asia.

Antiwar radicals looked forward to the Chicago convention for a different reason. It was a perfect opportunity to expose the "party of death" in all its ugliness and hypocrisy. The National Mobilization Committee (or "Mobe"), an umbrella body of antiwar groups, planned a large but peaceful march to the amphitheater where the delegates would be meeting. Hundreds

Robert F. Kennedy, during his 1968 presidential campaign. Source: *Chicago Historical Society*

of SDS activists came in hopes of convincing McCarthy supporters that change within the party system was unattainable.

Then there were the Yippies, apostles of comic revolution. "Rise up and abandon the creeping meatball! Come all you rebels, youth spirits, rock minstrels, truth seekers, peacock freaks, poets, barricade jumpers, dancers, lovers and artists. . . . We demand the politics of ecstasy. . . . Begin preparations now! Chicago is yours! Do it!"[24] The invitation was concocted by a small circle of friends—antiwar organizers, rock musicians, Beat artists, freelance hippie activists—who were living and getting high in the lower part of Manhattan Island.

Abbie Hoffman and Jerry Rubin were the ringleaders of the group, but the whole point of Yippie was to defy the top-down structure of mainstream politics and the inhumanity that allegedly flowed from it. "We're not leaders, we're cheerleaders," Hoffman told a reporter.[25] Yippies viewed America much the way the Beats had in the 1950s: as a boring, sexually repressive place, run by anxious men who made war against the poor, the powerless, and the unconventional. Make "revolution for the hell of it" proclaimed Hoffman in a 1968 book. Yippies eschewed the usual repertoire—long-winded analysis, fist-shaking slogans, orderly street protests—that had been main-stays of the Left since the nineteenth century. Instead, they devised humor-ous events made for television and watched by millions of incipient young rebels who had little interest in a politics that was not entertaining.

The Yippies intended Chicago to be a coming-out party for their vision, "a festival of life" to confront the party of death. They talked about letting greased pigs loose in the streets and then nominating one of the porcine anarchists for president; they mused about lacing the city's water supply with LSD and pre-dicted that thousands of young rebels would float nude in Lake Michigan, af-ter making love in the parks and on the beaches. Hardly any of this was seri-ous, but media outlets lapped it up. By early August Yippie had begun to fulfill the hopes of its creators; it had become a myth steeped in a crazy brew of what Abbie Hoffman called "risk, drama, excitement, and bullshit."[26]

Richard J. Daley was not amused. To the mayor, who lived in the same working-class Catholic neighborhood near the Stockyards where he had been raised, the Yippies and their more earnest allies were a dire threat to the con-servative values of most Chicagoans and to the civic order. In response, Da-ley mobilized, with help from the Johnson administration, a security force more massive than the one that had quelled the urban riots in Detroit and Newark the previous summer. All 12,000 city police were put on 12-hour shifts (at least a thousand were outfitted in scruffy clothes to infiltrate the protesters' ranks), some 6000 National Guardsmen were called up and trained to fight mock battles with "hippies," and another 7500 Regular Army troops flew in from their Texas base to squelch any riot that might occur in the black community. The mayor also warned the press: "We don't anticipate or expect [trouble] unless certain commentators and columnists cause trou-ble."[27] Daley's Chicago would show the nation how to deal with this un-American rabble.

The armed front certainly chilled the Movement. The Yippies had talked about inspiring half a million people to come to dance and demonstrate, but no more than 10,000 attended any protest during the four-day convention in late August. The mostly male contingent that did show up was brave or fool-hardy enough to go ahead with their plans. And Daley's policemen were an-gry enough to make them suffer.

Images of the conflicts that resulted have become as common as any that emerged from the 1960s: Yippies nominating a pig named Pigasus for the na-tion's highest office and then immediately losing him to police custody, cops smashing the cameras and heads of journalists trying to cover rampaging pro-testers, an orderly Mobe march to the amphitheater being turned back by tear gas, helmeted police and National Guardsmen clubbing and maceing thousands of demonstrators and bystanders in front of the Hilton Hotel in downtown Chicago—where the only live camera in town (outside the con-vention hall) beamed the violence to the entire nation for a full 17 minutes.[28]

Democrats watched it all from inside their air-conditioned amphitheater and then denounced one another in the most incendiary terms. From the podium, Connecticut senator Abraham Ribicoff, an antiwar delegate, accused the police of using "Gestapo tactics," and Richard Daley roared back, "Fuck you you Jew son of a bitch you lousy motherfucker go home." Fortunately for the mayor, no microphone was close enough to pick up his words. Much later, lip-readers used news footage to decipher them.[29]

To the outmanned demonstrators and their sympathizers, what occurred in Chicago seemed self-evident: sadistic police, encouraged by the authorities, had trampled on the rights of protesters, most of whom had behaved in a peaceful manner. The attacks on photographers and TV cameramen were viewed as blatant assaults on the First Amendment. The cops were trying to hide their brutality from the nation.

They need not have worried. Most Americans sided with Richard Daley and his police. After both Democrats and protesters had departed, the mayor refused to apologize: "This administration and the people of Chicago," he said, "would never permit a lawless, violent group of terrorists to menace the lives of millions of people, destroy the purpose of a national political convention and take over the streets."[30] Pollsters found that respondents, by a margin of almost 2 to 1, approved of his actions. CBS, the leading network at the time, received thousands of letters, 90 percent of which were critical of coverage perceived as favoring the demonstrators.

The war at home: National Guard jeeps outfitted for a riot during the Democratic Convention in Chicago, August 1968. Source: Chicago Historical Society

Fear of disorder and disgust at the protesters' unruly, sometimes obscene manner led many Americans to identify with any authority willing to do something to stop the "troublemakers." African Americans, who had their own stories of police misconduct to tell, were a noticeable exception: 63 percent believed the Chicago cops had used too much force, compared with only 10 percent of whites who felt that way.[31]

With the election just two months away, Republicans were quietly exultant. Hubert Humphrey emerged from his convention 12 points behind Richard Nixon in the polls. To press their advantage, GOP campaign officials quickly produced a television ad entitled "Failure." Over images of the violence in Chicago, an announcer asked, rhetorically: "How can a party that can't keep order in its own backyard hope to keep order in our fifty states?"[32]

A week later in Atlantic City, a different kind of institution came under attack in a fashion as novel as anything the Yippies had invented. On September 7 some 200 women staged a theatrical demonstration against the Miss America contest. They crowned a sheep, insisted on speaking only to female reporters, and threw a variety of "beauty products"—girdles, false eyelashes, wigs, and bras—into a huge "freedom trash can." Inside the convention hall, the telecast was briefly halted when 20 ululating protesters unfurled a banner reading "Women's Liberation."

By the late '60s, the pageant, begun almost half-a-century earlier, was no longer held in high esteem across the cultural spectrum. Liberal commentators made fun of its ever smiling, verbally vapid contestants and pointed out that no black competitor had ever made it to the finals. One columnist for *Life* magazine branded the contest "dull and pretentious and racist and exploitative and icky and sad."[33] But, for millions of people, Miss America still symbolized how young women were supposed to look and behave. As such, the event held in a declining resort town by the sea was an inviting target for a new kind of movement.

The protest was organized by New York Radical Women, a small group of friends with experience in civil rights and the larger New Left. Gradually, these women had grown disenchanted with the "macho" leadership of radical men who preferred their female comrades to stay in the background of what was supposed to be a common struggle. Remarkably, the Miss America protest was the first that any of the women involved had ever organized on her own. It also became a coming-out party for the feminist upsurge that, over the next decade, would change the lives of millions of women in the United States and around the world.

In spirit and ideology, the demonstrators owed a good deal to the New Left they were leaving. They chose the pageant because, in the words of organizer Robin Morgan, "Where else could one find such a perfect combination of American values—racism, materialism, capitalism—all packaged in one 'ideal' symbol, a woman." Particularly egregious were the absence of black participants and the fact that recent winners flew off, with comedian Bob Hope, to entertain U.S. troops in Vietnam. Morgan described Miss Illinois, the woman named Miss America in 1968, as being crowned with "her smile still blood-flecked from Mayor Daley's kiss."[34]

But Morgan and her sisterly comrades were also out to make a point their erstwhile brethren on the Left had neglected: it was a moral outrage (and, of course, a boon to the garment and cosmetics industries) to judge women primarily by their looks, by a standard of beauty borrowed from popular magazines like *Playboy* and *Cosmopolitan* as much as from the Miss America contest. The *New York Times* article about the protest provided unwitting confirmation of the problem. Reporter Charlotte Curtis described Robin Morgan wearing a "black-and-white pajama suit" and mentioned the dress and hat color of another protester who was in her middle sixties.[35] Outside the fashion pages, the *Times* never mentioned a man's sartorial choices.

But few people then considered sexual images a cause for political protest. Under way at the same time in Atlantic City was a Miss Black America contest dedicated to redressing the exclusion of African Americans from the white pageant. "We'll show black beauty for public consumption," announced a male organizer, "herald her beauty and applaud it."[36] A few years later, debates about the depiction of women's bodies in advertising and films and on television would become too heated and prevalent to ignore.

Neither the *Times* reporter nor other mainstream journalists recognized the historic nature of the event. The protest, Morgan later wrote, "was the first major action of the current Women's Movement . . . years of meetings, consciousness-raising, thought, and plain old organizing had made it possible."[37] Ecstatic about what they'd done, the demonstrators ended the day with a "funeral dance" by candlelight on Atlantic City's famous Boardwalk.

As with other radical actions in 1968, this one immediately spurred a backlash. Critics in the media began referring to "bra-burning feminists," even though no woman in Atlantic City had set fire to anything. During the protest, male onlookers shouted, "Go home and wash your bras" and urged demonstrators to throw themselves into the "freedom trash can." A former contestant from Wisconsin named Terry Meewsen got so angry that she rushed off to paint her own protest sign. "There's only one thing wrong with Miss America," it read, "She's beautiful." On her dress, Meewsen proudly wore a Nixon-for-president button.[38]

Autumn: Campaign

It was unusual that fall to hear much enthusiasm for either man running on a major party ticket for the most powerful job in the world. Most of the conservatives dominating the Republican Party would have preferred to nominate one of their own, such as California governor Ronald Reagan. But, fearing a repeat of the Goldwater debacle, they settled on Nixon, who had already campaigned three times for national office and was skilled at bridging the party's ideological factions. Few Americans, whatever their ideology, were happy with the state of the nation. The radicals of SDS expressed their disgust with politics as usual by organizing election day marches under the slogan, "Vote with your feet, Vote in the streets." If the GOP could wage a united, uncontroversial campaign, Nixon should be able to waltz into the White House.

Humphrey, by contrast, seemed a forlorn figure in his bitterly divided party. Anti-war liberals scorned the vice president as LBJ's lackey. White southerners and urban ethnics mistrusted Humphrey's long record of support for black rights and anti-poverty programs. To have any chance to win, he would have to cling to the organizational might of big labor unions and the fact that a large plurality of voters were still registered Democrats. In early September, Humphrey's campaign manager had a candid talk with the nominee over breakfast. "Look, I'm going to work my tail off for you," confided Larry O'Brien. "but as your manager I have to say to you—right now, you're dead."[39]

It took a pugnacious third-party candidate to prevent the Republicans from winning an easy victory. George Wallace, who created the American Independent Party in order to secure a ballot line, knew he would not be elected president; his reputation as a bigot gave him little prospect of winning any state outside the South. But his strong regional base also threw open the possibility that, if Humphrey could make it a close race, no man would win a majority of the electoral vote. If that occurred, the Constitution left the choice up to the House of Representatives, with each state having one vote. Wallace might have driven a hard bargain for his support—perhaps even repeal of the landmark civil rights and voting rights acts.

As it was, the Alabamian defined one of the two main issues of the campaign and forced his major-party rivals to sing his tune. The issue was "law and order." Four years of ghetto riots and campus protests and a growing rate of street crime had left over 80 percent of Americans believing, according to a September poll, that public order had "broken down."[40] Wallace's response was curt and uncompromising. "No one has a grievance in this country that gives him a right to . . . endanger the health and life of every citizen," he announced. And his solution was equally tough: "Let the police run this country for a year or two and there wouldn't be any riots," he told white working-class audiences that were more ardent than the large but rather passive throngs Humphrey and Nixon were drawing.[41] At the end of September, Wallace was scoring 21 percent in opinion polls, less than 10 points behind the vice president.

The second major issue was the war in Vietnam, key cause of the Democrats' internal hemorrhage and the GOP's opportunity. Wallace took the safe position of supporting the troops under fire without endorsing U.S. policy; after the Tet offensive, even his own stalwarts no longer believed that Americans were effectively defending the freedom of South Vietnamese. Nixon and Humphrey tried to sound "presidential." Knowing there was no public consensus about how to exit the Indochina quagmire, each tried to strike a balance between wooing doves and reassuring hawks. The Republican candidate promised he had "a secret plan" to end the war but made clear it did not involve surrendering South Vietnam to the enemy. At the end of September, Humphrey departed gingerly from his full-throated endorsement of administration policy; "I would be willing to stop the bombing of North Vietnam as an acceptable risk for peace," he told a TV audience. But he quickly added that the bombs would start falling again if the other side showed "bad faith."[42]

Such statements were drafted with exquisite care and the advice of advertising professionals. In 1968, to craft their appeal to voters, both major parties employed companies whose normal business was to persuade Americans to buy automobiles, soup, and laundry detergent. For the Nixon campaign, a market research firm tested how voters from key states felt about a blizzard of issues. The candidate's TV commercials, more ingenious than those shown in earlier campaigns, unsettled voters, on purpose, with rapid editing and electronic music to remind them that "America is in trouble today," trouble only a change in leadership could remedy.

To counter, Humphrey hired Doyle, Dane, Bernbach—an agency known, fittingly, for creating the slogan, "We're only Number Two. We have to try harder," for the Avis rental car company.[43] But his managers thought the ads the agency created were dry and stilted, and they turned instead to liberal TV producers. They filmed an emotional telebiography in which Humphrey played with his retarded, 5-year-old granddaughter. She "taught me the meaning of true love," the Democrat told viewers.[44]

George Wallace had neither the money nor the inclination to employ such methods. His campaign was a technological throwback; aside from the usual buttons and bumper stickers (which his supporters had to purchase), the candidate's personal appearances were virtually his entire campaign.

Wallace's rallies were exhibitions of political fury, a mirror image of the passions unleashed at many an outdoor rock concert. The typical event would begin with a country music band and a prayer. Then, after a warm-up speaker urged the crowd to donate "to the fastest-growing political movement in the history of our nation," the man himself strutted on stage, waving to his fans and the handful of (multiracial) hecklers who had been allowed, even encouraged, to attend. Wallace knew his people hungered for a way to fight back against liberals and the counterculture. So he first let hecklers have their (often obscene) say. Then he reduced them to slovenly parasites: "You young people seem to know a lot of four-letter words. But I have two four-letter words you don't know: S-O-A-P and W-O-R-K."[45]

The three candidates did have one thing in common. Whether through sophisticated advertising or bellicose one-liners, each spoke directly to voters. In the past, party bosses and local organizations had carried much of the burden of selling their candidate. Presidential nominees began advertising on TV in the 1950s, but, beginning in 1968, campaigns were completely dominated by the well-spun image of the man in the spotlight. One consequence was an increase in the number of independent voters who disdained participation in either party. And, beginning in 1968, voter turnout began a long-term decline.

But the presidential race that year almost ended in an upset. Humphrey slowly rose from his political grave to challenge Nixon in the big industrial states. Essential to his comeback were the publicists and precinct walkers of organized labor. Union officials feared that a Republican victory would put in jeopardy the economic gains of millions of blue-collar Americans who had only recently lifted themselves into the middle class. The AFL-CIO and United Auto Workers flooded union members with hard-hitting leaflets that called a vote for Wallace a vote for Nixon. The man from Alabama was blamed for his state's high illiteracy rate, poor record of adhering to child labor laws, and letting racists and members of the John Birch Society run his campaign. The attacks helped reverse Wallace's surge, as did the customary reluctance to "waste" a vote on a third-party hopeful. In the end, Wallace won only 13.6 percent of the vote, most of it in the South. And the strong union states of Michigan, Washington, and Pennsylvania all went for Humphrey. A heavy black vote also pulled the veteran liberal within sight of the White House.

It wasn't enough. Nixon drew only half a million more ballots than Humphrey (and 43 percent overall) yet easily won a majority of the electoral vote. Cries of "law and order" paid big dividends, particularly among those Americans who were leery of agitators of another race or from another region. In the South, the Republican candidate essentially split the vote with George Wallace; only 10 percent of whites in Dixie pulled the Democratic lever. This pattern (absent Wallace) would hold in presidential elections for the rest of the century. Except when the Democrats nominated a southerner (Jimmy Carter or Bill Clinton), the newly prosperous but still conservative white South voted solidly Republican. In the North, Democrats remained competitive (Humphrey won Michigan, Pennsylvania, and New York) but needed big turnouts from unionists, working women, and racial minorities.

So the 1968 election marked the end of a political era. Although Humphrey's party remained in control of Congress, the initiative gradually shifted to the Right. Advocates of liberal reform had to play defense against a growing and confident conservative movement. A year that rang with shouts of "revolution" and an angry backlash ended with the triumph of Richard Milhous Nixon—a brilliant if uninspiring man whose only strong faith was in his own fierce ambition. On the day after the election, the victor recalled a sign he had seen a teenage girl carrying as he campaigned through Ohio. "Bring Us Together," it read. As with many promises made by politicians in the 1960s, this one proved impossible to fulfill.

CHAPTER 13

Many Faiths

THE '60s REFORMATION

EVERY DAY PEOPLE ARE STRAYING AWAY FROM THE CHURCH AND GOING BACK
TO GOD.

—Comedian Lenny Bruce, c. 1965[1]

Nothing changed so profoundly in the United States during the 1960s as
American religion. That may seem a startling statement. So many aspects of
national life underwent turmoil during that decade and the years surrounding it—from race relations and relationships between the sexes to the citi-
zenry's trust in politicians. The most familiar images of the period depict
Americans protesting, dancing, taking drugs, or fighting a war—anything but
praying.

Yet an era when little could be taken for granted was also a time when
millions of people rethought and re-formed the place of the spiritual in their
lives. Following a tradition as old as the nation, Americans made sense of
rapid social and moral change in religious terms. Some expressed their faith
by participating in the same movements for human rights and against war
that attracted secular activists; a greater number confined their hopes and energies to matters of the spirit.

Whatever the choice, a good many citizens, particularly young adults,
broke away from the churches and synagogues of their childhoods. Between
the mid-1950s and the mid-1980s, over a third of all Americans left the denomination in which they'd been raised. Hungry for a faith both authentic
and fervent, they created new styles of Christian and Jewish worship and
joined new kinds of religious communities that promised a direct link to the
Almighty. At the same time, a small but growing minority of Americans rejected the beliefs and institutions of Western religion altogether. They explored the transcendent paths blazed by one variety or another of Buddhism,
Hinduism, and Islam. Spiritual discipline, voluntarily chosen, came back into

fashion. Millions more dabbled in less rigorous pursuits like astrology and sprinkled their conversations with terms like "karma," "mantra," "yin and yang." By the mid-'70s, the United States was in the throes of a religious revival—one in a series that has periodically rolled across the land since the colonial era.

Ironically, this spiritual surge was, in part, a revolt against the successes of established religion in the years immediately following World War II. During the late '40s and '50s, the major Christian and Jewish denominations all grew larger and more prosperous. Families rushed to join, particularly in the booming suburbs, and construction firms raced to keep up with demand. In 1960 over a billion dollars was spent on building churches, 40 times the total in 1945.[2] In formal ways, Americans seemed more devout than ever. More than half the population regularly attended a church or synagogue (an historic high), and over 90 percent told pollsters they prayed to God and said grace before meals.[3]

But some critics felt such signs of spiritual health concealed a certain hollowness of purpose. With the Cold War at its height, piety often seemed a patriotic reflex, even a civic obligation. Political leaders like Dwight D. Eisenhower regularly reminded citizens, "Without God there could be no American form of government. . . . Recognition of the Supreme Being is the first—and most basic—expression of Americanism."[4] During Ike's first term as president, the phrase "under God" was added to the Pledge of Allegiance and "In God We Trust" was inscribed on the currency. The ubiquitous slogan "The family that prays together stays together," a creation of the Advertising Council, betrayed a more anxious sentiment: Was religion little more than a device for keeping the social order together?

A number of theologians, both Christian and Jewish, complained about the banal character of worship. They worried that the blare of ideology and the glisten of fresh concrete and stained glass were muffling the cry of the soul. Attending a house of God had become, for many Americans, little more than a social occasion. "Our services are conducted with pomp and precision," wrote Abraham Joshua Heschel of the Jewish Theological Seminary. "Everything is present: decorum, voice, ceremony. But only one thing is missing: Life." A certain superficiality may even have crept into scripture reading. Over 80 percent of American adults agreed that the Bible was the "revealed word of God," but a majority could not name any of the four gospels in the New Testament.[5]

The weakening of spiritual passion did have a side benefit: it helped encourage a growing tolerance for religious minorities. The United States had been founded, unofficially, as a Protestant nation. Followers of other faiths long had to prove they posed no threat to the Protestant dominion associated, as it was for many Americans, with the nation's "freedom" from the religious tyrannies of the Old World. Ironically, bigotry went hand in hand with claims of religious liberty. Notwithstanding the First Amendment, numerous Protestant bastions—universities, country clubs, entire neighborhoods—restricted Catholics and/or Jews or barred them altogether.

But, after 1945, many of the cultural walls began to come down. In the "one nation under God" that had triumphed over Hitler and was now resisting communism, interfaith hostilities seemed out of place. Marriage between Protestants and Catholics steadily gained acceptance, as, more grudgingly (on both sides), did unions between Christians and Jews. Pollsters in the mid-'50s found Americans far less willing than a decade before to believe the worst about religious minorities—for example, that Catholics were ignorant dupes of the pope or that Jewish businessmen were dishonest. Such Jews as composer Leonard Bernstein and actress Barbra Streisand became cultural icons, while Ivy League colleges abandoned their restrictive Jewish quotas. Meanwhile, it no longer seemed unusual for Catholics to occupy top spots in corporations, and John F. Kennedy skillfully parried the fears of Protestant bigots on his way to the White House.

At the beginning of the 1960s, American religion was thus snared in a paradox. The more citizens dutifully attended a church or synagogue, the less the traditional content of their faith seemed to matter to them. Did God really mind if His people just went through the motions?

Billy Graham and Martin Luther King, Jr. certainly thought so. The two men were the nation's most celebrated Protestant ministers during the late '50s and '60s. In quite different ways, each injected the majority faith with a fresh dose of revivalistic spirit. For their admirers, passionate conversion became, once again, the central duty of any serious Christian.

Graham smoothed the ragged edges—the faith healing and flagrant anti-intellectualism—from white Protestant evangelism and thrust it into the television age. Beginning in 1949, he took his "crusade"—featuring a large, racially integrated cast of singers, musicians, and warm-up speakers—to city after American city and to many foreign lands. "All who are weak and heavy-laden, come unto me," Graham would appeal from a stage drenched in light. "The coming of the Lord draweth nigh." Millions responded, whether in person or after watching the spectacle on TV. Proudly and with restrained emotion, they made a "decision for Christ" and were "born again" in his service. In the process, orthodox Protestantism gradually shed its image as an old-time religion.

Simultaneously, King was preaching an updated version of the social gospel. To be a sincere Christian, he told audiences of all races, was to combat, nonviolently, the injustice meted out to racial minorities and the poor. His Southern Christian Leadership Conference (whose city-by-city campaigns consciously emulated Graham's "crusades") mobilized devout church members who insisted that God was on their side. "We cannot compromise with evil authority," King wrote from his Birmingham cell in 1963 to local white ministers who warned him against taking "extreme measures." We will put our beliefs into practice and suffer accordingly; either join us or get out of our way. King's messianic style converted people to the cause as much as did agreement with the black movement's demands. Many liberal white Protestants, confronting their churches' racist past, tried to follow the example black Christian militants were setting.

Although King occasionally cooperated with Graham in the late '50s, their brands of Christian witness were headed in opposite directions.[6] The civil rights leader, despite his firm grounding in the Bible, symbolized a current that flowed toward an ecumenical, consciously modern approach to Christianity. Modernists urged Protestant churches to jettison mystical dogmas and puritanical ethics. One group of theologians even heralded the "death of God" and counseled Christians to emphasize moral principles and abandon a doctrine grounded in faith. They and other liberal thinkers urged believers to throw themselves into the battle for social change alongside people of other religions and none at all. In contrast, Graham became the most prominent spokesman for Christians who believed, as a fellow evangelist put it, that "Jesus Christ is God's *only* provision for man's sin."[7] Churches that neglected to spread the traditional gospel were, they maintained, not really religious bodies at all.

Through most of the 1960s, the modernists seemed to have the upper hand—or at least to represent the future of American Protestantism. They were prominent voices in all the best-established denominations—the United Methodists, the Episcopalians, the United Presbyterians, and the United Church of Christ—whose wealth and numbers guaranteed a serious reception from the mass media and intellectuals. They dominated the National Council of Churches (NCC), an umbrella body that saw itself as the social conscience of Protestant America. In the 1960s, the NCC financed civil rights organizing in the Deep South and debated the virtue of draft resistance.

The liberal call to action galvanized many young Protestants who had not expected their staid churches to participate in changing anything. On scores of college campuses, Methodist student groups agreed it was a Christian's duty to "support all those movements which open up opportunities for God's children to be their best selves," as one professor put it.[8] Around the country, seminarians and devout laypeople alike got arrested for opposing racism and the Vietnam War and for supporting farmworkers' strikes. Desiring a more "relevant" faith, some ministers invited folk and jazz musicians to play during services. Loyal congregants in the established denominations were often shocked at the turn toward grassroots politics and popular culture; they came to church seeking comfort not conflict. But an aggressive moral agenda seemed to fit the era; one could not return to the quieter order of the '50s.

And African Americans kept the fires of Christian justice burning. In the mid-'60s, a black theology emerged as the spiritual component of the larger turn to black nationalism (whose stand against integration Martin Luther King opposed). Protestant ministers competed with the Nation of Islam to express the anger welling up in black urban neighborhoods against "the white power structure"—its clergy as well as its police. African-American churches began displaying statues and paintings of a dark-skinned, woolly-haired Christ, while liberal theologians, and an increasing number of preachers, both black and white, stressed Biblical passages like Luke 4:18, in which Jesus adopted the cause of "the poor . . . the brokenhearted . . . the captives" and vowed "to set at liberty them that are bruised."

But the new social gospelers ignored an embarrassing detail: the mainstream, mostly white churches were fast losing members. The slide began in the mid-'60s and accelerated over time. Between 1965 and 1975, the size of every major white liberal denomination shrank: the number of Episcopalians dropped by 17 percent, of United Presbyterians by 12 percent, of United Methodists by 10 percent, and of congregants in the United Church of Christ by 12 percent.[9] Immersion in activism had certainly invigorated the purpose of some old-line churches; the ranks of the clergy opened up to African Americans and to women. But many laypeople saw no reason to remain in denominations that were merely pasting Christian labels on essentially secular causes. They either abandoned organized religion or searched for a more intensely spiritual alternative.

Many a quest ended up in the evangelistic camp. "The Unchanging Gospel for a Changing World," promised Billy Graham's magazine *Decision*, whose circulation climbed into the millions during the 1960s. The slogan suggests the major reason why the appeal of conservative Protestant churches grew at the same time that of their modernist counterparts was dwindling. The former offered troubled individuals what the latter could not: the balm of simple answers to perennial questions of the soul.

American Protestantism had always been a deeply personal faith. Believers longed for an intimacy with the Almighty and, typically, did not feel "saved" unless they were sure that, as one young evangelist put it in the early 1970s, "God is a real person. . . . He actually walks among His people. He listens to them, talks to them, and affects their daily lives."[10] The enthusiasm of participants in past "great awakenings" always stemmed from this kind of relationship—and the dedicated missionaries who spread the good word. Now, it was happening again.

Every conservative denomination spurted in membership during the decade beginning in 1965. The Southern Baptists grew by 18 percent to become the largest Protestant group in the nation, while the smaller Assemblies of God and Nazarenes also made impressive gains. Evangelicals did not share the same theology or worship in the same way. Fundamentalists who stress the literal truth of the Bible and worship in a sober fashion differed from pentecostalists who believe the Holy Ghost takes over their bodies and leads them to display ecstatic "gifts of the Spirit" such as speaking in tongues. But evangelical Protestants agreed on two bedrock elements of their faith: Jesus is the only path to salvation, and the Bible is the unerring word of God. These united the world-famous Billy Graham with the humblest small-town preacher. To redeem the sinful was their common motivation.

Evangelists found a natural constituency among those marooned by sex, drugs, and rock and roll. The hedonistic trinity of the youth culture gave some Americans, for a time at least, the hope that one could transcend a life of drudgery and compromise. But it left other young people bruised and unhappy. They had glimpsed a vision of salvation—at the peak of an LSD trip or amid the collective rapture of a rock festival. But it quickly faded, leaving their lives in chaos. For some of these prodigal sons and daughters, the path of Jesus seemed the surest way home.

Of course, they couldn't get there without a guide. The Campus Crusade for Christ was eager to fill the role. Organized in 1951 by Southern California businessman Bill Bright, the group grew slowly for a decade with aid from the Graham juggernaut and a handful of evangelical churches. In 1960 it had 109 employees. Then, in the mid-'60s, Bright and a nucleus of young staff members set out to create their own brand of counter-culture. In 1967 the Crusade held a public convention at the University of California in Berkeley. On the steps of Sproul Hall (birthplace of the Free Speech Movement three years before), Jon Braun proclaimed "Jesus Christ, the world's greatest revolutionary." Soon, Braun and some other young evangelists were, in the way of earlier missionaries, going native: they grew their hair long, donned tie-dyed and fringed clothing, and spoke the hip idiom. Former Campus Crusaders took on new names like the Christian World Liberation Front and Jesus Christ Light and Power Company. They published graphically inventive papers (the one in Berkeley was christened *Right On*) and opened crash pads for kids strung out on drugs.

New Leftists made fun of these "Jesus freaks," but the appeal of the young crusaders outlasted that of their secular detractors. Evangelists, both of the hip and more conventional variety, converted thousands of lapsed Christians and the previously irreligious who dwelled in and around youth communities. By the mid-'70s, Campus Crusade boasted a staff of 6500 and a budget of $42 million. And Bright's brigade was only the largest of its kind. In Orange County, California, Rev. Chuck Smith baptized hippies in his swimming pool and set up a series of communal houses in which converts lived and studied the Bible. The pentecostalist Bobbi Morris organized the Living Word Fellowship and convinced thousands of mostly white, working-class young people to accept her strict, maternal authority and "get high on Jesus."

Young evangelists rally for Christ at the University of Texas, Austin, 1969. Source: *Campus Crusade for Christ, Intl.*

A murmur of armageddon ran through this sprouting network. Leading evangelists believed the world was approaching the end of time. Very soon, Jesus would return to earth and render His judgment. In 1970, Hal Lindsey, former leader of the Campus Crusade at UCLA, published a dramatic synopsis of these ideas, entitled *The Late, Great Planet Earth*. Over the next decade, his book, which referred to the Antichrist as "The Weirdo Beast" and "the Rapture" as "The Ultimate Trip," sold more than 9 million copies.[11] Serious theologians scoffed, but Lindsey had tapped into the same sense of dire crisis and wild optimism that gripped many on the secular Left. SDS and the Black Panthers expected some kind of socialism would emerge from the ashes of the U.S. empire. Lindsey and his fellow premillennialists (at times, including Billy Graham) were similarly convinced that the Second Coming would perfect the world.

Yet it was the spiritual security to be found in the conservative churches that best explains why they grew. "God *loves* you and offers a wonderful *plan* for your life," wrote Bill Bright in a 1965 pamphlet distributed all over the world. If one accepted this gospel, an eternity of contentment might result. It did require adopting a rigorous lifestyle and denying oneself certain sensual pleasures. But that only enhanced the appeal of the faith for people who had taken too many drugs or left bad marriages or simply felt their lives were devoid of meaning. The Bible made clear how God wanted his people to behave. For those who believed, surrender felt like freedom.

During the 1960s, the world of American Catholicism imploded and had to be rebuilt. No denomination underwent more rapid or more wrenching changes than did the nation's largest (which boasted some 48 million members in 1970). A decade that began with the election of the first Catholic president (even if he downplayed his religious identity) ended with Catholics, both laypeople and clergy, battling among themselves over the most basic matters of their faith: its liturgy, its authority structure, its moral obligations, and its definition of sin. The most tradition-laden of Western churches suddenly became the site of furious innovation—and of an equally vehement backlash among the defenders of old ways.

The prime cause of tumult occurred across the Atlantic, underneath the ornate dome of St. Peter's Basilica in Rome. Priests and bishops from all over the world gathered there for the Second Vatican Council, which convened periodically from 1962 to 1965. Called together by Pope John XXIII and completed by his successor, Paul VI, the council encouraged the breezes of theological pluralism and democracy to blow through church doctrines and practices essentially unchanged for centuries. The result was a Catholicism that invited "the active participation" of the laity, was open to dialogue and perhaps even future unity with Protestants, and encouraged debate and experimentation about its forms of worship.

Vatican II also updated the church's own kind of social gospel. Since the late nineteenth century, the Catholic hierarchy had alternated between preaching obedience to rulers and giving support to movements of workers and the poor—as long as they spurned Marxists and other secular radicals. But the final document of Vatican II announced that the modern church would no longer stand aloof from the worldly struggles of ordinary people. Henceforth, "the followers of Christ" would treat "the joys and the hopes, the griefs and the anxieties of the men of this age, especially those who are poor or in any way afflicted" as their own.[12]

In the United States the statement lent a measure of legitimacy to what thousands of Catholic brothers and sisters were already doing. Daniel Berrigan, a Jesuit, spoke out early and often against the Vietnam War. In 1968 he led a small group that entered a Selective Service office in Maryland and burned hundreds of draft files. American bishops could not, of course, endorse the destruction of federal property, but neither did they defrock the flamboyant priest. Breaking with Cold War orthodoxy, thousands of devout Catholics attended mass marches to protest the war being fought against Asian Communists. In New York City, two seminarians passed out leaflets accusing Cardinal Terence Cooke, an honorary military chaplain, of abetting war crimes—on the same day the cardinal ordained them in the Jesuit order.[13]

The black freedom movement also inspired innumerable acts of Catholic solidarity. Just before the 1963 March on Washington, Godfrey Diekmann of the Benedictine order told an enthusiastic gathering of fellow clergy that to "refuse to accept the Negro as our daily table guest" was to "trumpet the blasphemous triumph of Satan."[14] In 1965, white and black nuns dressed in their habits marched through New York and other cities in sympathy with demonstrators who were facing billy clubs and tear gas in Selma, Alabama. No longer would sisters accept being treated, as one put it, "like the children most of them spend their lives with." For their part, African-American Catholics, most of whom lived and worshiped in segregated areas, began to articulate a proud, separate identity. Black images of Jesus and Mary proliferated in inner-city churches, and parishioners demanded priests of their own race. "We have given up the myth," a black priest explained to a bishops' meeting in 1969, "that if we did all things in proper and approved fashion, we could be acceptable to the white people."[15]

A liturgical upheaval accompanied the political one. Many parish priests quickly applied the new ideas about worship that emerged from the Vatican Council. They began reciting the mass in English (or Spanish) instead of Latin, faced the flock instead of turning their backs to them, and encouraged parishioners to get off their knees, greet one another in a "kiss of peace," and join together in singing hymns and reading the Bible. Before Vatican II, a pastor who allowed any one of these activities would have been courting excommunication. By the 1970s, they had all become standard practice.

At the same time, groups of laymen and laywomen were fulfilling their spiritual needs with only occasional aid from a priest. In the early '60s, some Mexican-American laymen in California (the fastest-growing group of Catholics in the U.S.) began meeting on their own to study Scripture and discuss how the Holy Book might improve their lives and address the problems of their ethnic community. These *cursillos,* or "little courses," soon grew in popularity and emotional intensity, attracting farmworkers' leader Cesar Chavez, among others. The male-centered movement spawned a larger "charismatic" revival among Catholics nationwide, who tearfully displayed a personal connection to God, in the fashion long practiced in Pentecostal churches. At least one archbishop, Joseph McGucken of San Francisco, publicly regretted a singular result of the *cursillo* movement; in Mexican-American parishes, it was cutting down the number of people receiving Communion—still the core ritual of the Catholic mass.

But the archbishop's misgivings were small compared to those of conservatives who dissented from nearly everything Vatican II had wrought. "What in the Name of God Is Going On in the Catholic Church?" asked *National Review* in a 1965 cover story. In its erudite fashion, the magazine spoke for a fair number of lay Catholics who felt the new liturgy, in the rush to be worldly, was shattering the sublime mysteries of their faith. "Where else can one find robed priests like purple kings holding cups of silver and gold?" mused writer Garry Wills, who had once considered joining their ranks. Journalist Richard Rodriguez complained, "The [vernacular] mass is less ornamental; it has been 'modernized,' tampered with, demythologized, deflated. . . . No longer is the congregation moved to a contemplation of the timeless."[16] In a small-town Wisconsin parish, an anonymous writer lampooned the changes, "Latin's gone, peace is too; singin' and shoutin' from every pew. Altar's turned around, priest is too; commentators yellin': 'page 22.' . . . rosary's out, psalms are in; hardly ever heard a word against sin."[17] However, according to opinion polls, more than two-thirds of the laity welcomed the new rituals.

The embrace of social activism elicited a more negative response. Conservative intellectuals like William F. Buckley, Jr. were predictably outraged at figures like the brothers Daniel and Phillip Berrigan for sympathizing with a godless revolution in Vietnam. On the right, priests and nuns who marched in antiwar demonstrations and cheered on Black Power were seen as fools: Why enlist in a Left that had always despised their church and all its works? But a growing number of ordinary white Catholics also bristled at the demand that they support the civil rights movement. One Cleveland woman wrote to her diocesan paper that the sight of marching nuns made her "sick at heart." "Instead of public protests," she wrote, the sisters "should be down on their knees . . . praying."[18]

A flash point in this intrachurch conflict occurred in Milwaukee, a city whose white population was almost half Catholic. In the mid-'60s, James Groppi, white pastor in the mostly black parish of St. Boniface, led a lengthy series of peaceful marches that aimed at the full integration of the city's schools and neighborhoods. Television coverage made Groppi a well-known figure around the country. Some of his coreligionists regarded him as a hero. One Boston priest hailed Groppi for "unmask[ing] the hypocrisy of the lilywhite Catholic community. . . . St. Boniface is prophetic voice of the Church— not only the Catholic Church but religion itself."[19] Black leaders, including Martin Luther King, Jr., praised him too. And Groppi's protests bore fruit. After 200 straight days of marches, the Milwaukee City Council finally passed an open housing ordinance.

However, many white Catholics in Milwaukee despised Groppi and his followers. Like their counterparts in such cities as Chicago and Detroit, they believed integration would mean a sharp rise in violent crime and sexual tension, and a quick drop in property values. For these immigrants and second-generation Americans of eastern and central European ancestry, the neighborhood parish had been both a cultural refuge and a base from which to rise. They had built the Catholic community, literally and figuratively, and saw no reason to open it up to poorer Americans of a different race and, usually, a Protestant faith.

In Milwaukee, the fact that a man in a clerical collar was leading the assault occasioned cries of anguish that, at times, spilled over into a critique of recent changes in the church itself. "I am a very strong Catholic," Mae Bax-

Father James Groppi, civil rights activist, conducting a street Mass in Milwaukee, mid-1960s.
Source: *Archdiocese of Milwaukee Archives*

tis wrote to Father Groppi, "I should say, I *was*, but demonstrations like yours sicken me." Referring to Vatican II, she bewailed "what 2000 men could do to a 2000 year old Church." The crowds who harassed Groppi's marches with fists, spit, and racist slurs failed to dent his determination. But a self-described "old scrub lady" who told him that "Instead of making converts you are making enemies for our Religion" could not be so easily dismissed.[20] She spoke for many American Catholics upon whom the new dawn of pluralism had somehow failed to shine. In questioning the authority of liberal priests and bishops, she was invoking the greater authority of the stable faith she remembered.

On one major issue—sex—the church hierarchy refused to break with the past. In the wake of Vatican II, American Catholics hoped, or feared, that Pope Paul would soon extend his liberal outlook to the most intimate of matters. Millions of laywomen and laymen were already engaging in premarital sex, using birth control devices, and even having abortions (illegally, in most cases). In private, priests and nuns often looked the other way, while a growing minority chafed under their vow of celibacy.

And science was making it easier to flout tradition. A Catholic doctor, John Rock from Massachusetts, had been instrumental in developing the birth control pill. Amid much controversy, he claimed that Catholic women who took the pill were not really violating church teachings. Unlike such "artificial" means as condoms and diaphragms, the chemicals, he argued, did not impede the act of intercourse.

In 1968 Pope Paul VI stepped in to reassert the old-time morality. His encyclical *Humanae Vitae* barred Catholics from using contraceptives of any kind and suggested that abstinence was preferable to the "rhythm method." The Pope's reasoning echoed one element of the feminist critique. Sexual freedom, announced the pontiff, was just a means of exploiting another human being. Men who take advantage of birth control devices "lose respect for the woman and . . . come to the point of considering her as a mere instrument of selfish enjoyment."[21] Paul VI neglected to discuss abortion or the vow of celibacy.

In the United States, many priests, nuns, and theologians publicly protested his encyclical. The archbishop of Washington, D.C. ordered 51 outspoken priests to recant or never again be allowed to minister to the laity. Conservative Catholics hailed the pope for standing by his principles and began to build what became a powerful "pro-life" movement.

But most ordinary Catholics acted as if the encyclical had never been written. By the mid-'70s, Catholic women used "artificial" birth control as frequently as did Americans of other faiths. Abortion opposition remained strong among parishioners, yet this did not stop many Catholic women from seeking medical help to end their pregnancies, particularly after the Supreme Court's 1973 *Roe v. Wade* ruling struck down state laws prohibiting the procedure.

Among Protestants in the '60s, doctrinal conflicts led to the growth of larger, more vital conservative denominations. But Catholics had only one Church, and the shattering of that rock could only diminish its size and ability to inspire men and women to make a life-long commitment. The Vatican Council had emboldened Catholics to think for themselves. Many priests and nuns felt they deserved more personal freedom and concluded that church discipline would never allow it. So, with a mixture of sadness and rage, thousands abandoned their vows and left their orders. By 1980, the number of women in religious orders had declined 30 percent from its height in 1966. Only a third as many men were training for the priesthood as in the mid-'60s. In many parishes, full-time, married lay ministers were taking up the slack.

For American Catholics in the 1960s, the fires of "modernization" both cleansed and destroyed. What had been a church of immigrants wary of Protestant America changed into an institution as flamboyant, disputatious, and troubled as any other pillar of the postwar establishment. In their forms of worship and personal behavior, Catholics now resembled the majority of their fellow citizens. It was an ironic conclusion to a spiritual revolution.

In the mid-'60s, Jews were a tiny piece of America's religious mosaic— only 3 percent, according to pollsters.[22] The heyday of immigration from eastern Europe that had established a vibrant Jewish presence, both pious and secular, in major U.S. cities was half-a-century in the past. The nightmare of Hitlerism was more recent, of course, but most American Jews had lost no immediate relative in the Holocaust. And, in the wake of Auschwitz, public anti-Semitism was no longer acceptable. As beneficiaries of a newly tolerant ethnic order, Jews were thriving in nearly every profession and most lines of business.

Synagogues affiliated with all three main branches of the faith (Orthodox, Conservative, and Reform) burst with members and donations. In 1960 more than half of all American Jews belonged to a temple, double the percentage before World War II. But spiritual content often seemed secondary to the sparkling new gift shops, secular music performances, and athletic programs offered by many Reform and Conservative congregations. Jews denied that their religion separated them from other Americans. In the official Conservative prayer book one could find "America the Beautiful" as well as English translations of the traditional services. And the bar mitzvah, the coming-of-age ritual for males usually celebrated at age 13, often became an occasion notable as much for the conspicuous consumption of food, liquor, and gifts as for an adolescent's skill at reading and interpreting a portion of the Torah.

Then, during six days in June 1967, Israel fought and won a war against the armies of its Arab neighbors. The swift, complete victory was followed by a long and wrenching occupation of Palestinian lands. For many American Jews, the 1967 conflict awakened and inspired passions that did much to transform the meaning of their identity. No longer was Israel just a reason for Jewish pride, a desert miracle of orange groves and thriving kibbutzes, whose creation was romanticized in *Exodus*—a popular novel and film of the late '50s and early '60s. Israel was now the homeland of fellow Jews who had fought alone for their survival and were resigned to living in perpetual danger. The threat came not just from Arab militants but from communist powers, their Third World allies, and a good many American leftists who were eager to prove their "anti-imperialist" credentials. In the face of extinction, Israel became "the ultimate reality in the life of every Jew living today," as a graduate student at Brandeis University put it, "In dealing with those who oppose Israel, we are not reasonable and we are not rational. Nor should we be."[23]

This combative urgency did more than spur a huge increase in donations and travel to Israel as well as a new resolve to help shape its future. The Six-Day War turned many American Jews back to the sources of their religion, to a proud sense of themselves as belonging to a "people" who had been maligned and persecuted through most of recorded history yet had kept intact a distinctive faith and cultural style. The war heightened interest in the Holocaust itself, adding to the renown of articulate survivors like the writer Elie Wiesel and spawning the militant Jewish Defense League, whose slogan was "Never Again!" It also kindled a spiritual renewal among younger and more intellectual Jews, many of whom had joined the New Left and were now re-considering the secular cast of that commitment.

This renewal took a variety of forms. Some individuals and families began to observe the Jewish Sabbath the way their grandparents had—lighting candles and eating *challah* (a traditional bread) on Friday evening and then refraining from work until sundown on Saturday. Others kept kosher homes or studied Yiddish in an effort to recapture the texture of life in the European *shtetls* (villages) their forebears had fled. By 1970, almost 400 colleges offered programs in Jewish studies, often financed by wealthy donors and staffed by academics engaged with topics like Qabbalah (mystical texts) once relegated to the margins of scholarship. Forty Jewish student newspapers were being published at the time.

Young people returning to Judaism did not necessarily abandon the heretical spirit of the counterculture. *The Jewish Catalog*, a 1973 book that sold more than 200,000 copies, offered an eclectic menu of ritual, politics, and the arts liberally sprinkled with wit. One section was entitled, "Using the Jewish Establishment—A Reluctant Guide."[24]

A more profound, if less popular, feature of the renewal consisted of new communities of believers dubbed *havurah* (Hebrew for fellowship). Started by Jews in their twenties who sought a spiritual intensity unavailable in the synagogues of their youth, the *havurah* were egalitarian and emotional places where traditional blessings and the interpretation of religious texts mingled with sexual openness and popular music. As such, they posed a stark alternative to what one New York City participant called "the oppressive dullness and standardization of feeling . . . [the] artificial politeness and even-temperedness" of mainstream Jewish life.[25]

These communities borrowed much from the larger realm of hip culture and radical politics. Rabbi Itzik Lodzer, founder of the Boston *havurat*, credited psychedelics for generating the same "feeling of the true oneness of God and man" experienced by earlier Jewish mystics. When Paul Cowan left SDS to build a new kind of Judaism, he did not abandon his political values. Both the New Left and the *havurah* movement, he wrote, "encouraged intimacy and virtually outlawed authority. . . . Both organizations. . . . arrived at all their decisions by consensus, not by votes or by the decree of some central committee."[26] As in the secular Left, women in the new collectives set forth their views and capacity for leadership, claiming a role still unacceptable in most synagogues.

But Judaism gave the new fellowships a binding power that SDS and most hippie communes had lacked. Anchored in the Torah and a shared identity both ethnic and religious, thousands of young Jews now felt equipped to raise families and engage in politics in a more grounded and reflective manner. Their rejection of assimilation—either into middle-class America or its vaguely defined radical alternative—echoed lines from the film *Exodus* that

Sally Priesand, the first American woman ordained as a rabbi, 1972. Source: *American Jewish Archives, Cincinnati Campus, Hebrew Union College, Jewish Institute of Religion*

Paul Newman, playing a Jewish guerrilla fighter, threw at his Christian lover (played by Eva Marie Saint): "People are different. They have a right to be different. They like to be different. It's no good pretending that differences don't exist."[27] The assertion of Jewish distinctiveness articulated the same hunger for an authentic, moral life that was moving many Christians away from liberal churches and back to a living God.

In one major way, the '60s reformation was quite unlike earlier episodes of mass religious zeal in U.S. history: it burst through the confines of what mainstream commentators fondly called "the Judeo-Christian tradition." A small but growing minority of Americans, most of them young, no longer felt comfortable with faiths allegedly drenched in the polluted stream of the commercialized, competitive, power-hungry West. They looked instead for fulfillment from traditions rooted in Asia that seemed to promise an affinity with nature and the cosmos—one that did not rely on the medium of psychedelic drugs. A larger number of people attached themselves to homegrown guides who mingled the familiar ideology of self-help with the new language of "enlightenment." The consequence was a dizzying fragmentation of the religious landscape; many people browsed freely among unconventional theologies and subcultures without committing themselves to any one for very long. Best-selling books by such authors as Hermann Hesse and Carlos Casteneda popularized notions of reincarnation and of a "second consciousness" that might enable one to speak with animals and to fly.

The exotic names of new groups, gurus, and rituals conveyed the dizzying instability of the alternative religious marketplace. There were Tibetan Buddhists and Zen Buddhists, Moslem Sufis and Hindu Hari Krishnas, devotees of yoga and transcendental meditation (TM). Disciples flocked around such "teachers" (some living, some dead) as Meher Baba, Maharishi Mahesh Yogi, Gurdjieff, Maharaj Ji, Oscar Ichazo of Arica, Ron Hubbard of Scientology, and Werner Erhard of EST. Some Americans practiced witchcraft to link themselves to a nonpatriarchal past, ate peyote buttons to glimpse a holistic present, or "threw" the I Ching (title of a Chinese mystical text) to divine the future. One of the most popular rock groups of the era, the Grateful Dead, took its name from a Tibetan Buddhist guide to the afterlife. Other famous musicians like George Harrison of the Beatles communed with Indian gurus and learned to play the sitar.

Of course, such spiritual alternatives never attracted more than a small fraction of the Americans who adhered to one variety or another of Judaism and Christianity. Even in the San Francisco Bay Area, mecca for unorthodox faiths, fewer than 10 percent of the population seems to have taken part in any manifestation of the new religions.[28] Still, they drew a good deal of attention from journalists and theologians alike who agreed that a "New Age" might be at hand. Part of the reason was that the devotees tended to come from highly educated, economically comfortable backgrounds; they spoke easily with academics and the media and had the resources to create and sustain an impressive array of spiritual communities and businesses. And what they were communicating was a more elaborate version of the same longing for an honest, compassionate, "meaningful" life that was animating the larger counter culture. The "Great Refusal" of what was perceived as a system addicted to making war and profits was finding a counterpart in the emerging faiths of the affluent young.

Two distinct paths ran through this thicket of holy quests and fantasies. One required a disciplined regimen of thought and practice and separation from the world of work, family, and individual competition. Converts to Hare Krishna gave all their money and possessions to the temple, took a Sanskrit name, donned orange or yellow robes, and typically spent hours each day chanting and playing music on urban street corners.[29]

The second path offered a quicker and easier salve for the soul, group therapy garbed in the language of Oriental spirituality. Adherents to groups like EST and Arica were promised a happier and less alienated existence through mastery of a few basic exercises for mind and body. EST asked each "trainee" to devote two weekends, at a cost of $250 per head, to seminars where they were alternately cajoled, shouted at, and embarrassed into what founder Werner Erhard called "an expanded state of consciousness, without judgment—what is actually so with regard to specific areas in his life." Such tactics, shorn of their controversial edges, soon became common elements of a "human potential movement" adapted by corporations seeking to mold a happier and thus more efficient workforce. But their root was spiritual. According to the Sufis, Muhammad had counseled that, "The one who knows his self knows God."[30]

The Zen Center in San Francisco represented a more diligent break with Western norms. Shunryu Suzuki, a Japanese "roshi" or Zen master, arrived in the United States in 1958. The slight, middle-aged teacher soon attracted a nucleus of students in the city where Beat writers like Kenneth Rexroth and Allen Ginsberg had already seeded curiosity about his esoteric creed. By the late '60s, hundreds more had joined. Located in a former synagogue, the center taught the acceptance of one's thoughts and sensations through the arduous repetition of spiritual exercises. The primary of these was *zazen*— collective meditation for long periods each day (up to three hours) in a seated mode known as the "lotus position." The goal of all this sitting was to transcend worldly desires and fears, the insistent needs for love or fame or security that allowed one no permanent rest or satisfaction.

At the end of the '60s, philosopher Jacob Needleman spent several weeks at the Zen Center and at Tassajara, a mountain retreat Suzuki and his students had bought and renovated 150 miles south of San Francisco. He was quite won over. "The principal difference between the monastic society and ours," wrote Needleman, "is surely not that ours is more real, but that in this monastery everyone has a common aim . . . to awaken to his true nature, each to 'find his own way.'" He met the roshi and discovered that he was neither glum nor authoritarian. "One's overwhelming first impression is of openness and warmth. He laughs often, noiselessly—and when I was with him, trying to discuss 'profound questions,' I found myself laughing with him throughout the interview."[31]

Most members of the Zen community came from privileged backgrounds. Overwhelmingly white and college-educated, many had been part of the antiwar movement; most had at least dabbled in psychedelics. About half were raised as Jews. Zen seemed to appease their common yearning for a life pared down to intimate essentials. Instead of pursuing professional careers, members served the center as cooks and gardeners, printers and carpenters. After working for three years as head cook at Tassajara, one Zen devotee in his twenties wrote a book of baking recipes that quickly found a place in thousands of countercultural kitchens. But, by then, the author (who donated all earnings to his community) had become "exhausted of food" and was busy erecting stone walls at the mountain retreat.[32]

A more worldly beneficiary of the eastward gaze was Transcendental Meditation. Maharishi Mahesh Yogi traveled from India to the United States in 1959 to promote TM as a Hindu form of spiritual therapy. "Expansion of happiness is the purpose of life," he wrote, predicting that anyone who followed his method could achieve it. To become "well-intentioned, warm, loving and clear," a student had only to accept a mantra (sacred sound) from a TM "initiator" and then learn to concentrate on it while sitting for 20 minutes each morning and each evening before meals. The maharishi believed his simple teaching could do more than help one individual at a time. "The wars that break out," he claimed, "are the result of the build-up of tension generated by tense, irritable people" rather than economic or political conflicts.[33] TM might liberate the world!

Such blissful pronouncements earned the maharishi the derision of skeptics. But they also helped make him a celebrity, one who gained disciples at a rapid clip after cameras recorded the Beatles, the Rolling Stones, and several actors (Mia Farrow, most notably) arriving for brief periods to sit by his feet and imbibe his wisdom. The Indian was fully aware of his allure as a man from the "mysterious" East. As Jacob Needleman reported, "Here was a 'classic' guru, delivered by Central Casting: the flowing hair, the white robes, the floral cascades, the gnomelike twinkly eyes and the 'Eastern serenity.'"[34]

Early in the 1970s, the maharishi, who had returned to India, engineered a shift away the counterculture and toward a more practical, even rationalistic appeal. He and his disciples began to describe TM as the "science of cre-

Maharishi and the Beatles. Source: *Popperfoto/Archive Photos*

ative intelligence" rather than a religion in any traditional sense. Affluent believers and large speaking fees financed the establishment of Maharishi International University in the small town of Fairfield, Iowa. There, on a bucolic campus, students using medical instruments discovered that meditation slowed down the heart rate and relieved stress; others sought to translate sensations described in sacred Hindu texts into the discourse of human biology.[35]

Despite its commercial trappings, TM was more than an exotic fad, the soft and superficial fringe of the '60s Reformation. The meditation method helped Americans from diverse backgrounds—as many as half a million by the mid-1970s—to focus, in a relaxed manner, on their emotional troubles and, perhaps, to begin to solve them.[36] At the beginning of the century, the philosopher William James dubbed a similar kind of faith "the religion of healthy-mindedness." He wrote, "If a creed makes a man feel happy, he almost inevitably adopts it. Such a belief ought to be true; therefore it is true— such, rightly or wrongly, is . . . the religious logic used by ordinary men."[37]

Two common elements stand out from the bewildering mix of religions that characterized spiritual life in the '60s. First, many Americans were developing and others were coming to accept styles of worship and piety that would have been considered bizarre, even demonic, as recently as the 1950s. Sermons in favor of civil disobedience, jazz music played from the altar, Torah study mixed with LSD, and the belief in quiet sitting certainly had their vociferous critics. But even such fundamentalist detractors as Campus Crusaders for Christ sometimes adopted one or another rite of the youth culture, if only to attract more of the young. Increasing numbers of Americans turned away from the religious communities of their parents and sought personal, therapeutic routes to the divine.

Second, a new kind of division was emerging among faithful Christians and Jews. Denominational lines had less and less salience in a nation split between theological liberals and conservatives.[38] The former tended to be college-educated and to support the new social movements that advocated equality among the races and between men and women; the latter were convinced that such beliefs were wrenching American culture away from its moral roots and risked destruction of the sacred realm. Here lay the immediate roots of the culture wars—over abortion, public art, affirmative action, and other issues—which did much to define American politics during the last quarter of the twentieth century. The fires of that conflict continued to burn.

CHAPTER 14

"No Cease-Fire"

1969–1974

WASHINGTON, JAN. 23—AMERICA IS MOVING OUT OF VIETNAM AFTER THE LONGEST AND MOST DIVISIVE CONFLICT SINCE THE WAR BETWEEN THE STATES. . . . THERE HAS BEEN A SHARP DECLINE IN RESPECT FOR AUTHORITY IN THE UNITED STATES AS A RESULT OF THE WAR—A DECLINE IN RESPECT NOT ONLY FOR THE CIVIL AUTHORITY OF GOVERNMENT, BUT ALSO FOR THE MORAL AUTHORITY OF THE SCHOOLS, THE UNIVERSITIES, THE PRESS, THE CHURCH AND EVEN THE FAMILY. THERE WAS NO CEASE-FIRE ON THIS FRONT.
—James Reston, New York Times, January 24, 1973[1]

By the time Richard Nixon was sworn in as thirty-seventh president of the United States, it seemed to many Americans as though "the Sixties" had been going on forever. As the 1960s drew to an end, the war in Vietnam was costing the lives of hundreds of young Americans every week; American communities were torn with racial conflict; and the political and cultural gap between the generations had widened into what many believed was becoming an unbridgeable chasm. "I foresee the rest of this century as a dangerous time," Cornell University political scientist Andrew Hacker predicted in an essay in *Newsweek* in 1970. "We can no longer be a single nation, possessed of a common spirit. Neither 'class struggle' nor 'civil war' entirely describes the contours of this discord. Suffice it to say that increasingly we will encounter one another as enemies."[2]

Richard Nixon had promised Americans upon his election in 1968 that he would act decisively to "bring us together." This was an unlikely promise from a politician whose rise to national prominence had been based upon his willingness to create and exploit raw political division. But after the recent national traumas of having one president gunned down and another politically destroyed, many voters were eager to believe that the man they had just elevated to the White House was a "new Nixon," who would restore harmony and decorum to the nation's political life.

Born in 1913 in the small farming community of Yorba Linda in southern California, the second of five sons of pious Quaker parents, Richard Nixon grew up a solitary and unsmiling child.[3] His father, Frank Nixon, owned a general store and gas station, where his sons put in long hours. His mother, Hannah Milhous Nixon, was loving but distant; she discouraged any open display of affection by her sons. Money was scarce and family tragedies all too frequent; two of his brothers died of painful illnesses before Nixon reached 20. Early on he concluded that life was a grim and no-holds-barred struggle, in which success came only to those who persevered at any cost.

Unable to afford a more prestigious education, Nixon attended the local Quaker college in Whittier, California, and then, thanks to a scholarship, went on to earn a law degree from Duke University in North Carolina in 1934. After graduation, and military service in the South Pacific, Nixon returned to practice law at a small firm in Whittier.

In 1946 he ran for Congress. His Democratic opponent, incumbent Jerry Voorhis, was a staunch liberal, and also an anticommunist. But Nixon pilloried Voorhis as an advocate of "Communist principles." Two years earlier, such charges might have fallen flat, but in the Cold War atmosphere of 1946 they proved effective. Nixon's victory also reflected the emergence of southern California as a well-heeled bastion of conservative politics, its prosperity fueled by federal defense spending and real estate speculation. Nixon was taken up as a political champion by a group of wealthy patrons in the district, eager to roll back the political legacy of the New Deal.

Having been elected to Congress primarily on the issue of anticommunism, it was natural for Nixon to take a seat on the House Un-American Activities Committee (HUAC). In 1948 he got his biggest break when he helped reveal that Alger Hiss, a former State Department adviser in the Roosevelt administration, had been mixed up in the 1930s with a self-confessed Communist spy named Whittaker Chambers. Hiss was eventually sent to prison for perjury. The case brought Nixon national notoriety, which he parlayed into a successful campaign for a U.S. Senate seat in 1950 (during which he attacked Democratic opponent Helen Gahagan Douglas as a pro-Soviet "pink lady").

Two years later Eisenhower offered him the vice-presidential nomination. Although almost dropped from the ticket when it was revealed that he had accepted questionable if not illegal cash donations from wealthy contributors, Nixon managed to save his political career with a nationally televised speech, known as the "Checkers speech" ever after for its sentimental *non sequitur* reference to the Nixon family's cocker spaniel, also a gift from a political admirer ("Whatever they say," Nixon announced gravely, "we are going to keep her.").[4] During the campaign, Eisenhower stayed above the fray while Nixon hammered away at the Democrats for supposedly coddling Communists in government. Democrats retaliated by sticking the combative Nixon with the nickname "Tricky Dick."

Nixon's ambitions for moving on to the White House were thwarted in 1960. But in 1968 a "new Nixon" returned to the fray, with a carefully crafted image of mature statesmanship. He left his customary rabid partisanship to running mate Spiro Agnew (in the course of the campaign Agnew would call Democratic candidate Hubert Humphrey "squishy soft" on communism).[5] When Nixon took the oath of office, he placed his hand on his family Bible on the page that contained the reassuring lines from Isaiah, "They shall beat their swords into plowshares and their spears into pruning hooks."[6] And in his inaugural address, a celebration of good feeling and tolerance, he called on Americans to "lower our voices" and step away from "angry rhetoric that fans discontents into hatreds."[7]

There was one week in the year that followed that seemed to live up to the promise of the new president's call for national unity. That was the seven days in mid-July that witnessed the *Apollo XI* mission. Three American astronauts flew to the moon on the spacecraft *Columbia*, and two of them, Neil Armstrong and Edwin Aldrin, landed on its surface on July 20 in the module Eagle. People around the world watched live televised images of Armstrong and Aldrin standing before an American flag planted on the moon's surface, redeeming the pledge that John Kennedy had made eight years earlier. Before reboarding their landing module, Armstrong and Aldrin left behind them a plaque bearing the words "We came in peace for all mankind." Nixon flew to the South Pacific to be on hand on the U.S. aircraft carrier *Hornet* when *Apollo XI* splashed down three days later. Understandably elated,

President Richard Nixon, visiting the U.S. troops in South Vietnam, c. 1970. Source: *The Nixon Library*

the president declared the past few days had been "the greatest week in the history of the world since the Creation."[8]

But if for one week in 1969, Americans were able to put aside the conflicts of the past decade, there were 51 others in which the old battles continued to rage. Of all the issues raising voices in the first year of the Nixon presidency, none was as divisive as the war in Vietnam. Nixon acknowledged in his memoirs that, had he chosen to do so, he could have ended the war shortly after coming into office. He did not need to worry about being labeled the president who "lost Vietnam," as Truman had supposedly "lost China." It would have been easy for Nixon to blame the fiasco on his Democratic predecessors and refuse to send more young Americans to die in a lost cause. "If I brought our troops home [in 1969]," Nixon would later write, "I would be a hero regardless of what happened to South Vietnam and its people."[9]

In the spring of 1969, the new president announced a phased withdrawal of American forces from South Vietnam. The administration committed itself to the "Vietnamization" of the war, putting renewed emphasis on training and equipping the Army of the Republic of Vietnam (ARVN) to fight its own battles against the Communists. In July 1969, 814 men of the Third Battalion, Sixtieth Infantry, Ninth Division of the U.S. Army assembled on the tarmac of Tan Son Nhut airport in Saigon and boarded planes to return to the United States. They were the first of some 65,000 Americans withdrawn from Vietnam that year.[10] Nixon announced at a press conference in Washington that he expected *all* U.S. troops to come home from Vietnam before the end of the following year. His national security adviser, Henry Kissinger, pleaded privately with the administration's critics to suspend their opposition, promising that the war would soon be over. "Be patient," he told antiwar congressmen in the spring of 1969: "Give us another sixty or ninety days."[11]

Nixon promised peace, but he craved victory. As he stated on many occasions, he did not intend to be "the first President of the United States to lose a war."[12] Well aware of the unpopularity of the war, he understood that the only way he would be allowed to prolong it in pursuit of something he could label an American victory was if he was able to give the appearance at the same time of winding down the conflict.

Nixon made a deliberate policy of taking few members of his cabinet into his confidence; indeed, he often deceived them regarding his real plans. He relied for advice almost exclusively on his national security adviser Henry Kissinger, a former Harvard academic with a taste for grand international designs. Kissinger was a master of bureaucratic infighting and saw to it that other potential advisers, like Defense Secretary Melvin Laird, and Secretary of State William Rogers, enjoyed only limited access to the president. Kissinger's instincts were, in any event, completely in tune with those of the president he served. In a dangerous world, the leaders of the United States could not afford to be overly burdened with either candor or moral scruples. Like Nixon, he also relished the prospect of forcing others to do his bidding. Kissinger would tell NSC staff early on in the Nixon presidency to draw up plans for a "savage, decisive blow" against the enemy in Southeast Asia: "I refuse to believe that a little fourth-rate power like North Vietnam doesn't have a breaking point."[13]

Two months after coming into the White House, Nixon ordered American B-52s to begin bombing North Vietnamese supply routes that ran through the border regions of neutral Cambodia, as well as to locate and destroy what proved to be an elusive, if not mythical, North Vietnamese command center in Cambodia. Nixon probably would have preferred taking the war directly to the enemy, by immediately resuming bombing of North Vietnam itself, but that would have revealed too clearly to a restive American public his intentions of prolonging the war. The Cambodian operation, in contrast, allowed Nixon the means to step up the war without drawing a negative reaction. Coordinated by Kissinger, the bombing campaign was so secret that its existence was concealed even from top Air Force leaders; official records were falsified to make it seem that the B-52s dispatched to Cambodia were actually hitting targets in South Vietnam.

The bombings were ineffective in slowing the pace of North Vietnamese resupply and reinforcement. Their chief impact was to inflict heavy casualties on the civilian population living along the border regions, which led to increased support for the Khmer Rouge, the Cambodian Communist movement that was attempting to overthrow the neutralist government of Norodom Sihanouk. But the bombing of Cambodia was intended to be only the prelude to further attacks—hence its code name "Breakfast." Nixon planned to use the spring and summer of 1969 to secure sufficient public support for his policies in Vietnam to permit an open reescalatation of the war in the fall. If all had worked out as planned, the secret bombings in Cambodia were to be followed by a vast and open expansion of the air war in an operation code-named Duck Hook, tentatively scheduled to be launched at the beginning of November. American aircraft would then unleash the heaviest bombing of the war against North Vietnam, including among their targets the two principal North Vietnamese cities, heavily populated Hanoi and Haiphong. Nixon also planned to mine North Vietnam's ports and bomb the dikes that channeled water to North Vietnamese farmers. If the Communists still refused to capitulate, the bombing would be followed up by a land invasion of North Vietnam, and by the use of nuclear weapons against the Ho Chi Minh Trail.

Nixon hoped the mere prospect of such escalation would force North Vietnam to concede. He ordered Kissinger, who had already begun meeting secretly with North Vietnamese representatives in Paris in the spring of 1969, to inform them that he was contemplating "measures of the greatest consequences" should there be no progress in negotiations by November 1. He explained to White House aide Bob Haldeman his "madman theory" for winning the war in Vietnam:

> I want the North Vietnamese to believe I've reached the point where I might do *anything* to stop the war. We'll just slip the word to them that, "for God's sake, you know Nixon is obsessed about Communists. We can't restrain him when he's angry—and he has his hand on the nuclear button"—and Ho Chi Minh himself will be in Paris in two days begging for peace.[14]

Nixon and Kissinger, however, underestimated the resolve of their enemy. The Vietnamese Communists did not doubt the ability of the United States to deliver the "savage blows" the American leaders contemplated. But they were prepared to endure such blows for as long as it took to reach their own objective. As North Vietnam's chief military strategist Vo Nguyen Giap told an American journalist after the war, "If we had focused on the balance of forces, we would have been defeated in two hours."[15] Giap, Ho Chi Minh, and other North Vietnamese leaders had outlasted the French; they had outlasted American presidents Kennedy and Johnson; and they were confident that they would outlast Nixon.

For all the talk in 1969 of the war "winding down," Americans were still dying there by the hundreds every week. In a so-called mini-Tet offensive in February 1969, Communist forces killed over 1100 Americans. Nearly 9500 Americans would die in Vietnam in 1969—5000 fewer than the previous year's record casualties, but more than had died in the heavy fighting of 1967.

As Nixon marshaled his forces for implementing his "madman theory" in November, the antiwar movement was also preparing for the fall. The movement had fallen on hard times in the months after the 1968 Chicago Democratic convention. Although the campuses remained restive, there were no antiwar marches of the scale of earlier years in the first nine months of the Nixon presidency. Most Americans were willing to give the new president a chance to carry out his stated intention of ending the war quickly. In addition, the New Left wing of the antiwar movement was beginning to fragment, at least as a nationally organized movement. While Students for a Democratic Society grew to perhaps a hundred thousand loosely affiliated members in the 1968–69 academic year, SDS leaders became increasingly enamored of such Old Left diversions as theory mongering and internal heresy hunts.

Matters came to a head at the SDS national convention held in Chicago in June 1969. The organization splintered into rival factions, each proclaiming itself the true vanguard of the revolution. The best-known of the splinter groups to survive the crackup were the Weathermen, who took their name from a Bob Dylan lyric, "You don't need a weatherman to know which way the wind blows," and believed that New Leftists had to shed their "white skin privilege" by joining Third World revolutionaries in the violent overthrow of the American empire.

Weatherman assembled a few hundred militants in Chicago in early October 1969 with the avowed intention to "bring the war home." They held several days of street demonstrations marked by random vandalism and running battles with the police. Within a few months, Weatherman's most prominent leaders, including Mark Rudd and Bernadine Dohrn, "went underground," and launched a bombing campaign that went on sporadically for several years. (The only casualties in the campaign proved to be three of the Weatherman, who accidentally blew themselves up while constructing bombs in a Greenwich Village townhouse in March 1970.[16])

Since the student movement had always relied as much upon local initiative as central direction, the demise of SDS did not spell an immediate end to the New Left. In cities and college towns across the country, radical communities thrived in the late 1960s, centered around underground newspapers, coffeehouses, food co-ops, and local antiwar and community organizing projects.

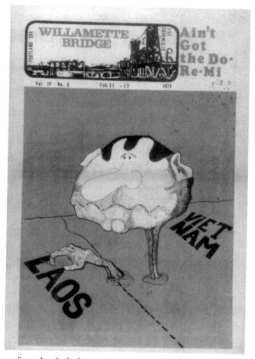

Nixon in the quagmire after the failed invasion of Laos, February 1971. Source: Author's Collection. Cartoon by James Beller

A national poll of college students taken in 1970 found that fully 11 percent of them described their politics as "radical or far left." When students were polled on political attitudes, rather than asked to adopt labels with possibly negative connotations ("far left"), the potential radical constituency on campus grew even larger. A full 75 percent of the students polled believed that "basic changes in the system" were necessary in the United States, while 44 percent agreed that social progress was more likely to come from "radical pressure from the outside" than through established procedures and institutions.[17]

Such political sentiments in the majority of cases proved ephemeral. The New Left made few recruits outside college campuses, and despite repeated efforts to form "adult" left-wing groups that would provide a vehicle for postgraduate activism, most of the would-be revolutionaries of 1968–1970 would sooner or later drift away from the ideological stances and organizational commitments of their student years.[18] But the moderate majority of the antiwar movement was nonetheless drawn into direct action by the example set earlier in the decade by SDS, and by others on the Left, who had collectively broken down inhibitions against mass public displays of dissent over foreign policy. The presence of the radicals also raised the question for those in power of what would happen if the moderate majority of the peace movement swung round to their point of view. "The reaction of noisy radical groups was considered all the time," Admiral Thomas Moorer, chairman of the Joint Chiefs of Staff during the Nixon years, would recall. "And it served to inhibit and restrain the decision makers."[19]

In the fall of 1969, as it became apparent that the dying was going to go on indefinitely in Vietnam, the antiwar movement not only revived but attained its greatest breadth of support and legitimacy. A new antiwar coalition, the Vietnam Moratorium Committee, came into existence, drawing upon the support of student government leaders, liberal Democratic activists, clergy, trade unionists, and veterans, among other mainstream groups. More than a million people nationwide participated in the Moratorium's first activity, a day of protest against the war on October 15. There were demonstrations, vigils, and other antiwar activities in hundreds of communities across the country.

Among those taking part in the protests were the children of White House aides Bob Haldeman and John Ehrlichman, as well as Defense Secretary Laird. Vice President Agnew was the administration's point man in its offensive against the antiwar movement; that fall he had described antiwar protesters as "an effete corps of impudent snobs." But even Agnew's own household wasn't solidly in the administration's camp; his 14-year-old daughter, Kim, wanted to participate in the Moratorium, but her father wouldn't let her.[20]

A subsequent antiwar demonstration in mid-November brought a record-breaking half million protesters to Washington, D.C. The participation in the days of protest by American soldiers serving in South Vietnam was another unprecedented development. In October the *New York Times* reported that a combat platoon from the Americal Division had worn black armbands on patrol in solidarity with the Vietnam Moratorium demonstrators at home. (Four of the protesting soldiers were wounded by booby traps on the patrol, a grim reminder of the unrelenting carnage of the war.) And in November, more than a hundred GIs serving in a field evacuation hospital in Pleiku boycotted Thanksgiving dinner in November to display their opposition to the war.[21]

Nixon was furious at public opposition to his policies. He struck back by questioning the patriotic loyalties of his critics. In a televised address to the nation on November 3, he appealed to the "silent majority" of pro-war Americans: "North Vietnam cannot defeat or humiliate the United States," he declared. "Only Americans can do that."[22] Many Americans agreed with Nixon. If the war was increasingly unpopular, so was the antiwar movement, which could not shake the unfavorable imagery generated by its more radical wing. But popularity, as measured in public opinion polls, is not necessarily a reliable measure of political effectiveness.

The protests in the streets were a continual reminder to Nixon of the political fate suffered by his predecessor in the White House. In the fall of 1969, the antiwar movement spoke more loudly than Nixon's silent majority.[23] Fearing the consequences of stepping up the war as they had planned the previous spring, Nixon quietly shelved plans for Operation Duck Hook. From that point on, although the killing went on for the next three years, Nixon no longer had any grand strategy for bringing the war to a successful conclusion. There was little he could now accomplish in Vietnam, except stave off Communist victory for a few more years.

When Nixon forgot in the spring of 1970 just how limited a mandate he had been granted for conducting the war, he was given a swift, sharp reminder by antiwar Americans. In April the president announced plans for the withdrawal of an additional 150,000 American troops from Vietnam in the coming year. At the same time, he decided to send American forces into Cambodia in a hastily concocted mission supposedly designed to root out the North Vietnamese supply depots and command centers that had survived a year of secret bombing unscathed. Nixon also intended the invasion to demonstrate support to the new military ruler of Cambodia Lon Nol, who had overthrown the neutralist Prince Sihanouk in March. Many of Nixon's advisers were skeptical about the likelihood of military success and worried about the political consequences of the invasion, but the one man who really guided the president's thinking on foreign policy matters, Henry Kissinger, encouraged him to go through with it. Nixon steeled his resolve before giving his final orders for the invasion by heavy drinking, and by sitting through repeated private screenings of *Patton,* his favorite World War Two epic.[24]

On the evening of April 30 President Nixon went on television to announce his decision to send U.S. ground forces into Cambodia. The stakes he said, could not be higher: "If, when the chips are down, the world's most powerful nation, the United States of America, acts like a pitiful, helpless giant, the forces of totalitarianism and anarchy will threaten free nations and free institutions throughout the world."[25]

But this latest crisis supposedly testing American resolve existed only because Richard Nixon had manufactured it. The war was supposed to be winding down, not moving on to new territory. The argument that the war had to be prolonged and even expanded in order to protect American credibility no longer persuaded many Americans. The response to the invasion of Cambodia was immediate and dramatic, and included a national student strike that swept up hundreds of thousands of students on over 700 campuses, ranging from such hotbeds of New Left sentiment as Berkeley and Madison to community colleges, religiously affiliated schools, and southern state universities previously untouched by antiwar activism. A hundred thousand protesters poured into Washington for a march on the White House.

On a number of campuses protests turned violent; four students were shot dead by Ohio National Guardsmen on the campus of Kent State University on May 4, and two more died at Jackson State College in May when Mississippi state police let loose a hail of gunfire into a crowd of black students. Several dozen ROTC buildings were burned down on campuses across the nation. On the overwhelming majority of campuses, however, the protests were peaceful.

And it wasn't just students who were protesting. GIs demonstrated at many bases in the United States; former Peace Corps volunteers occupied offices in the Peace Corps headquarters in Washington, D.C.; United Auto Worker president Walter Reuther, the foremost labor liberal, criticized the invasion; and the Senate passed a bill prohibiting the deployment of U.S. ground forces in Cambodia after July 1.[26] Henry Kissinger recalled the atmosphere in the circles in which he traveled in Washington in those May days as that of "a besieged city," with "the very fabric of government . . . falling apart." Kissinger worried about Nixon's stability; the president, he would later write, "reached a point of exhaustion that caused his advisers deep concern."[27]

Nixon did find support from one quarter. On May 8 a group of about 200 hard-hatted construction workers attacked antiwar protesters in New York City, assaulting them with fists, boots, and hammers, chanting "Love it or Leave it." A few weeks later tens of thousands of building trades workers marched through the city's streets in support of the war. A delegation of building trades leaders was invited to the White House to receive thanks from the president, presenting him with a hard hat labeled "Commander in Chief."[28]

Although Nixon found such gestures of support from his "silent majority" gratifying, he was quick to back down from the Cambodian invasion, withdrawing all U.S. ground forces from the country by the end of June. In a self-fulfilling prophecy Nixon had indeed revealed himself as a "pitiful, helpless giant," and despite claims that the U.S. invasion was the "most successful" military operation of the war, few Americans felt cheered by the adventure.[29] If North Vietnamese leaders had any doubts in April 1970 on the question of just how far the American people would allow Nixon to reescalate the war, thanks to Nixon's hasty pullback from Cambodia, they now had their answer.

Still the war dragged on. Although the ultimate fate of South Vietnam stirred few Americans, many cared passionately about the inhumane conditions endured by American prisoners of war in North Vietnamese captivity. Nixon accordingly recast his public justifications for the war so that it sometimes seemed the only the reason the United States was fighting in Vietnam was to gain the release of the POWs—a circular argument, since the longer the country fought, the more American POWs there were who needed release from captivity.

With the continued withdrawal of American forces, American casualties declined; just over 6000 died in 1970 and under 3000 in 1971. Military morale, however, declined even more precipitously. Drug abuse, including heroin addiction, was rampant. Thousands of soldiers had deserted or gone AWOL for extended periods of time. The number of instances of enlisted men attempting to kill their own officers—so-called fragging incidents, because they frequently involved the use of fragmentation grenades—climbed into the hundreds in 1970–1971. There were also many incidents of individuals and, on occasion, entire units refusing orders to go into combat.[30]

On the homefront, there was another flurry of antiwar protests in the spring of 1971. There were scattered protests around the country in February, when South Vietnamese troops ferried by American helicopters made an ill-fated foray into neighboring Laos. April and May saw much larger demonstrations, including an encampment on the Capitol Mall in Washington by over a thousand members of Vietnam Veterans Against the War (VVAW). Many of the antiwar veterans who gathered for that protest were in wheelchairs, or missing limbs, or wearing Purple Hearts on their combat fatigues. Hundreds tossed the medals they had received in Vietnam onto the Capitol steps. John Kerry, former lieutenant (j.g.), U.S. Navy, and decorated veteran of the war, spoke on behalf of VVAW in testimony before the Senate Foreign Relations Committee. Noting President Nixon's avowal that he wouldn't be the first president to "lose a war," Kerry demanded to know: "How do you ask a man to be the last man to die in Vietnam? How do you ask a man to be the last man to die for a mistake?"[31]

As important as Vietnam was as an issue dividing Americans in the late

1960s, it was racial conflict that made Richard Nixon president. Nixon came to see in the nation's endemic racial problems not only an opportunity to secure his own reelection in 1972, but to create an enduring Republican majority in the United States.

On coming into the White House in 1969, he enjoyed a record as a racial moderate. As vice president in the 1950s, Nixon had publicly endorsed the Supreme Court's decision in *Brown v. Board of Education* (something President Eisenhower never did), and supported proposals before Congress for civil rights legislation. He also met with Martin Luther King, Jr. in 1957 and assured the civil rights leader of the administration's goodwill. In 1964 Nixon maintained a studied silence about President Johnson's Civil Rights Act, since Republican presidential nominee Barry Goldwater was among the bill's opponents, but after the election Nixon endorsed the act, as he did the Voting Rights Act of 1965.

In the company of close associates, Nixon vented less tolerant views; according to White House aide John Ehrlichman, Nixon "thought, basically, blacks were genetically inferior. . . . He thought they couldn't achieve on a level with whites."[32] But unlike other practitioners of the politics of divisiveness such as George Wallace, Nixon did not allow his prejudices to define his racial politics. When Nixon embraced a "southern strategy" that involved turning his back on the civil rights movement, his actions were dictated more by a cool calculation of political advantage, than by any personal racial animosities.

Once in the White House, Nixon's handling of racial issues continued to be dictated by political considerations.[33] He hoped to head off or blunt a possible Wallace electoral challenge in 1972, while extending Republican inroads into formerly Democratic constituencies in the South and in white working-class neighborhoods in the North. A young Republican strategist named Kevin Phillips published a book in 1969 entitled *The Emerging Republican Majority*, in which he argued that the days of the New Deal coalition were numbered by the growing population and conservatives of the Sunbelt states of the South and Southwest, and by the disenchantment of ethnic working-class whites with Democrats' racial policies. Nixon read the book over Christmas 1969 and took its prescriptions to heart.[34]

Nixon's new urban affairs adviser, Daniel Patrick Moynihan, suggested to him in a memo a few weeks later that the problems of blacks had been "too much talked about" in recent years. It may be, Moynihan suggested, that "the issue of race could benefit from a period of 'benign neglect.'" ("I agree!" Nixon scribbled in the margin of his copy of the memo.)[35]

Economic issues had provided the underpinning of the New Deal coalition. Republicans could attract a majority of voters only if they changed the nature of the political debate. As presidential speechwriter Patrick Buchanan argued, Republicans had to "focus on those issues that divide the Democrats, not those that unite Republicans." The Nixon administration's social policies should be attuned to the issues that divided Americans into quarreling interest groups. "When RN [Nixon] comes out for aid to parochial schools," Buchanan wrote in a memo circulated within the administration, "this will drive a wedge right down the Middle of the Democratic Party. The same is true of abortion [meaning Nixon should oppose abortion]; the same is true of hardline anti-pornography laws."[36]

And the same was true of race. Already, in 1969, the strategy the Nixon administration would follow on racial issues was clear. With Nixon's approval, Attorney General John Mitchell sought to delay the enforcement of court-ordered desegregation of Mississippi's school districts. "Do only what the law requires [on integration]," Nixon ordered officials in the Justice Department and HEW, "not one thing more."[37] Government officials who sought to enforce desegregation too zealously, or who protested the new administration's delaying tactics, were purged. Nixon sought legislation in Congress to impose a moratorium on court-ordered busing. The administration also sought, unsuccessfully, to persuade Congress not to renew the Voting Rights Act of 1965, due to expire in 1970.

Nixon found the Supreme Court a convenient foil for his southern strategy. To fill vacancies on the Court, he nominated conservative judges from the South, who he knew would not win Senate approval. When nominee G. Harrold Carswell of Florida was rejected by the Senate, Nixon welcomed the vote as an opportunity to fan regional resentments. He declared himself in sympathy with "the bitter feeling of millions of Americans who live in the South about the act of regional discrimination that took place in the Senate yesterday."[38]

The Nixon administration introduced one new policy seemingly at odds with the entire thrust of the southern strategy, and that was federally mandated guidelines for "affirmative action" hiring of minorities in private employment. In 1969 Nixon's secretary of labor, George Schultz, announced the introduction of the Philadelphia Plan (so-called for the city where it was first to be put in practice). This plan required contractors on government-funded building sites to hire minority workers in skilled trades to fit government-determined quotas (euphemistically referred to as "numerical goals and timetables"); in 1970 the program was expanded to cover all federally funded hiring and contracting.

The term "affirmative action" had first been used in the Kennedy administration, and was enshrined in a section of the Civil Rights Act of 1964. However, throughout the presidencies of the two liberal Democrats in the 1960s, the term was understood to require color-blind principles in hiring. If a job applicant could prove that racial discrimination had denied him or her a given position, there was to be legal redress available. The Nixon's administration's approach, which involved setting aside a certain number of positions that could be filled only by black or other minority candidates, turned the original definition of affirmative action on its head.

Nixon liked affirmative action for several reasons. Compared to job-training programs, or public works, it was a low-cost strategy for the government to boost black employment. It also fit in with his belief that "black capitalism" would prove the solution to America's racial problems; government regulations also required the "set-aside" of a percentage of government contracts for minority businesses. The new black middle class who were the beneficiaries of federal largesse, might well decide that economic self interest dictated a vote for Republican candidates in the future.

Finally, Nixon was delighted at the prospect of presenting the Democrats with an apparently insoluble political dilemma. If they supported affirmative action, they would offend their labor allies (building trades unions in particular vehemently opposed the plan, since it challenged their control of the hiring process on building sites). And if they opposed it, they would offend their black constituency—although it is worth noting that the NAACP, mistrusting Nixon's motives, opposed the Philadelphia Plan. In the end, Democrats would come down strongly in support of affirmative action—and it would soon be forgotten by those who resented the policy that it was Richard Nixon who first put it into practice. By 1972 Nixon was condemning the Democrats for frightening Americans with "the spectre of a quota democracy"—as if he had never heard of a Philadelphia Plan.[39]

Nixon's southern strategy was intended to score points with white voters. What he did not intend (and could not have achieved had he wanted to) was to turn the clock back on civil rights to the 1950s. The gains of the 1960s as enshrined in the Civil Rights Act and the Voting Rights Act were secure. Jim Crow—the legally enforced separation of the races—was dead. Throughout the South, public schools, public transportation, and public accommodations were opening up to black and white alike. Blacks were registering and voting in record numbers in the region, and electing scores of political officials, from the county to the federal level. Even George Wallace began to sound new themes in response to the new political arithmetic. In 1971, in a speech to the National Press Club, the man who had eight years earlier vowed to support "Segregation forever!" now declared himself in favor of "public accommodations open to all."[40]

Blacks also made significant political gains in the North during these years. A new generation of black urban politicians challenged the power of the old white ethnic political machines; in 1967, for the first time, black men were elected as mayors of major northern cities: Carl Stokes in Cleveland, and Richard Hatcher in Gary, Indiana. Black voters in cities like Detroit, Newark, and Philadelphia would soon follow suit. But these proved ambiguous victories, hastening the flight of white voters to the suburbs, and leaving the new black mayors to attempt to cope with the problems of ever greater and more concentrated poverty in the inner cities, with ever dwindling resources. The combination of the end of Jim Crow in the South, and deteriorating economic and social conditions in northern cities brought the "great migration" of blacks northward in the twentieth century to an end. Between 1970 and 1975, for the first time in the history of the nation, more black Americans moved to the South from the North than the reverse.[41]

While a new black leadership took seats in city councils and in the halls of Congress, the "old" black leadership of the civil rights era faded into obscurity or irrelevance. King was dead, and the SCLC, under the uninspired direction of King's successor, Ralph Abernathy, survived only on the fading glory of the memories of Birmingham and Selma. SNCC collapsed in the early 1970s, with the flamboyant leaders of its later years either in jail, like H. Rap Brown, or living in self-imposed exile in Africa, like Stokely Carmichael (who had taken the name of Kwame Toure).

The Black Panther Party continued to make headlines through Richard Nixon's first term in office; J. Edgar Hoover pronounced the organization a major threat to national security, and the group's shoot-outs with police became the stuff of radical legend. But Huey Newton's increasingly erratic leadership disenchanted many of the Panthers' former admirers, both black and white. Released from prison on appeal in 1970, Newton soon wandered into cocaine addiction and megalomania; the most interesting part of each new issue of the Black Panther Party newspaper was learning what title Newton had decided to award himself that week (ranging from "Supreme Commander of the People" to "Supreme Servant of the People"). Though they continued to be regarded as folk heroes by many on the white New Left, and as dangerous adversaries by the FBI and local police agencies, by 1972 the Panthers were reduced to a hard core of fewer than 200 members in Oakland, California. There they dug in and survived for a time, operating more as a protection racket for black businesses than as a revolutionary movement.[42]

The greatest setback the civil rights movement suffered in these years was not so much a question of organization as it was one of moral legitimacy. The movement had lost its claim to speak for a larger vision of an inclusive and democratic America. Increasingly it was seen, at least by whites, as simply another "special interest" group, looking out for the selfish interests of its own members. The last years of the civil rights movement, John Lewis would later write, were a time of "groping lostness."[43]

As some of the old social movements waned, new ones came to the fore. Male homosexuals, long the victims of derision, physical attack, and police harassment, took to the streets of Greenwich Village in June 1969 in response to a police raid on a gay bar known as the Stonewall Inn on Christopher Street. For four nights they battled police in what became known as the

Stonewall Rebellion. This was an event notable for two reasons: first, because it was the only riot of the 1960s that included a Rockettes-style chorus line (with rioters mocking the police by kicking their heels in the air, and singing, "We are the Stonewall girls/We wear our hair in curls/We wear no under-wear/We show our pubic hair.").[44] And second, and more importantly, the Stonewall events sparked the organization of a new activist-oriented homo-sexual rights movement. Lesbians, too, were beginning to organize. Many of them had first been drawn into radical activism through the women's liber-ation movement; by 1969–1970 they were organizing openly as gay women, sometimes joining forces with gay men in local "Gay Liberation Fronts." Just as the Black Power movement had proclaimed "Black is beautiful," the new movement proclaimed "Gay is beautiful" and called for "Gay pride" as well as gay rights. In some cities, especially gay meccas like San Francisco, the new movement developed impressive electoral clout.[45]

Another insurgency making headway in the years of the Nixon presidency was the environmental movement. In September 1969, Wiscon-sin Senator Gaylord Nelson, proposed that a national "teach-in" be held the

At a gay rights demionstration, 1970. Source: *Author's collection*

following spring on environmental issues. Planning for the event soon took on a momentum of its own, as politicians and youthful volunteers around the country began planning their own activities for what came to be called Earth Day, scheduled for April 22, 1970. Earth Day was modeled on the decentralized organizational strategy pioneered by the antiwar movement, in the campus teach-ins of 1965, and the Moratorium activities of 1969. But in contrast to the antiwar protests, Earth Day was intended by its national organizers to be a strictly nonpartisan, nonconfrontational event, one that stressed the common interests of all Americans in a healthy environment. For its part, the Nixon administration was eager to back Earth Day, in part because of the popularity of the environmental issue, in part because it hoped that relatively innocuous sentiments associated with the movement would drain youthful support from more radical causes. As Nixon proclaimed in his State of the Union address in January, Americans must "make our peace with nature" by means of "reparations for the damage we have done to our air, to our land and to our water."[46] Corporations, including some major polluters, also jumped on the bandwagon, providing financial backing, advertising, and speakers for the teach-in.

Earth Day proved an enormous success. Twenty million Americans participated in one or more local observances, which often took such forms as parades, street fairs, and tree plantings. But the environmental issue was not as easily tamed as some of Earth Day's sponsors hoped. Administration and corporate spokesmen were booed off the stage in some cities; and there were also sit-ins, picket lines, and other disturbances sponsored by more radically inclined groups. The influence of 1960s protest movements lived on through the 1970s, in the anticorporate rhetoric and civil disobedience tactics embraced by youthful environmentalists, particularly those involved in attempts to shut down the nation's nuclear power industry.[47]

Perhaps the most enduring legacy of the Nixon presidency was the relegation of liberals to the margins of American politics. But their fate was not apparent at the start of Nixon's presidency. The Republican recapture of the White House seemed to liberals an aberration, a product of the exceptional circumstances of 1968, rather than the harbinger of a long-term rightward shift in American politics. In that year's congressional races, Nixon's coattails proved very short, gaining the Republicans only four seats in the House of Representatives and five in the Senate, making the new president the first since the 19th century to enter the White House without his party controlling either house of Congress. In the 1970 midterm elections, the Democrats would lose two more seats in the Senate (while still retaining control of that body), but gaining nine in the House of Representatives, as well as picking up eleven governorships around the nation. If there was an "emerging Republican majority" in American politics, it was emerging at a sedentary pace.

No prominent Democratic opponents of the war in Vietnam lost their House or Senate seats in 1968. Freed of the albatross of "Johnson's war," Democrats emerged from the election more united on foreign policy issues than they had been since 1965. In a symbolic show of strength in April 1970, the Senate Foreign Relations Committee voted unanimously to repeal the Gulf of Tonkin resolution that President Johnson had cited as the "functional equivalent" to a declaration of war in Vietnam.

Reunited on foreign policy issues, liberals also continued to set the agenda for the nation's domestic policy during Nixon's first term in office—with what, ironically, proved in some ways a stronger ally in the White House than they had known during the last embattled years of the Johnson presidency. Nixon may have despised liberals as political opponents, but he was by no means a doctrinaire conservative. He didn't care much about domestic policy issues, and did not have strong principled objections to the many liberal domestic programs that had been initiated over the past decade. Just as John Kennedy had been content to allow domestic policy to drift along in essentially the same directions it had taken in the preceding Republican administration, so Nixon allowed those policies to drift further along the liberal lines of the past half-decade. Moreover, Nixon was impressed by the argument made by his urban policy adviser, Democrat Daniel Patrick Moynihan.

Moynihan urged Nixon to conceive of his role as that of an enlightened conservative reformer, on the order of the nineteenth century British Tory leader and prime minister Benjamin Disraeli. After reading a biography of Disraeli, at Moynihan's suggestion, Nixon would opine: "Tory men and liberal policies are what have changed the world." Herbert Stein, who joined the Nixon administration as an economic adviser in 1969 and became chairman of the Council of Economic Advisers in 1971, would later note, somewhat ruefully, that "more new regulation was imposed on the economy during the Nixon administration than in any other presidency since the New Deal."[48]

In Nixon's first term in office, he signed into law acts creating such new federal regulatory agencies as the Occupational Safety and Health Administration (OSHA) and the Environmental Protection Agency (EPA). (Nixon's newly developed interest in environmental issues may have had something to do with the fact that his most likely Democratic challenger in 1972 was seen as being Edmund Muskie, who had spent the past half-decade forging a strong environmental record in the Senate.[49]) Nixon also went along with congressional initiatives to increase spending on social welfare programs, from AFDC to food stamps to Social Security.

No one one could plausibly suggest that the era of big government came to an end during the Nixon first term in office. "Vigorously did we inveigh against the Great Society," Nixon's archconservative speechwriter Pat Buchanan would complain in disgust in 1975, "enthusiastically did we fund it."[50]

With Nixon paying liberals the flattery of stealing their programs, their return to control of the White House seemed a strong possibility as a new election cycle began. In 1972 as in 1960, "liberal" remained an honorific in Democratic Party circles. There was a big change, however, in the process through which the Democratic Party would choose its presidential candidate in 1970. In a sop to the party's liberals in 1968, the same Democratic convention that nominated Hubert Humphrey also established a commission under the direction of Senator George McGovern to reform the way the party selected its delegates for future conventions. The McGovern Commission sought to wrest control of delegate selection out of the hands of the old party bosses by requiring state party organizations to hold primaries or other open forms of delegate selection, such as well-advertised caucuses. The commission's recommendations were adopted by the Democratic National Committee (DNC) in 1971, and as a result 60 percent of convention delegates the following year were chosen by primary voters, as opposed to only 40 percent so chosen in 1968. The new rules also established quotas for the number of blacks, women, and young people chosen as delegates, requiring their numbers to be "in reasonable relationship to [the group's] presence in the population of the State."[51]

In August 1968 McGovern had been put forward as a last-minute presidential candidate by some of Bobby Kennedy's political supporters, including Arthur Schlesinger, Jr. In the next three years, he emerged as the favorite of Democratic liberals, if not of the party establishment, who would have preferred either to run Humphrey again, or his 1968 vice-presidential candidate, Senator Edmund Muskie of Maine.

More conservative Democrats favored the unreconstructed cold warrior Henry "Scoop" Jackson of Washington, or George Wallace (whose own campaign for the Democratic nomination came to an abrupt end in a Maryland parking lot when he was shot and left paralyzed by a young man named Arthur Bremer—yet another in the string of deranged lone gunmen who had become a familiar feature of American political life over the past decade).

The new party rules, plus a widespread resentment among rank-and-file Democratic activists against the old party regulars, worked to McGovern's advantage. The number of women and minority delegates tripled from 1968 to 1972, the number of delegates under the age of 30 increased tenfold. The delegates to the 1972 convention were also inordinately well-educated; although there was no formal quota on graduate degrees, nearly 40 percent of the delegates held one. The Reform Democrats had finally come into their own. Going in to the climactic primary campaign in California in June, McGovern led Humphrey by 560 delegates to 311; with his victory there, McGovern secured an additional 271 delegates, and a lock on the party nomination when the Democrats met in their national convention in July in Miami Beach.

After fielding a tightly organized and smoothly run primary campaign, McGovern stumbled badly in the general election. Among the most famous gaffes of the campaign was McGovern's decision to first offer the vice-presidential nomination to Senator Thomas Eagleton of Missouri, and then, after it was revealed that Eagleton had been hospitalized for mental problems (and after McGovern pledged to stand "one thousand percent" behind his nominee) to dump Eagleton for Sargent Shriver. The Eagleton affair struck hard at McGovern's public image as a man of high principle, making him look instead like just another poll-driven, wavering politician. As a liberal standard-bearer, McGovern also lacked the stage presence of a John or Bobby Kennedy. The son of a Methodist minister, McGovern came across to many listeners as a kind of mild and ineffective pastor, disappointed in the worldly ways of his flock. *Rolling Stone*'s political correspondent Hunter S. Thompson, who

Gloria Steinem (hands on knees), speaking with a consciousness-raising group, c. 1970. Source: *Sophia Smith Collection*

admired McGovern, nonetheless brooded over his lack of charisma: "Crowds seem to turn him *off*, instead of on." To be a viable candidate, Thompson thought, "McGovern would need at least one dark kinky streak of Mick Jagger in his soul."[52]

There were constituencies energized by the McGovern campaign, primarily drawn from the ranks of younger cause-oriented liberals—antiwar activists, feminists, environmentalists, and the like, who had come to be known collectively as advocates of the "new politics." The 1972 campaign was the first time since the constitutional passage of women's suffrage that an organized feminist movement played an important role in a national presidential campaign. The newly founded *Ms.* magazine endorsed McGovern's primary candidacy, calling him "the only candidate who consistently makes women's concerns a part of his campaign."[53] Feminists were so well represented at the Miami convention that they came close to nominating one of their own, Frances "Sissy" Farenthold, a former Texas legislator, as McGovern's running mate. The 1972 election was also notable as the first in which 18-year-old American citizens were given the vote (as a result of the Thirty-sixth Amendment to the Constitution, adopted the previous year). McGovern strategists banked heavily on the youth vote, and the political campaign was staffed in good measure by men and women in their early twenties (among them a politically ambitious 26-year-old named Bill Clinton, who codirected McGovern's Texas state campaign).

But McGovern did considerably less well among traditional Democratic constituencies. With the exception of some of the more liberally oriented trade unions, like the UAW, organized labor stood aloof from his campaign. The bosses of important big city machines were similarly unenthusiastic. Many traditional working-class Democratic voters were put off by televised scenes from Miami of McGovern's youthful, shaggy-haired backers, and by gestures of political retribution like the unseating of Mayor Richard Daley in a credentials challenge. ("Anybody who would reform Chicago's Democratic Party by dropping the white ethnic," wrote Chicago newspaper columnist Mike Royko, "would probably begin a diet by shooting himself in the stomach."[54]) A number of Democratic southern governors, including Jimmy Carter of Georgia, refused to endorse the national ticket. And so did the "neoconservatives"—a small but influential group of formerly liberal intellectuals, writers, and editors who had grown disenchanted with Great Society social programs, black militancy, and the New Left, and would soon depart the Democrats for the more congenial company of the Republican party.[55]

The prospective "new politics" majority proved an illusion—to a great extent, the victim of political mistakes committed by the McGovern camp in 1972. But McGovern was also doomed by contingencies that were beyond his control—or, for that matter, any other potential Democratic nominee that year. It seems unlikely, in fact, that Muskie, Humphrey, or any other of the leading contenders for the Democratic nomination in 1972 could have prevailed over Richard Nixon, although someone else might have held down the magnitude of Democratic defeat—or perhaps not, since the nomination of any candidate other than McGovern would likely have precipitated a third party effort by disgruntled Democratic liberals. Richard Nixon enjoyed a virtually unassailable political position in 1972.

Nixon had both peace and prosperity going for him in 1972—a quite remarkable political phenomenon, considering the fact that the country was at war and its overall economic situation increasingly precarious. But Nixon, who had stumbled so badly over so many issues in 1969–1971, hit his stride in 1971–1972, and masterfully wielded the advantages of incumbency.

Nixon was able to bring his first-term record in international relations to a triumphant conclusion in the spring of 1972 by boldly seeking the normalization of relations with the People's Republic of China. For nearly a quarter century, the United States had tried to isolate the Communist regime in China, pretending that the legitimate seat of Chinese government was lodged in exile on Taiwan, where the anticommunist generalissimo Chiang Kai-shek had been forced to flee in 1949. As tensions with the Soviet Union eased after the Cuban missile crisis, China emerged in the minds of many Americans as the most dangerous adversary that the United States had to confront abroad. As late as 1965, Nixon was calling the war in Vietnam in reality a war against Red China.[56]

Once in office, however, Nixon reversed course, sending diplomatic signals through intermediaries that United States was ready to fashion a new relationship with Communist China. This dramatic shift in Nixon's thinking was part of a broader vision that he and Kissinger shared, of a new world firmly based upon the principles of geopolitics rather than ideology. The world's superpowers would cooperate in a system of international trade and peacekeeping, respecting one another's regional interests, and accepting the differences in their official political philosophies. Nixon hoped that in exchange for diplomatic recognition and trade with the United States, the Chinese would see it in their own interest to force the North Vietnamese to settle the conflict in Indochina. He also hoped that a U.S.–Chinese rapprochement would serve to make the Soviet Union more amenable to cooperating with the United States, since the last thing Moscow wanted was to have to face the combined might of Beijing and Washington.

The Chinese were interested, although they made it clear that their price for better relations would be the withdrawal of U.S. military forces from Taiwan, and the handing over of the United Nations seat currently held by the Taiwanese to the government in Beijing. It took three years of subtle diplomatic interplay (including, famously, an invitation to American ping-pong players to visit China) to reach the threshold of open contact. Nixon and

Kissinger both delighted in this kind of intrigue. Nixon's public announcement of the proposed opening to China created a sensation, and his 10-day visit to the nation in February 1972 was a political and public relations triumph. Americans were fascinated by their first extensive televised view into the mysterious land of Red China.

Mao and Nixon got along in Beijing like two old political cronies. In their bantering exchanges there was a sense of pragmatism—heavily laced with cynicism—that rendered irrelevant the tired ideological formulas of the Cold War. Upon their first introduction, Mao claimed he had "voted" for Nixon in 1968, to which Nixon responded that he had obviously "voted for the lesser of two evils." "I like rightists," the old revolutionary responded. Nixon understood perfectly. "I think the most important thing to note is that in America, at least at this time, those on the right can do what those on the left can only talk about." Mao agreed.[57]

As Nixon hoped, the Chinese–American rapprochement thoroughly alarmed the Russians and made them even more eager to have him visit Moscow for a long-scheduled summit. Nixon flew to Moscow in May, and signed agreements with the Soviets banning deployment of antiballistic missile systems, as well as an interim agreement limiting the development of offensive nuclear weapon systems. Both sides found ways to increase their nuclear arsenals in the years that followed, but the Strategic Arms Limitation Treaty (SALT) set an important precedent as the first treaty placing any limitation on the spread of nuclear weapons. Nixon also was able to announce a deal with the Soviets to purchase large supplies of American wheat—welcome news to the United States farm belt, and to Republican political strategists.

Meanwhile, a few thousand miles to the east, American bombers were attacking cities in North Vietnam for the first time since 1968 in response to a North Vietnamese offensive that, for awhile that spring, seemed on the verge of toppling the Saigon regime. The North Vietnamese were beaten back by heavy United States air attacks, and the war dragged on through the summer of 1972. But in early October, the long-stalled peace negotiations in Paris were finally making progress, as American negotiators were instructed by Kissinger to make a key concession. For four years, the United States had insisted that there could no settlement of the war that left North Vietnamese troops still operating in South Vietnam. A month before the U.S. presidential election, over the objections of South Vietnamese president Thieu, the United States dropped that condition. The warring Vietnamese sides would now simply declare a cease-fire, leaving their troops in control of whatever territory they controlled at the war's end. The Americans would complete their own withdrawal of forces from Vietnam. In exchange, the North Vietnamese made a concession of their own, accepting Thieu as interim leader of the South Vietnamese government until elections could be arranged in which the Communists would be free to participate. Nixon also pledged to provide vast military supplies to South Vietnam (which would soon have the world's fourth largest air force as a result), and secretly assured Thieu that in the event of a new Communist offensive the U.S. would renew bombing of North Vietnam. In reality, none of the parties involved expected that the proposed peace agreement could possibly work in practice, although it served the interests of both Richard Nixon and the North Vietnamese leaders to pretend for awhile that it would. The war would not so much come to an end as be put on hold.

There was still one more spasm of violent destruction in store for Vietnam before even this sham peace could be achieved. Immediately following the election, Nixon ordered Kissinger to present stiffer terms to the North Vietnamese than those already agreed upon. Then, arguing that it was North Vietnamese recalcitrance that was preventing a final peace settlement, he launched a new offensive against North Vietnam. For 12 days U.S. B-52s engaged in massive around-the clock bombing attacks on Hanoi and Haiphong. Fifteen bombers and 93 U.S. airmen were lost before the offensive was finally called off. The "Christmas bombing," coming so close upon the promise of a peace agreement, sparked outrage around the world and in the United States. Even some Republican senators wondered aloud if Nixon had taken leave of his senses.[58]

Although Nixon claimed that the bombing had been necessary to bring the North Vietnamese back to the bargaining table, the peace treaty as finally signed in mid-January differed in no essential degree from the one previously agreed upon. As one of Kissinger's aides remarked to a friend, "We bombed the North Vietnamese into accepting our concession."[59] Nixon made the most of the settlement, declaring on the day the peace accords were signed: "We have finally achieved peace with honor." There were no victory parades in American cities, but 591 POWs returned home from Vietnam shortly afterward to a tumultuous welcome. About 2500 Americans remained listed as missing in action. Total U.S. dead in the war came to over 58,000. Of those, 20,492 had died during the four years since Richard Nixon became their commander-in-chief.

When Nixon entered the White House, he inherited a troubled national economy.[60] The Vietnam War, initially a boon to the economy as the government pumped money into defense industries and unemployment dropped to record low levels, was beginning to have other, less desirable economic effects. Johnson's tax increase succeeded, at least temporarily, in eliminating the budget deficit. It did not, however, have much impact on inflation. American consumers, schooled by now to expect the prosperity of the postwar years to last forever, hardly noticed the loss of disposable income. They kept spending on new cars and new houses at presurcharge levels. Inflation, averaging under 2 percent from 1961 to 1965, and still running at less than 3 percent in 1967, was up to 4.5 percent by 1971, with no end in sight. The war in Vietnam would come to an end long before its economic consequences stopped being felt.

Another kind of economic bill was coming due in the late 1960s, and this, ironically, was a product of successful American foreign policy. In the years following the Second World War, international trade was a key component of U.S. strategy to contain the Soviet Union. A prosperous Europe and Asia would be a bulwark against the spread of communism, and the U.S., through generous lending policies and by providing easy access to U.S. domestic markets, helped rebuild the shattered industries and economies not only of its World War II allies, but also of its former enemies, Germany and Japan. When goods from those countries began appearing in American marketplaces in the 1950s, they were treated as curiosities—like the German Volkswagen and Japanese transistor radios, sprightly additions to the American-made cornucopia of consumer durables. What no one expected was how quickly or completely some foreign-manufactured goods would come to supplant those produced by their American competitors. The United States slipped into a deficit in trade with Japan for the first time in 1965; by 1971 its trade deficit with Japan had climbed to $3 billion.[61] The boom in defense industry employment in the later 1960s obscured another consequence of the growing share of the U.S. domestic market taken over by foreign manufacturers, and that was deindustrialization. Between 1966 and 1971, the United States economy lost nearly a million manufacturing jobs in such core industries as steel, auto, electrical manufacturing, and garment manufacturing.[62]

Unemployment, at a postwar low of under 4 percent when Nixon took office, gradually crept upward over the next two years to over 6 percent as the nation slipped into recession. The stock market was jittery, and unions increasingly militant; there were major strikes against General Electric and General Motors during Nixon's first two years in office, as well as a wildcat strike by postal workers that only ended only when Nixon sent in the army to move the mail. Gleeful Democrats began talking about "Nixonomics" and compared the president to Herbert Hoover.

Nixon had hoped that social issues would trump economic issues in the 1970s, allowing him to woo disaffected Democrats into his own new majority coalition. That didn't happen in the midterm elections of 1970, as blue-collar Democrats cast their ballots for Democratic congressional candidates. "The guy who is worried about crime and about the blacks moving into his neighborhood might . . . be tempted to vote Republican, but his paramount interest is his pay check," a Democratic adviser told the *Wall Street Journal* in the spring of 1970. "When he loses overtime pay, his standard of living is hurt, and he's going to blame the Administration for it. We'll see to that."[63]

In all fairness, there was little that Nixon could have done to stem the forces that soon would end a quarter-century of rising real wages. But politics is not about fairness, as Nixon understood as well as anyone. If the history of twentieth-century U.S. politics teaches any lesson, it is that incumbent presidents who face reelection during an economic downturn do not get reelected. And so in 1971 Nixon set about concocting a dramatic, if short-term fix for the economy. His New Economic Policy, announced in a nationally televised address in mid-August, included a 90-day federally imposed freeze on wage and price increases, a 10 percent tax on imports, and the end of the policy of allowing dollars to be traded for gold on the international currency market. The gold decision, taken without consulting of any of America's allies, destroyed the system of currency exchange that had functioned since the Bretton Woods agreements of 1944.

In taking these steps, Nixon was violating some fundamental canons of his party's free market orthodoxy; the influential conservative economist Milton Friedman predicted that the wage–price freeze would end "in utter failure and the emergence into the open of the suppressed inflation."[64] But, in the short run, the measures helped damp down inflation and increase employment. So did increased government spending on Social Security, veterans benefits, and the like, put into place by the Democratic-controlled Congress over the past few years. Finally, Nixon ordered government agencies to stock up on supplies, with the Defense Department, for example, laying in several years worth of everything from trucks to toilet paper. These measures temporarily reignited the economic boom. Unemployment fell to 5.5 percent, and workers' real earnings increased 4 percent between 1971 and 1972.

With peace and prosperity as well as McGovern's missteps all working for him, Nixon was free to follow the traditional "Rose Garden" strategy of incumbent presidents. He took every opportunity to appear in the role of the nation's elected leader rather than as a candidate in his own right. Nixon left most of the partisan mudslinging to surrogate campaigners, and refused to debate McGovern.

In the closing days of the campaign Nixon provided a philosophical justification for his reelection, offering a consistent conservative vision that had been lacking for most of the first four years of his presidency, a vision cast significantly in the form of a condemnation of "the sixties" and all they had wrought in American society. "What we have to realize," the president told a reporter, "is that many of the solutions of the sixties were massive failures. They threw money at problems and for the most part they failed." Profligate government spending had created a host of other problems, including crime, drug abuse, and welfare fraud, by undermining American traditions of self-reliance. In "the thoughts of the sixties," Nixon declared,

it was the government's job every time there was a problem, to make people more dependent upon it to give way to their whims. The welfare mess is an example. The escalation of the numbers of welfare, much of it is a result simply of running down what I call the work ethic.

The "leadership class" of the nation, particularly the "limousine liberals" of the Northeast were to blame. What they failed to recognize, Nixon suggested, in a telling image, is that the "average American is just like the child in the family. You give him some responsibility and he is going to amount to something." On the other hand, if "you make him completely dependent," it will only result in the creation of a "soft, spoiled and eventually a very weak individual."[65] Nixon apparently intended in his second term in office to finally return to the conservative principles of government he had honored in rhetoric but not in action during his first four years in the White House.

On November 7, Nixon won his expected landslide, taking over 60 percent of the popular vote, and the electoral votes of every state except Massachusetts. Nixon's supporters included a majority of Catholics, a majority of blue-collar workers, a majority of members of union families, and more than a third of registered Democrats. Of the traditional Democratic constituencies, only blacks and Jews remained loyal to McGovern. Democrats, however, retained majorities in Congress, gaining two seats in the Senate, losing a dozen in the House.

Liberal politicians survived the 1972 election: even George McGovern went back to his seat in the U.S. Senate, and was reelected by his South Dakota constituents two years later. But liberalism was fatally wounded, stuck not only with a reputation for promoting failed policies ("throwing money at problems" in Nixon's memorable phrase), but also as failed politics. For the remainder of the twentieth century, Democratic liberals could not shake the marks of their apparently decisive repudiation by the electorate in 1972. The term "liberalism" itself, proudly claimed by virtually every national figure in the Democratic party for a generation, fell into disrepute. It become the "L-word," and the "L" could just as easily have stood for "loser" as for "liberal." Though Republicans would continue to campaign against the memory of George McGovern (as generations of Democrats had campaigned against Herbert Hoover), the Democrats themselves would not choose another genuine "McGovernite" to run for the presidency in the twentieth century.

Republican strategist Kevin Phillips would argue that the Democrats had made the fatal mistake in the 1960s of abandoning "programs taxing the few for the benefit of the many (the New Deal)" to passing "programs taxing the many on behalf of the few (the Great Society)."[66] That was something of an exaggeration since Medicare—the single most expensive Great Society program—was precisely the kind of universal entitlement that had secured the loyalty of previous generations of voters behind the New Deal. For his own part in 1972, McGovern sought to continue this New Deal tradition by including in his platform a proposal for national health insurance. But it was the *perception* of a changing and narrowing set of Democratic loyalties and priorities that counted, much more than the reality. In the public mind, liberals had become the partisans of "special interests"—blacks, feminists, the elderly, welfare recipients, and so on, while it was the Republicans who spoke confidently in the name of an overriding national interest.

Liberals suffered too from the declining faith Americans had in government. The "credibility gap" that Johnson unleashed with his escalation of the war in Vietnam in 1965 had a far-reaching impact in domestic affairs as well as foreign policy. The percentage of Americans expressing "a great deal of confidence" in the executive branch of government declined from 41 percent in 1966 to 19 percent in 1973; for Congress the figure dropped from 42 percent to 29 percent.[67] Apathy and cynicism toward government was also measured by declining voter turnouts. In 1972 the voter turnout dropped 5 percentage points from the level of 1968, and the percentage continued to drop steadily over the next decade. The decline was greatest among lower-income groups who normally voted Democratic. The emerging Republican majority could almost as accurately be described as a shrinking Democratic electorate.[68]

Triumph did not mellow Richard Nixon: indeed, as the election neared, he savored the prospects of revenge. On September 15, 1972, the president met in the Oval Office with White House counsel John Dean and aide Bob Haldeman to discuss political problems that had arisen from the arrest of five intruders in the Watergate hotel and office complex in Washington, D.C., that previous June. The five men, and two others found outside the building, G. Gordon Liddy and E. Howard Hunt, had been attempting to break into the Democratic National Committee headquarters. Liddy was an ex-FBI agent, Hunt an ex-CIA man. It was soon discovered by investigators and the press that the two and the other defendants, also had links to President Nixon's reelection campaign. Nixon's press secretary, Ron Ziegler, dismissed the incident as a "third-rate burglary attempt." President Nixon denied that anyone in the White House had anything to do with it. Although Democrats protested, and reporters from the *Washington Post* and a few other newspapers tried to unravel the Watergate mystery, the country as a whole took little notice during that summer and fall.[69]

Nixon had given John Dean the task of monitoring the Watergate scandal to make sure it did not do any further damage to his reelection prospects. Dean could report to the president in September that all seemed to be going well. The president was pleased and praised Dean for putting his "fingers in the dikes every time that leaks have sprung there."

The two men went on to discuss postelection plans. What the president knew, and Dean did not know, was that their conversation was being recorded by a hidden, voice-activated recording system that had been installed in the Oval Office in 1971. The president suggested "watching the McGovern contributors and all that sort of thing." Dean assured him that he was keeping a "hawk's eye" on the president's opponents:

DEAN: Well, that's, uh, along that line, uh, one of the things I've tried to do, is just keep notes on a lot of the people who are emerging as—
PRESIDENT NIXON: That's right.
DEAN: as less than our friends.
PRESIDENT NIXON: Great.
DEAN: Because this is going to be over some day and they're—we shouldn't forget the way that some of them (unintelligible)—
PRESIDENT NIXON: I want the most, I want the most comprehensive notes on all of those who have tried to do us in. Because they didn't have to do it.

Nixon, in other words, could understand why people would attack him if they expected to make personal or political gains by doing so. But since by this time no one could believe McGovern really had a chance to win, Nixon thought continued political attacks on his administration were illegitimate, perverse—and deserving of punishment.

PRESIDENT NIXON: They didn't have to do it. I mean, if . . . they had a very close election everybody on the other side would understand this game. But now [they] are doing this quite deliberately and they are asking for it and they are going to get it. And this, this—we, we have not used the power in this first four years, as you know.
DEAN: That's true.
PRESIDENT NIXON: We have never used it. We haven't used the Bureau [the FBI] and we haven't used the Justice Department, but things are going to change now. And they're going to change, and, and they're going to get it right—
DEAN: That's an exciting prospect.
PRESIDENT NIXON: It's got to be done. It's the only thing to do.[70]

Coming into office, Richard Nixon had promised to bring the country together in healing the divisions of the 1960s. In reality, the Nixon administration embodied rather than resolved the decade's conflicts—and this was nowhere as evident as in the unfolding of the Watergate crisis of 1973–1974. The roots of the crisis could be found in the very first months of Nixon's administration, when he ordered the "secret bombing" of Cambodia. Enraged that news of the attacks had leaked to a reporter for the *New York Times,* Nixon ordered the FBI to wiretap several of Henry Kissinger's aides, whom he suspected as the leakers, as well as several newsmen. The taps, undertaken without legal authority, turned up nothing of substance; in any event, the *Times* report on the Cambodia bombing aroused little interest or controversy.

Not so the publication of what became known as the Pentagon Papers in the *New York Times* and other newspapers in several installments in June 1971. The Pentagon Papers, a 7000-page classified report on the origins of U.S. involvement in South Vietnam, had been commissioned by Secretary of Defense Robert McNamara shortly before he left office. Secretly copied and then released to the press by a disillusioned former Defense Department consultant named Daniel Ellsberg, the papers provided a devastating indictment of the shady practices and deceptions (including self-deception) that characterized policymaking toward Vietnam in the Eisenhower, Kennedy, and Johnson administrations. Although there was nothing in the Pentagon Papers reflecting directly on the Nixon administration, the president was outraged by their release. He knew all too well what would happen if some of the darker secrets of his own administration began spilling out for public scrutiny. Invoking national security, the administration obtained a temporary injunction blocking publication of further installments, but it was soon overturned by Supreme Court decision.

Nixon's defeat in the Pentagon Papers case seemed to unhinge him. In the weeks that followed, he ranted in the Oval Office to a captive audience of political aides about the perfidy of Ellsberg, the press, antiwar activists, and liberals in general. On six separate occasions in late June and early July, the taping system in the Oval Office recorded Nixon as he ordered his aides to organize a break-in at the Brookings Institution, a liberal think tank in Washington, D.C., where he believed, incorrectly, that more pilfered classified documents were being stored. "Goddamnit, get in and get those files," he raged at Haldeman in mid-June. "Blow the safe and get it."[71]

In this instance the president's men showed better sense than their boss, and quietly ignored his orders. But that was the last time they showed such discretion. In July E. Howard Hunt and G. Gordon Liddy, members of a secret administration operation known as "the plumbers," organized at Nixon's behest the previous year to "plug leaks" in the administration, were dispatched to Los Angeles to break into the office of Daniel Ellsberg's psychiatrist, in the hope that they could turn up information useful in discrediting Ellsberg. Their mission was a failure; the inept presidential burglars turned up nothing of use. In September John Ehrlichman informed the president of the disappointing results—doing so in an elliptical fashion designed to maintain Nixon's official ignorance of the commission of an illegal act on his behalf: "We had one little operation. It's been aborted out in Los Angeles which, I think, is better that you don't know about." But, he hastened to assure the president, "we've got some dirty tricks underway. It may pay off."[72]

The ultimate payoff for the plumbers' future projects was not exactly what Nixon and Ehrlichman had in mind. After the arrests at the Watergate, the president's top aides, with Nixon's knowledge, secretly funneled tens of thousands of dollars to the defendants in bail money, legal fees, and other payments.[73]

It wasn't enough. With the conviction of the Watergate defendants in the spring of 1973, the cover-up of White House involvement in the break-in began to unravel. One of the defendants, James McCord, wrote to the trial judge John Sirica to reveal that "political pressure" from high places had led the defendants to perjure themselves during the trial. Meanwhile, McCord's fellow defendant E. Howard Hunt escalated his own demands on the White House for payoffs to ensure his silence, not only on Watergate but on the Ellsberg break-in. John Dean went to the Oval Office on March 21 to warn Nixon of "a cancer on the presidency," represented by "the problem of the continued blackmail" by Hunt and others, payments that would only "compound the obstruction of justice situation." The president reassured him: "We could get that. . . . [I]f you need the money, . . . you could get the money. . . . What I mean is, you could, you could get a million dollars. And you could get it in cash. I, I know where it could be gotten."[74]

Time was running out on the president's men. Six weeks later, Dean, Ehrlichman, Haldeman, and Attorney General Richard Kleindienst were all forced to resign their White House positions because of deepening evidence of their involvement with the Watergate cover-up. They and others, including former attorney general John Mitchell, would soon be under indictment for Watergate-related crimes—all of them were eventually convicted. A Senate committee investigating the Watergate break-in, under the chairmanship of a folksy Democratic Senator from North Carolina, Sam Ervin, opened hearings in mid-May, broadcast live over the next several months every weekday to an enormous television audience. John Dean had decided he was not going to be a scapegoat for the president's crimes. When Republican senator Howard Baker asked Dean, "What did the President know and when did he know it?" the former White House counsel testified freely about what he knew about the Watergate break-in and cover-up, including the payoff conversation of March 21.[75] And when, quite accidentally, a minor figure in the scandal named Alexander Butterfield revealed the existence of the White House taping system, the Watergate struggle shifted into a battle over the control of the tapes.

It would take another eventful year for the drama to play itself out—in the meantime, Vice President Spiro Agnew was forced to resign his office after he pleaded no contest to charges that he had accepted bribes while serving as governor of Maryland, House minority leader Gerald Ford was approved by congressional vote as Agnew's successor, and Nixon's personal approval rating in public opinion polls fell to 17 percent, an all-time low for an American president. The nation's newspapers, making up for their general indifference to the Watergate scandal during the 1972 election campaign, now zealously pursued every Nixon misdeed over the past half-decade, from the Cambodia bombings to underpaying his personal income taxes. In June 1974 a grand jury investigating Watergate named Nixon as an "unindicted co-conspirator" in the cover-up that had already sent many of his aides to prison. The president's popularity was not helped by the U.S. economy slipping into recession in 1973–1974, with unemployment climbing to over 7 percent, combined with the most rapid inflation since the immediate post–World War II period.

Finally, in late July 1974, the Supreme Court, headed by one of Nixon's appointees, Chief Justice Warren Burger, ruled unanimously that the president's taped conversations with aides were subject to subpoena by congressional investigating committees, notwithstanding any claim of "executive privilege." The House of Representatives immediately began impeachment hearings. On August 5, the president turned over a tape to the House Judiciary committee from a meeting in the White House on June 23, 1972, six days after the Watergate break-in, which became known as the "smoking gun" tape. At that meeting, the president unambiguously instructed Haldeman to order the CIA to intervene with the FBI in the name of "national security," asking them to curtail their investigation of the Watergate break-in because it supposedly had been a botched CIA operation.[76]

Even such formerly staunch supporters as Arizona senator Barry Goldwater and California governor Ronald Reagan now called for Nixon's resignation. With his remaining political support crumbling, there were fears in Washington that in desperation, Nixon might resort to military force to stave off his removal from office, either by provoking war abroad or by staging a military coup at home. Secretary of Defense James Schlesinger went so far as to instruct the U.S. military commanders not to respond to a call from the president for military action without first clearing it with him.[77]

In the end, Nixon went quietly, resigning on August 9. The country breathed a collective sigh of relief at the conclusion of its worst constitutional crisis since the Civil War. With Nixon gone, with direct American involvement in the war in Vietnam concluded, with campus protest and racial rioting fading into unpleasant memory, many Americans hoped that August 1974 would mark a new beginning for the nation, a time of healing, and an end to discord. As President Gerald Ford declared upon taking the oath of office as thirty-eighth president of the United States, "our long national nightmare is over."[78]

He proved mistaken.

Winners, Losers, and Consequences

"THE PAST IS NEVER DEAD. IT'S NOT EVEN PAST."
—*William Faulkner*[1]

Who won the battles of the 1960s? No one would think to ask that question about the bloody conflict between North and South that cleaved the nation during the nineteenth century. As a consequence of the Civil War, the Union was preserved and chattel slavery abolished, although racial inequality remained a tormenting reality of American life. But many of the clashes in the United States a century later were fought on the terrain of cultural politics: two camps—one composed of left-liberals and radicals, the other of conservatives—hotly disputed the morality of their opponents' values, language, and behavior and differed sharply and, at times, violently about how to build a society of individuals at peace with themselves and with the rest of the world. Since beliefs tend to persevere longer than do rebel armies, the cultural civil war of the 1960s produced no clear victor.

In the early years of the twenty-first century, there remains a lively contest over the meanings of the 1960s. The battle is joined by Christian conservatives and homosexual activists, by proponents of English only and defenders of bilingual education, by ardent feminists and defenders of the "traditional" family, by advocates of pre-emptive war against hostile nations and critics of U.S. power and motives, by scholars who view America's past through the prism of multiculturalism and gender and those who argue that the thought and achievements of great national leaders ought to be the main focus of historical study.

In the 1990s, conservatives portrayed Bill and Hillary Clinton as the champions of a slew of lamentable liberal causes—from abortion rights to government-funded child care to sexual license. Such commitments, charged many on the Right, stemmed from a "self-indulgent" attitude that the Clintons had imbibed in the counterculture of the '60s and George McGovern's 1972 campaign for president. As Republicans tried, unsuccessfully, to drive her husband from office, the first lady responded with dark charges about "a vast right-wing conspiracy" to hamstring the agenda of the first Democratic chief executive to be reelected since Franklin D. Roosevelt.

The rhetorical skirmish among some of the nation's top leaders indicated that, after three decades, many of the key conflicts of the 1960s had neither healed nor driven either side from the field of battle. As columnist George Will has observed, "So powerful were—are—the energies let loose in the sixties that there cannot now be, and may never be, anything like a final summing-up. After all, what is the 'final result' of the Civil War? It is too soon to say."[2]

Still, some judgments can be made.[3] In the realm of electoral politics and policymaking, conservatives did far better than anyone expected at the dawn of the '60s. By the end of the 1970s, as the New Left and civil rights insurgencies lost numbers and energy, the Right could boast the largest and best-financed grassroots force in the land. Its influence, particularly among business executives and evangelical Protestants, did much to propel Ronald Reagan, George Bush, Sr. and George W. Bush into the White House and to establish a handful of conservative opinions as the conventional wisdom of American politics: antipoverty programs do not help the poor; taxes should always be lowered; "preferential treatment" for minorities is wrong; business is overregulated; and the size of government ought to be reduced—in every area but the military.

During the first Bush administration, the Right was granted its most cherished wish: Communists fell from power throughout eastern Europe. Elsewhere, former revolutionaries quickly became apostles, in practice if not ideology, of entrepreneurial capitalism. In Ho Chi Minh City, prosperous Vietnamese could feast on Kentucky Fried Chicken and ice cream from Baskin-Robbins while wearing clothes designed by Donna Karan and Calvin Klein. Meanwhile, thousands of their poorer compatriots toiled, for meager wages, making athletic shoes for the American market. With astonishing speed, and little violence, socialism was reduced to an ideology no longer taken very seriously even in nations ruled by parties of the Marxist Left.

Liberalism wasn't faring much better. Widely blamed for the turmoil of the late '60s, liberals were unable to regain the aura of a political force that could master the future. Instead, their very name became grist for ridicule by those on the Right seeking to put an opponent on the defensive. At the beginning of the new century, no Republican and only a handful of Democrats embraced it. Although Bill Clinton was attacked as a "liberal" throughout his presidency, two of his major accomplishments in office were ones that conservatives had long advocated: a balanced budget and the end of guaranteed welfare payments to single mothers with small children.

The coalition of wage earners and intellectuals of all races and most regions that Franklin D. Roosevelt forged in the 1930s cracked apart during the late '60s and has not been rebuilt. That alliance was forged during a period of economic growth and patriotic unity that ended in the debacle of Vietnam. Taking its place on the left of American politics was a melange of social movements—feminist, gay and lesbian, black nationalist, Mexican American, environmentalist—that swelled in size and became skilled at defending the rights and cultural identities of people who, before the '60s, had been scorned or ignored. But conservatives usually set the terms of debate about economic and social policy—and usually wielded a voting majority on the Supreme Court, as the 5-4 ruling that resolved the 2000 election for George W. Bush made spectacularly clear.

The Right, however, did not have everything its own way in politics. Notwithstanding the resentment of "big government," millions of Americans clung fiercely to benefits they received as a result of programs initiated by liberal Democrats in the 1960s and early '70s: Medicare, Medicaid, food stamps, the Occupational Health and Safety Act, the Higher Education Act (which mandates equal treatment for women), and the Environmental Protection Agency. In fact, protecting the environment quickly became one '60s cause that no politician could afford to oppose—even though some on the Right grumbled, in the teeth of scientific consensus, that the danger of global warming was much exaggerated.

Neither were conservatives able to unite the nation behind a militant policy abroad. The demise of world Communism did not lead most Americans to abandon their "Vietnam Syndrome"—fear of sending large numbers of troops to fight abroad for uncertain ends. Following the terrorist attacks on September 11, 2001, President George W. Bush asserted the need to "take the battle to the enemy, disrupt his plans, and confront the worst threats before they emerge."[4] But opinion polls registered a sizeable opposition to open-ended, preventive wars; unlike during the height of the Cold War and the early years of U.S. intervention in Indochina, many Democrats in Congress were reluctant to follow the administration's lead. A bipartisan foreign policy thus remained more the exception than the rule, as had been true since Lyndon Johnson sent half-a-million American troops to fight an unwinnable conflict almost four decades earlier.

What is more, conservatives had little success in reversing larger social changes that the New Left and the youth culture had helped set in motion. The most obvious legacy was that of issues radical feminists made prominent at the end of the '60s. The central tenet of their ideology was that "the personal is political." The most intimate details of private life—housework and child care, sexuality and childbirth—were viewed as fundamentally linked to social and political power. By the mid-'70s, the media had stopped calling feminists "bra burners" and were giving their demands a respectful hearing. Mainstream politicians refused, despite the pleas of a growing right-to-life movement, to negate the Supreme Court's 1973 ruling in *Roe v. Wade* that essentially legalized abortion.

Thirty years later, feminists often had to defend themselves against charges that they were out to destroy "family values." But the embattled reputation of their movement obscured the fact that relationships between the genders had changed in fundamental ways during the last third of the century. Most young women, at least in the middle class, expected to have access to the same careers and to receive the same compensation as men. It was no longer surprising to see women leaders in formerly "men's" fields like television production (Oprah Winfrey), diplomacy (Secretary of State Madeleine Albright), or the Supreme Court (justices Sandra Day O'Connor and Ruth Bader Ginsburg). Even conservative Republicans recruited female candidates and urged them to be as aggressive on the stump as men. The idea that husbands and wives (or unmarried partners) should share the housework and child rearing was all but universally accepted. So were suits for sexual harassment, which was not even considered a crime until the 1970s. Near the end of the century, a majority of American women under 30 agreed, in a national poll, that "The women's movement has made your life better."[5] It was as if U.S. society had been waiting for decades, with mounting nervousness and impatience, for some group to have the courage to state the obvious about problems between the sexes.

Personal issues not directly linked to women's equality remained more controversial—such as the teaching of sex education in public schools and tolerance toward homosexuals in the military and ministry. Many American parents wanted to retain a sphere of privacy about intimate matters and feared that gays and lesbians were out to "convert" the young. Still, the fact that millions of homosexuals were open about their sexual identity—and had a sizable movement to lobby for their interests—was a remarkable change from the Eisenhower years when police routinely raided gay bars and every state declared "sodomy" illegal.[6]

What about the black freedom movement, inspiration for all the "liberations" that followed? After the black insurgency split into integrationist and nationalist camps late in the '60s, its power and elan gradually declined. During the next decades, black activists railed against the Right's ability to dismiss their cause as a selfish "special interest" but were unable to regain the political momentum. Meanwhile, deteriorating schools, inadequate transportation, and the disappearance of urban manufacturing jobs conspired to leave the black poor in worse shape than they had been during the heyday of the movement. By century's end, "benign neglect" of the inner city had become, in fact if not rhetoric, the unofficial policy of the nation.

This is a dismal portrait. But it conceals a number of more encouraging realities. The landmark civil rights bills passed by lawmakers under the influence of the black freedom movement proved irreversible, and they helped to pry open opportunities for millions of African Americans. Since the '60s, the number of black political officials, elected and appointed, skyrocketed; their ranks included mayors of the biggest cities, a southern governor, and the chairman of the Joint Chiefs of Staff, who later became Secretary of State. By the mid-1990s, young blacks were graduating from high school at the same rate as whites (albeit usually from schools with fewer resources). With the aid of affirmative action, black graduates enjoyed access to every university in the land. Middle-class African Americans (the name itself popularized by Jesse Jackson, King's former lieutenant) no longer occupied a mere beachhead on a vast Euro-American shore. They owned businesses and practiced professions in totals far beyond what earlier generations had achieved.[7]

For a growing number of black Americans, the cultural mainstream no longer seemed as alien as it had during the era of Jim Crow. In the 1990s, major newspapers ran cheery features about Kwanzaa alongside ones on other "ethnic" traditions, big corporations sponsored Kwanzaa Expos, and President Bill Clinton hailed "the meaning and energy of this inspiring festival." A new generation of black politicians, who had often attended integrated schools, won votes from whites and new immigrants by speaking less about racism and more about promoting business and reforming education. Even hip-hop music, a quintessential creation of "the 'hood," gained a huge following among nonblacks, and spawned Eminem, a vengeful white lyricist whose popularity crossed racial lines.[8]

It was more difficult to tell how much racial attitudes had changed since the '60s. Certainly, Americans had not attained the paradise of racial tolerance that white and black organizers dreamed about in the early years of the freedom movement. Most people socialized only within their own race, and blacks remained deeply suspicious of law enforcement, even when police departments were thoroughly integrated.

Meanwhile, old-fashioned styles of racism continued to fester. Numbers of real estate agents still steered black tenants away from white neighborhoods, and both talk radio and the Internet hummed with "darky jokes" and other forms of racist banter. In 1994 two conservatives wrote a best-selling book that argued, in sober tones, that African Americans were genetically less intelligent than whites and Asians.[9] In response, some black nationalists railed against "white devils," whom they accused of spreading AIDS and crack cocaine to inner-city neighborhoods.

Fortunately, millions of Americans rejected such talk. They made friends across the color line, particularly at work, and enjoyed a popular culture whose relaxed, multiracial character defied grim descriptions of a country deeply divided in the bad old ways. The study of the history and culture of minority groups became a staple of public and private education, especially in metropolitan areas. And a growing number of voices opposed viewing all issues, political and personal, through a racial mirror in which one must think and act as either black or white. In 1997, the sociologist Orlando Patterson, an immigrant from Jamaica, called on his fellow blacks to commit themselves anew to the "glorious ideal of America as the 'beloved community': free, egalitarian, and as integrated in its social life as it already is in the triumphant global culture that Afro-Americans have done so much to fashion."[10] But if black people followed his advice, would Americans of other races follow?

While activists, politicians, and intellectuals continue to fight over the meaning of the '60s, other Americans retired from the fray. Thousands of military veterans and Robert McNamara, the former defense secretary, made pilgrimages back to Vietnam and were greeted warmly by their erstwhile enemies; Pete Peterson, the first U.S. ambassador to that nation since the war ended, had spent seven years as a POW. Toward the end of his life, George Wallace repeatedly apologized for the harm he caused black Americans. Like Union and Confederate veterans who staged joint reunions at the turn of the last century, such figures seek to end disputes that once set them and their fellow citizens at odds. Fortunately, this time around, abrogating the rights of black citizens has not been the price of reconciliation.

For their part, Americans born since the 1960s have grown up surrounded by a surfeit of images—musical, visual, and literary—that convey the polarized passions of the era but do little to explain them. The '60s hits of Marvin Gaye and James Brown, of the Rolling Stones and Bob Dylan, of Janis Joplin, Jimi Hendrix, and the Beatles (not to speak of dozens of less famous artists) supply a mildly stimulating soundtrack that overwhelms memories of cultural and racial conflict. No wonder that when the U.S. Postal Service asked Americans, in 1998, to vote for "the subjects that best commemorate the 1960s," the winners were a trio of cultural products whose enduring popularity (in legend and the marketplace) seems to transcend conflict entirely: the Beatles, Woodstock, and *Star Trek*.[11]

One reason why young Americans show little inclination to refight the '60s is that they realize how much the nation has changed. The United States now exhibits a degree of ethnic diversity that defies the biracial model that reigned from the beginnings of the nation through the heyday of the civil rights movement and the backlash against it. Intermarriages—between all combinations of peoples—have steadily increased since the 1960s. In 2000, 6.8 million Americans (two percent of the total population) told the U.S. Census they belonged to more than one race; the government had never before included such an option on its questionnaire.[12] Thanks in part to liberalized immigration laws, the numbers of U.S. residents from Central and South America, East and South Asia, and Africa mushroomed during the last third of the twentieth century. The 2000 Census reported there were more Hispanic Americans than black Americans. The Hispanic category itself, invented by federal officials in 1973, is somewhat artificial: What, besides the same mother tongue, does an Argentinian psychoanalyst in Washington, D.C., have in common with a Mexican laborer who crosses the border into California to harvest crops?[13] But, at least in demographic terms, the United States has, since the '60s, become a different country.

Newcomers have transformed the human face of the economy: the first language of most meatpackers in Iowa and Kansas is Spanish, immigrants from South Asia drive thousands of New York City taxicabs, and Chinese women are ubiquitous in the garment trades. By 2000, a majority of residents of the nation's one-hundred largest cities hailed from non-European backgrounds. Unlike the European immigrants who flooded into industrial America at the turn of the last century, most newcomers can now stay in more or less constant touch with their homelands. Many travel back and forth on a regular basis. And the influence of Latinos, particularly those from Mexico and Cuba, in politics and popular culture is swiftly growing.[14] They are a pivotal voting bloc in the populous states of Florida, California, and Texas—and make up about one-third of major league baseball rosters.

The comparative ease with which immigrants and U.S. citizens alike cross borders is but one feature of the global economy whose contours were just coming into view at the end of the 1960s. The quarter-century of growth following World War II delivered secure jobs for millions of Americans at rising wages in big corporations. Increasing numbers of these newly prosperous workers bought homes, paid taxes, and sent their children to colleges where alternative cultures and politics flowered. But after the '60s, most of these workers and their offspring had to adapt, quickly, to an unstable world in which products and labor increasingly cut loose from their national moorings. The rapid computerization of a myriad of tasks also took a toll, even as it made life easier and smoother for many. During the 1970s, the number of long-distance phone calls made in the United States tripled, while the ranks of telephone operators assigned to handle them dropped by 40 percent.[15] A gradual decline in the membership and economic clout of labor unions based in manufacturing, mining, and construction helped stretch the income gap between classes and reminded some historians of conditions during the Gilded Age that followed the Civil War.

Of course, some of the hype about computer capitalism was valid. Fewer Americans needed to work at jobs that were nasty, brutish, and shortened life—even if they still paid a union wage. As information became a commodity of universal value, more and more Americans rushed to learn new skills and subjects; as a result, cultural tolerance probably increased. Thanks to the Internet—created in the late '60s by federal scientists to communicate with each other more efficiently—anyone with a modem could connect to vast storehouses of data. Some who gazed endlessly at their monitors were only pursuing loneliness, but others found new pleasures, profits, or a blend of the two.[16]

The visions and perils of globalized capitalism may seem without precedent, but the emerging culture owes a good deal to aspects of the 1960s that some critics considered selfish and amoral. During the Vietnam War, young rebels had opposed the draft with the cry, "Not with my life you don't" and argued that society should prize the quality of life over laboring diligently for a brighter future. Since then, "postmaterialist values" of individual liberty, self-expression, and sexual relativism have gained around the world—in bad economic times and good.[17] At the start of the twenty-first century, even the Communist rulers of a poor nation like Vietnam were encouraging their people to buy American goods associated with ease and luxury (often marketed by former compatriots who had crossed the Pacific and made it rich). The traditional morality of saving, diligence, and sexual self-denial was nearly everywhere on the run.

In the United States, neither the Right nor the Left that emerged from the '60s was overjoyed by the triumph of this kind of "freedom." Conservatives saw moral discipline breaking down under the assault of cyberpornography and the increasing acceptance of homosexuality. Liberals and radicals complained that the wealthy lacked any sense of social responsibility, particularly to their own workers. Neither camp welcomed the fact that the global marketplace was diluting the meaning of American citizenship—although, in contrast to earlier periods, hostility toward new immigrants failed to activate a mass movement.

The amoral economic order did help generate an alternative of sorts in the spiritual realm. The great awakening that began in the '60s gained strength through the rest of the century. Every major world religion achieved a foothold in the United States, and fundamentalists—whether Jewish, Christian, Muslim, Buddhist, or Hindu—gained adherents by preaching obeisance to the laws and texts of their faith.[18] New Age religions grew as well, driven by a longing to understand the "inner self" that traditional congregations could not satisfy. For many Americans, writes sociologist Robert Wuthnow, "Faith is no longer something people inherit but something for which they strive."[19]

The Civil War of the 1860s was a terrible and humbling experience. As Lincoln suggested in his second inaugural address, delivered in March 1865, it was the price the nation had to pay for the sin of slavery:

> Fondly do we hope, fervently do we pray, that this mighty scourge of war may speedily pass away. Yet, if God wills that it continue until all the wealth piled by the bondman's two hundred and fifty years of unrequired toil shall be sunk, and every drop of blood drawn with the lash shall be paid by another drawn with the sword, as was said three thosuand years ago, so still it must be said, "The judgments of the Lord are true and righteous altogether."[20]

Lincoln himself would not live to see the end of the war. One night in early April he had a dream in which he foresaw his own death. A few nights later, on April 14th, 1865—Good Friday on the Christian religious calendar—he was struck down by an assassin's bullet.

On another April evening, 103 years later, Martin Luther King, Jr. spoke of the possibility of his own death as he addressed a crowd of supporters gathered in a Memphis church. He reflected on the dramatic events of the 1960s, and how glad he was that he had been a part of them. Had he died before the start of the decade, he reminded his audience:

> I wouldn't have been around here in 1960, when students all over the South started sitting-in at lunch counters. And I knew as they were sitting in, they were really standing up for the best in the American dream, and taking the whole nation back to those great wells of democracy which were dug deep by the founding fathers in the Declaration of Independence and the Constitution.[21]

Lincoln and King were kindred spirits living in kindred eras. They fashioned and spoke a language of civic virtue and redemptive sacrifice that continues to inspire new generations of Americans. We may not envy them for the difficult times in which they lived and died. But we should recognize that it is in just such eras of discord and conflict that Americans have shown themselves most likely to rediscover and live out the best traditions to be found in our national experience.

Critical Events During the Long 1960s

1946   War begins between France and the Viet Minh for control of Vietnam

1947   Jackie Robinson becomes first black man to play major league baseball in the twentieth century

1948   President Harry S Truman orders desegregation of the military

1954   French withdraw from Vietnam; Geneva accords partition the country into North and South, with the U.S. supporting the latter (the Republic of Vietnam)

In *Brown v. Board of Education,* Supreme Court rules that segregated schools violate the Fourteenth Amendment and are thus unconstitutional.

Elvis Presley releases first record on Sun label

Senator Joseph McCarthy censured by his colleagues.

1955   Montgomery, Alabama, bus boycott begins

Founding of *National Review*

Merger of American Federation of Labor and Congress of Industrial Organizations (AFL-CIO); union membership at historic high

Allen Ginsberg reads "Howl" in public for the first time

1956   After Supreme Court sides with Montgomery boycotters, buses in that city are desegregated

Dwight Eisenhower wins reelection in a landslide

The USSR crushes the Hungarian revolution

The first enclosed shopping mall opens in Minneapolis

The Platters become the first black group to have a no. 1 record on the popular music chart

1957   President Eisenhower sends troops to Little Rock, Arkansas to enforce school desegregation

Congress passes first civil rights legislation since the nineteenth century

Southern Christian Leadership Conference (SCLC) organized, with Martin Luther King, Jr. as president

Communist-led insurgency begins in South Vietnam

USSR launches *Sputnik*, initiating the space race

1958   Recession begins, boosting unemployment to postwar high of 6 percent

Democrats make big gains in congressional elections

Publication of John Kenneth Galbraith's *The Affluent Society*

Formation of John Birch Society

1959   Soviet Premier Nikita Khrushchev visits United States

Revolutionaries, led by Fidel Castro, take power in Cuba

First American soldiers die in Vietnam

1960   Founding of Students for a Democratic Society (SDS)

Founding of Young Americans for Freedom (YAF)

YAF issues the Sharon Statement

Black college students stage sit-ins at lunch counters in the South and then found Student Non-Violent Coordinating Committee (SNCC)

Publication of Barry Goldwater's *The Conscience of a Conservative*

At Harvard, Timothy Leary and Richard Alpert begin experimenting with psychedelic drugs

John F. Kennedy narrowly elected president, first Catholic to hold that office; Lyndon Baines Johnson elected vice president

First birth control pill approved for sale by Food and Drug Administration

1961   Invasion of Cuba at Bay of Pigs a complete failure

Yuri Gagarin, of the USSR, becomes first human in space

Erection of Berlin Wall

Publication of Joseph Heller's *Catch 22*

Freedom Riders force integration of interstate travel facilities in the South

1962   SDS issues Port Huron Statement

Supreme Court, in case of *Engel v. Vitale*, rules against prayer in public schools

Pope John XXIII opens the Second Vatican Council

John Glenn becomes first American to orbit the earth

Cuban missile crisis

George C. Wallace elected governor of Alabama

Beatles attain their first no. 1 record (in Britain), "Love Me Do"

Release of Bob Dylan's first album

1963   U.S. and USSR sign treaty banning atmospheric nuclear tests

Battle of Ap Bac in South Vietnam

SCLC stages mass protests in Birmingham, Alabama; Martin Luther King, Jr. writes *Letter from a Birmingham Jail*

Publication of Betty Friedan's *The Feminine Mystique*

March for Jobs and Freedom attracts a quarter-million people to Washington, D.C.

Release of Stevie Wonder's "Fingertips, Part 2" and the Kingsmen's recording of "Louie Louie"

Four black girls are murdered in bombing of Sixteenth Street Baptist Church in Birmingham

Fall and assassination of Ngo Dinh Diem in Saigon

Assassination of Medgar Evers in Jackson, Mississippi

Assassination of John F. Kennedy in Dallas; Lyndon Johnson becomes president

1964   Malcolm X breaks with the Nation of Islam

Congress passes landmark Civil Rights Act

Congress passes Economic Opportunity Act, initiating war on poverty

Mississippi Summer Project; three volunteers murdered by southern whites

Gulf of Tonkin resolution gives President Johnson authority to prosecute an unlimited war in Vietnam

Free Speech Movement at University of California in Berkeley

President Johnson reelected in a landslide over Barry Goldwater, but conservatives take over the Republican Party

Beatles' first tour of the United States helps make them the most popular musical group in the English-speaking world

Nikita Khrushchev toppled from power in the USSR

Cassius Clay wins heavyweight championship of the world and then announces he has joined the Nation of Islam and changed his name to Muhammad Ali

Martin Luther King, Jr. awarded the Nobel Peace Prize

1965   First U.S. combat troops begin fighting in South Vietnam

In Washington, D.C., SDS stages the first large national demonstration against the war

Teach-ins against the war begin

Twenty thousand U.S. troops intervene in the Dominican Republic

In Selma, Alabama, SCLC and SNCC lead marches for voting rights

Malcolm X is assassinated in New York City

Congress passes Voting Rights Act

United Farm Workers Organizing Committee launches a strike against grape growers in California

Congress passes Immigration Reform Act

Insurrection in Watts section of Los Angeles

1966   Formation of the National Organization for Women (NOW)

Formation of the Black Panther Party

Stokely Carmichael, chairman of SNCC, begins popularizing the slogan "Black Power"

SCLC undertakes a major civil rights campaign in Chicago which fails to crack white resistance

Publication of *Quotations of Chairman Mao,* or "the little red book," as Cultural Revolution rages in China

Publication of *Human Sexual Response* by Masters and Johnson

Ronald Reagan elected governor of California

1967   Martin Luther King, Jr. begins speaking out against the Vietnam War

Antiwar protesters march on the Pentagon

Thurgood Marshall is appointed the first black justice of the Supreme Court

Carl Stokes of Cleveland is elected the first black mayor of a major American city

Israel defeats Egypt, Syria, and Jordan in a six-day war and takes control of formerly Arab lands

Large insurrections rock the black ghettos of Newark and Detroit

Publication of Robert Crumb's *Zap*, first underground comic book to gain a mass readership

"Summer of Love" in San Francisco

Muhammad Ali is stripped of his heavyweight championship because he refuses to serve in the armed forces

1968 Tet offensive throughout South Vietnam turns most Americans against President Johnson's policy

President Johnson announces he will not run for reelection

Massacre of Vietnamese civilians at My Lai

United States and government of North Vietnam begin peace talks in Paris

Assassination of Martin Luther King, Jr. in Memphis

Assassination of Senator Robert F. Kennedy in Los Angeles

Black and white radicals take over buildings at Columbia University in New York City

Insurrection by students and workers shuts down France

USSR and its allies crush reformist government in Czechoslovakia

Mexican government crushes student movement in advance of Olympic Games there

Antiwar demonstrators clash with police at Democratic Convention in Chicago

Feminists stage a protest at the Miss America contest in Atlantic City

George Wallace mounts a serious third-party campaign for the presidency

Richard Nixon narrowly elected president, with Spiro Agnew as his vice president

1969 Huge rock festivals in Bethel, New York and Altamont, California

United States puts man on the moon

Soviet and Chinese troops clash along their Central Asian border

President Nixon initiates "Vietnamization" of the war and decreases number of U.S. combat troops in Indochina

Ho Chi Minh dies

Earl Warren retires as chief justice of the Supreme Court; he is succeeded by Warren Burger

SDS splits into competing factions

YAF throws out its libertarian faction

Moratorium draws largest turnout for an antiwar demonstration in U.S. history

Stonewall riot in New York's Greenwich Village initiates the gay liberation movement

In Denver, the first La Raza conference declares pride in the heritage of Latino-Americans

Internet begun (under a different name) by Pentagon scientists

1970   Earth Day inaugurates a mass environmental movement

Congress creates the Environmental Protection Agency and the Occupational Safety and Health Administration

U.S. invasion of Cambodia touches off student strikes at hundreds of college campuses

During protests, authorities kill four students at Kent State in Ohio and two at Jackson State in Mississippi

Congress repeals Gulf of Tonkin resolution

New York, Hawaii, and Alaska become first states to pass liberal abortion laws

New York City postal workers go on strike, the first in the history of the postal service; President Nixon breaks it with U.S. troops

Jimi Hendrix and Janis Joplin die from drug overdoses

The Beatles disband

1971   U.S. voting age is lowered to 18 by the Twenty-sixth Amendment

New York Times publishes the Pentagon Papers

Congress passes the Military Service Act, which gradually ends the draft and institutes an all-volunteer army

1972   President Nixon visits the People's Republic of China

The Watergate break-in

Last U.S. combat troops withdraw from South Vietnam

Richard Nixon defeats Democrat George McGovern in a 49-state landslide

Congress sends the Equal Rights Amendment to the states for ratification

1973   The Supreme Court, in *Roe v. Wade*, overturns most restrictions on abortion

United States signs a peace treaty with North Vietnam and the Viet Cong; the Communist side releases American prisoners of war

Members of the American Indian Movement occupy the village of Wounded Knee, South Dakota, to protest the U.S. government's treatment of Native Americans

Vice President Spiro Agnew resigns and pleads no contest to a charge of tax evasion; Gerald Ford succeeds him

Oil-producing nations cut supplies to the United States, beginning a recession

1974   House Judiciary Committee votes articles of impeachment against President Nixon

Richard Nixon resigns from the presidency and is succeeded by Gerald Ford

Inflation reaches double digits

Frank Robinson of the Cleveland Indians becomes the first black manager in major league baseball

1975   Communist forces occupy Saigon, ending the Vietnam War and beginning the reunification of the country

Communists take control in Cambodia and Laos

First personal computer goes on sale

Bibliographical Essay

In recent years, the 1960s has become an exciting field for research and writing in which both academics and journalists have participated. This brief essay indicates a few of the works that have most influenced our own thinking.

General Works

For masterful insights and nuggets of information on the postwar world, see Eric Hobsbawm, *The Age of Extremes* (1995). Daniel Bell's *The Cultural Contradictions of Capitalism* (1976) and *The Coming of Post-Industrial Society* (1973) provide a brilliant theoretical context. Michael Barone's *Our Country* (1990) is an indispensable guide to political history since the 1930s. James Patterson's *Grand Expectations* (1996) is the most intelligent survey about the United States during the quarter-century following the end of World War II. But one should also consult Godfrey Hodgson's *America in Our Time* (1976), which was ahead of its time in analyzing the rise and fall of the liberal establishment. For the '60s itself, general texts that provoke thought as well as supply detail include David Farber, *The Age of Great Dreams* (1994); David Burner, *Making Peace with the Sixties* (1997); and Allen J. Matusow, *The Unravelling of America* (1984). A thoughtful anthology about key aspects of culture and politics is *The Sixties: From Memory to History*, edited by David Farber (1994).

Economic and Social Life

There is no good overview of how U.S. society changed during "the long '60s." But there are splendid studies of some aspects of that transformation. On residential shifts, see Kenneth T. Jackson, *Crabgrass Frontier: The Suburbanization of the United States* (1984); and Adam Rome, *The Bulldozer in the Countryside; Suburban Sprawl and the Rise of American Environmentalism* (2001). On working people, see the relevant chapters in American Social History Project, *Who Built America?*, Vol. 2 (1992). On unionism, see Nelson Lichtenstein, *The Most Dangerous Man in Detroit: Walter Reuther and the Fate of American Labor* (1995); and Joshua Freeman, *Working-Class New York: Life and Labor Sinc World War II* (2000). On the military–industrial complex, see Ann Markusen et al., *The Rise of the Gunbelt* (1991). On cultural and intellectual life, see John P. Diggins, *The Proud Decades: America in War and in Peace, 1941–1960* (1988) and Stephen Whitfield, *The Culture of the Cold War* (1991). On family life, see the relevant chapters of Steven Mintz and Susan Kellogg, *Domestic Revolutions* (1988); Jessica Weiss, *To Have and to Hold: Marriage, The Baby Boom and Social Change* (2000), Elaine Tyler May, *Homeward Bound* (1989) and Stephanie Coontz, *The Way We Never*

Were (1992). For stirrings of rebellion among women before the '60s, see *Not June Cleaver*, edited by Joanne Meyerowitz (1994), and Ruth Rosen, *The World Split Open: How the Modern Women's Movement Changed America* (2000).

Black Ordeal, Black Freedom

This subject has been graced with an abundance of intelligent and engaged works. On the problems to be confronted, see David Goldfield, *Black, White, and Southern* (1990); *The "Underclass" Debate*, edited by Michael Katz (1993); and Thomas Sugrue, *Origins of the Urban Crisis* (1996). A good overview of the movement is Robert Weisbrot, *Freedom Bound* (1990). Also see *Women in the Civil Rights Movement*, edited by Vicki L. Crawford et al. (1993). Unparalleled in their narrative sweep are two volumes by Taylor Branch that focus on Martin Luther King, Jr.—*Parting the Waters* (1988) and *Pillar of Fire* (1998). On SNCC, see Clayborne Carson, *In Struggle* (1981), and Charles M. Payne, *I've Got the Light of Freedom* (1995). Fine local studies include William Chafe, *Civilities and Civil Rights* (1980), on Greensboro; John Dittmer, *Local People* (1994), on Mississippi; Robert Norrell, *Reaping the Whirlwind* (1985), on Tuskegee and Stephen J. Whitfield, *A Death in the Delta: The Story of Emmett Till* (1988). On the integration of baseball, see Jules Tygiel, *Baseball's Great Experiment* (1983); on legal battles, see Jack Greenberg, *Crusaders in the Courts* (1994). On the resurgence of black nationalism, see *The Autobiography of Malcolm X* (1965) and William L. Van Deburg, *New Day in Babylon* (1992). On international pressures, see Mary L. Ovdziak, *Cold War Civil Rights* (2000).

Youth Culture

This area is just beginning to attract talented scholars and writers. A mammoth, transnational overview is Arthur Marwick, *The Sixties: Cultural Revolution in Britain, France, Italy, and the United States, c. 1958–c. 1974* (1998). Also see *Imagine Nation: The American Counterculture of the 1960s and '70s,* ed. Peter Braunstein and Michael William Doyle (2002). Still valuable is the critique that gave a name to the phenomenon, Theodore Roszak, *The Making of a Counter Culture* (1969). For a lively and provocative look at the corporate side of the hip phenomenon, see Thomas Frank, *The Conquest of Cool* (1997). On the Beats, see John Tytell, *Naked Angels* (1976). Deft interpretations of sexual life include the relevant chapters of John D'Emilio and Estelle B. Freedman, *Intimate Matters* (1997), as well as Barbara Ehrenreich et al., *Re-Making Love* (1986), David Smith Allyn's *Make Love, Not War* (2000); and Beth Bailey, *Sex in the Heartland* (1999). On psychedelics and other drugs, see Martin A. Lee and Bruce Shlain, *Acid Dreams* (1992); Jay Stevens, *Storming Heaven: LSD and The American Dream* (1987); and Geoffrey O'Brien's quasi-memoir, *Dream Time* (1988). The literature on rock music is vast, but the best of it focuses on individual artists or genres. Pungent overviews include Greil Marcus, *Mystery Train* (1982) and Ellen Willis, *Beginning to See the Light* (1992). On particular subjects, see Peter Guralnick, *Sweet Soul Music* (1986) and (on Elvis), *Last Train to Memphis* (1994); Dave Marsh, *Louie Louie* (1993); and (on Motown) Gerald Early, *One Nation Under a Groove* (1995); and David Hajdu, *Positively 4th Street: The Lives and Times of Joan Baez, Bob Dylan, Mimi Baez Farina, and Richard Farina* (2001). Developments in an older style that also surged in popularity during the '60s are detailed in Bill C. Malone, *Country Music, USA* (1985).

Conservatism

A phenomenon of such influence during the 1960s and after is just beginning to gain recognition from historians. Pioneering works about conservative ideology and thinkers include George Nash, *The Conservative Intellectual Movement in America Since 1945* (1976), John B. Judis, *William F. Buckley, Jr.: Patron Saint of the Conservatives* (1988), and Patrick Allitt, *Catholic Intellectuals and Conservative Politics in America, 1950–1985* (1993). On the Right's growing clout in electoral politics, see Rick Perlstein, *Before the Storm: Barry Goldwater and the Unmaking of the American Consensus* (2001); Robert Alan Goldberg, *Barry Goldwater* (1995), Lou Cannon, *Reagan* (1982), and Mary C. Brennan, *Turning Right in the Sixties* (1995). On Young Americans for Freedom, see John A. Andrew III, *The Other Side of the Sixties* (1997); and Gregory L. Schneider, *Cadres for Conservatism* (1999). The best study of George Wallace is Dan T. Carter's *The Politics of Rage* (1995). On grassroots conservatism, see Ronald P. Formisano, *Boston Against Busing* (1991) and Lisa McGirr's *Suburban Warriors* about Orange Country, California (2001). On the motivations of activists on both edges of the political spectrum, see Rebecca Klatch, *A Generation Divided: The New Left, the New Right, and the 1960's* (1999).

Religion

Two overviews by Robert Wuthnow stand out from a welter of monographic works: *The Restructuring of American Religion* (1988) analyzes the waning of older, denominational divisions and the new split into liberal and conservative camps; while *After Heaven* (1998) explores the spiritual practices of Americans since the 1950s. A fine study that discusses the awakening of the '60s is William G. McLoughlin, Jr., *Revivals, Awakenings, and Reform* (1978). A brief but valuable study of evangelists is David Harrington Watt, *A Transforming Faith* (1991). Still enlightening is William G. McLoughlin, Jr.'s *Billy Graham* (1960). On the Catholic upheaval, see John T. McGreevy, *Parish Boundaries* (1996), and the relevant chapters in Jay Dolan, *The American Catholic Experience* (1985). The best survey of the Jewish revival is Edward S. Shapiro's *A Time for Healing* (1992). New Age religions are cogently analyzed in *The New Religious Consciousness*, edited Charles Y. Glock and Robert N. Bellah (1976) and Wade Clark Roof, *A Generation of Seekers* (1993).

Liberalism

Two valuable overviews of the history of liberalism in the 1960s can be found in Allen J. Matusow, *The Unravelling of America: A History of Liberalism in the 1960s* (1984) and David Steigerwald, *The Sixties and the End of Modern America* (1995). But the best sources on liberalism remain biographies. On John F. Kennedy, see Arthur Schlesinger, Jr.'s classic, *A Thousand Days: John F. Kennedy in the White House* (1965), and, from a very different perspective, Thomas C. Reeves, *A Question of Character: A Life of John F. Kennedy* (1991). For Lyndon Johnson, see Robert Dallek's excellent biography *Flawed Giant, Lyndon Johnson and His Times, 1961–1973* (1998), Doris Kearns's interesting combination of oral history and biography, *Lyndon Johnson and the American Dream* (1976); and Michael S. Beschloss, ed., *Taking Charge: The Johnson White House Tapes, 1963–1964*

(1997). Also see the engaging memoir by Kennedy and Johnson speechwriter Richard Goodwin, *Remembering America: A Voice from the Sixties* (1989). For an overview of liberal social policy in these years, see Irwin Unger *The Best of Intentions: The Triumph and Failure of the Great Society Under Kennedy, Johnson and Nixon* (1996); and Gareth Davies, *From Opportunity to Entitlement: The Transformation and Decline of Great Society Liberalism* (2000). For a critical history by a conservative scholar of one key figure in sixties liberalism, see Vincent J. Cannato, *The Ungovernable City: John L. Lindsay and his Struggle to Save New York City* (2001). For studies of advocacy groups and social movements associated with liberalism in the 1960s, see Steven Gillon, *Politics and Vision: The ADA and American Liberalism, 1947–1985* (1987); John D. Skrentny, *The Minority Rights Revolution,* (2002); Walter A. Jackson, *Gunnar Myrdal and America's Conscience: Social Engineering and Racial Liberalism, 1938–1987* (1990); William H. Chafe, *Never Stop Running: Allard Lowenstein and the Struggle to Save American Liberalism* (1993); Kevin Boyle, *The UAW and the Heyday of American Liberalism 1945–1968* (1995); Flora Davis, *Moving the Mountain: The Women's Movement in America Since 1960* (1991); Daniel Horowitz, *Betty Friedan and the Making of the Feminine Mystique: The American Left, the Cold War, and Modern Feminism* (1998); and Robert Gottlieb, *Forcing the Spring: The Transformation of the American Environmental Movement* (1993).

The New Left

The history of the New Left is increasingly contested terrain. One of the divisions in the field is between those old enough to have participated in the events they describe, and those who came along later. Among the former are works such as Todd Gitlin's lucid memoir/history *The Sixties: Years of Hope, Days of Rage* (1987), James Miller's *"Democracy Is in The Streets": From Port Huron to the Siege of Chicago* (1987), and Maurice Isserman's, *If I Had a Hammer, the Death of the Old Left and the Birth of the New Left* (1987). Among the rapidly increasing latter category, see David Farber's *Chicago '68* (1988) Douglas C. Rossinow's *The Politics of Authenticity: Liberalism, Christianity, and the New Left in America* (1998); and Rusty L. Monhollon, *"This is America?" The Sixties in Lawrence, Kansas* (2002). For an insightful essay on the New Left and its legacy, see Paul Berman, *A Tale of Two Utopias: The Political Journey of the Generation of 1968* (1996). Most of these authors, regardless of generation, are generally sympathetic to the motives and goals of the New left if not uncritical of where those motives and goals led the movement. For a thoroughly unsympathetic critique from a conservative perspective, see Peter Collier and David Horowitz, *Destructive Generation: Second Thoughts About the '60s* (1989). On the highly charged relationship between women and the New Left, see Sara Evans, *Personal Politics: The Roots of Women's Liberation in the Civil Rights Movement and the New Left* (1980), and Alice Echols, *Daring to Be Bad: Radical Feminism in America, 1967–1975* (1989). On what happened to New Leftists after the 1960s, see the important work by Jack Whalen and Richard Flacks, *Beyond the Barricades: The Sixties Generation Grows Up* (1989).

Vietnam

The best starting place for understanding the war in Vietnam is provided by the documents collected in Neil Sheehan et al., *The Pentagon Papers, as published in the New York Times* (New York: 1971). For a recent account that challenges the "inevitability" of the war, see Fredrik Logevall: *Choosing War: The Last Chance for Peace and*

The Escalation of the War in Vietnam (1999). Good overviews of the history of the war included Stanley Karnow, *Vietnam: A History* (1983), George Herring, *America's Longest War: The United States and Vietnam, 1950–1975* (1986), Marilyn Young, *The Vietnam Wars, 1945–1990* (1991), Robert D. Schulzinger, *A Time for War: The United States and Vietnam, 1941–1975* (1997), Loren Baritz, *Backfire: A History of How American Culture Led Us into Vietnam and Made Us Fight the Way We Did,* 2nd ed. (1998); and A. J. Langguth, *Our Vietnam: The War 1954–1975* (2000). Neil Sheehan's beautifully written combination of memoir, history, and biography, *A Bright Shining Lie: John Paul Vann and American in Vietnam* (1988), is in a class by itself. Also see correspondent Michael Herr's classic reflection on the war, *Dispatches* (1978), Robert S. McNamara's fascinating if problematic memoir, *In Retrospect: The Tragedy and Lessons of Vietnam* (1995), and his subsequent co-authored study, Robert S. McNamara, *et al., Argument Without End: In Search of Answers to the Vietnam Tragedy* (1999). For opposition to the war in Vietnam, see Tom Wells, *The War Within: America's Battle Over Vietnam* (1994) the essays in Melvin Small and William D. Hoover, eds., *Give Peace a Chance: Exploring the Vietnam Antiwar Memorial* (1992) and Daniel Ellsberg, *Secrets: A Memoir of Vietnam and the Pentagon Paper* (2002). On the experience of Vietnam veterans returning from the war, see Jerry Lembcke's provocative study *The Spitting Image: Myth, Memory and the Legacy of Vietnam* (1998).

The Nixon Presidency

The complex, tortured, and fascinating figure of Richard Nixon is a biographer's dream, as is evident in such works as Roger Morris, *Richard Milhous Nixon: The Rise of an American Politician* (1990), Tom Wicker, *One of Us: Richard Nixon and the American Dream* (1991), and Stephen E. Ambrose's exhaustive three-volume work, *Nixon: The Education of a Politician 1913–1962* (1987), *Nixon: The Triumph of a Politician, 1962–1972* (1990), and *Nixon: Ruin and Recovery, 1973–1990* (1991). Nixon's domestic policies as president are explored in Kenneth O'Reilly, *Nixon's Piano: Presidents and Racial Politics from Washington to Clinton* (1995), and Allen J. Matusow, *Nixon's Economy: Booms, Busts, Dollars, and Votes* (1998). For foreign policy during these years, see Seymour M. Hersh, *The Price of Power: Kissinger in the Nixon White House* (1983), and William Bundy, *A Tangled Web: The Making of Foreign Policy in the Nixon Presidency* (1998). The events leading to Nixon's downfall are chronicled in Stanley Kutler, *The Wars of Watergate: The Last Crisis of Richard Nixon* (1990), and documented in Nixon's own words in Stanley Kutler, ed., *Abuse of Power: The New Nixon Tapes* (1997). Michael Schudson provides a useful coda for the Nixon presidency in his fine study, *Watergate in American Memory: How We Remember, Forget, and Reconstruct the Past* (1992).

Notes

Introduction

1. Robert Penn Warren, *The Legacy of the Civil War* (New York: Random House, 1961), pp. 107–108.
2. Quoted in "Centennial of the Civil War . . . Business Booms Like the Gettysburg Cannon," *Newsweek,* March 27, 1961, p. 77.
3. H. N. Meyer, "Rally Round What Flag?" *Commonweal,* LXXIV (June 9, 1961), p. 271.
4. Quoted in Dan Wakefield, "Civil War Centennial: Bull Run with Popcorn," *Nation,* CXC (January 30, 1960), pp. 95–97. The Centennial Commission did, in the end, decide to mark the occasion of hundredth anniversary of the Emancipation Proclamation with a ceremony at the Lincoln Memorial. "Centennial Rites Hail Emancipator," *New York Times,* September 23, 1962, p. 1.
5. " 'Please Don't Start Another War,' " *Newsweek,* LVII (April 24, 1961), p. 40. Also see Thomas J. Pressly, *Americans Interpret Their Civil War,* 2nd ed. (New York: Free Press, 1965), p. 8.
6. Quoted in Dan T. Carter, *The Politics of Rage: George Wallace, the Origins of the New Conservatism, and the Transformation of American Politics* (New York: Simon & Schuster, 1995), p. 11.
7. Quoted in Dewey W. Grantham, *Recent America: The United States Since 1945* (Wheeling, IL: Harlan Davidson, 1998), p. 241.
8. Quoted in Stephen B. Oates, *Let the Trumpet Sound: The Life of Martin Luther King, Jr.* (New York: New American Library, 1982), p. 364.
9. Norman Mailer, *Miami and the Siege of Chicago* (New York: World Publishing Company, 1968), pp. 197–198.
10. James Reston, "War Leaves Deep Mark on U.S.," *New York Times,* January 24, 1973, p. 1.
11. Warren, *The Legacy of the Civil War,* pp. 3–4.

Chapter 1

1. Quoted in James MacGregor Burns, *The Crosswinds of Freedom* (New York: Knopf, 1989), p. 267.
2. As the historian Eric Hobsbawm puts it, "For 80 per cent of humanity the Middle Ages ended suddenly in the 1950s, or perhaps better still, they were *felt* to end in the 1960s." Hobsbawm, *The Age of Extremes: A History of the World, 1914–1991* (New York: Vintage Books, 1996), p. 288.
3. Quoted in James T. Patterson, *America's Struggle Against Poverty, 1900–1994* (Cambridge, MA: Harvard University Press, 1994), p. 113.
4. "Turn of the Decade," *New York Times,* January 3, 1960, p. 8E.
5. Quotes from Fred Siegel, *Troubled Journey: From Pearl Harbor to Reagan* (New York: Hill & Wang, 1984, p. 121; Hobsbawm, *The Age of Extremes,* p. 231.

6. James Baldwin, "Fifth Avenue, Uptown," originally published in *Esquire,* July 1960; reprinted in Baldwin, *The Price of the Ticket: Collected Nonfiction, 1948–1985* (New York: St. Martin's/Marek, 1985), p. 230.

7. John Patrick Diggins, *The Proud Decades: America in War and Peace, 1941–1960,* quoted in Robert Griffith, ed., *Major Problems in American History Since 1945* (Lexington, MA: D.C. Heath, 1992), p. 229; American Social History Project, *Who Built America?*, Vol. 2 (New York: Pantheon, 1992), p. 525.

8. Quoted in Kenneth T. Jackson, *Crabgrass Frontier: The Suburbanization of the United States* (New York: Oxford University Press, 1985), p. 231.

9. Quoted in Sara M. Evans, *Born for Liberty: A History of Women in America* (New York: Free Press, 1989), pp. 245–246.

10. Steven Mintz and Susan Kellogg, *Domestic Revolutions: A Social History of American Family Life* (New York: Free Press, 1988), pp. 199, 186; Marya Mannes, "Female Intelligence: Who Wants It?" *New York Times Magazine,* January 3, 1960, p. 48.

11. The loosening of puritanical mores extended to homosexuals as well. Gay bars were a commonplace of big city life, although many proprietors had to pay off the police to avoid harassment. The beginnings of a movement for what was then called "homophile rights" had appeared in the form of the Mattachine Society (for men) and the Daughters of Bilitis (for women). Both groups equated the cause of sexual liberty with the nation's struggle against "totalitarianism" abroad.

12. *Time,* January 18, 1960, pp. 75–76.

13. Quoted in American Social History Project, *Who Built America?*, Vol. 2, p. 519.

14. For these and other details, see *Statistical Abstract of the United States, 1961* (Washington, DC: Government Printing Office, 1961).

15. C. Wright Mills, *The Power Elite* (New York: Oxford University Press, 1956), p. 361; Mills, "Culture and Politics," in Gerald Howard, ed., *The Sixties* (New York: Washington Square Press, 1982), p. 78.

16. Quoted in Alonzo L. Hamby, *Liberalism and Its Challengers: F.D.R. to Reagan* (New York: Oxford University Press, 1985), p. 121.

17. Quoted in Kenneth O'Reilly, *"Racial Matters": The FBI's Secret File on Black America, 1960–1972* (New York: Free Press, 1989), p. 51.

18. Quoted in Godfrey Hodgson, *America in Our Time* (New York: Random House, 1976), p. 120.

19. Joseph Heller, *Catch-22* (New York: Simon & Schuster, 1961), p. 40.

20. Norman Mailer, "The White Negro," *Dissent,* IV (Summer 1957), pp. 276–292.

21. Quoted in Erik Barnouw, *Tube of Plenty: The Evolution of American Television,* 2nd rev. ed. (New York: Oxford University Press, 1990), p. 247.

22. Life, January 11, 1960, p. 83.

23. David M. Goldfield, *Black, White, and Southern: Race Relations and Southern Culture, 1940 to the Present* (Baton Rouge: Louisiana State University Press, 1990), pp. 111–112; *Washington Post,* issues of January 1960.

24. *Washington Post,* January 2, 1960, p. A9.

Chapter 2

1. James Hicks, quoted in Henry Hampton and Steve Fayer with Sarah Flynn, *Voices of Freedom: An Oral History of the Civil Rights Movement from the 1950s Through the 1980s* (New York: Bantam Books, 1990), p. xxiv.

2. Quoted from *Souls of Black Folk,* in David Levering Lewis, *W.E.B. DuBois: Biography of a Race, 1868–1919* (New York: Holt, 1993), p. 281.
3. Quoted in Jack Greenberg, *Crusaders in the Courts: How a Dedicated Band of Lawyers Fought for the Civil Rights Revolution* (New York: Basic Books, 1994), p. 118.
4. Kenneth Clark, "Racial Progress and Retreat: A Personal Memoir," in Herbert Hill and James E. Jones, Jr., eds, *Race in America: The Struggle for Equality* (Madison: University of Wisconsin Press, 1993), p. 13.
5. Quoted in Jules Tygiel, *Baseball's Great Experiment: Jackie Robinson and His Legacy* (New York: Oxford University Press, 1983), p. 302.
6. Quoted in Neil R. McMillen, *Dark Journey: Black Mississippians in the Age of Jim Crow* (Urbana: University of Illinois Press, 1989), p. 18.
7. Cited in David R. Goldfield, *Black, White, and Southern: Race Relations and Southern Culture, 1940 to the Present* (Baton Rouge: Louisiana State University Press, 1990), pp. 64, 73.
8. John Dittmer, *Local People: The Struggle for Civil Rights in Mississippi* (Urbana: University of Illinois Press, 1994), p. 7.
9. For examples, see Robin D. G. Kelley, "The Black Poor and the Politics of Opposition in a New South City, 1929–1970," in Michael B. Katz, ed., *The "Underclass" Debate: Views from History* (Princeton, NJ: Princeton University Press, 1993).
10. A good summary of these beliefs is James H. Cone, *A Black Theology of Liberation,* 2nd ed. (Maryknoll, NY: Orbis, 1986).
11. Quoted in Hampton and Fayer, *Voices of Freedom,* p. 19.
12. Quoted in Goldfield, *Black, White, and Southern,* p. 99.
13. Parts of this work and of his student papers were plagiarized, although it is likely that King didn't realize that he had committed a violation of the academic code. For a full discussion, from several viewpoints, see "Becoming Martin Luther King, Jr.—Plagiarism and Originality: A Round Table," *Journal of American History* LXXVIII (June 1991), pp. 11–123.
14. Quoted in Robert Weisbrot, *Freedom Bound: A History of America's Civil Rights Movement* (New York: Norton, 1990), p. 16.
15. Quoted in Goldfield, *Black, White, and Southern,* p. 102.
16. Quoted in David Alan Horowitz, "White Southerners' Alienation and Civil Rights: The Response to Corporate Liberalism," *Journal of Southern History* LV (May 1988), p. 178.
17. Goldfield, *Black, White, and Southern,* p. 87.
18. Quoted in William H. Chafe, *Civilities and Civil Rights: Greensboro, North Carolina, and the Black Struggle for Freedom* (New York: Oxford University Press, 1980), p. 16.
19. Chafe, *Civilities and Civil Rights,* pp. 93, 56.
20. Quoted in Chafe, *Civilities and Civil Rights,* p. 119.
21. Quoted in Clayborne Carson, *In Struggle: SNCC and the Black Awakening of the 1960s* (Cambridge, MA: Harvard University Press, 1981), p. 17.
22. Quoted in Taylor Branch, *Parting the Waters: America in the King Years, 1954–63* (New York: Simon & Schuster), p. 291.
23. Quoted in Hampton and Fayer, *Voices of Freedom,* p. 75.
24. Quoted in Kay Mills, *This Little Light of Mine: The Life of Fannie Lou Hamer* (New York: Dutton, 1993), p. 32.
25. Quoted in Weisbrot, *Freedom Bound,* p. 95.
26. Interview with Moses by Clayborne Carson, quoted by Dittmer, *Local People,* p. 104.

27. Quoted in Mills, *This Little Light of Mine*, p. 14.
28. Quoted in Bernice Johnson Reagon, "Women as Culture Carriers in the Civil Rights Movement: Fannie Lou Hamer," in Vicki L. Crawford, Jacqueline Anne Rouse, and Barbara Woods, eds., *Women in the Civil Rights Movement: Trailblazers and Torchbearers, 1941–1965* (Bloomington: Indiana University Press, 1993), p. 214.
29. Ralph Ellison, "Harlem is Nowhere," in Ellison, *Shadow and Act* (New York: Random House, 1964), p. 296.
30. Hansberry successfully concealed her lesbianism from a public she believed wasn't ready to accept that fact.
31. Ellison, "Harlem Is Nowhere," p. 298.
32. Nathan Glazer and Daniel P. Moynihan, *Beyond the Melting Pot*, 2nd ed. (Cambridge: MIT Press, 1970 [1963]), p. 55.
33. *South Deering Bulletin*, 1955, quoted in Arnold R. Hirsch, *Making the Second Ghetto: Race and Housing in Chicago, 1940–1960* (New York: Cambridge University Press, 1983), p. 211.
34. Quoted in Charles E. Silberman, *Crisis in Black and White* (NY: Random House, 1964), p. 46.
35. James Baldwin, "Fifth Avenue, Uptown," originally published in *Esquire*, July 1960; reprinted in Baldwin, *The Price of the Ticket: Collected Nonfiction, 1948–1985* (New York: St. Martin's/Marek, 1985), p. 210.
36. Quoted in C. Eric Lincoln and Lawrence H. Mamiya, *The Black Church in the African American Experience* (Durham, NC: Duke University Press, 1990), p. 361.
37. Baldwin, "Fifth Avenue, Uptown," in *The Price of the Ticket*, p. 210.
38. Quoted in Thomas L. Blair, *Retreat to the Ghetto: The End of a Dream?* (New York: Hill & Wang, 1977), p. xviii.
39. Quotes from Weisbrot, *Freedom Bound*, pp. 174, 175.

Chapter 3

1. Quoted in Richard Reeves, *President Kennedy: Profile of Power* (New York: Simon & Schuster, 1994), p. 100.
2. For thoughtful versions of this argument, see David Steigerwald, *The Sixties and the End of Modern America* (New York: St. Martin's Press, 1995), and Allen J. Matusow, *The Unravelling of America: A History of Liberalism in the 1960s* (New York: Harper & Row, 1984). For a more ideologically extravagant version of the same argument, see Myron Magnet, *The Dream and the Nightmare: The Sixties' Legacy to the Underclass* (New York: Morrow, 1993).
3. As the conservative policy analyst Charles Murray, no friend of the liberal tradition, would write: "In 1960 'liberal' connoted a forward-looking, problem-solving, pragmatic, sleeves-rolled-up stance toward the world." Murray, *Losing Ground: American Social Policy, 1950–1980* (New York: Basic Books, 1984), p. 22.
4. Arthur Schlesinger, Jr., *The Vital Center: The Politics of Freedom* (Boston: Houghton Mifflin, 1949), pp. 244, 250. For contrasting views of Schlesinger's career, see Michael Wreszin, "Arthur Schlesinger, Jr., Scholar–Activist in Cold War America: 1946–1956," *Salmagundi*, No. 63-6, 1984, pp. 255–285; and the essays in John Patrick Diggins, *The Liberal Persuasion: Arthur Schlesinger, Jr. and the Challenge of the American Past* (Princeton, NJ: Princeton University Press, 1997), especially the preface by Diggins and Michael Lind, "The Vital Historian," pp. 3–15. Also see Stephen P. Depoe, *Arthur M.*

Schlesinger, Jr., and the Ideological History of American Liberalism (Tuscaloosa: University of Alabama Press, 1994).

5. Arthur M. Schlesinger, Jr., *The Age of Jackson* (Boston: Little, Brown, 1945); *The Age of Roosevelt*, Vol. I, *The Crisis of the Old Order* (Boston: Houghton Mifflin, 1957), Vol. II, *The Coming of the New Deal* (Boston: Houghton Mifflin, 1959), Vol. III, *The Politics of Upheaval* (Boston: Houghton Mifflin, 1960).

6. Arthur Schlesinger, Jr., "The Challenge of Abundance," *The Reporter*, May 3, 1956, pp. 8–9. Also see, Depoe, *Arthur M. Schlesinger, Jr.*, pp. 33–38.

7. John Kenneth Galbraith, *The Affluent Society* (Boston: Houghton Mifflin, 1958), pp. 252–253.

8. John Keats, *The Crack in the Picture Window* (Boston: Houghton Mifflin, 1956); William H. Whyte, Jr., *The Organization Man* (New York: Simon & Schuster, 1956); Vance Packard, *The Hidden Persuaders* (New York: David McKay, 1957), *The Status Seekers* (New York: David McKay, 1959). Also see Daniel Horowitz, "Social Criticism in an Age of Conformity and Anxiety," in Horowitz, ed., *American Social Classes in the 1950s: Selections from Vance Packard's The Status Seekers* (Boston: Bedford Books, 1995), pp. 6–7.

9. Gunnar Myrdal, *An American Dilemma: The Negro Problem and Modern Democracy* (New York: Harper & Brothers, 1944), pp. 928–929 (emphasis in original). Also see Walter A. Jackson, *Gunnar Myrdal and America's Conscience: Social Engineeering and Racial Liberalism, 1938–1987* (Chapel Hill: University of North Carolina Press, 1990).

10. The black college students who launched the sit-in movement in Greensboro, North Carolina, in 1960 would cite Myrdal as one of the authors who had influenced their decision to challenge segregation in public facilities. Jackson, *Gunnar Myrdal*, p. 294.

11. Myrdal, *An American Dilemma*, pp. 1021–1022.

12. In the summer of 1960 Gallup pollsters asked the respondents in a polling sample to explain "what is meant by the terms 'liberal' and 'conservative.'" It turned out that a majority of those polled either said they didn't know or offered answers that were "generally incorrect." The pollsters then asked a second question of that minority of their sample—44 percent who could offer a "generally correct" definition of the two terms: "Suppose there were only two major parties in the United States, one for liberals and one for conservatives. Which one would you be most likely to prefer?" Opinion split nearly equally, with 43 percent choosing the liberal alternative, and 45 percent choosing the conservative alternative. *The Gallup Poll of Public Opinion, 1935–1971* (New York: Random House, 1972), p. 1673.

13. Thomas J. Sugrue probes these tensions in *The Origins of the Urban Crisis: Race and Inequality in Postwar Detroit* (Princeton, NJ: Princeton University Press, 1996).

14. David Brody, *Workers in Industrial America Essays on the 20th Century Struggle* (New York: Oxford University Press, 1980), pp. 229–230; Robert Zieger, *American Workers, American Unions, 1920–1985* (Baltimore, MD: Johns Hopkins University Press, 1986), pp. 137–167. Also see Samuel Lubell's classic account of postwar political transformation, *The Future of American Politics* (New York: Harper & Row, 1952).

15. Quoted in Zieger, *American Workers*, p. 174.

16. James Q. Wilson, *The Amateur Democrat: Club Politics in Three Cities* (Chicago: University of Chicago Press, 1962), p. 159 (emphasis in the original).

17. Quoted in Carolyn Heilbrun, *The Education of a Woman: The Life of Gloria Steinem* (New York: Dial Press, 1995), pp. 86–89.

18. William H. Chafe, *Never Stop Running: Allard Lowenstein and the Struggle to Save American Liberalism* (New York: Basic Books, 1993), pp. 104–105, 138–139.

19. The "typical reader" was also, in accordance with the cultural assumptions of the era, apparently a male. The report noted that about one quarter "of the subscribers' wives work"; whether any of the "wives" also read *The New Republic* was a question the magazine neglected to ask.

20. "Find the Typical Reader," *New Republic*, CIIL (May 18, 1963), pp. 5–6. In 1963 the magazine had over 83,000 readers.

21. A quarter of the magazine's readers lived in New York, Connecticut, New Jersey and Massachusetts (readers in Mississippi, in contrast, accounted for 0.2 percent of *New Republic* subscribers).

22. The term "conscience constituency" was coined in 1965 by Michael Harrington in "Pragmatists and Utopians: The New Radicalism," *Commonweal*, LXXXII (September 3, 1965), p. 627. For "new class" see David T. Bazelon, *Power in America: The Politics of the New Class* (New York: New American Library, 1967).

23. Jane Jacobs, *The Life and Death of Great American Cities* (New York: Random House, 1961); Rachel Carson, *Silent Spring* (Boston: Houghton Mifflin, 1962); Betty Friedan, *The Feminine Mystique* (New York: Norton, 1963); Ralph Nader, *Unsafe at Any Speed: The Designed-In Dangers of the American Automobile* (New York: Grossman, 1965).

24. John Dewey, *The Public and Its Problems* (New York: Holt, 1927), p. 184.

25. Quoted in David Burner, *John F. Kennedy and a New Generation* (Glenview, IL: Scott, Foresman, 1988), p. 10. Useful biographies of Kennedy include Garry Wills, *The Kennedy Imprisonment: A Meditation on Power* (Boston: Little Brown, 1981); Thomas C. Reeves, *A Question of Character: A Life of John F. Kennedy* (New York: Free Press, 1991), and Hugh Brogan, *Kennedy* (London: Longman, 1996).

26. David Halberstam, *The Best and the Brightest* (New York: Random House, 1972), p. 121.

27. Norman Mailer, "Superman Comes to the Supermarket," originally published in *Esquire*, November 1960, reprinted in Gerald Howard, ed., *The Sixties* (New York: Washington Square Press, 1982), p. 158.

28. Halberstam, *The Best and the Brightest*, pp. 11–14.

29. Schlesinger quoted in Steven Gillon, *Politics and Vision: The ADA and American Liberalism, 1947–1985* (New York: Oxford University Press, 1987), p. 135. Also see Matusow, *The Unravelling of America*, p. 16.

30. Kennedy quoted in Arthur Schlesinger, Jr., *A Thousand Days: John F. Kennedy in the White House* (Boston: Houghton Mifflin, 1965), pp. 1005–1006.

31. Taylor Branch, *Parting the Waters: America in the King Years 1954–63* (New York: Simon & Schuster, 1988), pp. 357–374. Also see Irving Bernstein, *Promises Kept: John F. Kennedy's New Frontier* (New York: Oxford University Press, 1991), pp. 28–30, 34–35; James Sundquist, *Politics and Policy: The Eisenhower, Kennedy, and Johnson Years* (Washington, DC: The Brookings Institution, 1968), pp. 33–34; and Matusow, *The Unravelling of America*, pp. 25–28.

32. Quoted in Schlesinger, *A Thousand Days*, p. 733.

33. Quoted in Halberstam, *The Best and the Brightest*, p. 77.

34. D. Halberstam, *The Best and the Brightest*.

35. Ronald E. Powaski, *March to Armageddon: The United States and the Nuclear Arms Race, 1939 to the Present* (New York: Oxford University Press, 1987), p. 93; Andreas Wenger, *Living with Peril: Eisenhower, Kennedy, and Nuclear Weapons* (New York: Rowman and Littlefield, 1997), pp. 248–255.

36. Quoted in Walter A. McDougall, . . . *The Heavens and the Earth: A Political History of the Space Age* (New York: Basic Books, 1985), p. 303.

37. Quoted in Stanley Karnow, *Vietnam: A History* (New York: Viking Press, 1983), p. 248.
38. Trumbull Higgins, *The Perfect Failure: Kennedy, Eisenhower, and the CIA at the Bay of Pigs* (New York: Norton, 1987).
39. Hugh Brogan, *Kennedy*, pp. 126–129.
40. On the Cuban missile crisis, see A. A. Fursenko and Timothy Naftali, *One Hell of a Gamble: Khrushchev, Castro, and Kennedy, 1958–1964* (New York: Norton, 1997), and Mark J. White, *Missiles in Cuba: Kennedy, Khrushchev, Castro, and the 1962 Crisis* (Chicago: Ivan R. Dee, 1997).
41. Quoted in Gillon, *Politics and Vision*, p. 143.
42. Dewey W. Grantham, *Recent America: The United States Since 1945* (Arlington Heights, IL: Harlan Davidson, 1987), p. 240; Gillon, *Politics and Vision*, p. 148.
43. Sundquist, *Politics and Policy*, pp. 34–40. Kennedy had already given business tax breaks in the form of generous investment credits and deprecation allowances in the Revenue Act of 1962, but had not cut taxes for individual taxpayers.
44. Irwin Unger, *The Best of Intentions: The Triumph and Failure of the Great Society Under Kennedy, Johnson and Nixon* (New York: Doubleday, 1996), pp. 30–31. Congress also rejected or refused to consider other Kennedy proposals for domestic spending on behalf of migrant workers, unemployed youth, and public transportation. William Chafe, *The Unfinished Journey: America Since World War II* (New York: Oxford University Press, 1995), p. 193.
45. Flora Davis, *Moving the Mountain: The Women's Movement in America Since 1960* (New York: Simon & Schuster, 1991), pp. 34–38.

Chapter 4

1. Quoted in Mieczyslaw Maneli, *War of the Vanquished* (New York: Harper & Row, 1971), p. 154.
2. The account that follows draws upon Stanley Karnow, *Vietnam: A History* (New York: Viking Press, 1983); George Herring, *America's Longest War: The United States and Vietnam, 1950–1975* (New York: Knopf, 1986); Neil Sheehan, *A Bright Shining Lie: John Paul Vann and America in Vietnam* (New York: Random House, 1988); Marilyn Young, *The Vietnam Wars, 1945–1990* (New York: HarperCollins, 1991); Robert D. Schulzinger, *A Time for War: The United States and Vietnam, 1941–1975* (New York: Oxford University Press, 1997); and other sources as noted.
3. Quoted in Gareth Porter, ed., *Vietnam: The Definitive Documentation of Human Decisions*, Vol. I (Stanfordville, NY: Earl M. Coleman Enterprises, 1979), pp. 64–65.
4. Quoted in Porter, *Vietnam*, Vol. I, p. 11.
5. Quoted in Stephen E. Ambrose, *Rise to Globalism: American Foreign Policy Since 1938*, 7th rev. ed. (New York: Penguin Books, 1993), p. 75.
6. Quoted in Porter, *Vietnam*, Vol. I, p. 95.
7. Quoted in Karnow, *Vietnam*, p. 189.
8. Quoted in A.J. Langguth, *Our Vietnam: The War 1954–1975* (New York: Simon and Schuster, 2000), p. 70.
9. Dwight Eisenhower, *The White House Years*, Vol. 1, *Mandate for Change, 1953–1956* (Garden City, NY: Doubleday, 1963), p. 372.
10. *Dwight D. Eisenhower, Public Papers* Vol. 3. (Washington, D.C.: U.S. Govt. Printing Office 1955), pp. 382–384.
11. Neil Sheehan, et al., *Pentagon Papers* (New York: Bantam Books, 1971), p. 25.
12. Quoted in Young, *The Vietnam Wars*, p. 58.

13. Quoted in Harry Maurer, *Strange Ground: Americans in Vietnam, 1945–1975: An Oral History* (New York: Henry Holt, 1989), pp. 85–86.
14. Joseph Alsop, "A Man in a Mirror," *New Yorker*, June 25, 1955, quoted in Young, *Vietnam Wars*, p. 55.
15. Schulzinger, *A Time for War*, pp. 92–96.
16. Quoted in Karnow, *Vietnam*, p. 248.
17. Quoted in Porter, *Vietnam*, Vol. II, p. 134.
18. E. W. Kenworthy, "Kennedy Warns Buddhist Dispute Imperils Vietnam," *New York Times,* September 3, 1963, p. 1.
19. Quoted in Young, *The Vietnam Wars*, p. 94.
20. Quoted in Karnow, *Vietnam*, p. 249.
21. David Halberstam, *The Best and the Brightest*, (New York: Random House, 1972), pp. 123–124.
22. Michael Herr, *Dispatches* (New York: Avon Books, 1978), p. 61.
23. Quoted in Howard Zinn, *Vietnam: The Logic of Withdrawal* (Boston: Beacon Press, 1967), p. 48.
24. Tom Mangold and John Penycate, *The Tunnels of Cu Chi* (New York: Random House, 1985), pp. 61–65.
25. Quoted in Karnow, *Vietnam*, p. 406. Viet Cong numbers and weaponry are described in Eric M. Bergerud, *The Dynamics of Defeat: The Vietnam War in Hau Nghia Province* (Boulder, CO: Westview Press, 1991), pp. 93–95.
26. Kenneth Babbs quoted in John Clark Pratt, ed., *Vietnam Voices: Perspectives on the War Years, 1941–1982* (New York: Penguin Books, 1984), pp. 115–116.
27. Quoted in Porter, *Vietnam*, Vol. II, pp. 141–142.
28. Robert McNamara, *In Retrospect, the Tragedy and Lessons of Vietnam* (New York: Random House, 1995), pp. 38–39, 41.
29. Quoted in Neil Sheehan, *A Bright Shining Lie*, p. 290.
30. Arthur M. Schlesinger, Jr., *A Thousand Days: John F. Kennedy in the White House* (Boston: Houghton Mifflin, 1965), p. 547.
31. Robert S. McNamara, et al., *Argument Without End: In Search of Answers to the Vietnam Tragedy* (New York: Public Affairs, 1999), p. 378.

Chapter 5

1. Quoted in Taylor Branch, *Parting the Waters: America in the King Years, 1954–63* (New York: Simon & Schuster, 1988), p. 734.
2. *The Gallup Poll*, Public Opinion 1935–1971, Vol. III (New York: Random House, 1971), p. 1800.
3. Quoted in Stephen E. Ambrose, *Nixon: The Triumph of a Politician, 1962–1972* (New York: Simon & Schuster, 1989), p. 11.
4. Richard Reeves, *President Kennedy: Profile of Power* (New York: Simon & Schuster, 1993), p. 461.
5. *The Kennedy Presidential Press Conferences* (Stanfordville, NY: Earl M. Coleman Enterprises, 1978), p. 416.
6. Quoted in Neil Sheehan, *A Bright Shining Lie: John Paul Vann and America in Vietnam* (New York: Random House, 1988), p. 204.
7. Quoted in Stanley Karnow, *Vietnam: A History* (New York: Viking Press, 1983), p. 261.
8. Quoted in Sheehan, *A Bright Shining Lie*, p. 259.

9. Sheehan, *A Bright Shining Lie*, p. 265.
10. Dan T. Carter, *The Politics of Rage: George Wallace, the Origins of the New Conservatism, and the Transformation of American Politics* (New York: Simon & Schuster, 1995), p. 479, note 29.
11. Quoted in Carter, *The Politics of Rage*, p. 85.
12. Quoted in David Garrow, *Bearing the Cross: Martin Luther King, Jr. and the Southern Christian Leadership Conference* (New York: Morrow, 1986), p. 227.
13. Quoted in Branch, *Parting the Waters*, p. 692.
14. Quoted in Garrow, *Bearing the Cross*, p. 239.
15. Branch, *Parting the Waters*, p. 757.
16. Quoted (without attribution) in Richard Reeves, *President Kennedy*, p. 487.
17. "Letter from a Birmingham Jail," in Thomas R. West and James W. Mooney, eds., *To Redeem a Nation: A History and Anthology of the Civil Rights Movement* (St. James, NY: Brandywine Press, 1993), pp. 119–20.
18. Quoted in Branch, *Parting the Waters*, p. 793.
19. Quoted in Carter, *Politics of Rage*, p. 149, and Branch, *Parting the Waters*, pp. 821–822.
20. Quoted in Carter, *Politics of Rage*, p. 156.
21. Quotes from Branch, *Parting the Waters*, p. 824.
22. Quoted in Carter, *Politics of Rage*, p. 154.
23. On Hoover's campaign against King, see David Garrow, *The FBI and Martin Luther King, Jr.: from "Solo" to Memphis* (New York: W.W. Norton, 1981), passim. On Robert Kennedy's role in King's wiretapping, see Evan Thomas, *Robert Kennedy, His Life* (New York: Simon and Schuster, 2000), pp. 259–264.
24. On the Detroit march, see Suzanne E. Smith *Dancing in the Street: Motown and the Cultural Politics of Detroit*, (Cambridge: Harvard University Press, 1999). Branch, *Parting the Waters*, 842–3.
25. Quotes from Peter Guralnick, *Last Train to Memphis: The Rise of Elvis Presley* (Boston: Little Brown, 1994), pp. 253, 437.
26. Dave Marsh, *The Heart of Rock & Soul: The 1001 Greatest Singles Ever Made* (New York: New American Library, 1989), p. 333.
27. Quoted in Smith, " 'Dancing in the Street'," p. 22.
28. "Heat Wave" quoted in Marsh, *Heart of Rock & Soul*, p. 38.
29. Bob Dylan, "Song to Woody," in Dylan, *Lyrics, 1962–1985* (New York: Knopf, 1990), p. 6. Copyright Dutchess Music Corp., 1965.
30. Bob Dylan, "A Hard Rain's A-Gonna Fall," in *Lyrics*, p. 59.
31. Quoted in Anthony Scaduto, *Bob Dylan* (New York: New American Library, 1971), p. 160.
32. Quoted in Scaduto, *Bob Dylan*, p. 177.
33. Quoted in Karnow, *Vietnam*, 289. The main source for this section is Ellen J. Hammer, *A Death in November: America in Vietnam, 1963* (New York: Dutton, 1987).
34. Quoted in Karnow, *Vietnam*, p. 289. The most complete study of Diem's overthrow is Hammer's *A Death in November*.
35. Quoted in Hammer, p. 288.
36. Quoted in Hammer, p. 300, 301.
37. Quoted in Jim Bishop, *The Day Kennedy Was Shot* (New York: Funk & Wagnalls, 1968), p. 25.
38. Quoted in Gerald Posner, *Case Closed: Lee Harvey Oswald and the Assassination of JFK* (New York: Random House, 1993), p. 233.

39. Bruce Catton, Introduction, *Four Days: The Historical Record of the Death of President Kennedy*, compiled by United Press International and American Heritage Magazine (no city: American Heritage and UPI, 1964), pp. 3, 5.

40. For a brief guide to conspiracy theories by one of the more perceptive sleuths, see Carl Oglesby, *The JFK Assassination: The Facts and the Theories* (New York: Penguin Books, 1992).

41. For this detail and a provocative argument that Oswald, acting alone, killed Kennedy to revenge the administration's attempts to topple Castro, see Max Holland, "After Thirty Years: Making Sense of the Assassination," *Reviews in American History*, XXII (June 1994), pp. 191–209.

42. Quoted in Bishop, *The Day Kennedy Was Shot*, pp. 225–226.

Chapter 6

1. Quoted in "Oral Histories of the Johnson Administration," University Publications of America Microfiche, Part I, # 4, interview with John Roche.

2. Quoted in Robert Dallek, *Flawed Giant, Lyndon Johnson and His Times, 1961–1973* (New York: Oxford University Press, 1998), p. 56.

3. Quoted in Dallek, *Flawed Giant,* p. 54.

4. Theodore H. White, *The Making of the President, 1964* (New York: Atheneum Publishers, 1965), p. 57.

5. Many years later, Johnson would speak candidly to interviewer Doris Kearns about his fears in 1964 of being regarded as a usurper in the White House, "a naked man with no presidential covering." See Doris Kearns, *Lyndon Johnson and the American Dream* (New York: Harper & Row, 1976), p. 177.

6. Quoted in David Steigerwald, *The Sixties and the End of Modern America* (New York: St. Martin's Press, 1995), p. 23. Also see Richard Goodwin, *Remembering America: A Voice from the Sixties* (Boston: Little, Brown, 1989), p. 243.

7. This biographical sketch of Johnson's background draws upon Robert Caro, *The Years of Lyndon Johnson: The Path to Power* (New York: Knopf, 1982); Robert Dallek, *Lone Star Rising: Lyndon Johnson and His Times, 1908–1960* (New York: Oxford University Press, 1991); Dallek, *Flawed Giant;* and Kearns, *Lyndon Johnson and the American Dream.*

8. Quoted in Caro, *The Path to Power,* p. 271.

9. Quoted in Bruce J. Schulman, *Lyndon B. Johnson and American Liberalism: A Brief Biography with Documents* (Boston: Bedford Books, 1995), p. 19. Roosevelt doubtless meant the "first Southern President" since the Civil War; not counting the southern-born but northern-residing Woodrow Wilson, the last president to come from the South had been Zachary Taylor.

10. Quoted in Dallek, *Flawed Giant,* p. 12.

11. Quoted in Kearns, *Lyndon Johnson and the American Dream,* p. 178.

12. Quoted in John Lewis, *Walking with the Wind: A Memoir of the Movement* (New York: Simon & Schuster, 1998), p. 240.

13. Dallek, *Flawed Giant,* pp. 38, 111–120. The circumstances that led to women's rights being enshrined in the 1964 civil rights bill are described in Flora Davis, *Moving the Mountain: The Womens' Movement in America Since 1960* (New York: Simon & Schuster, 1991), p. 43.

14. The discussion of the war on poverty that follows is drawn from Daniel Patrick Moynihan, *Maximum Feasible Misunderstanding: Community Action in the War on Poverty*

(New York: Free Press, 1969); Allen J. Matusow, *The Unravelling of America: A History of Liberalism in the 1960s* (New York: Harper & Row, 1984), pp. 217–271; Nicholas Lemann, *The Promised Land: The Great Black Migration and How It Changed America* (New York: Knopf, 1991), pp. 111–221; and Irwin Unger, *The Best of Intentions: The Triumph and Failure of the Great Society Under Kennedy, Johnson and Nixon* (New York: Doubleday, 1996).

15. Michael Harrington, *The Other America* (New York: Macmillan, 1962), pp. 10, 14, 159.

16. Whether Kennedy actually read *The Other America*—or just read a review of it that appeared in *The New Yorker*—remains in dispute. For differing accounts, see, for example, Arthur Schlesinger, Jr., *A Thousand Days: John F. Kennedy in the White House* (Boston: Houghton Mifflin, 1965), p. 1010, and Lemann, *The Promised Land*, p. 131.

17. Quoted in John Morton Blum, *Years of Discord: American Politics and Society, 1961–1973* (New York: Norton, 1991), p. 149.

18. Quoted in Dallek, *Flawed Giant*, p. 75.

19. Quoted in Michael R. Beschloss, ed., *Taking Charge: The Johnson White House Tapes, 1963–1964* (New York: Simon & Schuster, 1997), p. 211.

20. James L. Sundquist, "Origins of the War on Poverty," in Sundquist, ed., *On Fighting Poverty, Perspectives from Experience* (New York: Basic Books, 1969), pp. 26–27. Johnson quoted in Lemann, *The Promised Land*, p. 149.

21. John Kenneth Galbraith, *The Affluent Society* (Boston: Houghton Mifflin, 1958), p. 198.

22. Michael L. Gillette, ed., *Launching the War on Poverty: An Oral History* (New York: Twayne Publishers, 1996), p. xiii; Polenberg, *One Nation Divisible*, pp. 194–195. For typical coverage from the period, see, for example, the cover of the special issue of *Newsweek* devoted to exploring "Poverty USA," *Newsweek*, February 17, 1964.

23. Harry M. Caudill, *Night Comes to the Cumberlands: A Biography of a Depressed Area* (Boston: Little Brown, 1963), p. vii. On the influence of Caudill's book, see Schlesinger, *A Thousand Days*, p. 1007.

24. *The Gallup Poll of Opinion, 1935–1971* (New York: Random House, 1972), p. 1870.

25. Quoted in Goodwin, *Remembering America*, p. 278.

26. *Remembering America*, p. 281.

27. Quoted in White, *The Making of the President, 1964*, pp. 371–372.

28. Quoted in David Halberstam, *The Best and the Brightest* (New York: Random House, 1972), p. 305.

29. National Security Action Memorandum No. 273 by McGeorge Bundy, November 26, 1963, in *Pentagon Papers*, p. 233.

30. Memorandum, "Vietnam Situation," from Secretary of Defense Robert S. McNamara to President Lyndon B. Johnson, Dec. 21, 1963, in *Pentagon Papers*, p. 271.

31. Memorandum, "South Vietnam," from Secretary of Defense McNamara to President Johnson, March 16, 1964, p. 279.

32. Michael R. Beschloss, ed., *Taking Charge: The Johnson White House Tapes, 1963–1964* (New York: Simon and Schuster, 1997), pp. 95, 363–370.

33. Quoted in Stanley Karnow, *Vietnam: A History* (New York: Viking Press, 1983), p. 325.

34. Quoted in Marilyn Young, *The Vietnam Wars, 1945–1990* (New York: HarperCollins, 1991), p. 118.

35. Halberstam, *The Best and the Brightest*, p. 422.

36. Quoted in Karnow, *Vietnam*, p. 374.

37. Quoted in Michael Hunt, *Lyndon Johnson's War: American's Cold War Crusade in Vietnam, 1945–1968* (New York: Hill and Wang, 1996), p. 85.

38. Gulf of Tonkin resolution, August 7, 1964, quoted in Gareth Porter, *Vietnam: The Definitive Documentation of Human Decisions*. Vol. II (Stanfordville, NY: Earl M. Coleman Enterprises, 19), p. 307.

39. Quoted in *Pentagon Papers*, p. 311.

40. Quoted in Unger, *The Best of Intentions*, p. 104.

41. Quoted in Dallek, *Flawed Giant*, p. 198.

42. Michael Harrington, "Afterword," *The Other America* (New York: Penguin Books, 1981) pp. 208–209; Unger, *The Best of Intentions*, pp. 109–116, 204; James T. Patterson, *America's Struggle Against Poverty, 1900–1985* (Cambridge, MA: Harvard University Press, 1986), p. 167.

43. Quoted in Patterson, *American's Struggle Against Poverty*, p. 134.

44. Patterson, *America's Struggle Against Poverty*, pp. 117–128, 139–144.

45. The discussion of the Supreme Court that follows is based, except where otherwise noted, on Morton J. Horwitz, *The Warren Court and the Pursuit of Justice* (New York: Hill & Wang, 1998).

46. On importance of the concept of "rights" in American history and to American identity see Daniel T. Rodgers, *Contested Truths: Keywords in American Politics Since Independence* (New York: Basic Books, 1987), pp. 45–79, and Mary Ann Glendon, *Rights Talk: The Impoverishment of Political Discourse* (New York: Free Press, 1991), pp. 1–17.

47. On Earl Warren's career, see Jack Harrison Pollack, *Earl Warren: The Judge Who Changed America* (Englewood Cliffs, NJ: Prentice-Hall, 1979).

48. Jacqueline Van Voris, *Carrie Chapman Catt: A Public Life* (New York: Feminist Press, 1987), p. 153.

49. The ACLU was an exception to this rule. In the early 1950s its leaders began a membership drive that expanded the organization from 10,000 members to more than five times that number between 1951 and 1960. In the ACLU's case, McCarthyism was actually a spur toward rather than a detriment to expansion. On ACLU membership figures, see Samuel Walker, *In Defense of American Liberties: A History of the ACLU* (New York: Oxford University Press, 1990), pp. 206–207, 262. For the Sierra Club, see Michael Cohen, *The History of the Sierra Club, 1892–1970* (San Francisco: Sierra Club Books, 1988), p. 275. ADA membership statistics are from Steven Gillon, *Politics and Vision: The ADA and American Liberalism, 1947–1985* (New York: Oxford University Press, 1987), p. 107. For SANE, see Lawrence S. Wittner, *Rebels Against War: The American Peace Movement, 1933–1983* (New York: Columbia University Press, 1969), pp. 257–260. And for the NAACP, see Martin N. Marger, "Social Movement Organizations and Response to Environmental Change: The NAACP, 1960–1973," *Social Problems*, XXXII (October 1984), p. 23.

50. Walker, *In Defense of American Liberties*, pp. 262–263.

51. Cohen, *History of the Sierra Club*, pp. 362, 395–434, 442.

52. For the impact of the 1960s on the environmental movement, see Robert Gottlieb, *Forcing the Spring: The Transformation of the American Environmental Movement* (Washington, DC: Island Press, 1993). For the Santa Barbara oil spill, see Hal K. Rothman, *The Greening of a Nation? Environmentalism in the United States Since 1945* (Fort Worth, TX: Harcourt Brace College Publishers, 1998), pp. 101–105.

53. Chavez is quoted in American Social History Project, *Who Built America?*, Vol. 2 (New York: Pantheon, 1992), p. 565. Other good sources on the farmerworkers include Robert B. Taylor, *Chavez and the Farm Workers* (Boston: Beacon Press, 1975), and Jacques Levy, *Cesar Chavez: Autobiography of La Causa* (New York: Norton, 1975).

54. Quoted in *Who Built America?*, p. 565.

55. Daniel Horowitz, *Betty Friedan and the Making of the Feminine Mystique: The American Left, the Cold War, and Modern Feminism* (Amherst: University of Massachusetts Press, 1998), p. 217.

56. Betty Friedan, *The Feminine Mystique* (New York: Norton, 1963), p. 378.

57. Davis, *Moving the Mountain*, p. 46.

58. On the growth of the women's movement from the mid-Sixties through the early Seventies see Sara Evans, *Personal Politics: The Roots of Women's Liberation in the Civil Rights Movement and the New Left* (New York: Vintage Books, 1980), and Alice Echols, *Daring to Be Bad: Radical Feminism in America, 1967–1975* (Minneapolis: University of Minnesota Press, 1989).

59. Goodwin, *Remembering America*, p. 543.

60. Michael Harrington, *Toward a Democratic Left: A Radical Program for a New Majority* (New York: Macmillan, 1968), p. 270.

Chapter 7

1. "1965: The Prime Task," *The Nation*, January 11, 1965, p. 21.

2. Kenneth Crawford, "Most Hopeful Times," *Newsweek*, January 4, 1965, p. 19.

3. Doris Kearns, *Lyndon Johnson and the American Dream* (New York: Harper & Row, 1976), p. 170.

4. Kearns, *Lyndon Johnson and the American Dream*, p. 1959.

5. "Set for a Fifth Fat Year," *Business Week*, January, 2, 1965, pp. 11, 13; Robert M. Collins, "Growth Liberalism in the Sixties," in David Farber, ed., *The Sixties: From Memory to History* (Chapel Hill: University of North Carolina Press, 1994), p. 19.

6. *The Military Balance: 1965–1966* (London: Institute for Strategic Studies, 1966), pp. 23–27.

7. *The Gallup Poll, Public Opinion 1935–1971*, Vol. III (New York: Random House, 1972), p. 1924.

8. Quoted in Ronald Steel, *Walter Lippmann and the American Century* (Boston: Little, Brown, 1980), p. 556.

9. "Plan of Action for South Vietnam," September 3, 1964, quoted in Neil Shoehan, et al. *Pentagon Papers* (New York: Bantam Books, 1971), pp. 355–356.

10. Quoted in Robert Dallek, *Flawed Giant, Lyndon Johnson and His Times, 1961–1973* (New York: Oxford University Press, 1998), p. 243.

11. Quoted in Stanley Karnow, *Vietnam: A History* (New York: Viking Press, 1983), p. 405.

12. Quoted in Larry Berman, *Planning a Tragedy: The Americanization of the War in Vietnam* (New York: Norton, 1982), p. 37.

13. Quoted in Fredrik Logevall, *Choosing War: The Lost Chance for Peace and the Escalation of War in Vietnam* (Berkeley: University of California Press, 1999), p. 347.

14. Quoted in Karnow, *Vietnam*, p. 415.

15. Robert S. McNamara, *In Retrospect: The Tragedy and Lessons of Vietnam* (New York: Random House, 1995), p. 174.

16. Dallek, *Flawed Giant*, p. 257.

17. Quoted in Dallek, *Flawed Giant*, p. 243.

18. Christian G. Appy, *Working-Class War: American Combat Soldiers and Vietnam* (Chapel Hill: University of North Carolina Press, 1993), pp. 155, 182–183.

19. Appy, *Working-Class War*, p. 37.

20. Quoted in *Pentagon Papers*, p. 432.

21. Quoted in John Lewis, *Walking with the Wind: A Memoir of the Movement* (New York: Simon & Schuster, 1998), p. 328.

22. David Garrow, *Protest at Selma: Martin Luther King, Jr., and the Voting Rights Act of 1965* (New Haven, CT: Yale University Press, 1978), pp. 31–34.

23. Garrow, *Protest at Selma*, p. 134. Also see Kearns, *Lyndon Johnson and the American Dream*, p. 228.

24. Howard Zinn, *SNCC: The New Abolitionists* (Boston: Beacon Press, 1964), p. 147.

25. Quoted in Garrow, *Protest at Selma*, p. 39.

26. Quoted in Howell Raines, *My Soul Is Rested: The Story of the Civil Rights Movement in the Deep South* (New York: Penguin Books, 1983), p. 200.

27. David Garrow analyzed SCLC's shift from a strategy of "nonviolent persuasion" to what he described one of "nonviolent provocation" in *Protest at Selma*, pp. 212–236.

28. The account that follows draws upon Garrow's *Protest at Selma*, passim, and his *Bearing the Cross: Martin Luther King, Jr. and the Southern Christian Leadership Conference* (New York: Morrow, 1986), pp. 357–430, as well as Taylor Branch, *Parting the Waters: America in the King Years: 1954–63* (New York: Simon & Schuster, 1988), pp. 552–613, and other sources as noted.

29. Quoted in *Flawed Giant*, p. 217. Also see Dan Carter, *The Politics of Rage: George Wallace, the Origins of the New Conservatism, and the Transformation of American Politics*, (New York: Simon & Schuster, 1995), pp. 253–254.

30. Quoted in Garrow, *Bearing the Cross,* pp. 408–409.

31. Gallup Poll, pp. 1933–1934.

32. The southern newspaper editor Hodding Carter expressed his dismay at the use of the Confederate flag as a symbol of resistance to civil rights in "Furl That Banner?" *New York Times Magazine*, July 25, 1965, p. 8.

33. Carter, *Politics of Rage*, pp. 108–109.

34. Quoted in Lewis, *Walking with the Wind*, p. 346.

35. Michael Harrington, "A New Populism," *New York Herald Tribune*, March 28, 1965, p. 24.

36. Allen J. Matusow, *The Unravelling of America: A History of Liberalism in the 1960s* (New York: Harper & Row, 1984), pp. 187–188.

37. Quoted in Thomas Byrne Edsall and Mary D. Edsall, *Chain Reaction: The Impact of Race, Rights, and Taxes on American Politics* (New York: Norton, 1991), p. 37.

38. Theodore White, *The Making of the President, 1964* (New York: Atheneum Publishers, 1965), p. 304.

39. Harrington, "A New Populism,"p. 24.

40. Quoted in Richard Hofstadter and Michael Wallace, eds. *Violence in America: A Documentary History* (New York: Knopf, 1970), pp. 264–265.

41. *Violence in the City–An End or a Beginning?* (Los Angeles: Governor's Commission on the Los Angeles Riots, 1965), p. 1; Gerald Horne, *Fire This Time: The Watts Uprising and the 1960s* (Charlottesville: University Press of Virginia, 1995), p. 3.

42. "Races: Trigger of Hate," *Time*, August 20, 1965, p. 13.

43. Quoted in Horne, *Fire This Time*, p. 281.

44. Edward C. Banfield, *The Unheavenly City: The Nature and Future of Our Urban Crisis* (Boston: Little Brown, 1970), p. 196.

45. Quoted in Hofstadter and Wallace, eds., *Violence in America*, pp. 264–265.

46. *Washington Post,* October 4, 1965, p. A7.

47. Quoted in *Immigration and National Act with Notes and Related Laws* (Washington, DC: Government Printing Office, 1995), p. 585.

48. Quoted in Ruben Rumbaut, "Passages to America: Perspectives on the New Immigration," in Alan Wolfe, ed., *America at Century's End* (Berkeley: University of California Press, 1991), p. 190.

49. *Washington Post,* October 4, 1965, p. 1.
50. The best accounts of the Ia Drang Valley battle can be found in Lt. Gen. Harold G. Moore (Ret.) and Joseph L. Galloway, *We Were Soldiers Once . . . And Young, Ia Drang: The Battle That Changed the War in Vietnam* (New York: Random House, 1992), and in Harry G. Summers, Jr., "The Bitter Triumph of Ia Drang, *American Heritage,* XXXV (February 1984), pp. 50–58.
51. Quoted in Moore and Galloway, *We Were Soldiers Once . . . ,* p. 339. Also see McNamara, *In Retrospect,* pp. 221–222.
52. " 'A Busy Life Came to a Close . . . ,' " *Newsweek* (December 27, 1965), pp. 18–19.

Chapter 8

1. Mick Jagger/Keith Richard "Wild Horses," ADKCO, Inc., 1971.
2. Allen Ginsberg, *Howl and Other Poems* (San Francisco: City Lights Books, 1956), p. 9.
3. Quoted in David Smith Allyn, "Make Love, Not War: The Sexual Revolution in America, 1957–1977," Ph.D. dissertation, Harvard University, 1996, pp. 75–76.
4. Quoted in Miles, *Ginsberg,* 232.
5. Allyn, "Make Love, Not War," pp. 227–228.
6. Only one letter required alteration; the group's previous name was Beetles. Steve Turner, *Angelheaded Hipster: A Life of Jack Kerouac* (New York: Viking Press, 1996), pp. 20–21.
7. Bob Dylan, "Mr. Tambourine Man," in Dylan, *Lyrics, 1962–1985* (New York: Knopf, 1990), p. 172.
8. For abundant examples, see Thomas Frank, *The Conquest of Cool: Business Culture, Counterculture, and the Rise of Hip Consumerism* (Chicago: University of Chicago Press, 1997). Quote on p. 120.
9. *The Essential Lenny Bruce,* John Cohen, ed. (New York: Ballantine Books, 1967), pp. 200–201.
10. Quoted in Barbara Ehrenreich, Elizabeth Hess, and Gloria Jacobs, *Re-Making Love: The Feminization of Sex* (Garden City, NY: Anchor Books, 1986), p. 60.
11. Beth Bailey, "Sexual Revolution(s)," in *The Sixties: From Memory to History,* ed. David Farber (Chapel Hill: University of North Carolina Press, 1994), pp. 249–52.
12. Allyn, "Make Love, Not War," p. 208.
13. John D'Emilio and Estelle B. Freedman, *Intimate Matters: A History of Sexuality in America,* 2nd ed. (Chicago: University of Chicago Press, 1997), p. 294.
14. Quoted in Allyn, "Make Love, Not War," p. 288.
15. Quoted in Bailey, "Sexual Revolution(s)," p. 256.
16. Quoted in Todd Gitlin, *The Sixties* (New York: Bantam Books, 1987), p. 372.
17. Quoted in Paul Potter, *A Name for Ourselves* (Boston: Little Brown, 1971), pp. xv–xvi.
18. Marquee cited in Geoffrey O'Brien, *Dream Time: Chapters from the Sixties* (New York: Viking Press, 1988), p. 97.
19. O'Brien, *Dream Time,* p. 41.
20. Ginsberg quoted in O'Brien, *Dream Time,* p. 59; Snyder quoted in Jane Kramer, *Allen Ginsberg in America* (New York: Random House, 1969), p. 33.
21. Theodore Roszak, *The Making of a Counter Culture: Reflections on the Technocratic Society and Its Youthful Opposition* (Garden City, NY: Anchor Books, 1969), p. 177.
22. This paragraph and the ones that follow about LSD are indebted to Martin A. Lee and Bruce Shlain, *Acid Dreams: The Complete Social History of LSD: The CIA, The Sixties, and Beyond* (New York: Grove Weidenfeld, 1992). Quote on p. xviii.

23. Quoted in Lee and Shlain, *Acid Dreams*, p. 30.

24. Timothy Leary, *Flashbacks: An Autobiography* (Los Angeles: Tarcher, 1983), p. 159.

25. David Farber, *The Age of Great Dreams: America in the 1960s* (NY: Hill & Wang, 1994), p. 188.

26. Quoted in Lee and Shlain, *Acid Dreams*, p. 47.

27. Quoted in Lee and Shlain, *Acid Dreams*, p. 81.

28. Joan Didion, *Slouching Toward Bethlehem* (New York: Farrar Straus & Giroux, 1968), pp. 127, 122.

29. Greil Marcus, *Mystery Train: Images of America in Rock 'n' Roll Music*, rev. ed. (New York: Dutton, 1982), p. 4.

30. Norman Mailer, "The White Negro," *Dissent* IV (Summer 1957), 276-92.

31. Quoted in Peter Guralnick, *Last Train to Memphis: The Rise of Elvis Presley* (Boston: Little Brown, 1994), p. 289.

32. "Won't Get Fooled Again," from *Who's Next*, MCA 1971.

33. Quoted in Godfrey Hodgson, *America in Our Time* (New York: Random House, 1976), p. 341.

34. Ellen Willis, "Janis Joplin," in *Beginning to See the Light: Sex, Hope, and Rock-and-Roll*, 2nd ed. (Hanover, NH: Wesleyan University Press, 1992), p. 63.

35. Quoted in Willis, "Janis Joplin," p. 64.

36. The lyrics are quoted in many places. See, for example, http://vlibnet.mtsu.edu/ ~bubba/bub1096/0903.html.

37. Quoted in Dave Marsh's indispensable *Louie Louie* (New York: Hyperion, 1993), p. 98.

38. Quoted in Marsh, *Louie Louie*, p. 116.

39. Quoted in John Patrick Diggins, *The Rise and Fall of the American Left* (New York: Norton, 1992), p. 273.

40. Quoted by Paul Goodman, "The New Reformation," in Irving Howe, ed., *Beyond the New Left* (New York: McCall, 1970), p. 90.

41. Quoted in William L. Van Deburg, *New Day in Babylon: The Black Power Movement and American Culture, 1965–1975* (Chicago: University of Chicago Press, 1992), p. 192.

42. Baraka quoted in Ibid., 181; "Haiku," in Sonia Sanchez, *homegirls & handgrenades* (New York: Thunder's Mouth Press, 1984), 9. For a critical view of Baraka's art and career, see Jerry Gafio Watts, *Amiri Baraka: The Politics and Art of a Black Intellectual* (New York: New York University Press, 2001).

43. Van Deburg, *New Day*, 172; Ariana Hernandez-Reguant, "Kwanzaa and the U.S. Ethnic Mosaic," in Jean Mutaba Rahier, ed. *Representations of Blackness and the Performance of Identities,* (Westport, CT: Bergin and Garvey, 1999), p. 101–122.

44. Timothy Miller, *The 60s Communes: Hippies and Beyond* (Syracuse: Syracuse University Press, 1999), p. xx. This is the only book-length historical study of the phenomenon.

45. Rosabeth Moss Kanter, "Communes in Cities," in John Case and Rosemary C.R. Taylor, eds. *Co-ops, Communes, and Collectives: Experiments in Social Change in the 1960s and 1970s,* (New York: Pantheon, 1979), p. 118.

46. Edward Bellamy, *Looking Backward* (New York: New American Library, 1960 [1888]), p. 190.

47. Stephen Gaskin, quoted in Timothy Miller, "The Sixties Era Communes," in Peter Braunstein and Michael William Doyle, eds. *Imagine Nation: The American Counterculture of the 1960s and '70s* (New York: Routledge, 2002), p. 337.

48. This contrast is borrowed from Judson Jerome, a poet who lived in a commune and traveled to many others. Judson Jerome, *Families of Eden: Communes and the New Anarchism* (New York: The Seabury Press, 1974), p. 58 and passim.
49. Miller, "The Sixties Era Communes," p. 343.

Chapter 9

1. Lyric from "Bob Dylan's Dream," *The Freewheelin' Bob Dylan*, 1963.
2. W.J. Rorabaugh, *Berkeley at War: The 1960s* (New York: Oxford University Press, 1989), p. 8. Many Peace Corps volunteers, upon their return to the United States, were then drawn into radical activism, especially against the war. Tom Wells, *The War Within: America's Battle Over Vietnam* (New York: Henry Holt, 1994), pp. 117–118, 427.
3. Maurice Isserman, *If I Had a Hammer, the Death of the Old Left and the Birth of the New Left* (New York: Basic Books, 1987), pp. 196–197.
4. Bob Dylan, "The Times They Are A-Changin'," 1963.
5. Kenneth Keniston, *Young Radicals: Notes on Committed Youth* (New York: Harcourt, Brace and World, 1968), p. 85 (emphasis in original).
6. Quoted in Rorabaugh, *Berkeley at War*, p. 164.
7. Rorabaugh, *Berkeley at War,* pp. 34, 36.
8. The most detailed account of the writing of the Port Huron Statement can be found in James Miller, *"Democracy Is in the Streets": From Port Huron to the Siege of Chicago* (New York: Simon & Schuster, 1987), pp. 78–125. Also see Isserman, *If I Had a Hammer*, pp. 209–214.
9. The Port Huron Statement is reprinted as an appendix to Miller's *"Democracy Is in the Streets,"* pp. 329–374.
10. *Nation*, CC (May 10, 1965), p. 492.
11. Quoted in H. W. Brands, *The Wages of Globalism: Lyndon Johnson and the Limits of American Power* (New York: Oxford University Press, 1995), p. 25. The account of the rise of the antiwar movement that follows is drawn from Wells, *The War Within*, pp. 9–65, and other sources as noted.
12. Quoted in Maurice Isserman, "You Don't Need a Weatherman But a Postman Can Be Helpful: Thoughts on the History of SDS and the Antiwar Movement," in Melvin Small and William D. Hoover, eds., *Give Peace a Chance: Exploring the Vietnam Antiwar Movement* (Syracuse, NY: Syracuse University Press, 1992), p. 25.
13. Quoted in Isserman, "You Don't Need a Weatherman," p. 22.
14. For SDS membership figures in 1966, see Kirkpatrick Sale, *SDS* (New York: Random House, 1973), pp. 271–272.
15. Letter from Timothy Tyndall of FSFA to Natoinal Office (NO), November 23, 1965, Reel 21, SDS Papers (microfilm of holdings in Wisconsin State Historical Society collection). For the formation of Dodge City Community College SDS, see letter from Bill Burrows to NO, January 11, 1965, Reel 21, SDS Papers.
16. Letter from John Allen to NO, February 1, 1966, Reel 19, SDS papers.
17. Carl Davidson, "Toward Institutional Resistance" (Madison, WI: SDS, 1967), pp. 3–4. This pamphlet can be found on Reel 36, SDS Papers. As a young Harvard University SDSer named Michael Kazin wrote approvingly in 1969: "SDS has progressed from marching plaintively to convince Lyndon Johnson of the error of his ways to striking at the core of the apparatus of American technical and intellectual power in the large private and public universities of the land." Michael Kazin, "Some Notes on SDS," *American Scholar*, XXXVIII (Autumn 1969), p. 649.

18. Jack Newfield, *A Prophetic Minority* (New York: New American Library, 1966), p. 99. Also see Howard Zinn, *SNCC, The New Abolitionists* (Boston: Beacon Press, 1964).

19. Doug McAdam, *Freedom Summer* (New York: Oxford University Press, 1988), pp. 5, 117. Clayborne Carson, *In Struggle: SNCC and the Black Awakening of the 1960s* (Cambridge, MA: Harvard University Press, 1981), pp. 160–161.

20. Quoted in Carson, *In Struggle*, p. 127.

21. Malcolm X, *The Autobiography of Malcolm X* (New York: Grove Press, 1965), p. 383.

22. Carson, *In Struggle*, pp. 134–136.

23. Julian Bond commented on the importance of the cultural differences between Lewis and Carmichael in an interview in Peter Joseph, *Good Times: An Oral History of American in the Nineteen Sixties* (New York: Charterhouse, 1973), p. 69.

24. Carson, *In Struggle*, pp. 204–211.

25. William L. Van Deburg, *New Day in Babylon: The Black Culture Movement and American Culture, 1965–1975*, (Chicago: University of Chicago Press, 1992) pp. 117–119. Also see Christopher Lasch, "Black Power: Cultural Nationalism as Politics," in *The Agony of the American Left* (New York: Vintage Books, 1969), pp. 117–168.

26. Carson, *In Struggle*, p. 274. Also see Stokely Carmichael and Charles V. Hamilton, *Black Power: The Politics of Liberation in America* (New York: Vintage Books, 1967), passim.

27. Julius Lester, "Notes of a Journey," in John J. Bunzel, ed., *Political Passages: Journeys of Change Through Two Decades, 1968-1988* (New York: Free Press, 1988), pp. 72–73. Also see Carson, *In Struggle*, pp. 229–230.

28. Carson, *In Struggle*, p. 282.

29. Kay Mills, *This Little Light of Mine: The Life of Fannie Lou Hamer* (New York: Penguin Books, 1993), p. 178.

30. Angus Campbell and Howard Schuman, "Black Views on Racial Issues," in Marcel L. Goldschmid, ed., *Americans and White Racism: Theory and Research* (New York: Holt, Rinehart & Winston, 1970), p. 347.

31. Hugh Pearson, *The Shadow of the Panther: Huey Newton and the Price of Black Power in America* (Reading, MA: Addison-Wesley, 1994), p. 113.

32. Letter from Steve Halliwell to Leo Haimson, August 2, 1967, Reel 19, SDS Papers.

33. Mary King, *Freedom Song: A Personal Story of the 1960s Civil Rights Movement* (New York: Morrow, 1987), pp. 437–455; Sara Evans, *Personal Politics: The Roots of Women's Liberation in the Civil Rights Movement and the New Left* (New York: Knopf, 1979), pp. 84–88. King and Hayden's position paper is reprinted as an appendix to *Freedom Song*, pp. 567–569.

34. The "kind of memo" is reprinted as an appendix to King, *Freedom Song*, pp. 571–574.

35. Alice Echols, *Daring to Be Bad: Radical Feminism in American, 1967–1975* (Minneapolis: University of Minnesota Press, 1989), pp. 65–69, 272.

36. Quoted in King, *Freedom Song*, p. 452.

37. Marge Piercy, "The Grand Coulee Damn," in Robin Morgan, ed., *Sisterhood Is Powerful: An Anthology of Writings from the Women's Liberation Movement* (New York: Vintage Books), 1970, p. 429.

38. Wells, *The War Within*, pp. 138–139, 168–170, 218.

39. Thomas Powers, *Vietnam: The War at Home* [1973; reprint, Boston: G.K. Hall, 1984], p. 200.

40. I. F. Stone, "Daydreams and Suicide Tactics," *New America,* June 18, 1965, p. 5.

41. Weissman's comments appeared in SDS's *National Vietnam Newsletter,* #2 (August 12, 1965).

42. Tom Hayden, *Reunion: A Memoir* (New York: Random House, 1988), p. 183.
43. Quoted in Barrie Thorne, "Resisting the Draft: An Ethnography of the Draft Resistance Movement," unpublished Ph.D. dissertation, Brandeis University, 1971, p. 61.
44. Lee Webb, "Conference Working Paper and Suggested Priorities for the NC" [n.d., late 1965], Reel 20, SDS papers.
45. Kirkpatrick Sale, *SDS*, p. 341.
46. Wells, *The War Within*, pp. 191–194.
47. Norman Mailer, *The Armies of the Night: History as a Novel, the Novel as History* (New York: New American Library, 1968), pp. 108–109.
48. Wells, *The War Within*, pp. 195–203.
49. McNamara, *In Retrospect*, p. 305; quoted in Wells, *The War Within*, p. 110.
50. Mailer, *Armies of the Night*, pp. 107–108.

Chapter 10

1. Quoted in Doris Kearns, *Lyndon Johnson and the American Dream* (New York: Harper & Row, 1976), pp. 286–287.
2. Feiffer cartoon, December 18, 1966, reprinted in the frontpiece to Marvin E. Gettleman and David Mermelstein, eds., *The Great Society Reader: The Failure of American Liberalism* (New York: Random House, 1967).
3. *The Gallup Poll, Public Opinion 1935–1971*, Vol. III (New York: Random House, 1972), p. 2011.
4. Quoted in Doris Kearns, *Lyndon Johnson and the American Dream*, p. 286.
5. Quoted in Robert Dallek, *Flawed Giant, Lyndon Johnson and His Times, 1963–1973* (New York: Oxford University Press, 1998), p. 312.
6. Nicholas Lemann, *The Promised Land: The Great Black Migration and How It Changed America* (New York: Knopf, 1991), pp. 188–189.
7. Quoted in Gareth Davies, *From Opportunity to Entitlement: The Transformation and Decline of Great Society Liberalism* (Lawrence: University Press of Kansas, 1996), p. 105.
8. Robert Sherrod, "Notes on a Monstrous War," *Life*, January 27, 1967, p. 22.
9. Sherrod, "Notes on a Monstrous War," p. 21.
10. Quoted in Irwin Unger, *The Best of Intentions: THe Triumph and Failure of the Great Society Under Kennedy, Johnson and Nixon* (New York: Doubleday, 1996), p. 255.
11. Quoted in Unger, *The Best of Intentions*, p. 110.
12. Kearns, *Lyndon Johnson and the American Dream*, p. 252.
13. Quoted in Neil Sheehan, *A Bright Shining Lie: John Paul Vann and American in Vietnam* (New York: Random House, 1988), p. 628.
14. "Shaping Up," *Time Magazine*, September 9, 1966, p. 36.
15. Quoted in Robert McNamara, *In Retrospect, the Tragedy and Lessons of Vietnam* (New York: Random House, 1995), p. 269.
16. Quoted in Stephen B. Oates, *Let the Trumpet Sound: The Life of Martin Luther King, Jr.* (New York: New American Liberary, 1982), pp. 433–434.
17. Quoted in Michael Harrington, *The New American Poverty* (New York: Holt, Rinehart & Winston, 1984), p. 20.
18. James T. Patterson, *America's Struggle Against Poverty, 1900–1985* (Cambridge, MA: Harvard University Press, 1986), p. 151.
19. Michael L. Gillette, *Launching the War on Poverty: An Oral History* (New York: Twayne Publishers, 1996), p. 74.
20. Bernard R. Gifford, "War on Poverty: Assumptions, History and Results, a Flawed But

Important Effort," in Marshall Kaplan and Peggy L. Cuciti, eds., *The Great Society and Its Legacy* (Durham, NC: Duke University Press, 1986), p. 68.

21. Quoted in Kevin Boyle, *The UAW and the Heyday of American Liberalism, 1945–1968* (Ithaca, NY: Cornell University Press, 1995), p. 217.

22. Patterson, *America's Struggle Against Poverty*, pp. 160, 162.

23. Frances Fox Piven and Richard A. Cloward, *Poor People's Movements: Why They Succeed, How They Fail* (New York: Pantheon, 1977) p. 264.

24. The most influential statement of this view can be found in Charles Murray, *Losing Ground: American Social Policy, 1950–1980* (New York: Basic Books, 1984). Also see George Gilder, *Wealth and Poverty* (New York: Basic Books, 1981).

25. Linda Gordon, *Pitied But Not Entitled: Single Mothers and the History of Welfare* (Cambridge, MA: Harvard University Press, 1994), p. 1. On the long history of the notion of the "deserving poor" see, Michael Katz, *In the Shadow of the Poorhouse: A Social History of Welfare in America* (New York: Basic Books, 1986).

26. Martha Davis, *Brutal Need: Lawyers and the Welfare Rights Movement, 1960–1973* (New Haven, CT: Yale University Press, 1993), pp. 36–37.

27. For the history of one such effort in radical community organizing, the "Economic Research and Action Project," launched by Students for a Democratic Society (SDS), see Wini Breines, *Community and Organization in the New Left, 1962–1968: The Great Refusal* (New York: Praeger, 1982), pp. 123–149, and Sara Evans, *Personal Politics: The Roots of Women's Liberation in the Civil Rights Movement and the New Left* (New York: Knopf, 1979), pp. 126–155.

28. William Ryan, *Blaming the Victim* (New York: Random House, 1971), p. 106.

29. Quoted in Davis, *Brutal Need*, p. 70.

30. Charles Noble, *Welfare as We Knew It: A Political History of the American Welfare State* (New York: Oxford University Press, 1997), p. 98; Gareth Davies, *From Opportunity to Entitlement: The Transformation and Decline of Great Society Liberalism* (Lawrence: University Press of Kansas, 1996), pp. 158, 214–215.

31. Quoted in Davis, *Brutal Need*, p. 120.

32. The deteriorating image of the poor in this period is discussed in Herbert J. Gans, *The War Against the Poor: The Underclass and Antipoverty* (New York: Basic Books, 1995).

33. The Moynihan Report, along with many published reactions to it, can be found in Lee Rainwater and William L. Yancey, eds., *The Moynihan Report and the Poltics of Controversy* (Cambridge, MA: MIT Press, 1967).

34. Quoted in Davies, *From Opportunity to Entitlement*, p. 71.

35. Gus Tyler, "White Workers/Blue Mood," in Irving Howe, ed., *The World of the Blue Collar Worker* (New York: Quadrangle Books, 1972), pp. 198–200; Jill Quadagno, *The Color of Welfare: How Racism Undermined the War on Poverty* (New York: Oxford University Press, 1994), p. 179.

36. Quadagno, *The Color of Welfare*, p. 131.

37. Edward C. Banfield, *The Unheavenly City: The Nature and Future of Our Urban Crisis* (Boston: Little Brown, 1970), p. 196.

38. Quadagno, *The Color of Welfare*, p. 30.

39. Quoted in David Garrow, *Bearing the Cross: Martin Luther King, Jr. and the Southern Christian Leadership Conference* (New York: Morrow, 1986), p. 439.

40. Quoted in James Ralph, *Northern Protest: Martin Luther King, Jr., Chicago, and the Civil Rights Movement* (Cambridge, MA: Harvard University Press, 1993), p. 101.

41. Quoted in Ralph, *Northern Protest*, p. 120.

42. Quoted in Ralph, *Northern Protest*, p. 189.

43. Quoted in Ralph, *Northern Protest*, p. 188.
44. Quoted in Ralph, *Northern Protest*, p. 127.
45. Quoted in Jonathan Rieder, *Canarsie: The Jews and Italians of Brooklyn Against Liberalism* (Cambridge, MA: Harvard University Press, 1985), pp. 133–134.
46. Studs Terkel, *Working* (New York: Pantheon, 1972), p. 6.
47. Quoted in Rieder, *Canarsie*, p. 133.
48. Quoted in Eric Cummins, *The Rise and Fall of California's Radical Prison Movement* (Stanford, CA: Stanford University Press, 1994), p. 126.
49. James Q. Wilson, *Thinking About Crime* (New York: Basic Books, 1975), pp. 5–7.
50. Wilson, *Thinking About Crime*, pp. 12, 16, 38.
51. Goldwater and Johnson are quoted in Michael William Flamm, "'Law and Order': Street Crime, Civil Disorder, and the Crisis of Liberalism," Ph.D. dissertation, Columbia University, 1998, pp. 115, 123.
52. Quoted in Flamm, " 'Law and Order'," p. 153.
53. Quoted in Thomas Byrne Edsall and Mary D. Edsall, *Chain Reaction: The Impact of Race, Rights, and Taxes on American Politics* (New York: Norton, 1991), p. 51. Flamm's "'Law and Order'" is an excellent study of this.

Chapter 11

1. Quoted in John A. Andrew III, *The Other Side of the Sixties: Young Americans for Freedom and the Rise of Conservative Politics* (New Brunswick, NJ: Rutgers University Press, 1997), p. 75.
2. Barry Goldwater, *The Conscience of a Conservative* (New York: Hillman Books, 1960), p. 3.
3. Clinton Rossiter, *Conservatism in America: The Thankless Persuasion* (1962); Richard Hofstadter, "Goldwater and Pseudo-Conservative Politics," in *The Paranoid Style in American Politics and Other Essays* (New York: Vintage Books, 1967), p. 104.
4. Goldwater, *The Conscience of a Conservative*, pp. 5, 23, 38, 127.
5. The best guide to such writings is George Nash, *The Conservative Intellectual Movement in America Since 1945* (New York: Basic Books, 1976). Also see Patrick Allitt, *Catholic Intellectuals and Conservative Politics in America, 1950–1985* (Ithaca, NY: Cornell University Press, 1993).
6. Friedrich von Hayek, *The Road To Serfdom* (Chicago: University of Chicago Press, 1994 [1944]), p. 101.
7. Milton Friedman with the assistance of Rose Friedman, *Capitalism and Freedom* (Chicago: University of Chicago Press, 1962), p. 3.
8. Russell Kirk, *The Conservative Mind: From Burke to Eliot*, 7th rev. ed. (Chicago: Regnery, 1986 [1953]), pp. 8–9.
9. Will Herberg, "Pure Religion and Secularized Society," *National Review*, September 10, 1963, p. 189.
10. Daniel Bell has made this argument for the modern West as a whole in *The Cultural Contradictions of Capitalism* (New York: Basic Books, 1976).
11. Quoted in Hayek, *The Road to Serfdom*, pp. 31–32.
12. Kirk, *The Conservative Mind*, p. 9.
13. Quoted in Charles E. Rice, *The Supreme Court and Public Prayer: The Need for Restraint* (New York: Fordham University Press, 1964), p. 3.
14. Quotes from Robert S. Alley, *School Prayer: The Court, the Congress, and the First Amendment* (Buffalo, NY: Prometheus Books, 1994), pp. 109, 124, 123.

15. Russell Kirk, "From the Academy," *National Review*, January 16, 1962, p. 27. Among the magazine's regular contributors were Garry Wills and Joan Didion, whose essays helped build both their magazine's and their own reputations for literary excellence.

16. Quoted in Paul Gottfried and Thomas Fleming, *The Conservative Movement* (Boston: Twayne, 1988), 10.

17. Frank Meyer, "Principles and Heresies," *National Review*, June 18, 1963, p. 496.

18. Quoted in Sara Diamond, *Roads to Dominion: Right-Wing Movements and Political Power in the United States* (New York: Guilford Press, 1995), p. 53.

19. Schlafly quoted in Garry Wills, *Reagan's America: Innocents at Home* (Garden City, NY: Doubleday, 1987), p. 286.

20. See Lisa McGirr, *Suburban Warriors: The Origins of the New American Right* (Princeton: Princeton University Press, 2001).

21. The Sharon statement was only 400 words long. Quoted in M. Stanton Evans, *Revolt on the Campus* (Chicago: Regnery, 1962), p. 118.

22. Evans, *Revolt on the Campus*, pp. 118, 123 ("arrogance"), p. 53.

23. Lee Edwards, *Goldwater* (Washington, DC: Regnery, 1995), p. 180.

24. Jeb Magruder, later convicted during the Watergate scandal, quoted in Robert Alan Goldberg, *Barry Goldwater* (New Haven, CT: Yale University Press, 1995), p. 219.

25. Quoted in Goldberg, *Goldwater*, pp. 196–197.

26. Quoted in Goldberg, *Goldwater*, p. 237.

27. Mary C. Brennan, *Turning Right in the Sixties* (Chapel Hill: University of North Carolina Press, 1995), p. 102.

28. Quoted in Lou Cannon, *Reagan* (New York: Putnam's, 1982), 111. The author of the Open Housing Act was Byron Rumford, a black Democrat from Berkeley.

29. Quoted in Cannon, *Reagan*, p. 115.

30. Hale Champion quoted in Michael Barone, *Our Country* (New York: Free Press, 1991), p. 416.

31. Quoted in Cannon, *Reagan*, p. 117.

32. Quoted in Ronald P. Formisano, *Boston Against Busing: Race, Class, and Ethnicity in the 1960s and 1970s* (Chapel Hill: University of North Carolina Press, 1991), p. 36.

33. *Meet the Press*, June 2, 1963 (copy at Library of Congress). This section on Wallace is drawn in large part from Michael Kazin, *The Populist Persuasion: An American History*, rev. ed (Ithaca, NY: Cornell University Press, 1998), pp. 233–235. See that source for complete citations.

34. Wallace quoted in Thomas Edsall and Mary Edsall, *Chain Reaction* (New York: Norton, 1991), p. 78.

35. From *Meet the Press*, June 30, 1968, Recorded Sound Division, Library of Congress.

36. Quoted in Edsall and Edsall, *Chain Reaction*, p. 77.

37. James Jackson Kilpatrick, "What Makes Wallace Run?" *National Review*, April 18, 1967, p. 400.

38. George Wallace, *"Hear Me Out"* (Anderson, SC: Drake House, 1968), p. 62.

Chapter 12

1. *Bartlett's Familiar Quotations*, 15th ed. (Boston: Little Brown, 1980), p. 913. The quote is c. 1968.

2. Cronkite quoted in Stanley Karnow, *Vietnam: A History* (New York: Viking Press, 1983), p. 547; Clifford quoted in the documentary, *LBJ*, Vol. 2, PBS Video, 1991.

3. Quoted in Neil Sheehan, *A Bright Shining Lie: John Paul Vann and American in Vietnam* (New York: Random House, 1988), p. 719.

4. See Ronald H. Spector, *After Tet: The Bloodiest Year in Vietnam* (New York: Free Press, 1993).

5. Quoted in Gabriel Kolko, *Anatomy of a War: Vietnam, the United States, and the Modern Historical Experience* (New York: Pantheon, 1986), p. 314.

6. Quoted in Todd Gitlin, *The Sixties* (New York: Bantam Books, 1987), p. 299.

7. Among those attending the meeting were Dean Acheson, Douglas Dillon, McGeorge Bundy, Henry Cabot Lodge, John J. McCloy, Robert Murphy, and Arthur Dean.

8. Quoted in Sheehan, *A Bright Shining Lie*, p. 722.

9. David Garrow, *Bearing the Cross: Martin Luther King, Jr. and the Southern Christian Leadership Conference* (New York: Morrow, 1986), pp. 591–592.

10. Garrow, *Bearing the Cross*, pp. 581–582.

11. Garrow, *Bearing the Cross*, p. 618.

12. Garrow, *Bearing the Cross*, pp. 611–612.

13. Quoted in Garrow, *Bearing the Cross*, pp. 607, 621.

14. Quotes from Stephen B. Oates, *Let the Trumpet Sound: The Life of Martin Luther King, Jr.* (New York: Harper & Row, 1982), p. 490; Garrow, *Bearing the Cross*, p. 622.

15. Quotes from Robert V. Daniels, *Year of the Heroic Guerrilla: World Revolution and Counterrevolution in 1968* (New York: Basic Books, 1989), pp. 99, 102–103.

16. Quoted in Robert Weisbrot, *Freedom Bound: A History of America's Civil Rights Movement* (New York: Norton, 1990), p. 269.

17. Mark Rudd, "Columbia," in *The Movement*, March 1969, reprinted in Immanual Wallerstein and Paul Starr, eds., *The University Crisis Reader, Volume II: Confrontation and Counterattack* (New York: Vintage Books, 1971), p. 179.

18. Quoted in *1968: A Student Generation in Revolt—An International Oral History*, Ronald Fraser, ed. (New York: Pantheon, 1988), p. 199.

19. Theodore Kheel, quoted in Jerry Avorn et al., *Up Against the Ivy Wall: A History of the Columbia Crisis* (New York: Atheneum, 1968), p. 173.

20. Brown quoted in Avorn et al., *Up Against the Ivy Wall*, p. 134; Hayden in *Ramparts*, June 15, 1968; reprinted in *University Crisis Reader*, Wallerstein and Starr, eds., pp. 162–165. The SDS leader was paraphrasing the Latin American revolutionary Che Guevara who had called for "two, three, many Vietnams" to weaken U.S. power.

21. Quoted in Terry Anderson, *The Movement and the Sixties* (New York: Oxford University Press, 1995), p. 199. The FBI took careful note of the events at Columbia, and used them in May 1968 as the justification for launching COINTELPRO operations against the white New Left as a whole. FBI field offices around the country were instructed to use tactics such as instigating "personal conflicts and animosities" between New Left leaders, creating the impression that New Left leaders were "informants for the Bureau or other law enforcement agencies, and sending anonymous letters about New Leftists' activities to "parents, neighbors, and the parents' employers" to undermine groups like SDS. U.S. Senate, Select Committee to Study Governmental Operations, "Intelligence Activities and the Rights of Americans," Book II (1976), pp. 88–89.

22. Richard Hofstadter, "The 214th Columbia University Commencement Address," *The American Scholar*, XXXVII (Autumn 1978), p. 583.

23. Quoted in David Farber, *Chicago '68* (Chicago: University of Chicago Press, 1988), p. 117. Many details in this section are drawn from Farber's rich account.

24. Yippie manifesto, January 1968, quoted in Farber, *Chicago '68*, p. 17.
25. Quoted in Jonah Raskin, *For the Hell of It: The Life and Times of Abbie Hoffman* (Berkeley: University of California Press, 1996), p. 129.
26. Quoted in Raskin, *For the Hell of It*, p. 129.
27. Quoted in Farber, *Chicago '68*, p. 160.
28. For the detailed investigation by a quasi-governmental commission, see *Rights in Conflict: The Walker Report* (New York: Bantam Books, 1968).
29. Gitlin, *The Sixties*, pp. 333–334.
30. Quoted in Farber, *Chicago '68*, p. 250.
31. Farber, *Chicago '68*, p. 206.
32. Quoted in Michael William Flamm, "'Law and Order': Street Crime, Civil Disorder, and the Crisis of Liberalism," Ph.D. dissertation, Columbia University, 1998, p. 445.
33. Shana Alexander, "Hooray! Getting Back to Normal," *Life*, September 20, 1968, p. 28.
34. Robin Morgan, "Women Disrupt the Miss American Pageant," reprinted in Morgan, *Going Too Far: The Personal Chronicle of a Feminist* (New York: Random House, 1977), pp. 64, 64–65.
35. Charlotte Curtis, "Miss America Pageant Is Picketed by 100 Women," *New York Times*, September 8, 1968, p. A81. I have used the higher figure of protesters, based on Ruth Rosen's *The World Split Open: How the Modern Women's Movement Changed America*, (New York: Viking Press, 2000).
36. J. Morris Anderson, quoted in Curtis, "Miss America Pageant Is Picketed."
37. Morgan, "Women Disrupt the Miss American Pageant," p. 62.
38. Curtis, "Miss America Pageant Is Picketed."
39. Quoted in Lewis Chester, Godfrey Hodgson, and Bruce Page, *An American Melodrama: The Presidential Campaign of 1968* (New York: Viking Press, 1969), pp. 632–633.
40. Harris poll cited in Flamm, "'Law and Order'," p. 468.
41. Wallace quoted in Flamm, "'Law and Order'," p. 454; Michael Kazin, *The Populist Persuasion: An American History*, rev. ed. (Ithaca, NY: Cornell University Press, 1998), p. 236.
42. Humphrey speech in Salt Lake City, September 30, 1968. Quoted in Chester et al., *American Melodrama*, p. 649.
43. Chester, *American Melodrama*, p. 637.
44. Edwin Diamond and Stephen Bates, *The Spot: The Rise of Political Advertising on Television* (Cambridge, MA: MIT Press, 1984), p. 180.
45. Quoted in Garry Wills, *Nixon Agonistes: The Crisis of the Self-Made Man* (Boston: Houghton Mifflin, 1970), p. 50.

Chapter 13

1. Quoted in John Cohen, ed., *The Essential Lenny Bruce* (New York: Ballantine Books, 1967), p. 57.
2. Sydney E. Ahlstrom, *A Religious History of the American People* (New Haven, CT: Yale University Press, 1972), p. 953.
3. See the statistics gathered in Gallup Report, *Religion in America: 50 Years: 1935–1985* (Princeton, NJ: Gallup, Inc., 1985).
4. Eisenhower in 1946. Quoted in Robert Wuthnow, *The Restructuring of American Religion: Society and Faith Since World War II* (Princeton, NJ: Princeton University Press, 1988), p. 67.
5. Heschel quoted in Edward S. Shapiro, *A Time for Healing: American Jewry Since World War II* (Baltimore: Johns Hopkins University Press, 1992), p. 164; Bible statistic cited

in Will Herberg, *Protestant-Catholic-Jew: An Essay in American Religious Sociology* (Chicago: University of Chicago Press, 1983 [1955]), p. 2.

6. King gave a prayer during Graham's 1957 crusade in New York City and applauded the white evangelist for holding rallies in Harlem and including black ministers on his planning committees. But the heated racial climate of the '60s, and Graham's drift toward the mainstream Right, made any future joint ventures impossible. See Taylor Branch, *Parting the Waters: America in the King Years, 1954–63* (New York: Simon & Schuster, 1988), pp. 227–228.

7. Quotation from Bill Bright's *Have You Heard of the Four Spiritual Laws?* (1965), as quoted in David Harrington Watt, *A Transforming Faith: Explorations of Twentieth-Century Evangelism* (New Brunswick, NJ: Rutgers University Press, 1991), p. 23.

8. William Walzer, quoted in Sara Evans, *Personal Politics: The Roots of Women's Liberation in the Civil Rights Movement and the New Left* (New York: Knopf, 1979), p. 32.

9. Jackson W. Carroll et al., *Religion in America: 1950 to the Present* (San Francisco: Harper & Row, 1979), p. 15.

10. An anonymous member of the Living Word Fellowship, c. 1971. Quoted in Steven M. Tipton, *Getting Saved from the Sixties: Moral Meaning in Conversion and Cultural Change* (Berkeley: University of California Press, 1982), p. 33.

11. Paul Boyer, *When Time Shall Be No More: Prophecy Belief in Modern American Culture* (Cambridge, MA: Harvard University Press, 1992), pp. 5, 127.

12. *Gaudium et Spes*, quoted in John T. McGreevy, *Parish Boundaries: The Catholic Encounter with Race in the Twentieth-Century Urban North* (Chicago: University of Chicago Press, 1996), p. 160.

13. Garry Wills, *Bare Ruined Choirs: Doubt, Prophecy, and Radical Religion* (Garden City, NY: Doubleday, 1972), p. 192.

14. Quoted in McGreevy, *Parish Boundaries*, p. 206.

15. Quotes in McGreevy, *Parish Boundaries*, pp. 166, 225.

16. Wills, *Bare Ruined Choirs*, p. 3; Richard Rodriguez, *Hunger of Memory: The Education of Richard Rodriguez* (New York: Bantam Books, 1983), p. 101.

17. Quoted in Jay Dolan, *The American Catholic Experience* (New York: Harper & Row, 1985), p. 429.

18. Quoted in McGreevy, *Parish Boundaries*, p. 171.

19. Letter quoted in McGreevy, *Parish Boundaries*, p. 202.

20. Quoted in McGreevy, *Parish Boundaries*, pp. 205, 204.

21. Quoted in Patrick Allitt, *Catholic Intellectuals and Conservative Politics, 1950–1975* (Ithaca, NY: Cornell University Press, 1993), p. 174.

22. Gallup Report, "Religion in America," May 1985, p. 27. This was a decline from the 5 percent recorded in 1947.

23. Michael J. Rosenberg, "Israel Without Apology," in James A. Sleeper and Alan L. Mintz, eds., *The New Jews* (New York: Vintage Books, 1971), p. 82.

24. *The First Jewish Catalog: A do-it-yourself kit*, Richard Siegel et al., ed. (Philadelphia: Jewish Publication Society of America, 1973).

25. Alan Mintz, "Along the Path to Religious Community," in Sleeper and Mintz, eds., *The New Jews*, p. 29.

26. Itzik Lodzer (aka Arthur Green), "Psychedelics and the Kabbalah," in *The New Jews*, Sleeper and Mintz, eds., p. 191. Cowan quoted in Riv-Ellen Prell, *Prayer and Community: The Havurah in American Judaism* (Detroit: Wayne State University Press, 1989), p. 90.

27. Quoted in Deborah Dash Moore, *To the Golden Cities: Pursuing the American Jewish Dream in Miami and Los Angeles* (New York: Free Press, 1994), p. 254.

28. This figure is based on a large sample gathered and interpreted, in the early 1970s by a team of religious sociologists at the University of California, Berkeley. Robert Wuthnow, *Experimentation in American Religion: The New Mysticisms and their Implications for the Churches* (Berkeley: University of California Press, 1978), p. 16.
29. Gregory Johnson, "The Hare Krishna in San Francisco," in Charles Y. Glock and Robert N. Bellah, eds. *The New Religious Consciousness* (Berkeley: University of California Press, 1976), p. 39.
30. Quotes from Donald Stone, "The Human Potential Movement," in Glock and Bellah, eds., *The New Religious Consciousness*, pp. 97, 93.
31. Jacob Needleman, *The New Religions* (Garden City, NY: Doubleday, 1970), pp. 66, 50.
32. Edward Espe Brown, *The Tassajara Bread Book* (Berkeley: Shambala, 1970), p. 141.
33. Maharishi Mahesh Yogi quoted in Needleman, *The New Religions*, pp. 133, 134.
34. Needleman, *The New Religions*, p. 132.
35. On these changes in TM, see Mikael Rothstein, *Belief Transformations* (Aarhus, Denmark: Aarhus University Press, 1996).
36. The figure comes from TM itself. Stone, "The Human Potential Movement," p. 100.
37. William James, *The Varieties of Religious Experience* (New York: Penguin Books, 1982 [reprint]), pp. 78–9.
38. For the fullest examination of this point, see Wuthnow, *The Restructuring of American Religion*, pp. 132–172.

Chapter 14

1. James Reston, "War Leaves Deep Mark on U.S.," *New York Times*, January 24, 1973, p. 1.
2. Andrew Hacker, "'We Will Meet as Enemies'," *Newsweek*, July 6, 1970, p. 25.
3. The portrait of Richard Nixon that follows is drawn from Roger Morris, *Richard Milhous Nixon: The Rise of an American Politician* (New York: Henry Holt, 1990); Stephen E. Ambrose, *Nixon: The Education of a Politician 1913–1962* (New York: Simon & Schuster, 1987), and *Nixon: The Triumph of a Politician, 1962–1972* (New York: Simon & Schuster, 1990); and Tom Wicker, *One of Us: Richard Nixon and the American Dream* (New York: Random House, 1991).
4. Quoted in Wicker, *One of Us*, p. 45.
5. A classic account of Nixon's 1968 campaign strategy can be found in Joe McGinniss, *The Selling of the President 1968* (New York: Simon & Schuster, 1969).
6. Richard Nixon, *RN: The Memoirs of Richard Nixon* (New York: Grosset & Dunlap, 1978), p. 366.
7. Quoted in Ambrose, *The Triumph of a Politician*, p. 244.
8. Quoted in Ambrose, *The Triumph of a Politician*, p. 285.
9. Richard Nixon, *No More Vietnams* (New York: Arbor House, 1985), pp. 103–104.
10. "Beginning of the End?," *Newsweek*, July 21, 1969, p. 24.
11. Quoted in Seymour M. Hersh, *The Price of Power: Kissinger in the Nixon White House* (New York: Summit Books, 1983), pp. 79–80.
12. Quoted in Ambrose, *The Triumph of a Politician*, p. 301.
13. Quoted in Loren Baritz, *Backfire: A History of How American Culture Led Us into Vietnam and Made Us Fight the Way We Did*, 2nd ed. (Baltimore: Johns Hopkins University Press, 1998), p. 196.
14. Quoted in William Bundy, *A Tangled Web: The Making of Foreign Policy in the Nixon Presidency* (New York: Hill & Wang, 1988), p. 53.

15. Stanley Karnow, "Giap Remembers," *New York Times Magazine*, June 24, 1990, p. 36.
16. The collapse of SDS is chronicled in Kirkpatrick Sale, *SDS* (New York: Vintage Books, 1973); Todd Gitlin, *The Sixties: Years of Hope, Days of Rage* (New York: Bantam Books, 1987); and James Miller, *"Democracy Is in The Streets": From Port Hurton to the Siege of Chicago* (New York: Touchstone, 1987). For a vivid firsthand account of this period, see Susan Stern, *With the Weathermen: The Personal Journal of a Revolutionary Woman* (Garden City, NY: Doubleday, 1975).
17. For figures on the dimension of campus radicalism in the 1960s, see Helen Lefkowitz Horowitz, "The 1960s and the Transformation of Campus Cultures," *History of Education Quarterly,* XXVI (Spring 1986), pp. 12, 18; *The Report of the President's Commission on Campus Unrest* (Washington, D.C.: Government Printing Office, 1970), pp. 18, 39, 48; Kirkpatrick Sale, *SDS,* p. 636.
18. The drift away from radical activism did not, however, mean that former New Leftists simply "sold out," embracing conservatism and materialism, as the familiar "Yippie"-to-"Yuppie" stereotype would have it. See, for example, Jack Whalen and Richard Flacks, *Beyond the Barricades: The Sixties Generation Grows Up* (Philadelphia: Temple University Press, 1989).
19. Quoted in Tom Wells, *The War Within: America's Battle Over Vietnam* (New York: Henry Holt, 1994), p. 579.
20. Agnew is quoted in Wells, *The War Within,* p. 382. On the participation in protests by children of administration officials, see *ibid.,* pp. 373–374.
21. "Some GI's in Vietnam Protest," *New York Times,* October 16, 1969, p. 1; "100 G.I.'s in Pleiku Fast for Holiday," *New York Times,* November 28, 1969, p. 1.
22. Quoted in Ambrose, *The Triumph of a Politician,* p. 310.
23. On the impact of the antiwar movement on public opinion and on Nixon's policies in the fall of 1969, see Melvin Small, *Johnson, Nixon, and the Doves* (New Brunswick, NJ: Rutgers University Press, 1988), pp. 162–192. For a differing appraisal, see John E. Mueller, *War, Presidents and Public Opinion* (New York: Wiley, 1973).
24. Henry Kissinger, *White House Years* (Boston: Little, Brown, 1979), pp. 497–498
25. Nixon quoted in Ambrose, *The Triumph of a Politician,* p. 345. Also see Kissinger, *White House Years,* p. 505.
26. Wells, *The War Within,* p. 427.
27. Kissinger, *White House Years,* pp. 511, 513, 514.
28. Peter Levy, *The New Left and Labor in the 1960s* (Urbana: University of Illinois Press, 1994), pp. 1–2.
29. Nixon quoted in "The Cambodian Venture: An Assessment," *Time,* July 6, 1970, p. 16.
30. Colonel Robert D. Heinl, Jr., "The Collapse of the Armed Forces,", *Armed Forces Journal,* June 7, 1971. Also see Christian G. Appy, *Working Class War: American Combat Soldiers and Vietnam* (Chapel Hill: University of North Carolina Press, 1993), pp. 245–247.
31. Quoted in David Thorne and George Butler, eds., *The New Soldier, by John Kerry and Vietnam Veterans Against the War* (New York: Collier Books, 1971), p. 18. Also see Richard Stacewicz, *Winter Soldiers: An Oral History of the Vietnam Veterans Against the War* (New York: Twayne Publishers, 1997).
32. Quoted in Nicholas Lemann, *The Promised Land: The Great Black Migration and How It Changed America* (New York: Knopf, 1991, p. 204.
33. Except where otherwise noted, this account of Nixon's racial policies is based upon Kenneth O'Reilly, *Nixon's Piano: Presidents and Racial Politics from Washington to Clin-*

ton (New York: Free Press, 1995), pp. 277–329, and Thomas Byrne Edsall and Mary D. Edsall, *Chain Reaction: The Impact of Race, Rights, and Taxes on American Politics* (New York: Norton, 1991), passim.

34. Dan T. Carter, *The Politics of Rage: George Wallace, the Origins of the New Conservatism, and the Transformation of American Politics* (New York: SImon & Schuster, 1995), p. 380. Also see Kevin Phillips, *The Emerging Republican Majority* (New Rochelle, NY: Arlington House, 1969).

35. Quoted in Ambrose, *The Triumph of a Politician*, p. 332.

36. Quoted in John Skrentny, *The Ironies of Affirmative Action: Politics, Culture, and Justice in America* (Chicago: University of Chicago Press, 1996), pp. 218–219.

37. Quoted in Ambrose, *The Triumph of a Politician*, p. 364.

38. Quoted in Ambrose, *The Triumph of a Politician*, p. 338. In 1948, when he was a candidate for the Florida state legislature, Carswell had declared, "Segregation of the races is proper and the only practical and correct way of life. . . ." Ambrose, *ibid.*, p. 330.

39. Skrentny, *The Ironies of Affirmative Action*, pp. 177–221.

40. Quoted in Carter, *The Politics of Rage*, p. 417.

41. John Cromartie and Carol B. Stack, "Reinterpretation of Black Return and Non-Return Migration to the South, 1975–1980," *The Geographical Review*, LXXIX (July 1989), p. 300.

42. On the later history of the Panthers, see Hugh Pearson, *The Shadow of the Panther: Huey Newton and the Price of Black Power in America* (Reading, MA: Addison-Wesley, 1994), pp. 217–250. For SNCC, see Clayborne Carson, *In Struggle: SNCC and the Black Awakening of the 1960s* (Cambridge, MA: Harvard University Press, 1981), pp. 287–306.

43. John Lewis, *Walking with the Wind: A Memoir of the Movement* (New York: Simon & Schuster, 1998), p. 376.

44. Quoted in Paul Berman, *A Tale of Two Utopias: The Political Journey of the Generation of 1968* (New York: Norton, 1996), p. 149. Also see Martin Duberman, *Stonewall* (New York: Dutton, 1993).

45. See, for example, Randy Shilts, *The Mayor of Castro Street: The Life and Times of Harvey Milk* (New York: St. Martin's Press, 1982).

46. Quoted in Robert Gottlieb, *Forcing the Spring: The Transformation of the American Environmental Movement* (Washington, DC: Island Press, 1993), p. 108.

47. Gottlieb, *Forcing the Spring*, pp. 177–184.

48. Nixon is quoted in Jonathan Schell, *The Time of Illusion* (New York: Vintage Books, 1976), p. 49. Stein is quoted in Allen J. Matusow, *Nixon's Economy: Booms, Busts, Dollars, and Votes* (Lawrence: University Press of Kansas, 1998), p. 241.

49. Gottlieb, *Forcing the Spring*, p. 109.

50. Pat Buchanan, *Conservative Votes, Liberal Victories* (New York: Quadrangle, 1975), p. 13.

51. Quoted in Everett Carll Ladd, Jr., and Charles D. Hadley, *Transformations of the American Party System: Political Coalitions from the New Deal to the 1970s* (New York: Norton, 1975), p. 315.

52. Hunter S. Thompson, *Fear and Loathing: On the Campaign Trail, '72* (New York: Fawcett, 1973), p. 127.

53. Quoted in Peter N. Carroll, *It Seemed Like Nothing Happened: The Tragedy and Promise of America in the 1970s* (New York: Holt, Rinehart & Winston, 1982), p. 36.

54. Quoted in Carroll, *It Seemed Like Nothing Happened*, p. 86.

55. Peter Steinfels, *The Neo-Conservatives: The Men Who Are Changing American Politics* (New York: Simon & Schuster, 1979).

56. Nixon's foreign policy triumphs in 1972 are described in Hersh, *The Price of Power*, pp. 363–382, 489–502; and Bundy, *A Tangled Web*, pp. 303–350.

57. The Mao–Nixon exchange is quoted in Nixon, *RN*, pp. 562–563. Also see Kissinger, *White House Years*, pp. 1061–1062.

58. Stephen Ambrose, *Nixon: Ruin and Recovery, 1983–1990* (New York: Simon & Schuster, 1991), pp. 41–43.

59. Quoted in Ambrose, *Nixon: Ruin and Recovery*, p. 50.

60. The section on the American economy in the first years of the Nixon presidency, except where otherwise noted, is drawn from Allen J. Matusow, *The Unravelling of America: A History of Liberalism in the 1960s* (New York: Harper & Row, 1984), pp. 159–179, and Matusow, *Nixon's Economy*, passim, and especially pp. 182–213.

61. Matusow, *Nixon's Economy*, p. 134.

62. David Brody, *Workers in Industrial America: Essays on the Twentieth Century Struggle* (New York: Oxford University Press, 1980), p. 240.

63. Quoted in Matusow, *Nixon's Economy*, p. 62.

64. Quoted in Matusow, *Nixon's Economy*, p. 157.

65. Quoted in Michael Harrington, "The Myth That Was Real," *Nation*, November 27, 1972, p. 519.

66. Phillips, *The Emerging Republican Majority*, p. 37.

67. Figures are from a chart in Kevin Phillips, *Post-Conservative America: People, Politics, and Ideology in a Time of Crisis* (New York: Random House, 1982), p. 29.

68. The New York Times 1998 Almanac (New York: Penguin Books, 1998), p. 109.

69. The account of the Watergate scandal that follows is based on Stanley Kutler, *The Wars of Watergate: The Last Crisis of Richard Nixon* (New York: Norton, 1990), except where otherwise noted.

70. Quoted in Stanley Kutler, ed., *Abuse of Power: The New Nixon Tapes* (New York: Free Press, 1997), pp. 149–150.

71. Quoted in Kutler, *Abuse of Power*, p. 3.

72. Quoted in Kutler, *Abuse of Power*, p. 28.

73. See, for example, the discussion of paying off E. Howard Hunt and other defendants that took place between Nixon and Haldeman on August 1, 1972, quoted in Kutler, *Abuse of Power*, p. 111.

74. Quoted in Kutler, *Abuse of Power*, p. 254.

75. Quoted in Ambrose, *Ruin and Recovery*, p. 190.

76. The conversation of June 23, 1972 is reprinted in Kutler, *Abuse of Power*, pp. 67–70.

77. Michael Schudson, *Watergate in American Memory: How We Remember, Forget, and Reconstruct the Past* (New York: Basic Books, 1992), p. 12.

78. Quoted in Ambrose, *Ruin and Recovery*, p. 445.

Conclusion

1. Faulkner, *Requiem for a Nun* (New York: Random House, 1951).

2. George Will, "Foreword," in Stephen Macedo, ed., *Reassessing the Sixties* (New York: Norton, 1997), p. 8.

3. For other thoughtful attempts to do so, see John Judis, "The Spirit of '68," *The New Republic*, August 31, 1998, pp. 20–27; Todd Gitlin, in "Afterword," in Macedo, ed.,

Reassessing the Sixties, pp. 283–297; Rick Perlstein, "Who Owns the Sixties?" *Lingua Franca,* May–June, 1996, pp. 30–37.

4. Speech at West Point, June 2002, quoted in Nicholas Lemnn, "The War on What?: Letter from Washington," *The New Yorker,* September 16, 2002, 36.

5. Sarah Boxer, "One Casualty of the Women's Movement: Feminism," *New York Times,* December 14, 1997, IV, p. 3.

6. On lingering distaste for homosexuality see Alan Wolfe, *One Nation, After All* (New York: Penguin, 1999).

7. For a statistical argument, see Orlando Patterson, *The Ordeal of Integration: Progress and Resentment in America's "Racial" Crisis* (Washington, DC: Civitas/Counterpoint, 1997), pp. 15–82.

8. Clinton quoted (from 1996) in Ariana Hernandez-Reguant, "Kwanzaa and the U.S. Ethnic Mosaic," *Representations of Blackness and the Performance of Identities,* ed. Jean Muteba Rahier (Westport, Ct.: Bergin and Garvey, 1999), 102; Darryl Fears, "Confined by a Label That Once Empowered: Some Ambitious Young Politicians Say 'Black Leader' Unfairly Defines Them," *Washington Post,* August 28, 2002, A1; Lynette Holloway, "The Angry Appeal of Eminem is Cutting Across Racial Lines," *New York Times,* October 28, 2002, C1.

9. Richard J. Herrnstein and Charles Murray, *The Bell Curve: Intelligence and Class Structure in American Life* (New York: Free Press, 1994).

10. Patterson, *Ordeal of Integration,* p. 203.

11. "Memories," *New York Times,* July 9, 1998, p. B1.

12. The states with the highest multiracial percentages were the Pacific crossroads of Hawaii, with 21.4% and Alaska, home to a large Native American population, with 5.4%. But not far behind was California, the nation's largest state, with 4.7% (1.6 million people), representing a true rainbow of ethnic varieties. *www.prb.org/AmeristatTemplate.cfm.*

13. "Hispanics" were designated one of five ethnic classifications (the others being American Indian or Alaskan native, Asian or Pacific islander, black, and white) in 1973 by several federal agencies. Michael Lind, *The Next American Nation: The New Nationalism and the Fourth American Revolution* (New York: Free Press, 1995), p. 119.

14. The United States is not alone in hosting large numbers of immigrants. For a comparative discussion, see Stephen Castles and Mark J. Miller, *The Age of Migration: International Population Movements in the Modern World* (New York: Guilford Press, 1993).

15. Eric Hobsbawm, *The Age of Extremes: A History of the World, 1914–1991* (New York: Pantheon, 1994), p. 413.

16. For the technological history, see Katie Hafner and Matthew Lyon, *Where Wizards Stay Up Late: The Origins of the Internet* (New York: Simon & Schuster, 1996).

17. For a thorough cross-national survey, see Ronald Inglehart, *Culture Shift in Advanced Industrial Society* (Princeton, NJ: Princeton University Press, 1990). For a witty critique of the new, hip elite, see David Brooks, *Bobos in Paradise: The New Upper Class and How They Got There* (New York: Simon and Schuster, 2000).

18. For an excellent survey, see Martin E. Marty and R. Scott Appleby, *The Glory and the Power: The Fundamentalist Challenge to the Modern World* (Boston: Beacon Press, 1992).

19. Robert Wuthnow, *After Heaven: Spirituality in America Since the 1950s* (Berkeley: University of California Press, 1998), p. 8.

20. Abraham Lincoln, "Second Inaugural Address," in Henry Steele Commager, ed., *Fifty Basic Civil War Documents* (New York: Von Nostrand Reinhold Company, 1965), pp. 168–169.

21. Quoted in David Garrow, *Bearing the Cross: Martin Luther King, Jr., and the Southern Christian Leadership Conference* (New York: William Morrow and Company, 1986), p. 620.

Index

Note: Page numbers followed by the letter *f* indicate figures.